European Yearbook of International Economic Law

EYIEL Monographs - Studies in European and International Economic Law

Volume 44

The European Yearbook of International Economic Law (EYIEL) is a Springer-publication in the field of International Economic Law (IEL), a field increasingly emancipating itself from Public International Law scholarship and evolving into a fully-fledged academic discipline in its own right. With the yearbook, editors and publisher make a significant contribution to the development of this "new" discipline and provide an international source of reference of the highest possible quality.

The EYIEL covers all areas of IEL, in particular WTO Law, External Trade Law of major trading countries, important Regional Economic Integration agreements, International Competition Law, International Investment Regulation, International Monetary Law, International Intellectual Property Protection and International Tax Law.

EYIEL publishes articles following a substantive review by the editors and external experts as appropriate.

The editors have published extensively in the field of IEL and European Law alike. They are supported by an international Advisory Board consisting of established scholars of the highest reputation.

EYIEL Monographs is a subseries of the European Yearbook of International Economic Law (EYIEL). It contains scholarly works in the fields of European and international economic law, in particular WTO law, international investment law, international monetary law, law of regional economic integration, external trade law of the EU and EU internal market law. The series does not include edited volumes. EYIEL Monographs are peer-reviewed by the series editors and external reviewers.

Güneş Ünüvar

The Transformation of International Investment Law and Its Principles

Indirect Expropriation and Fair and Equitable Treatment

Springer

Güneş Ünüvar
Luxembourg Centre for European Law
University of Luxembourg
Luxembourg, Luxembourg

ISSN 2364-8392 ISSN 2364-8406 (electronic)
European Yearbook of International Economic Law
ISBN 978-3-032-01109-1 ISBN 978-3-032-01110-7 (eBook)
https://doi.org/10.1007/978-3-032-01110-7

This Springer imprint is published by the registered company Springer Nature Switzerland AG
The registered company address is: Gewerbestrasse 11, 6330 Cham, Switzerland

Foreword

International investment law has developed into a significant field for examining how law mediates the intersection of global economic interdependence and national sovereignty. Investment treaties, once seen as specialised instruments for regulating cross-border economic activities, now operate as sites of negotiation over competing values such as investor protection, regulatory autonomy, and the broader legitimacy of economic governance. These instruments and their adjudication no longer simply reflect legal commitments; they embody the dynamic interplay of power, policy, and principles in a globalised world.

This evolving complexity of investment treaties finds expression in the dynamic relationship between arbitration and treaty-making. Güneş Ünüvar takes as his point of departure the proposition that investment arbitration and treaty-making are not distinct or linear processes. Rather, they exist in a state of iterative co-production, where arbitral jurisprudence interprets and reconstitutes the substantive content of investment law. This dual role of arbitration (as both a mechanism of dispute resolution and a driver of normative evolution) positions tribunals not merely as passive adjudicators. Instead, they have emerged as active contributors to the legal architecture of investment governance.

The central intellectual ambition of Güneş Ünüvar's work lies in the reconceptualisation of how substantive principles such as FET and indirect expropriation function within the legal system. These principles, often criticised for their vagueness, are not static rules awaiting application but, as the author demonstrates, evolving normative constructs. Through their interpretative practices, tribunals engage in a form of jurisprudential creativity, drawing boundaries around these principles while simultaneously expanding their conceptual reach. This dynamic interaction compels us to rethink the nature of the legal certainty in international investment law. Certainty emerges as a processual outcome rather than a fixed endpoint, modelled by the recursive interplay between treaties and tribunals. What distinguishes this work is its capacity to frame the evolution of these principles not merely as technical adjustments but as reflective of deeper tensions within the international legal order. For instance, FET is not simply about protecting investors' legitimate expectations; it is also a vessel through which tribunals negotiate competing concepts of fairness, accountability, and regulatory flexibility. Similarly, the principle of indirect expropriation is shown to operate along a continuum of legal reasoning, balancing the economic impact of state actions against their regulatory intent and proportionality.

One of the most significant contributions of Ünüvar's analysis is his demonstration of how arbitral jurisprudence drives iterative refinement of investment treaties. The argument advanced is not that tribunals dictate treaty design but that their interpretative practices generate lessons (both positive and cautionary) that inform states' drafting strategies. This reciprocal relationship is conceptualised as a dynamic feedback loop, where adjudication provides raw material for legal innovation in treaty-making. This iterative process raises important theoretical questions regarding the nature of legitimacy in international investment law. If tribunals, through their interpretative authority, shape the substantive content of future treaties, what does this mean for the traditional dichotomy between adjudication and legislation? The book challenges us to move beyond this dichotomy, proposing instead a vision of international investment law as a hybrid system in which the boundaries between interpretation, norm creation, and policy adaptation are fluid and interconnected.

The originality of Ünüvar's work lies in its capacity to reconceptualise foundational principles and practices within international investment law. For instance, the development of the "Effect-Intent Scale" for indirect expropriation is not merely a new analytical framework; it is a theoretical intervention that reframes the understanding of the balance between economic harm and regulatory purposes. Similarly, the reclassification of FET as an objective standard tied to proportionality, transparency, and legitimate expectations challenges conventional views, offering a more coherent framework for its application. The broader implication of these insights is the reconceptualisation of international investment law as a system in flux, characterised by a constant negotiation of values. It seems that this dynamism does not undermine the legitimacy of the system; rather, it may underscore its capacity to adapt to and respond to evolving economic and political realities. More fundamentally, the book contributes to a growing body of scholarship that views international law as an ongoing project of normative construction, and not as a static repository of rules. Such an understanding positions his analysis as not only a study of the present contours of investment law but also a conceptual framework for evaluating its future trajectories in an increasingly contested global order.

Kowloon, Hong Kong
January 2025

Julien Chaisse

Acknowledgments

My first contact with international investment law took place in the summer of 2011, when I was doing my legal internship at Çakmak Attorney Partnership in Ankara. I was tasked with analysing and compiling more than eighty BITs that Türkiye had signed up to that point for a book that was being prepared at the law firm. I remember spending roughly three weeks carefully reading every line of each treaty and repeating the process to ensure that I did not miss any punctuation or spelling error in these texts. It was during this period that I learnt the basic provisions of this area of law and became acquainted with investment arbitration. It was also during this period that I started to take a special interest in principles such as indirect expropriation and FET, which are frequently encountered in investment arbitration cases. At the end of that summer, the above-mentioned book was published with a rather long appendix containing all the BITs I had analysed. I also had the opportunity to briefly contribute to the main text. This is how the long journey that led to this book began.

While this book is, in principle, based on my PhD thesis written between September 2013 and August 2016, the current version underwent an extensive revision in the past two and a half years. Since 9 December 2016, the date I defended my thesis, there have been many noteworthy developments in the field of investment law, which had to be incorporated into the text. This revision was inevitable and crucial and substantial to a point where it felt like I wrote a PhD all over again, after nearly a decade. Certain parts of the book are completely rewritten, some parts were entirely removed, the case analysis was expanded, and many of its conclusions were modified in light of the newer IIAs signed or negotiated since 2016.

This research is the foundation of my academic career, and to finally see it as a book invokes a feeling that is difficult to describe. I am also immensely proud to have published a Turkish edition in early 2025 with *Onikilevha Yayıncılık*. With this English edition, I finally complete the circle. A special shout-out to Holger Hestermeyer is absolutely warranted for convincing me to publish this manuscript in English during a spontaneous coffee chat in Vienna. Without his encouragement, this edition would probably not exist.

There is a village to thank. I will take my time and be as exhaustive as possible. First of all, I would like to thank Frank Hoffmeister, who encouraged me to embark upon an academic career many years ago; and my PhD supervisor, long-time collaborator, and dear friend Joanna Lam for her encouragement and invaluable support during and after my PhD. I am also immensely grateful to Mikael Rask Madsen, the Director of the Centre of Excellence for International Courts (iCourts), University of Copenhagen, for his invaluable guidance in the past decade and a half. I would also like to thank Julien Chaisse for his unwavering support as a mentor, for his impeccable ability to lead by example, and agreeing to write the brilliant foreword for this book.

I am grateful to my dear friends and colleagues Ali Emir Bağış, Yunus Emre Bakiler, Okan Özen, Erman Özgür, Barış Seven, and Önder Kutay Şeker at Özgür Ünüvar Bakiler Attorney Partnership in Ankara for their massive support during this process. Some of them have been bearing with me for two decades now, and it is nothing short of commendable.

I would also like to extend my gratitude to the editors of the European Yearbook of International Economic Law: first and foremost to Marc Bungenberg; and to Jelena Bäumler, Christina Binder, Markus Krajewski, Giesela Rühl, Christian J. Tams, Jörg Philipp Terhechte, and Andreas R. Ziegler for offering this book a home. I am also grateful to Anja Trautmann and Pradeep Kuttysankaran from Springer for their assistance, guidance, and understanding throughout the editorial process.

In addition, I would like to thank my friends and colleagues for their support and encouragement, and everyone with whom I have had the privilege and pleasure of exchanging ideas: Aslı Arda, Ayşe Ece Acar, Julian Arato, Cristina Díaz Arias, Onur Çağdaş Artantaş, Randi Ayman, Simon Batifort, Başak Bağlayan, Daniel Friedrich Behn†, Tarald Gulseth Berge, Bruno Biazatti, Gabriel Bottini, Colin Brown, Ömer Erkut Bulut, Salvatore Caserta, Pola Cebulak, Yuliya Chernykh, Mikkel Jarle Christensen, Pierre-Henri Conac, Mesut Çakmak, Zeynep Çakmak, Joel Dahlquist, Eric De Brabandere, Lea Di Salvatore, Shai Dothan, Yulia Dragunova, Başak Etkin, Johannes Fahner, Steven Freeland, Harry Lars Ghillemyn, Charalampos Giannakopoulos, Lorenzo Gradoni, Ece Göztepe, Elisabeth Güllering, Elif Cemre Hazıroğlu, Ben Heath, Moshe Hirsch, Lena Hornkohl, Ekin Deniz İlhan, Lise Johnson, Pınar Kılıç, Meg Kinnear, Anne Lise Kjær, Ula Aleksandra Kos, Ursula Kriebaum, Irina Kühn, Aysel Küçüksu, Huaxia Lai, Malcolm Langford, Fenghua Li, Iryna Marchuk, Chrysoula Mavromati, Juan A. Mayoral, Ladan Mehranvar, Katharina Ó Cathaoir, Meltem Ece Oba, Bertil Emrah Oder, Jed Odermatt, Cem Çağatay Orak, Berkay Orhaner, Josef Ostřanský, Özgür Öner, Henrik Palmer Olsen, Yannis Panagis, Luca Pantaleo, Hugo Perezcano Díaz, Nathalie Perrin, Rodrigo Polanco, Lauge Poulsen, Sergio Puig, Hélène Ruiz Fabri, Karl P. Sauvant, Krista Nadakavukaren Schefer, Stephan Schill, Silvia Steininger, Xueji Su, Taylor St John, Catharine Titi, Takis Tridimas, Rosie Tomp, Gamze Erdem Türkelli, Maxim Usynin, Ana Maria Daza Vargas, Theodora Valkanou, Anıl Yılmaz Vastardis, Öykü İnci Yener-Roderburg, and Ezgi Yıldız.

Most importantly, I would like to thank my family—my mother Birsen Ünüvar, my father Recep Süha Ünüvar, my brother Ateş Ünüvar; my love, Hannah Deters—and of course Albus—for their unconditional love and invaluable support. This book is dedicated to you.

Luxembourg Güneş Ünüvar
December 2024

Competing Interests The author has no competing interests to declare that are relevant to the content of this manuscript.

Contents

Abbreviations

BIT	Bilateral Investment Agreement
CETA	Comprehensive Economic and Trade Agreement
CIL	Customary International Law
COMESAIA	COMESA Common Investment Area Investment Agreement
ECT	Energy Charter Treaty
EU	European Union
EUCAFA	EU–Chile Advanced Framework Agreement
EUMA	EU–Mexico Agreement
EUSIPA	EU–Singapore Investment Protection Agreement
EUVIPA	EU–Vietnam Investment Protection Agreement
FET	Fair and Equitable Treatment
FTA	Free Trade Agreement
ICJ	International Court of Justice
ICSID	International Centre for Settlement of Investment Disputes
IIA	International Investment Agreement
IMS	International Minimum Standard
IPA	Investment Protection Agreement
ISDS	Investor-State Dispute Settlement
MST	Minimum Standard of Treatment
NAFTA	North American Free Trade Agreement
OECD	Organisation for Economic Co-operation and Development
PCIJ	Permanent Court of International Justice
RCEP	Regional Comprehensive Economic Partnership
SICJ	Statute of the International Court of Justice
TPP	Trans-Pacific Partnership
TTIP	Transatlantic Trade and Investment Partnership
UNCITRAL	United Nations Commission on International Trade Law
UNCTAD	United Nations Conference on Trade and Development
USMCA	United States–Mexico–Canada Agreement
VCLT	Vienna Convention on the Law of Treaties
WTO	World Trade Organisation

Chapter 1
Introduction

Abstract This introductory Chapter sets the stage for the book by outlining the development and current state of international investment law as a rapidly evolving legal discipline. It highlights how the field has grown structurally and substantively through the proliferation of bilateral investment treaties (BITs) and the rise of investor-state dispute settlement (ISDS) mechanisms, which have played a critical role in shaping key protection principles such as Fair and Equitable Treatment (FET) and indirect expropriation. The Chapter frames the book's central inquiry into how the interpretation of these substantive principles by arbitral tribunals interacts with states' treaty-making practices, particularly in light of recent developments in new-generation international investment agreements like CETA and (CP)TPP. By establishing the framework, the Chapter underscores the ongoing challenges of legitimacy, coherence, and regulatory authority faced by international investment law, setting the foundation for a detailed examination of its legal-political evolution throughout the book.

> [There] shall succeed, in a more or less distant time, a civilisation founded on arbitration and justice, a superior civilisation which is neither force, nor power, nor riches, but rather the tranquil triumph of justice for the weak as well as for the strong.[1]—Luis Drago, 1907

1.1 Research Question

In academia, anthropomorphic references to international investment law are fairly common. Stephan Schill noted that the development of international investment law framework was still in its infancy.[2] Brigitte Stern likened the controversies of inter-

[1] Cited in Hull (1908), p. 341.

[2] Schill (2014), p. 334.

G. Ünüvar, *The Transformation of International Investment Law and Its Principles*, European Yearbook of International Economic Law 44,
https://doi.org/10.1007/978-3-032-01110-7_1

national investment law and policy system to a *crise de croissance*, or a teenager's crisis.[3] Anthea Roberts, similarly, referred to the evolution of the field of international investment law "from its infancy and awkward adolescence".[4] Besides the question of whether or not these analogies stem from a heartfelt sentiment towards this curious legal and political field, represented by an exponentially growing community of lawyers, political scientists, and sociologists; this personification of a field of law and policy surely draws attention to the particularities of its temporal, political, as well as legal development.

An in-depth examination reveals the unmistakable parallels between the development of this legal and political discipline and that of a human being—in fact, not unlike any other legal discipline. They are born out of the interaction among their predecessors. As they continue to exist through time, they are influenced by a plethora of factors, and shaped by the manner in which they perceive these factors. They both resist to change, yet eventually change; adapt, and repeat this process. They, at least ideally, learn from experience and act upon their experiences. One could say that it is this process of learning and development, which spans a lifetime, that defines a human. Similarly, for a legal discipline, it is this development process that defines what kind of legal field it may turn out to be, with its strengths, weaknesses, flaws, failures, as well as its aspirations.

Adolescence, therefore, accurately reflects the state in which international investment law is today; perhaps more precisely than intended by the aforementioned scholars. International investment law is in a fervent search of identity, and it strives for acknowledgment. It is struggling towards building its own legitimacy and reputation. It is surrounded by fiery criticism, and in many ways, it claims to be misunderstood. It is engulfed by new experiences, and is in a process of continuous development—both structurally (in terms of its instruments, actors, stakeholders), and substantially (its content, rules, and procedure); similar to a human's physical, and intellectual, transformation.

This book, generally speaking, concerns the story (so far) of the development, and future aspirations, of a legal and political domain. Despite being a relatively 'young' legal discipline, international investment law has had an interesting conjuncture, and has a rich, deep-rooted history of preceding legal and political disciplines. In mid-twentieth century, when the first BITs had emerged, the structural development of international investment law entered a critical phase. As BITs proliferated and became more popular, so did the disputes arising from them. They have installed an intrinsic network of similar, yet not identical, sets of provisions which established the backbone of international investment law, complemented with arbitral precedence. Today, there are more than three thousand IIAs in force,[5]

[3] Stern (2011), p. 174.

[4] Roberts (2013), p. 49.

[5] Most of the IIAs in force can be found at the UNCTAD IIA Navigator. https://investmentpolicy.unctad.org/international-investment-agreements.

and more than a thousand arbitral awards are known to exist.[6] Some scholars famously claim that despite the instrumentally fragmented structure of international investment law spread through thousands of IIAs, the overarching substance has become more multilateral and coherent.[7]

Such substantive multilateralism and coherence has been driven by the arbitral practice embedded within the IIA regime. Especially in the last three decades, *de facto* arbitral jurisprudence has transformed investment law into an autonomous body of law, recognisably distinct from other legal disciplines within international economic law and governance. A plethora of vaguely worded IIAs prompted the process of arbitral law-making, granting a framework to common yet obscure protection principles such as FET.[8] While it would be farfetched to claim that the arbitral practice has outlined an unmistakably coherent normative legal framework for vague principles such as FET, it is nonetheless notable how the understanding of substantive protection principles has transformed over the years.

Therefore, this book seeks to examine this very transformation of substantive protection principles. It examines whether, and how, they have evolved into more coherent rules through arbitral experience, as a crucial aspect of the development of international investment law. To that end, the book will particularly focus on two issues: interpretation of indirect expropriation and FET as *non-contingent* protection principles.[9] It will highlight the legal-political implications of the interpretative development of these two traditionally controversial notions as a case study. Besides the development of these protection clauses, the book will further delve into the interaction between this adjudicatory process and the transformation of different state/regional policies and the form and content of IIAs, the so-called new generation EU IIAs forming a centrepiece of the analysis.[10] Through this analysis, the book aims to qualitatively illustrate a direct, mutual, and highly influential link between interpretative trends and treaty-making practices of states.

In line with this background, the book asks the following question: **How does the interpretation of substantive protection principles in investor-state dispute settlement (ISDS) mechanisms, such as FET and indirect expropriation, interact with states' treaty-making practices?** In connection with this main inquiry, the book further asks, and seeks to answer throughout its Chapters, the following sub-questions:

- How does the protection of foreigners (and by extension foreign merchants) historically relate to current trends in arbitral practice and treaty-making?

[6] The most recent figures released by UNCTAD indicate that there are 1332 known cases as of September 2024. UNCTAD, Investment Dispute Settlement Navigator. https://investmentpolicy.unctad.org/investment-dispute-settlement.

[7] Schill (2009), p. 357.

[8] A wealth of scholarship exists on FET. *See* generally, Živković (2023); Dumberry (2018); Paparinskis (2013); Kläger (2011); Tudor (2008); Schreuer (2005).

[9] *See*, Fatouros (1962).

[10] Lam and Ünüvar (2019), p. 781.

- How did the so-called non-contingent protection principles (such as FET) develop over time as legal concepts?
- How does IIA regime interact with state sovereignty?
- Does the IIA regime really deprive states of their regulatory authority?
- Why and how did states readjust their IIAs, and what sorts of considerations played a role in this readjustment?
- How do arbitral tribunals differentiate between a non-compensable state act and an indirect expropriation?
- What is the relationship between CIL and FET, and to what extent it is established after nearly three decades of adjudication and treaty-making?

The negotiations for a number of regional and bilateral IIAs, some of which are FTAs, are either currently underway, or have been concluded in the past decade. Some of these treaties involve important global actors such as the US, the EU, and China. The book will argue that a number of IIAs, conceived and negotiated (and in some instances, already shelved) in the past decade, such as CETA,[11] (CP)TPP,[12] as well as TTIP,[13] generally indicate a direction towards regional consolidation, further clarity, as well as repossession of regulatory authority as a reaction towards the vague and highly unforeseeable outcomes of arbitral awards.

1.2 Scope of Research

The research concerns the mutual influence between adjudicatory activities and jurisprudence prompted by IIA-based disputes on the one hand, and IIA-making activities of states on the other. It argues that earlier generation IIAs, upon which the *jurisprudence constante* of international investment law has so far been constructed, affect and shape the future content of next generation IIAs in return. In line with this premise, the research question outlined above has been limited particularly in two main aspects: (a) Basis of the investor-state disputes analysed (treaty-based disputes), and (b) the protection principles, contained in IIAs, examined (indirect expropriation and FET).

First of all, the book primarily relates to treaty-based disputes, as opposed to contract based disputes between investors and states. Sornarajah defined the contract-based investment protection, from which said contract-based disputes arise, as "contractual structures of protection that were negotiated with the host state

[11] CETA (2017). https://policy.trade.ec.europa.eu/eu-trade-relationships-country-and-region/countries-and-regions/canada/eu-canada-agreement_en.

[12] CPTPP (2018), https://www.mfat.govt.nz/en/trade/free-trade-agreements/free-trade-agreements-in-force/cptpp/comprehensive-and-progressive-agreement-for-trans-pacific-partnership-text-and-resources.

[13] TTIP European Commission Draft Proposal, https://www.europarl.europa.eu/meetdocs/2014_2019/documents/inta/dv/tradoc_153807/tradoc_153807en.pdf.

at the time of the entry of the investment."[14] These disputes are possible through consent to arbitration, and jurisdictional specifications under a contract between an investor and a host state.

Treaty-based disputes, on the other hand, stem from the inter-state international economic treaties (the aforementioned IIAs) aimed at, *inter alia*, the protection and promotion of investments.[15] For the purposes of this book, an IIA can be a BIT, a trilateral investment treaty (TRIT),[16] an (investment chapter within an) FTA, a sectoral or regional economic treaty (such as the ECT)[17] or any other international instrument agreed upon between states which grants the international law protection to foreign investors in the territory of a host country. These IIAs grant private persons (both real and legal), who fall within the definition of an 'investor' as agreed upon in the applicable IIA, specific remedies which allow them to challenge state acts that interfere with their investments.

This limitation has several reasons. First reason is that the treaties, from which the treaty-based arbitral disputes arise, are largely comparable in terms of their content, context and scope.[18] This instrumental similarity co-exists with an *ad hoc* arbitration mechanism which, just as in general international law, has no *stare decisis* rule.[19] Despite this *ad hoc* nature, *de facto* precedent plays a significant role in how substantive protection principles are interpreted by arbitral tribunals. In spite of certain divergences and the multitude of applicable instruments to such disputes, the overlap in how different, yet somewhat similar, treaties are interpreted forms one of the foundational premises of this research.

The second reason is that the IIAs and (to a certain extent) disputes arising from these instruments are much more accessible than private contracts and contract-based awards.[20] A majority of IIAs contain comparable (often virtually identical) provisions, and the disputes that arise from them generally concern violations of similar obligations. In contrast, private contracts have no such similarity among themselves and each contract concerns only the investors which are the parties of that particular contract. Therefore, the variety and limited accessibility of these contracts inevitably hinder their systemic reviewability in this context. Therefore,

---

[14] Sornarajah (2010), p. 277.

[15] Ünüvar (2022), p. 383. Protection and promotion of investments are commonly articulated objectives of IIAs. For instance, the 2009 BIT between the People's Republic of China and Germany is officially called an agreement "on the Encouragement and Reciprocal Protection of Investments". Other examples include the 1997 BIT between Bulgaria and Turkey, an agreement on "Mutual Promotion and Protection of Investments"; and the 1995 BIT between Czech Republic and Thailand for the "promotion and protection of investments".

[16] One prominent example would be the 2014 TRIT between China, Japan, and the Republic of Korea.

[17] The Energy Charter Treaty (1998).

[18] Lowenfeld (2008), p. 555; De Mestral (2015), p. 2.

[19] Guillaume (2011), pp. 8–9; Schill (2011), p. 79; specifically, in regard to the NAFTA context, *see* Howse and Ünüvar (2022); Elcombe (2010), p. 84.

[20] According to Maupin, there are "tens of thousands" of investor-State contracts. Maupin (2013), pp. 144–151.

except for several contract-based disputes, such as *Biloune v. Ghana*,[21] the book will not examine investor-State contracts or contract-based disputes.[22]

The second limitation is framed by case study. The book focuses on two highly controversial protection principles which are found in thousands of IIA globally, namely FET and the concept of indirect expropriation.[23] The processes of consolidation and coherence in treaty interpretation, I argue, can be effectively demonstrated through the examination of these principles. The main reason for this contention is, first and foremost, their *non-contingent* nature. Non-contingent standards are assessed independently, and not in accordance with a comparative element. Besides these non-contingent principles are the relative, or contingent, standards such as Most-Favoured-Nation (MFN) and National Treatment (NT). When a standard is contingent, the required treatment is assessed by reference to the treatment accorded to another investment. In other words, whereas the question of whether a host state violated its NT obligation is determined by reference to the treatment extended to a domestic investor, the examination of an alleged violation of FET obligation will not, at least in principle, include such comparative assessment. Instead, the adjudicators will rely on facts, the evidence presented by the parties, rules on interpretation in international law, and essentially their own discretion on what could be deemed 'fair' in a given situation.

Scholarly work has demonstrated that contingent principles, such as MFN, establish an organic interpretative link between different IIAs by extending the rules in an IIA to another.[24] Non-contingent principles, which will entail independent analyses, do not necessitate such cross-referencing. MFN, by nature of its norms, requires consideration of the treatment accorded to the investors of a 'most favoured nation' and an assessment of the treatment accorded to a third-country investor *vis-à-vis* a third country investor. As for the analyses of FET and indirect expropriation, no such express link exists, and no rule prompts such instrumental comparison (on treaty level). Even despite the lack of such link, FET and indirect expropriation provisions in IIAs nonetheless demonstrate a *de facto* interpretative overlap and greatly contribute to the consolidation of interpretative streams in international investment law and ISDS. Therefore, the book will exclude what it considers to be contingent protection principles, namely NT, and MFN. It will only refer to these principles to the extent that they are relevant to the analysis of FET and indirect expropriation.

In addition, the book further excludes the principle of 'full protection and security'. While it has prompted debates on its exact content (particularly on whether it

[21] *Antoine Biloune (Syria) and Marine Drive Complex Ltd. v. Ghana Investments Centre and the Government of Ghana*. Award on Jurisdiction and Liability (27 October 1989) and Award on Compensation and Costs (30 June 1990) (*Biloune v. Ghana*).

[22] The *interpretation* of contracts by treaty-based ISDS tribunals is, however, a distinct matter. See, Chernykh (2022).

[23] Dolzer and Bloch (2003); Heiskanen (2007); Knahr (2007); Reinisch (2008).

[24] Schill (2009), pp. 121–193.

refers to the obligation of legal or physical security of the investment),[25] in comparison with FET and indirect expropriation, its role in the development of international investment law jurisprudence is less significant.

1.3 Structure of the Book

In light of the background and scope outlined above, the book comprises of four main Chapters.

Chapter 2, entitled *What is Fair? Treatment of Foreigners and Their Property Throughout History*, revolves around the notion of fairness in order to establish a historic-political background and context for the subsequent Chapters of the book. It maintains that, as far the interaction between a sovereign and a merchant is concerned, fairness has persistently existed through time and has played a part in shaping sovereigns' attitude towards each other, as well as towards foreigners. The Chapter argues that fairness and particularly fair treatment of foreigners, for most of history, has existed as a contingent notion, assessed by sovereign entities vis-à-vis the treatment accorded to other groups. It then asserts that it has developed into, or at least has aspired to become, an autonomous, non-contingent notion with a context-specific and objective definition attached to it. Overall, the Chapter aims at pinpointing the transformation of fairness, a core philosophical notion in legal and social studies, from an exclusively contingent notion into the contemporary, allegedly more universal and objectively defined, non-contingent principle found in thousands of IIAs today.

Chapter 3, entitled *State as a Sovereign and a (Respondent) Party in Investment Treaty Disputes*, concerns states and their dual role as sovereign treaty-makers, and dispute parties under treaty-based arbitration. Building upon the states' role as sovereigns, it puts to question the manner in which they create and direct international law and adjudication. It scrutinises the limits of sovereignty with an emphasis on states' self-limiting prerogatives.[26] This discussion is particularly illustrative as guidance for treaty-making, for relevant policy considerations (and in particular public interest and regulatory authority of states) which are intrinsically linked with such treaty-making practice. It further relates to coherence and clarity in the determination of the limits of protection principles. The Chapter further elaborates on the interpretative authority, i.e., whether or not (and to what extent) states, who are the creators and subjects of such treaties, should interfere with adjudicatory elaborations of how certain treaty principles are interpreted. For instance, in the course of an ongoing arbitral dispute, should states be able to amend or reaffirm the meaning of certain principles in applicable treaties? Pursuant to this background,

[25] *See*, for instance, Schreuer (2010); Malik (2011).

[26] Koskenniemi (2010), p. 62.

the Chap. 3, together with Chap. 2, essentially lays forth the foundation of the subsequent case study on the construction and transformation of FET and indirect expropriation provisions.

Chapter 4, entitled *(Indirect) Expropriation as a Sovereign Act: A Case for Balance*, is the first case study of the book. It mainly concerns indirect expropriation. It starts off with introductory remarks on expropriation as a concept in international law and a sovereign act, and briefly recounts lawful, unlawful, direct, as well as indirect expropriation. It gives an account of how states draft and adopt expropriation provisions, and how they specifically frame or limit indirect expropriation in their existing IIAs. It then delves into an in-depth case law analysis on how arbitral tribunals, pursuant to these IIAs, have interpreted and applied various expropriation provisions. While doing so, the Chapter applies what it calls an *Effect-Intent Scale*, to assess the interpretative tendencies of arbitral tribunals. It critically examines whether the effects, or the purposes, of an allegedly expropriatory act prevails over the other. It further divides cases under three doctrinal categories largely accepted by investment law scholarship: *sole effects*, which allegedly prioritises the effects of a measure while determining whether an act amounts to expropriation; *the police powers*, which, in the same scenario, gives more weight to the intent and purpose of the measure vis-à-vis its effects on the investment. A particularly notable contribution of this Chapter is its critical dissection of the infamous *sole effects* doctrine, an alleged interpretative strand in arbitral practice. Here, I argue that it is more of a theoretical benchmark than one that is systemically observed by arbitral tribunals—even by those who have been repeatedly cited as having rendered landmark awards following this doctrine. A loosely defined third group covers what the book refers to as the *proportionality margin*, and it collects the arbitral awards which strive to strike a balance between the two approaches. The Chapter includes an extensive case law analysis, spanning from some of the earliest cases to some of the most recent. The Chapter then analyses the new generation IIAs and expropriation provisions vis-à-vis this collective arbitral knowledge and experience, and reflects upon the effectiveness of these instruments in the making.

Chapter 5, entitled *The Fair and Equitable Treatment Principle and Its Thresholds*, concerns the second and final case study of the book on its namesake principle. Possibly the most controversial protection principle in IIAs, it has inspired countless academic debates regarding its definition, content, context, and purpose. The Chapter discusses the conceptual development of the FET as found in IIAs since its conception in mid-twentieth century. Then, similar to the expropriation analysis conducted under Chap. 4, Chap. 5 delves into FET practice in arbitration. It identifies interpretative trends which generally fall under two broad categories: FET as IMS/MST (interpreted according to what is thought to be CIL), and FET as an autonomous principle (interpreted independently from any references to CIL). Finally, following an analysis of the new generation IIAs and novel approaches to FET formulation, the Chapter demonstrates that there exists a causal link between the arbitral practice and the transforming framework of FET. By reference to the preceding Chapters in the book, Chap. 5 further contends that FET in fact aspires to become an objective, and increasingly clear-cut concept which drives adjudicatory tradition in international investment law. It represents a contemporary manifestation of non-contingent fairness in international law, and captures broader policy concerns of states regarding the delicate balance between public and private interests.

1.4 Theoretical Approach and Methodology

In its core, this book is an international law study with interdisciplinary elements. It borrows from disciplines such as history, social and political philosophy, and political science to bolster its central legal arguments. Chapter 2, for instance, is a historical account of the overall legal and political transformation of international investment law with a broad approach to its historic predecessors, which go as far back as the time of Aristotle. It further employs the notion of fairness as a timeless philosophical concept which is as relevant to today's legal and political issues as it was to societal issues thousands of years ago. The book, therefore, aims at exposing the historical link between the *then* and *now*.

One central presumption of this work is that international investment law, as an emerging field in international (economic) law, inherently and inseparably captures both law and policy.[27] As Sir Edward Fry noted during the Second Hague Peace Conference of 1907, "[a] law passed by a people is inseparable from the moral ideal which has inspired it; we [cannot] pronounce a divorce between the moral conception and the law which is its expression."[28] Therefore, the book, as a foundational premise, rejects that a purely legal study of the interpretation of international investment protection instruments is accurate, let alone useful. States, as creators of these legal instruments, have shaped their *raison d'etre* deeply entrenched within policy considerations such as promoting foreign investment and bolstering international economic relations. As the field developed, these policy considerations have diversified and adapted themselves to the needs of their time. Now, as is also relevant from the content of the academic and professional work in the field, it is virtually impossible to think of international investment law without states' concerns regarding regulatory authority and sustainable development on the one hand, and economic interests of foreign investors on the other. Therefore, also in line with historical and philosophical considerations which relate to fairness, this field establishes a bridge between states, public, and foreign investors. It looks into the classical question of how to establish a balance between competing interests of its actors.

The book notably employs two sets of theories to construct its theoretical background. The first set relates to state sovereignty, which looks into the nature of sovereignty as exercised by states. States' sovereignty, in fact, is the primary source

[27] Miles (2010), p. 1.

[28] Hull (1908), p. 343.

of public international law and instruments which create this legal and political network.[29] According to Shaw, "[i]n international law [...] it is the states themselves that create the law and obey or disobey it."[30] For the purposes of this book, what is strongly relevant is the limitation of state sovereignty in the domestic realm by way of international initiatives. The book approaches international agreements as a way of self-limitation of domestic sovereignty; a prerogative necessary for the rule of (international) law to prevail over the hegemony of sovereign powers and the adequate inclusion of the interests of other stakeholders in the establishment of international relations.[31]

The second set of theories relates to the so-called clash of paradigms in international investment law.[32] International investment law is a hybrid legal field which is born into public international law, but also encapsulates elements of private international, as well as public law. It is primarily a public international law field, because it is largely built upon a network of treaties executed between sovereign states—the primary actors of public international law. This being said, principal beneficiaries, at least in the *status quo*, seem to be foreign investors who are protected by this network of instruments. By consequence, this protective net which is established on a public international law level, and vertically protects foreign investors, have direct effects on others who are not directly covered by these agreements. These effects can relate to health, environment, security, sustainable development, or any other kind of public concern.[33] These different perspectives collectively create and drive the discourse in this legal domain.

Upon this framework, being primarily an international law study, the book is driven by more classical approaches to law. It examines international legal instruments, extensively engages with the case law which stems from these instruments, and interprets them in accordance with the contention that law should retain at least a certain degree of coherence and consistency.[34] The primary goal is to embed the above-mentioned theoretical and policy considerations within a solid legal review.

The intrinsic connection between the law and policy in this field necessitates an up-to-date, dynamic analysis. Such dynamism stems both from the theory and practice; and for the latter, the use of empirical data is crucial. In order to capture its

---

[29] Shaw (2012), p. 6.

[30] Shaw (2012), p. 6.

[31] A wealth of scholarship exists on the subject, which has proliferated significantly in the past decade. See, for instance, Deva and Van Ho (2023) and other contributions in Van Harten and Yılmaz Vastardis (2023); Küçüksu and Ünüvar (2023); Schneiderman and Van Harten (2023); Cotula (2021); Deva (2021); Ho and Sattorova (2021); Perrone (2016); Kulick (2012); Szazi (2012).

[32] Roberts (2013); Van Harten (2008), pp. 124–151.

[33] Muchlinski (2016); on an institutional level, large-scale initiatives are underway to address this issue, for instance see, OECD (2024).

[34] Alexy and Peczenik attempt to define what is meant by such coherence. See, Alexy and Peczenik (1990). For a more recent, in-depth analysis of the concept of coherence in international investment arbitration, *see*, Giannakopoulos (2022).

highly topical and relevant nature, in addition to an in-depth examination of the case law on the subject, the book further makes use of interviews. By doing so, the research aims at bolstering its empirical and practical relevance. The interviews, as far as this research is concerned, are not used as the primary evidence but mainly to support the theoretical and adjudicatory arguments conveyed in accordance with the methodology generally outlined above.

The interviews were conducted on a qualitative basis. It was particularly important to extract first-hand experience, impressions and accounts through such interviews to enhance the theoretical background. Therefore, rather than a survey-based methodology, I have personally met and conducted customised and semi-structured interviews with government officials, officials from international organisations, legal counsel, and arbitrators who have been active in the field of international investment law. A more detailed explanation regarding the interviews is provided below.

1.5 Sources

Article 38 of SICJ is often referred to as an articulation of the formal sources of international law. The said article counts (a) international conventions establishing rules expressly recognised by the contesting states, (b) international custom as evidence of a general practice accepted as law, (c) the general principles of law "recognised by civilised nations", (d) judicial decisions and the teaching of the most highly qualified publicists of the various nations, as subsidiary means for the determination of the rules of law.[35]

While the articulated list covers the primary sources used in this study, in order to capture the interdisciplinary methodology mentioned above, the book adopts a broader understanding of what sources are taken into account. To emphasise on the practical and topical relevance of the issues discussed in this book, soft law instruments have also been used. These include policy statements, communications, reports, letters or other correspondence (which are either public, or have been allowed for reference), and other instruments which outline the policy considerations. While legal instruments, such as treaties, may point towards certain policy considerations in various ways, they may not reveal the full picture of how law and policy may interact. In addition, news articles, public interviews and similar popular sources have also been used when relevant.

The analysis of available case law is crucial to the undergirding arguments of this book. As the research concerns the interpretation and application of actual IIAs in adjudicatory practice (and their subsequent juxtaposition to new generation IIAs), it was necessary to conduct an extensive case law review to identify prevalent

[35] Article 38, SICJ. Available at https://www.icj-cij.org/statute.

interpretative trends in international investment law. These cases are carefully picked in order to represent a variety of respondent states, different sectors, different wordings, and different timeframes so as to give a qualitatively holistic picture of the jurisprudence. They are analysed *vis-à-vis* the existing as well as future IIAs to assess how they have guided investment arbitration practice. The book emphasises the difference between interpretation and application of norms.[36] Therefore, in some cases and in addition to how an arbitral tribunal *interpreted* a provision, the book elaborates on how the provisions are *applied* to the facts of the case and deliberately distinguishes these two concepts.

Another important and distinct feature of this book is the use of empirical data in the form of semi-structured or informal interviews conducted in five countries. I conducted 21 high-level interviews with legal counsel, state officials involved in IIA negotiations as well as disputes between investors and states; policy-makers, prominent academics, as well as officers from international organisations between May 2015 and April 2016. The interviewees represented a total of 10 (developed and less developed) countries, covering the Americas (8), Asia (6), Europe (6), and Oceania (1). While the book includes several direct citations from the transcripts of these interviews where express and written consent of the interviewee is absent, they remain anonymous in terms of direct names or any specification which may indirectly reveal the identity of the person or persons. This being said, some general features have been indicated with regard to their roles to contextualise the insights and information contained therein. When interviewees refuse to be directly quoted even anonymously, I have paraphrased their remarks. Given the rules and principles with regard to client-lawyer confidentiality, secrecy regarding classified information at governmental level and other sensitive information is involved, I have shown utmost care and attention not to reveal any unauthorised information. Relevant guidelines have been included at the end of the book for reference (Annex 2).

Each interview is numbered, and information regarding the location, as well as date and time of each interview is provided (see Annex 1). Annex 1 further contains information on the interviewees' experience in the field. The citations are done in accordance with the assigned numbers, where interviewee consent is absent. Otherwise, the interviewees are directly quoted.

1.6 Research Value and Relevance

International investment law is an undeniably popular field, and an increasing number of scholars and professionals find themselves extensively dealing with its many conundrums and controversies. Particularly during the 1990s, a period when hundreds of IIAs (primarily BITs) entered into force, the implications of these treaties were largely unknown or drastically underestimated. With the emergence of

[36] Gourgourinis (2011).

NAFTA-based investor claims, followed by the Argentine economic crisis later in early 2000s, states slowly began to realise the so-called unintended consequences of these international agreements.[37] Besides the states, foreign investors, too, had had their own epiphany: they 'struck gold' when they became aware that these IIAs provide them with extensive protection and strong international remedies against states' interventions. This impact further transcended above this investor-state duality, particularly within the context of multinational corporations undertaking public services which had significant impact on, *inter alia*, health and environment. This is the primary reason why these so-called investment protection instruments have equally direct effects on the public sphere.

There are different directions to take while looking at these issues. While there is no clear-cut division in this regard, one tendency is to examine the procedural aspects of international investment law. In other words, one group in academia particularly focuses on the dispute settlement mechanisms, in this case arbitration, and examine its structural features vis-à-vis the nature of the disputes resolved. Given its inherently confidential nature and the manner in which the arbitrators are (party) appointed, many scholars have discussed whether or not arbitration is an appropriate means to resolve disputes which apparently have a strong and direct public angle.[38]

Another group, to which this book more readily belongs, focus more on the substantial rules encompassed by the thousands of IIAs in force today. This strand of scholarship focuses more on how substantial rules and principles which draw the framework of how investors are protected against states' acts, such as MFN, NT, FET, protection against expropriation, as outlined above (and discussed in detail in below Chapters). *Inter alia*, these works focus on what these principles mean, they critically analyse how they are drafted, and formulate proposals on how to optimise their structure in the light of a balanced, unbiased and impartial way to bolster the legitimacy of the international investment regime and dispute settlement.

This intellectual process is complemented by states' policy and treaty-making efforts which, with the guidance of the former, recalibrate and readjust the principle instruments which drive the system. States observe arbitral practice, get inspiration and (voluntary) instructions from academia, and reflect upon their IIAs which are in force. As a result of this process, they react in a multitude of ways. Firstly, they revise, specify, or altogether do away with certain provisions in IIAs in order to ensure that desired adjudicatory and policy-related outcomes are achieved, while seeking to remedy the criticism and shortcomings of the previous generations of instruments. Secondly, states engage in so-called systemic reform in multilateral fora, such as UNCITRAL and the OECD, to address various perceived shortcomings. For example, under the auspices of the former, the 'Working Group III' has been working under a mandate to, *inter alia*, "identify and consider concerns regarding ISDS" with an emphasis on the procedural aspects of dispute settlement since

---

[37] Skovgaard Poulsen (2015).

[38] Van Harten (2008), pp. 124–149; *compare* Brower and Blanchard (2014).

2017.[39] This work is ongoing as of early 2025. The distinction between substance and procedure becomes blurred in certain contexts, however, as the Working Group III ultimately picked up a number of 'cross-cutting' issues that arguably go beyond the conventional understanding of procedure: counterclaims, right to regulate, assessment of damages and compensation are a few examples.[40]

The work being conducted under the auspices of OECD focuses on substantive principles in two prongs: under 'Track 1', "government and non-government participants have initiated the first major sustained multilateral effort to explore how investment treaties factor into climate action", exploring, among other issues, how the Paris Agreement and net zero goals can be incorporated in IIAs. Under 'Track 2', stakeholders consider "merits and means to transition substantive clauses of older treaties with designs that are no longer used or are no longer considered satisfactory to newer designs where governments would wish to do so".[41] Broader policy considerations beyond the work of UNCITRAL Working Group III include right to regulate of states, the promotion of sustainable development, inclusion of investors' obligations and corporate social responsibility (CSR) clauses,[42] as well as transparency and public participation in dispute settlement proceedings.[43] The list goes on.

Therefore, this book comes at a time when international investment law is arguably undergoing its largest-scale recalibration. The effects of the abovementioned multilateral efforts, as well as unilateral steps taken by states to repossess and recalibrate their regulatory space are yet to be seen, but the short-term effects are imminent. A particularly noteworthy layer of this tectonic shift, showcasing the outcome of this global transformation, is made up of plurilateral and regional initiatives culminating into important treaties such as CETA, EUSIPA,[44] and EUVIPA,[45] as well as the now-shelved TTIP;[46] CPTPP among the Pacific Rim countries (notably

---

[39] UNCITRAL (2017) Report of Working Group III (Investor-State Dispute Settlement Reform) on the work of its thirty-fourth session – Part I (A/CN.9/930/Rev.1).

[40] UNCITRAL (2024) Possible reform of investor-State dispute settlement (ISDS): Draft Provisions on procedural and cross-cutting issues (A/CN.9/WG.III/WP.244). Specifically on the right to regulate, see more generally Titi (2014); Wandahl Mouyal (2015).

[41] OECD (2024), p. 14.

[42] Krajewski (2020), pp. 114–116. Some BITs already refer to investor obligations. See, for example, the Morocco-Nigeria BIT (2016).

[43] Lam and Ünüvar (2019); OECD (2005).

[44] EUSIPA (2018). https://investmentpolicy.unctad.org/international-investment-agreements/treaty-files/5714/download.

[45] EUVIPA (2019). https://investmentpolicy.unctad.org/international-investment-agreements/treaty-files/5868/download.

[46] European Commission, TTIP – Documents. https://policy.trade.ec.europa.eu/eu-trade-relationships-country-and-region/countries-and-regions/united-states/eu-negotiating-texts-ttip_en.

excluding the US)[47] which incorporates the original text of TPP; and RCEP[48] among ASEAN countries as well as several Pacific Rim countries (notably including China but excluding the US). These are but some examples of this global progress. In the midst of this novel political environment, an up-to-date, critical assessment of some of the key substantial provisions in these treaties (or negotiation texts) is a natural continuation of the above-mentioned multi-layered process. This research, therefore, aspires to provide an accurate and in-depth contribution with regard to these topical developments.

References

Alexy R, Peczenik A (1990) The concept of coherence and its significance for discursive rationality. Ratio Juris 3:130–147

Brower CN, Blanchard S (2014) What's in a Meme? The truth about investor-state arbitration: why it need not, and must not, be repossessed by states. Columbia J Transnatl Law 52:689–779

Chernykh Y (2022) Contract interpretation in investment treaty arbitration: a theory of the incidental issue. Brill Nijhoff, Leiden

Cotula L (2021) Public participation and investment treaties: towards a new settlement? In: De Brabandere E, Gazzini T, Kent A (eds) Public participation and foreign investment law. Brill, Leiden

De Mestral A (2015) Investor-state arbitration between developed democratic countries. Investor-State Arbitration Series, Paper no. 1

Deva S (2021) International investment agreements and human rights: assessing the role of the UN's business and human rights regulatory initiatives. In: Chaisse J, Choukroune L, Jusoh S (eds) Handbook of international investment law and policy. Springer, Berlin

Deva S, Van Ho T (2023) Addressing (in)equality in redress: human rights-led reform of the investor-state dispute settlement mechanism. JWIT 24(3):398–436

Dolzer R, Bloch F (2003) Indirect expropriation: conceptual realignments? International Law FORUM du droit international 5:155–165

Dumberry P (2018) Fair and equitable treatment: its interaction with the minimum standard and its customary status. Brill, Leiden

Elcombe J (2010) Regulatory Powers vs. Investment Protection under NAFTA's Chapter 1110: Metalclad, Methanex, and Glamis Gold. Univ Toronto Fac Law Rev 68:71–98

Fatouros A (1962) Government guarantees to foreign investors. Columbia University Press, New York

Gao H (2022) The investment chapter in the regional comprehensive economic partnership: enhanced rules without enforcement mechanism. In: Kimura F, Urata S, Thangavelu S, Narjoko D (eds) Dynamism of East Asia and RCEP: the framework for regional integration. ERIA, Jakarta, pp 201–222

[47] Australian Government Department of Foreign Affairs and Trade, CPTPP text and associated documents. https://www.dfat.gov.au/trade/agreements/in-force/cptpp/official-documents.

[48] RCEP (2020). https://investmentpolicy.unctad.org/international-investment-agreements/treaty-files/6032/download. Currently, RCEP does not include an ISDS mechanism. This being said, its Article 10.18 includes a so-called 'built-in agenda', noting that the parties shall enter into discussions on the settlement of investment disputes between a Party and an investor of another Party "no later than two years after the date of entry of this Agreement". While some commentators consider the subsequent inclusion of ISDS to be an "arduous task", others do not discount the possibility that it might nonetheless be included. Lugg et al. (2024), p. 462; Gao (2022), p. 216.

Giannakopoulos C (2022) Manifestations of coherence and investor-state arbitration. Cambridge University Press, Cambridge

Gourgourinis A (2011) The distinction between interpretation and application of norms in international adjudication. JIDS 2(1):31–57

Guillaume G (2011) The use of precedent by international judges and arbitrators. JIDS 2:5–23

Heiskanen V (2007) The doctrine of indirect expropriation in the light of the practice of the Iran-United States Claims Tribunal. JWIT 8:215–232

Ho J, Sattorova M (2021) Investors' international law. Bloomsbury, London

Howse R, Ünüvar G (2022) Sowing the seeds of an ISDS legitimacy crisis? The Notorious First Wave of NAFTA Chapter 11 Awards. In: Fabri HR, Stoppioni E (eds) International investment law: an analysis of the major decisions. Bloomsbury Publishing, London, pp 99–117

Hull W (1908) The two Hague conferences and their contributions to international law. Ginn and Co., Boston (reprinted in 1970 by Kraus Reprint Co, New York)

Kläger R (2011) 'Fair and equitable treatment' in international investment law. Cambridge University Press, Cambridge

Knahr C (2007) Indirect expropriation in recent investment arbitration. Austrian Rev Int Eur Law 12:85–102

Koskenniemi M (2010) What use for sovereignty today? Asian J Int Law 1:61–70

Krajewski M (2020) A nightmare or a noble dream? Establishing investor obligations through treaty-making and treaty-application. BHRJ 5(1):105–129

Küçüksu A, Ünüvar G (2023) Vulnerability theory as a paradigm shift in international investment law: reimagining the role of the state. BHRJ 8(3):309–328

Kulick A (2012) Global public interest in international investment law. Cambridge University Press, Cambridge

Lam J, Ünüvar G (2019) Transparency and participatory aspects of investor-state dispute settlement in the EU 'New Wave' Trade Agreements. Leiden JIL 32(4):781–800

Lowenfeld AF (2008) International economic law, 2nd edn. Oxford University Press, Oxford

Lugg A, Ganeson K, Elsig M, Chaisse J, Jusoh S (2024) Why is there no investor-state dispute settlement in RCEP? Bargaining and contestation in the investment regime. Bus Polit 26(4):449–476

Malik M (2011) The full protection and security standard comes of age: yet another challenge for states in investment treaty arbitration? IISD Best Practices Series. https://www.iisd.org/system/files/publications/full_protection.pdf

Maupin J (2013) Transparency in international investment law: the good, the bad and the murky. In: Bianchi A, Peters A (eds) Transparency in international law. Cambridge University Press, Cambridge, pp 142–171

Miles K (2010) International investment law: origins, imperialism and conceptualizing the environment. Colorado JIL 21:1–47

Muchlinski P (2016) Negotiating new generation international investment agreements. In: Hindelang S, Krajewski M (eds) Shifting paradigms in international investment law: more balanced, less isolated, increasingly diversified. Oxford University Press, Oxford, pp 41–64

OECD (2005) Transparency and Third Party Participation in Investor-State Dispute Settlement Procedures (OECD Working Papers on International Investment 2005/1)

OECD (2024) Strengthening sustainable investment through international investment agreements. OECD Publishing, Paris

Paparinskis M (2013) The international minimum standard and fair and equitable treatment. Oxford University Press, Oxford

Perrone N (2016) The international investment regime and local populations: are the weakest voices unheard? Transnatl Leg Theory 7(3):383–405

Reinisch A (2008) Legality of expropriations. In: Reinisch A (ed) Standards of investment protection. Oxford University Press, Oxford, pp 171–204

Roberts A (2013) Clash of paradigms: actors and analogies shaping the investment treaty system. AJIL 107:45–94

Schill SW (2009) The multilateralization of international investment law. Cambridge University Press, Cambridge

Schill SW (2011) Enhancing international law's legitimacy: conceptual and methodological foundations of a new public law approach. Virginia JIL 52:57–102

Schill SW (2014) International investment law as international development law. In: Bjorklund A (ed) Yearbook on international investment law & policy. Oxford University Press, Oxford, pp 327–356

Schneiderman D, Van Harten G (eds) (2023) Rethinking investment law: perspectives & prospects. Oxford University Press, Oxford

Schreuer C (2005) Fair and equitable treatment in arbitral practice. J World Invest Trade 6:357–386

Schreuer C (2010) Full protection and security. J Int Dispute Settlement 1(2):353–369

Shaw MN (2012) International law, 5th edn. Cambridge University Press, Cambridge

Skovgaard Poulsen LN (2015) Bounded rationality and economic diplomacy: the politics of investment treaties in developing countries. Cambridge University Press, Cambridge

Sornarajah M (2010) The international law on foreign investment, 3rd edn. Cambridge University Press, Cambridge

Stern B (2011) The future of international investment law: a balance between the protection of investors and the states' capacity to regulate. In: Alvarez JE, Sauvant KP (eds) The evolving international investment regime – expectations, realities, options. Oxford University Press, Oxford, pp 174–192

Szazi E (2012) NGOs: legitimate subjects of international law. Leiden University Press, Leiden

Titi C (2014) The right to regulate in international investment law. Nomos, Baden-Baden

Tudor I (2008) The fair and equitable treatment standard in the international law of foreign investment. Oxford University Press, Oxford

Ünüvar G (2022) The 'object and purpose' and incrementalism of investment treaties: can international investment law reinvent its identity? In: Egan M, Raube K, Chaisse J (eds) Contestation and polarization in global governance. Edward Elgar, Cheltenham, pp 379–398

Van Harten G (2008) Investment treaty arbitration and public law. Oxford University Press, Oxford

Van Harten G, Yılmaz Vastardis A (eds) (2023) Special Issue: Critiques of Investment Arbitration Reform 24(3)

Wandahl Mouyal L (2015) International investment law and the right to regulate: a human rights perspective. Routledge, London and New York

Živković V (2023) Fair and equitable treatment and the rule of law. Elgar Publishing, Cheltenham

Chapter 2
What Is Fair? Treatment of Foreigners and Their Property Throughout History

Abstract This Chapter examines the treatment of foreigners with an emphasis on the notion of 'fairness', highlighting its evolution from a subjective and contingent consideration guiding sovereign discretion, to an ostensibly objective international standard commonly referred in contemporary international investment law. With increased inter-communal interactions and the development of international law from the seventeenth century onward, a vague, yet influential international standard began to take shape, replacing more provincial, contingent conceptualisations of fairness. Despite its controversial foundation, the so-called international minimum standard (IMS) remains a key principle in international investment law today, influencing international adjudication and treaty-making practices of states. The analysis constructs the theoretical framework for the rest of the book, and underscores the necessity for more inclusive and clearly defined global rules guiding substantive protection principles in international investment law.

2.1 Introduction

The development of *substantive protection principles* in international investment law, the rules and principles in IIAs regulating the international sphere of protection of foreign investment in a host country, presents a peculiar story. One of the main reasons for this peculiarity is the very nature of their long-term transformation from an obscure and largely arbitrary set of behaviours solely stemming from sovereign discretion to a set of intertwined, highly technical rules and instruments embedded within the contemporary structure of international investment law. A thorough historical, political, and legal examination of this global transformation is not only helpful, but also crucial to understand the broader rationale behind the protection of foreigners in a host country.

G. Ünüvar, *The Transformation of International Investment Law and Its Principles*, European Yearbook of International Economic Law 44,
https://doi.org/10.1007/978-3-032-01110-7_2

The question of how foreigners should be treated in a host country is a very old one. While the question itself seems to have remained persistently relevant and unchanged, what keeps changing and adapting to the reality of each era is the answer, or answers, given to it. This book does not claim to be the first to look into this controversy. While the scholarly work which includes the historical development of international investment law is illuminating, it is rare that any of them go back in time further than de Vattel's treatise the Law of Nations,[1] or Francisco de Vitoria's lectures to explain the historic and philosophical origins of this intricate legal and political network.[2] Others examine the field's development from the beginning of the nineteenth or twentieth century, specifically focusing on the relatively recent institutional and instrumental milestones.[3]

Understandably, it is neither feasible nor possible to expect every work on investment law—and, by extension, rules and thoughts on protection of foreigners—to cover its daunting temporal expanse which spans from classical philosophers such as Aristotle to today. This Chapter neither claims nor intends to cover every aspect of it. While Aristotle may not have particularly dealt with the question of how Greek city-states should compensate foreign investors if the former expropriated the property of the latter, he was very much interested in how a foreigner should be treated in the Athenian city-state. The link between the latter, more general philosophical inquiry and the former, more technical and contemporary question is one of the nuances embedded within the historical background conveyed throughout this Chapter.

In order to establish a framework for the subsequent Chapters focusing on the FET and indirect expropriation provisions in IIAs, I will attempt to capture the transforming rationale and temporal expanse of the fair treatment of foreigners. Fair treatment in this case does not exclusively refer to the investment law context as encapsulated by the FET principle,[4] but rather the more general and basic notion of a sovereign treating foreigners *fairly*.

According to the Merriam-Webster Dictionary, 'fair' means either "marked by impartiality and honesty: free from self-interest, prejudice, or [favouritism]", or "in a manner that is honest or impartial or that conforms to rules".[5] According to the Black's Law Dictionary, fair means "[characterised] by honesty, impartiality, and candor; just; equitable; disinterested" and "[f]ree of bias or prejudice".[6] The choice

[1] De Vattel (1758).

[2] One comprehensive account of some of his lectures can be found in Anghie (2004), pp. 13–31.

[3] Newcombe and Paradell (2009), pp. 1–74.

[4] See Chap. 5.

[5] Definition of 'fair', Merriam-Webster Online Dictionary. http://www.merriam-webster.com/dictionary/fair.

[6] Definition of 'fair', Black's Law Dictionary (2019), p. 741. Notably, Black's Law Dictionary includes two contextual definitions of 'fair and equitable'. One of them, *fair-and-equitable requirement*, relates to bankruptcy, and denotes that 'a bankruptcy court must … consider the plan as a whole, and weigh all the circumstances surrounding the treatment of each impaired class of interests." The other contextual definition is of *fair and equitable treatment*, which is as follows: "In

of this particular term over other possible substitutes, such as 'just', might raise concerns. The first reason for this is its constant use in modern IIAs. While some earlier IIAs refer to "just and equitable" treatment instead of the term "fair and equitable",[7] there seems to be little difference in their meaning as far as these treaties are concerned. A second reason is the language in which this research is conducted—the words 'fair' and 'just' are distinct in the English language, unlike some other European languages.[8] Such distinction does not seem to exist when translated to other languages, such as French (*juste*), Spanish (*justo*), Italian (*giusto*), Greek (*δίκαιος* - *díkeos*), or Turkish (*adil*). Likewise, as far as the aforementioned FET clauses in translated IIAs are concerned, 'fair' seems to share the same meaning as 'just' also in arbitral practice and IIA treaty-making. In essence, I believe that fairness alludes to a more colloquial, general meaning;[9] however, as far as this work is concerned, fair, just and equitable are considered interchangeable. This presents a complex semantic and philosophical conundrum, and the Chapter will refrain from further discussing particular implications of their difference. For the sake of maintaining a somewhat uniform language throughout the Chapter and through different periods examined, this Chapter will refer to fairness and, unless such language is specifically referred to in a cited treaty, text or otherwise, will refrain from the use of 'just' or other semantic variations.

While the notion of fairness includes the basis of treatment being equivalent for all those within a given jurisdiction regardless of their origin, this does not capture all of its possible meanings, at least not in the contemporary context of international

international investment law, a host state's guarantee of transparency, nondiscrimination, due process, good faith, freedom from coercion and harassment, and access to justice for the investing party. This is the most important standard of treatment of foreign investments by a host state … Its most important feature is the protection of the investor's legitimate expectations."

[7] For instance, Article 3, Argentina – France BIT (1993).

[8] German language seems to have this distinction, as several European Commission documents in German refer to "*faire* Behandlung von Drittstaatsangehörigen", translated as "fair treatment of third party nationals". In the French version of the same text, the word "fair" is translated as "équitable". See, European Commission (2004) Mitteilung der Kommission an den Rat, das Europäische Parlament und den Europäischen Wirtschafts- und Sozialausschuss: Eine strategische Partnerschaft zwischen der EU und Indien, KOM (2004). http://eur-lex.europa.eu/LexUriServ/LexUriServ.do?uri=COM:2004:0430:FIN:DE:PDF. However, the German BIT language adopts the word "gerecht" for fair, which also translates as "just". Albania – Germany BIT (1995); Yemen – Germany BIT (2008).

[9] Rawls (1971). In his seminal work, Rawls discusses justice as a conception of fairness. Also see, for a linguistic comparison of 'justice' and 'fairness', Wierzbicka (2006), p. 160: "Justice could be 'seasoned' with mercy, but it would be impossible to say the same about fairness. Mercy implies inequality: the giver of mercy is in some sense above the recipient, who depends on the giver's benevolence […] Fairness […] implies equal standing of all the parties – at least in the sense that they are all bound by the same rules." From a paradigms theory perspective, discussed in Chap. 3 below, this description has interesting implications relating to the dual role of states as the rulemakers *and* respondents in disputes, as equal parties of arbitration.

investment law. Fairness is an inherently subjective, context-dependent, and vague[10] term. International investment law, however, presents a case where fairness is not a purely contingent principle that is comparatively assessed—in some cases, such as IMS, it seems to refer to an overarching meta-principle seemingly unaffected by the treatment accorded to the compared or contrasted subjects, i.e. nationals and foreigners. Such meta-principle, as I will demonstrate below in detail, carries with it the promise of a vague, yet over-arching fairness; resonating from more contemporary conceptualisations of justice. It points almost towards the elements of an international social contract among the nations, aspiring to be fair regardless of the vantage point.[11] This, therefore, prompts the following question: is it possible to devise a framework for universal fairness within an international law domain?

This Chapter, while serving as the historical background of the book, will introduce the historical roots of the concept of fairness as a contingent concept; bereft of a universal definition. It will elaborate on whether, or how, the notion of *fairness* evolved over time towards professed objectivity first in general international law; and then, in international investment law. More specifically, the core of the inquiry is its transformation from an exclusively contingent notion dependent on a sovereign's discretion with regards to the treatment it accorded to its own subjects, to a more universal, more specific yet non-contingent manifestation allegedly embedded in (customary) international law, such as IMS on the treatment of foreigners.[12] It will examine how this notion attached itself to the temporal, legal and political context throughout history and how the last few centuries prompted its alleged universality, shaping the very core substantial principles in investment law commonly invoked in investment arbitration. It will go over important historical examples and refer to documentary evidence spanning from Ancient times to present, to scrutinise the reasons why and how the above-mentioned transformation took place, how it contributed to the development of international investment law and why the discussion survived up until this day.

2.2 Early History

The foundations of what is called international investment protection originate from the more general (and preceding) issue of the status of foreigners in another country.[13] Contemporary rules of international investment law constitute the last link in a long chain of acts, disciplines, methods, and rules concerning the treatment of

[10] Poscher associates vagueness with "borderline cases", which is defined as "cases 'in which one just does not know whether to apply the expression of withhold it, and one's not knowing is not due to ignorance of the facts'". Poscher (2011), p. 3; also see Endicott (2000).

[11] Nicholson (1965), p. 401.

[12] Borchard (1940), p. 460. Borchard reiterated that "essential elements" of objective justice were required of all legal systems.

[13] Newcombe and Paradell (2009); Root (1910).

foreigners abroad. The issue of treatment of foreigners naturally encompasses the legal protection of foreigners, particularly against intrusion by the host country's government or hostile elements in the new environment. The protection would be instated either by a foreigner's own country, or by the sovereign of the lands in which he or she resided. Contemporary rules and mechanisms were conceived following a long tradition of diplomatic protection,[14] and diplomatic protection as a means of pacific settlement is preceded by more aggressive means of protection of nationals by their home state, such as the use of force,[15] and so on. The emergence of different, more contemporary means of protection of foreigners do not necessarily lead to the dissipation of preceding means, however, as the use of force had co-existed with diplomatic protection in nineteenth century, and diplomatic protection may still be an alternative to more direct remedies such as investor-state dispute settlement (ISDS), despite not being nearly as popular.

It is possible to trace some of the early reflections and societal ideas on how foreigners should be perceived and treated. Ancient Egyptian historical evidence dating back to twelfth century BC indicate that "alterity was tied predominantly to a different style of worship".[16] This is an interesting example of how some earlier societies saw an inherent belligerency in foreigners who, by extension, worshipped other Gods. This fact presents striking parallels to the relatively modern juxtaposition of Christendom with 'civilisation' later in sixteenth century and well into nineteenth century.[17]

A similar association also seems to have existed in Ancient Greece. Thucydides separated "Hellenes" and foreigners, collectively referring to them as "barbarians".[18] Same distinction appears to be the case with Plato who, in one of his dialogues,[19] recites a funeral oration attributed to Aspasia, which sets aside "pure Hellenes" and "descendants of Pelops or Cadmus or Aegyptus or Danaus, who are by nature barbarians".[20]

This being said, ancient Greek city-states had an elaborate legal framework which concerned foreigners, especially those who resided within their walls.[21] There seems to be three distinct groups of individuals based on their ethnicity and residency: the *politis*, citizens of a city-state who enjoyed full fights; the *metics*,[22] foreigners who legally resided in city-states and enjoyed limited privileges; and the *xenos*, foreigners who were present, but not resident, in these cities.[23] *Metics* were expected to obey the law of the city, they paid a special tax, and performed military

[14] Crawford (2012), p. 509.

[15] Lesaffer (2015), p. 46.

[16] Di Biase-Dyson (2013), p. 359.

[17] Armstrong (1993), p. 17.

[18] Thucydides (1914), p. 4.

[19] Plato (2008); Richter (2011), p. 97.

[20] Plato (2008).

[21] Dimopoulou-Piliouni (2008), p. 28.

[22] Dimopoulou-Piliouni (2008), p. 28; Whitehead (1977). Another group of *metics* were the freed slaves, who were almost always non-Greeks.

[23] Kamen (2013), p. 43.

service.[24] They were required to have a *prostates*, a patron, whom they could choose freely. While the patrons' exact role seems uncertain, one of the functions up until fourth century BC was to bring cases on behalf of the *metics* they supervised in case they needed legal assistance.[25] While it was possible for *metics* to sue and be sued, their cases were heard in separate courts. In terms of most rights and judicial remedies, foreigners were different than citizens of a state.

Aristotle discusses the differences between citizens and foreigners in his *Politics*.[26] He refers to certain non-Greeks as "natural slaves".[27] On this seemingly inherent inferiority reflected upon foreigners, Jill Frank stresses upon the implied nature of Aristotle's words:

> Aristotle's distinction between Greeks and certain non-Greeks [...] rests not on nature as something immutable, not on his conviction that Greeks were superior to foreigners, but on his observations about the (political and nonpolitical) behaviors of those foreigners.[28]

While many early communities either rejected legal rights and capacity to those who belonged to or originated from another political or social community, there is evidence that other civilisations accustomed to the presence of foreigners (mostly through means of commerce and trade) institutionalised their dealings with them. The Mauryan Empire, which ruled the northern Indian subcontinent between fourth and second century BC, had a sizeable Greek population, and its government had a department for foreigner affairs.[29]

Other communities segregated the sets of rules that applied to the members of the community and those aliens. Possibly one of the most famous early examples of segregation between the treatment of natives (or citizens) and foreigners is the division of *ius civile and ius gentium* in Rome.[30] *Ius civile* was the body of laws that applied exclusively to Roman citizens, whereas *ius gentium*, the "law of nations", covered all peoples including those who were not citizens of Rome and their dealings with the Roman citizens.[31] As cultural and commercial interactions between Romans and foreigners intensified, a praetorship for foreigner affairs (*praetor peregrinus*) was established in 242 BC.[32] Karadeniz Çelebican notes that the law created by the *praetor peregrinus*, often in the process of settling disputes between foreigners and citizens, constituted a large portion of what came to be known as *ius gentium*.

Foreigners in Roman Law can be examined under two categories: *peregrinus* (those who lived under the Roman rule without having the Roman citizenship), and *barbarus* (those who lived outside the Roman territories, or those belonged in

---

[24] Kamen (2013), p. 43.

[25] Kamen (2013), p. 43.

[26] Aristotle (1998), p. 2.

[27] Aristotle (1998), p. 11.

[28] Frank (2004), p. 101.

[29] Chaudhary (2008), p. 61.

[30] Anderson (2009), p. 47.

[31] Anderson (2009), p. 47.

[32] Karadeniz Çelebican (2014), pp. 147–149.

societies with which Rome had no cultural, economic or political relations).[33] Similar to those in ancient Greek city-states, neither category was granted the benefits of the Roman citizenship. Especially the *barbarus* were perceived as enemies or outcasts, as is also evident in the fact that the Law of the Twelve Tables uses the phrase *hostis* (under Table III), the Latin word for 'enemy', for foreigners.[34] The *barbarus* had no default rights or protection according to Roman law, insofar as they could be abducted, sold into slavery, or killed by Roman citizens. Less commonly, Rome had entered into agreements with foreign tribes which recognised certain rights to foreigners such as the right to conduct commerce in Rome (*ius commercii*), or to get married to a Roman citizen (*ius connubii*). The *peregrinus*, who were generally those who lived in Roman colonies and conquered lands under Roman control, did possess certain limited citizenship[35] rights.

Germanic tribes and other so-called barbarians, according to Cutler, "did not look beyond the tribe."[36] Foreigners, therefore, were strictly without any rights. They were under the protection of the tribe with which they resided, to the extent that no tribe member opposed to such protection.[37] Of course, such tentative or cautious attitude was not always the case—it is known that Scythians sacrificed foreigners to the mythical goddess Diana as offerings.[38]

2.3 The Medieval Sovereign

The gradual emergence of the concept of territoriality of the law,[39] growth of commerce in twelfth century[40] and increased complexity of economic relations between different sovereigns altered the perception and definition of foreigners. Factors such as inter-communal marriages, agricultural developments and the rise of feudalism bolstered and ensured the primacy of territoriality as a criterion, yet on the other hand, it did not completely supersede the individual application of law. Gradually, the law of the land applied to all within a kingdom or an empire without discrimination or segregation on the basis of origin.

Examination of medieval documents such as treaties and decrees allow for a deeper understanding of the dealings between a ruler and a foreigner, and the notions which governed this relationship. One interesting example is a charter issued by

---

[33] Karadeniz Çelebican (2014), pp. 147–149.

[34] Thatcher (1901), pp. 9–11. For a modernised Latin version of the Twelve Tables, see https://avalon.law.yale.edu/ancient/twelve_tables.asp.

[35] Karadeniz Çelebican (2014), pp. 148–149. For instance, a foreigner was not allowed to benefit from a Roman will.

[36] Cutler (1933), p. 225.

[37] Borchard (1913), pp. 497–498.

[38] O'Brien (1833), p. 173.

[39] Borchard (1913), p. 499.

[40] Cantor (1982), p. 18.

Henry II, in 1157, for merchants from Cologne. He ensured protection to the merchants, their possessions, and provided that they shall be in his custody and protection "as if they were [his] men and friends".[41] As another example, one of the lesser-known rules in 1215 Magna Carta in fact concerns foreign merchants.[42] It states that "if our merchants are safe [in the land that is at war with us], the other merchants are to be safe in our land."[43]

Both texts have interesting implications. They illustrate an obligation of the sovereign towards a group -in this case, merchants of foreign origin- that is defined with reference to the treatment accorded to another group. Both, while aiming at ensuring protection of foreigners, do so by setting a contingent treatment threshold. Henry II's protection, somewhat amiably, stems from the protection he accords to his own men and friends. Magna Carta, on the other hand, emphasises on the treatment accorded to English merchants abroad by another sovereign, and promises safety to the merchants hailing from these lands as long as his own men are safe there. Both examples implicitly set the limits of what would constitute *fair* treatment expected and promised by a sovereign—protecting others as friends and own men, and protecting others according to treatment that which accorded to one's own elsewhere. Magna Carta's contingent fairness, for instance, could mean that if English merchants in a land were to be killed, it would only be fair that foreign merchants are also executed—without prejudice to the safety to be accorded to them in case English merchants are safe. What is fair was directed, framed and executed entirely in accordance with the discretion of one sovereign, or the interaction between the sovereign discretion of two or more rulers. An intrinsically relative notion of fair treatment, strikingly similar to NT[44] and MFN[45] principles in contemporary trade and investment law, can be found embedded in these texts.

2.4 Towards 'Universal' Standards and Non-Contingent Fairness

Francisco de Vitoria, a sixteenth century theologian, jurist, and moralist;[46] is regarded as one of the founding figures of modern international law.[47] Two of his lectures, *De Indis Noviter Inventis* and *De Jure Bellis Hispanorum in Barbaros,*[48] in general dealt with issues related to the Spanish-Native American relations following

[41] Kim (2001), p. 27.

[42] Rule 30, Magna Carta (1215), p. 4.

[43] Rule 30, Magna Carta (1215), p. 4.

[44] Banifatemi (2009); Choukroune (2014); Nikièma (2017), p. 2.

[45] Bjorklund (2008); UNCTAD (2010).

[46] Hernandez (1991), p. 1042.

[47] Anghie (2004), p. 13; Scott (1934).

[48] De Vitoria (2009); Anghie (2004), p. 13. Anghie translates the titles as 'On the Indians Lately Discovered', and 'On the Law of War Made by the Spaniards on the Barbarians'.

the discovery of the New World. He examined the basis of this cultural, social and political interaction between the two very distinct peoples. The lectures are significant in terms of how it established the basis of, and the rationale behind, the Spanish existence in America.

What principally makes Vitoria's ideas stand out is how they seem to differ from the divine norms of fifteenth century, which would deprive Native Americans of their rights of ownership by virtue of their lack of belief in the Christian faith. This rationale, which granted or deprived the status of 'civilised' to indigenous peoples depending on their compatibility with the Christian faith, had been persistent until at least the nineteenth century.[49] Most of his premises in that regard seem to originate from his understanding of the society as rooted and flowing from nature, and his observations regarding Native Americans find their source in a more civil, secular system of law. As Anghie accurately points out:

> According to Vitoria [...], the Indians belong to the universal realm like the Spanish and all other human beings because [...] they have the facility of reason and hence a means of ascertaining jus gentium which is universally binding. [...] [H]owever, the Indian is very different from the Spaniard because the Indian's specific social and cultural practices are at variance from the practices required by the universal norms – which in effect are Spanish practices – and which are applicable to both Indian and Spaniard.[50]

Vitoria's work attaches an inherently universal character to European Christian norms and justifies war against those who do not comply with these set of rules and practices—in this case, the Native Americans. Being a jurist *and* a theologian (a combination strikingly visible in his views), his secular arguments concerning the Natives differ little from his theological arguments on how the 'justness' and Christendom are bound to each other despite the structurally secular discourse embedded in the former. On justness of war, his separation of Christians and others is express: he notes that if any subjective assessment of justness was valid, "even Turks and Saracens might wage wars against Christians".[51]

Except for the legitimisation and authorisation bestowed upon Christian sovereigns by divine law, fair treatment of foreigners had maintained its near-exclusive contingent nature up until the seventeenth and eighteenth centuries. Indeed, it is challenging to find any explicit reference to an overarching international legal standard with which sovereigns were to comply, detached from their sovereign discretion and regardless of the domestic treatment they accorded to foreigners.

Religion continued to maintain its importance in determining whether a community was civilised and peaceful and, by extension, its members were entitled to rights.[52] The rise of the modern concept of 'nationality' is intrinsically bound to the

---

[49] Anghie (2004), pp. 20–28; Yarrow (2011), p. 89.

[50] Anghie (2004), p. 22.

[51] Anghie (2004), p. 26.

[52] An unmistakable link between Christianity and statehood can be found in the Treaty of Westphalia, which speaks of a "Christian and universal peace". Article I, The Treaty of Westphalia (1648). http://avalon.law.yale.edu/17th_century/westphal.asp; Yarrow (2011).

Thirty Years' War which led a series of events including the Peace of Westphalia.[53] These events created the basis for the concept of sovereignty of states and maintained their role as international actors in the next few centuries.[54] Statehood constituted the core, legitimate polity[55] and served as a gateway to a system of inter-state endorsement of a particular territory as a fully-fledged subject of the newly forming international legal order.[56] The establishment of an international legal order naturally meant the clash of nations in terms of ideologies and the sovereignty they each possessed—indeed, which rules and principles were to guide this international order? This new understanding of public international law (and the innate controversies it brought along) changed forever the guiding rules for protection of foreigners—the emphasis has slowly, but surely, shifted towards the inter-state relations and protection of a foreigner by the *home* state, rather than an exclusive reliance on the *host* state.[57] Although contingent concepts, just like domestic rules, worked relatively well in a world composed of different domestic systems which had seldom interacted with each other, it showed signs of failure in the new international system, according to which an intricate network of economic, political and societal ties were maintained.

Before the conceptualisation of 'international standards' defining such international fairness among nations, states had established mechanisms, usually driven by the political power and maintained by military might, to readjust perceived insufficiencies to remedy the gap between two states in terms of rule of law and fairness—very much like Vitoria's insistence on compliance with values of allegedly universal nature. The modern notion of diplomatic protection was first conceptualised by Emmerich de Vattel in his famous work *Le Droit des Gens* (the Law of Nations) of 1758.[58] According to de Vattel, "whoever [treats] a citizen ill, indirectly offends [their] state, which is bound to protect that citizen."[59] With regards to the standard of treatment, he wrote that "as soon as [the sovereign] admits [foreigners], he engages to protect them **as his own subjects**, and to afford them perfect security, as far as depends on him.[60] This larger framework also covers the protection of cross-border commerce and alien property—de Vattel remarked that particularly the safety of commerce and foreigners' property was essential, and a state's mistreatment of such property was also an injury to the foreigner's state. De Vattel, not unlike Henry II's above-mentioned charter, primarily appraised the fairness of treatment of foreigners with reference to the treatment of the sovereign's own subjects, setting a contingent threshold. However, while one sovereign's discretion remained

---

[53] Schmidt (2011), p. 601.

[54] Philpott (2001), p. 82.

[55] Philpott (2001), p. 33.

[56] Philpott (2001), p. 33.

[57] Herdegen (2013), p. 74.

[58] De Vattel (1758).

[59] De Vattel (1758), p. 109.

[60] De Vattel (1758), p. 104. Emphasis added.

relevant (as the sovereign was bound to protect the foreigners as its 'own'), De Vattel's arguments also included a responsibility of the host state towards the home state, in case the former mistreated a national of the latter. By prescribing a right to 'avenge' for the home state, he included a mechanism to attempt to enforce this wrongdoing and either restore fair treatment or remedy the unfairness which the citizen had to endure. In other words, the home state espoused, and struggled for, the case of the mistreated citizen.[61]

The Treaty of Amity and Commerce between the United States and France of 1778 is one of many American commercial treaties which included an MFN clause (Article 2) and a mutual obligation to "protect and defend" the property owned by the other party.[62] In fact, both countries had spearheaded the eighteenth century economic liberalism—for the French and American thinkers of the Enlightenment era, free and unrestricted global trade and commerce would alter the very essence of the global political diplomacy, shifting its focus from the balance of power and military alliances to a purely commercial relationship. Particularly for the United States, as Gilbert noted, there were two foreign policy objectives: one of them was to "make trade as free as possible, because only a complete liberalisation of trade could provide full security against the danger that close commercial relations might create a political dependency";[63] and the second one was "to persuade other powers to the acceptance of principles of international which would mitigate the impact of war on civilian life."[64] The objective of achieving political independence and sustaining peace through international economic and political cooperation would also lead to the very foundation of a contemporary supranational regional union more than a century later, namely the EU.[65]

---

[61] Dolzer and Schreuer (2012), p. 232.

[62] Treaty of Amity and Commerce between the United States and France (6 February 1778). http://avalon.law.yale.edu/18th_century/fr1788-1.asp. Another highly important legal text in this regard would be the Treaty of Amity, Commerce and Navigation between the Great Britain and the United States of America (*Jay Treaty*, 19 November 1794). http://avalon.law.yale.edu/18th_century/jay.asp. In the words of Alexander Hamilton, "[t]he right of holding or having property in a country always implies a duty on the part of its government to protect that property, and to secure to the owner the full enjoyment of it … [w]henever therefore a Government grants permission to foreigners to acquire property within its territories or to bring & deposit it there, it tacitly **promises protection and security**. … It is neither natural nor equitable to consider him as subject to be deprived of [the possession and use of his property] for a cause foreign to himself especially for one which may depend on the volition or pleasure even of the very government to whose protection it has been confided: For the proposition, which affirms the right to confiscate or sequester, does not distinguish between offensive or defensive war, between a war of ambition on the part of the power which exercises the right or a war of self-preservation against the assaults of another." Hamilton (1795), Emphasis added.

[63] Gilbert (1970), pp. 68–69; Hagan (1973), p. 3.

[64] Gilbert (1970), p. 69.

[65] For a discussion on political and economic reasons why states would opt-in to join the European Union, *see*, Milward (2005), p. 37. A parallel rationale had also been expressed by Winston Churchill, who proposed in 1946 that European nations must "recreate the European family, or as much of it as we can, and provide it with a structure under which it can dwell in peace, in safety and in freedom." Mathijsen (2007), p. 12.

In 1818, in a letter to the Spanish Envoy to the United States Mr. Luis de Onís regarding American vessels and cargo seized within Spanish colonial territories by French cruisers, Secretary of State John Quincy Adams underlined the importance of the protection of alien property:

> There is no principle of the law of nations more firmly established than that which entitles the property of strangers within the jurisdiction of a country in friendship with their own to the protection of its sovereign by all the efforts in his power.[66]

A few years later, in 1823, he reiterated and expanded upon this standpoint by pointing towards the idea of a universal rule, which globally ensured equal protection of the foreigners with native citizens:

> The principle of 'placing the foreigner in regard to all objects of navigation and commerce upon a footing of equal favor with the native citizen' is altogether congenial to the spirit of our institutions, [however] the fairness of its operation depends upon its being admitted universally [...] The United States have nevertheless made considerable advances in their proposals to other nations towards the general establishment of this most liberal of all principles of commercial intercourse.[67]

American treaty practice in late nineteenth and early twentieth century was heavily influenced by the objective of protection of American citizens, their rights and their property abroad. John Milton Hay, Secretary of State between 1898 and 1905, perceptively explained this purpose, which also sheds light to overarching objectives of commercial treaties both contemporary and modern:

> The right of citizens of the United States to resort to and transact affairs of business or commerce in another country, without molestation or disfavor of any kind, is [...] a necessary feature of the mutual intercourse of civilized nations and confirming the principles of equality, equity, and comity which underlie their relations to one another.[68]

From early eighteenth century throughout nineteenth and early twentieth century, many international treaties have included provisions on the protection of foreigners,[69] depriving domestic sovereignty and discretion with regards to such protection of its legal monopoly. Foreign investors and traders from capital-exporting countries in countries to which they had brought capital began voicing discontent regarding the treatment they had been subjected. In case of failure by the host state to protect the alien, the home state of the foreign investor or trader would assume the role, and in its citizen's stead espouse the case and the claim of its citizen.[70] For more than two centuries, the principle of diplomatic protection sat at the core of the issue of protection of foreigners abroad, and it was the only plausible, applicable and enforceable

---

[66] Moore (1906), pp. 4–5.

[67] Extract of a letter from Mr. Adams, Secretary of State, to Mr. Anderson, Minister Plenipotentiary to Colombia, dates 27th May, 1823. In: British and Foreign State Papers (1814) H.M.S.O: London, p. 470. https://archive.org/details/britishandforei10offigoog/page/469/mode/2up.

[68] Moore (1906), p. 2.

[69] Brown (2013), p. 3.

[70] Newcombe and Paradell (2009), p. 5.

method—an obligation of the host state to protect the alien, and the right of the home state to intervene if its citizen abroad is mistreated. This notion, besides its innovative aspects so as to provide safety for citizens abroad, also caused various forms of abusive intervention by more powerful states, and in particular the infamous *gunboat diplomacy*.[71]

2.5 Colonial and Quasi-Colonial Trade

More contemporary discourse striving to explain the clashes between the capital-importing and capital-exporting states succeed, or at least largely relate to, the clashes of nineteenth and early twentieth century between colonial powers and colonies.[72] In a world dominated by the Western colonial empires, most conflicts and legal tools related to international law originated from the need to control of local resources and assets in colonies.[73] In accordance with the colonial structure, disputes would be settled within the imperial rule, as local administrations were subject to the rule of the colonial authorities. Imperial courts had the jurisdiction and the competence, thus, the nature of conflict was not between two independent, sovereign nations. International arbitration or any other form of alternative dispute settlement between a colony and the colonising empire was not an option.

There were, however, many independent states that were neither major colonial powers nor direct colonies which were described as "quasi-colonies".[74] Gallagher and Robinson, as a part of their theory of "the imperialism of free trade"; and later on McLean, to explain the influence of the British Empire on territories it controlled without formal colonial responsibility, referred to the term the "informal empire".[75] Similar 'informal' empires also existed within the context of others, such as the Netherlands or Portugal. Rapid industrialisation during nineteenth century led to rapid globalisation and economic global expansion. It was, *inter alia*, the search for new markets, resources and assets that eventually caused colonisation and other forms of economic and political control over weaker states to emerge. Foreign influence and extraterritorial applicability of foreign (particularly European and the US) law dominated the domestic judicial systems in many of these states to a remarkable

[71] For a detailed historic account, see Hood (1975); also see Anzola (2008), pp. 1–9; Miles (2013), pp. 52–69 (for a series of 19th century examples, *inter alia*, on the use of armed intervention or coercion for 'adjusting differences').

[72] Miles (2013), pp. 120–121.

[73] Schrijver (1997), pp. 173–174.

[74] Schrijver (1997), p. 174.

[75] Gallagher and Robinson (1953), pp. 1 and 6; McLean (1976), p. 291.

extent.[76] The investors retained their nationality, and their own laws applied to them rather than the domestic law of the host state. These juridical initiatives were not limited to states and their institutions—in fact, even private commercial entities went as far as acting as sovereign bodies.

This being said, foreign influence has exceeded beyond extraterritorial judicial activities. Countries such as the Ottoman Empire, China, Japan, Iran and Egypt were urged, sometimes by use of force, to grant economic capitulations to colonial powers so that they would have access to foreign businesses and capital flow.[77] One of the most prevalent examples is probably the Ottoman Empire and its nineteenth century trade agreements with other European countries. The Treaty of Balta Liman (*Baltalimanı Antlaşması* in Modern Turkish), an 1838 trade agreement between the Ottoman and the British empires, was a trade and commerce treaty which unmistakably favoured the latter party.[78] It was a treaty set to replace an 1820 customs duties scheme, which had already granted exceptional concessions to merchants from, *inter alia,* Britain; such as a 3% customs duty to British merchants (in comparison, Ottoman merchants had to pay 60% in Britain). While Balta Liman increased this customs duty to 12%, it granted additional exemptions and concessions, and lifted export bans for a broad variety of British goods. Not only the new treaty ensured the continuation of many previous concessions, it also extended the advantages by including not only an MFN provision for all concessions and privileges granted to third party nationals, but also an NT provision which ensured the application of the same taxation schemes as Ottoman Muslim merchants, who enjoyed certain economic privileges vis-a-vis other Ottoman (non-Muslim) communities. The Ottoman government had signed a similar trade agreement with France the same year, to be followed by agreements with Sweden, Norway, Spain, Netherlands, Prussia and Belgium in 1840; as well as Denmark and Tuscany in 1841.

2.5.1 The Curious Case of the Dutch East India Company

In other cases, foreign merchants did not only possess economic privileges, but nothing short of complete control over the territory in which they had operated. One of the most prominent examples in this regard is the Dutch East India Company (*Vereenigde Oost-Indische Compagnie*, hereinafter referred to as "VOC") and its activities in Southeast Asia. Founded in 1602 by the Dutch States General, it was conferred rights to enter into treaties, acquire land and keep armed soldiers, besides its exclusive rights with regards to regional commerce.[79] In line with these rights and competences, the VOC established a government in Jakarta and it took over the regulatory and policing

[76] For a retrospective analysis of the BITs vis-à-vis earlier extraterritorial judiciary activities focusing on 'civilising' the ostensibly 'uncivilised', see Alvarez (2011), p. 86.

[77] Van Harten (2008), p. 15.

[78] Geyikdağı (2008), pp. 50–55.

[79] Miles (2013), p. 35 et seq.

powers within its claimed territory. Many of the earlier international investment law principles and the so-called 'investor-centric' notion of protection within the scope of the legal field can be traced back to the activities of the VOC and other overseas trade companies. Among its advisors was Hugo Grotius, who had worked many years for the VOC – Miles argued that some of the theories that he had developed strove to justify the legality of the governance of the VOC.[80] Additionally, the company had competed against other Western powers in the region, particularly Portuguese and British companies whose activities were focused on the East Indies. The VOC had established an economic and political dominance in the region, and to this end, it had also engaged in warfare to eliminate commercial rivals. From this illustration, it is possible to trace back the roots of two important features of international investment law, namely the emergence of investors as private actors within the international law structure and secondly, the alleged investor bias in investment protection.

The manner in which the VOC exercised and enjoyed its administrative competences particularly through emulation of sovereign authority leads to the conclusion that the VOC acted not only on its behalf in order to pursue its commercial interests, but also on behalf of the Dutch state itself, given the company's dependency on the state to sustain the enjoyment of privileges in the region.[81] The VOC did not, at least in the sense that a state is defined, act on a basis of sovereignty. The powers it exercised were limited to the extent that the Dutch government considered appropriate or necessary. This relationship between the Dutch state and the VOC merged the interests of VOC and the interests upheld by the state in the region, effectively turning a primarily commercial entity to an extension of the sovereign. An attack on the VOC would be considered an attack on the Dutch state itself, while the intervention or any military action of the VOC was through the mandate of the Dutch state.[82]

The VOC demonstrates the extent to which sovereign states had gone to justify *de jure* acts undertaken by a private entity, and internalise them with that of the sovereign itself. It was necessary to adjust the activities and interests of private commerce, at least the reasoning behind them, so that they would overlap with the interests of the colonial states. As an overwhelmingly privileged private actor, the VOC is a particularly infamous example—instead of being subject to treatment by a sovereign in another territory, the VOC, by definition a foreign investor, assumed sovereignty.

This example is crucial in retrospect. The VOC may be the most illustrative case of a private entity acting as a direct actor in international relations, a feature that, *inter alia*, defines international investment law.[83] Although private companies do not directly assume sovereignty over territories in the twenty-first century, it comes without surprise that especially multinational corporations may exercise significant political influence over their host and home states.[84] One legal counsel from Türkiye,

[80] Miles (2013), p. 35.

[81] Miles (2013), p. 35 et seq.

[82] Miles (2013), p. 35 et seq.

[83] Vadi (2015), p. 46.

[84] Wandahl Mouyal (2015), p. 30.

particularly active in the energy sector, elaborated on the dynamics of such influence during an interview conducted in the summer of 2015:

> [Large corporations] engage with the state, and have influence [on it]. Especially for the state, if they are talking to a multinational energy company, and if their presence [in the domestic market] will give a good impression to the world of [their] domestic market, this is a success for the state. The state could say that this particular company chose us among all other potential target economies.[85]

Politically sensitive sectors, such as energy and telecommunications, are some prominent examples. The significance of the issue manifests itself in sectoral lobbying activities, third party consultations in the course of trade and investment deals, as well as ISDS itself. The latter is a truly peculiar feature of international investment law, a mechanism by which foreign investors can bring a claim against a host state should the acts of a state damage or destroy their investment. It is no surprise such an international remedy bestowed upon foreign investors in an exclusive manner within the contemporary international law structure echoes from, and is often linked with, more extreme historical examples such as the one above.

Secondly, from a historical point of view, the alignment of 'public' and 'private' interests of the state and private businesses should not be evaluated separately from some of the most criticised features of the current international investment law regime, namely the so-called bias in favour of investors.[86] While there is some empirical evidence that the international investment law structure does not favour investors vis-à-vis host states,[87] the bias claim stands as one of the outstanding reasons, if not in fact the main reason, of the more recent clashes between capital-importing and capital-exporting states which dominated the second half of twentieth century. It is also relevant within the context of the Investment Court System (ICS) and the Multilateral Investment Court (MIC) as envisaged by modern trade and investment deals such as CETA,[88] EU – Singapore,[89] and EU – Vietnam[90] IPAs.

---

[85] Interview #3.

[86] Chung (2007) (claiming that international investment law favours investors).

[87] According to the ICSID Caseload Statistics published in August 2024 (2024-2), 53% of all ICSID cases finalised in 2024 were at least partially in favour of the claimant investor. In 36% of all cases, the outcome was in favour of respondent states. In 11%, arbitral tribunals decided that they had no jurisdiction. In all ICSID cases to date, claimant investors received a favourable decision in 49% of all cases. Decisions against investors stand at 30%. Tribunals rejected jurisdiction in about 20% of all cases. See, ICSID Caseload – Statistics (Issue 2024-2) https://icsid.worldbank.org/resources/publications/icsid-caseload-statistics. For an earlier statistical study noting that of all ICSID claims, investors have prevailed in 33% (and 16% in the last 50 claims by 2015), see Miller and Hicks (2015).

[88] Comprehensive and Economic Trade Agreement between Canada and the European Union (CETA) (2017). https://policy.trade.ec.europa.eu/eu-trade-relationships-country-and-region/countries-and-regions/canada/eu-canada-agreement_en.

[89] EUSIPA (Signed in 2018; not in force as of January 2025). https://policy.trade.ec.europa.eu/eu-trade-relationships-country-and-region/countries-and-regions/singapore/eu-singapore-agreements/texts-agreements_en.

[90] EUVIPA (Signed in 2019, not in force as of January 2025). https://policy.trade.ec.europa.eu/eu-trade-relationships-country-and-region/countries-and-regions/vietnam/eu-vietnam-agreement/texts-agreements_en.

This topic may seem distinct from the fair treatment accorded to foreigners in a host country. However, to the exact contrary, it highlights the reciprocity of the concept of fairness. In other words, treatment of foreigners should be fair *towards* the foreigner, but also fair *for* the host state. Claims relating to investor bias imply that the system is partial and has been built upon unfair rules and standards largely disregarding the host states' interests.[91] Another aspect of this argument is how international investment law instruments contain a series of rules that protect the investor against acts of the state, rather than equally protecting the state against the wrongdoings of a foreign company. It is no coincidence that BITs are often officially referred to as agreements on reciprocal promotion and protection of *investments*.

2.5.2 East Asia

Southeast Asia was not the only region which had suffered from excessive interventionism and foreign control. For many subjugated Asian nations, mid- and late-nineteenth century was a period of political and economic pressure, mostly due to single-sided treaties that granted economic and legal capitulations to Western powers. The Treaty of Wangxia,[92] signed in 1844 between the United States and the Qing Empire in the Portuguese city of Macao, ensured "the special protection of the local authorities" for the US citizens who are "placed on a common footing of amity and goodwill with subjects of China".[93] However, it is completely mute with regard to the protection of Chinese subjects in the United States. Initially, the situation was not very different for Japan either—in 1853, Matthew Perry of the US Navy, commanding a naval fleet, entered into Tokyo harbour and forcefully negotiated a series of trade deals, such as the Treaty of Kanagawa, that eventually opened the Japanese ports to the US merchant ships the year after.[94]

Following the US example, other Western powers such as Russia, France, the Netherlands and the British Empire also imposed trade agreements on Japan and China.[95] Under Emperor Meiji, who ruled between 1868 and 1912,[96] Japan undertook a swift and effective industrialisation and Westernisation process.

[91] *See* generally, OECD (2004).

[92] Treaty of Wangxia (or 'Treaty of Wang-hsia' 望厦條約 – 18 May 1844). https://china.usc.edu/treaty-wangxia-treaty-wang-hsia-%E6%9C%9B%E5%BB%88%E6%A2%9D%E7%B4%84-may-18-1844.

[93] Article XIX, Treaty of Wangxia.

[94] Treaty of Kanagawa (31 March 1854). https://avalon.law.yale.edu/19th_century/japan002.asp. Notably, its Article IX prescribes an earlier version of the Most-Favoured-Nation provision: "It is agreed, that if, at any future day, the government of Japan shall grant to any other nation or nations privileges and advantages which are not herein granted to the United states and the citizens thereof, that these same privileges and advantages shall be granted likewise to the United States and to the citizens thereof without any consultation or delay."

[95] Lipson (1985), p. 43; Treaty of Peace, Friendship, and Commerce between Her Majesty [of Great Britain] and the Tycoon of Japan (26 August 1858); Treaty of Nanjing (Nanking – 28 December 1842). https://china.usc.edu/treaty-nanjing-nanking-1842.

[96] Murase (1976), p. 274; for a detailed analysis of the Meiji-era reforms, see Keene (2002).

2.5.3 The Latin American Experience

Finally, the Latin American states present an intriguing story with regards to the global influence of the Western powers on international commerce. Venezuela is a particularly salient example.[97] The series of intense interactions between Venezuela and the Western powers from mid to late nineteenth century is possibly one of the most vivid illustrations of this conflicting relationship between "The West and the Rest",[98] and as was argued by Hood, "[m]any of Latin America's reactions towards the United States today are the direct though long-term repercussions of those seemingly remote days".[99] While historical frictions surely played their part in the making of Latin American states' contemporary identities and largely shaped their relationship with other states; others assert, particularly with regards to socialist republics such as Venezuela and Bolivia, that populist political narratives are used in order to facilitate historical discourse based on colonial and quasi-colonial exploitation.[100]

Besides the relationship with the United States, Venezuela's relations with the United Kingdom, Italy, France and Germany, particularly the series of events that led to the Anglo-German blockade of 1902[101] play a remarkable role in the late nineteenth–early twentieth century developments in global commerce, debt enforcement and international dispute settlement. Especially from 1870 onwards, Venezuela's modern feudalism locally referred to as *caudillismo* remarkably intensified in governance with despotic rulers succeeding one another.[102] The reason for the blockade was that Cipriano Castro, the President of Venezuela between 1899 and 1908, had avoided paying Venezuela's debts to several European states. Venezuela had had a long exercise of avoiding debts, a political tradition first exercised by the infamous dictator Antonio Guzmán Blanco during his rule between 1870 and 1877. Despite the seeming reluctance of the United Kingdom to use force to collect its debt, intervention eventually became unavoidable when other creditors, such as Germany, voiced their discontent with the situation. An armada of British, Italian and German ships had thus blockaded the Venezuelan shoreline from December 1902 to February 1903 and bombarded Caracas, until a series of treaties was signed between the blockading states and Venezuela, unsurprisingly, largely to the former's advantage.[103] In February 1903, a mixed claims commission was estab-

[97] Miles (2013). Hood's (1975) account of the Venezuela – European relationship is highly illustrative.

[98] More recently, the term has been used by Niall Ferguson; see Ferguson (2011), pp. 96–140.

[99] Hood (1975); also see, Whitaker (1948), pp. 59–68.

[100] Gomez (2011), p. 227.

[101] Mitchell (1999), p. 64 et seq.

[102] Miles (2013).

[103] United Nations (2006) Reports of International Arbitral Awards, Mixed Claims Commission France – Venezuela, vol. X, pp. 9–355; United Nations (2006) Reports of International Arbitral Awards, Mixed Claims Commission Germany – Venezuela, vol. X, pp. 357–476; United Nations (2006) Reports of International Arbitral Awards, Mixed Claims Commission Great Britain – Venezuela, vol. IX, pp. 349–533; United Nations (2006) Reports of International Arbitral Awards,

lished to handle the cases regarding the wrongful seizure of (or injury to) property owned by foreign nationals. This practice of enforcement came to be known as the gunboat diplomacy, and its exercise marks an important turning point in international dispute settlement. It also exemplifies one of the most notorious practices of use of force to coerce one state to comply with 'international' rules.

The histories of the Latin American countries are intrinsically connected to one another, and an overall examination may prove to be more accurate and comprehensive in certain cases than a country-by-country analysis. Venezuela is not the only Latin American country that suffered from the use of force to collect debts, and it was not the first or the last country to be exposed to the Western expansionism during the eighteenth and nineteenth centuries. In 1868, the Argentine jurist Carlos Calvo developed a series of arguments to tackle this excessive use of force towards indebted states. As it came to be known later, the *Calvo Doctrine* dismissed the right to diplomatic protection or international remedies for foreign investors and proposed that foreigners should submit their disputes to national courts, and nowhere else.[104] An early version of the NT principle is embedded in this doctrine, since one of the prominent principles was that foreigners should not be entitled to more rights than the nationals of the host states. Calvo asserted that a foreigner should not be entitled to international remedies, exactly because a national, it his dealings with his own state, was not entitled to it.[105] In line with the foregoing analysis of contingent and reciprocal fairness, Calvo's line of reasoning clearly follows that what is fair for a foreigner is to be subject to treatment to which a national is entitled.

Another important standpoint of the doctrine was that it proposed a very limited use of force. The doctrine of state sovereignty is presented as a basis for the rule of non-intervention, both diplomatic and physical.[106] In a strict sense, Calvo's arguments did not confine a foreigner to whatever treatment a sovereign may deem appropriate for its nationals in an absolute sense, as he further suggested that if local remedies are exhausted, other international remedies, such as forceful intervention, may come into play.[107] During the escalation of crisis and the blockade in Venezuela before 1903, Venezuela based its arguments on NT and non-intervention principles, and refused to settle the conflict by means of arbitration. As Miles points out, their argument did not make a significant impact on the dispute and eventually British and German naval force determined the course of the matter.[108]

For more powerful states, the fact that a sovereign treated a foreigner in the same way it treated a national was not enough. Conceptualising and enforcing rights under international law by (usually forced and one-sided) trade agreements has many examples within the context of colonial powers and quasi-colonial territories

Mixed Claims Commission Italy – Venezuela, vol. X, pp. 477–692; United Nations (2006) Reports of International Arbitral Awards, Mixed Claims Commission United States – Venezuela, vol. IX, pp. 113–318.

[104] Shea (1955), pp. 16–21.

[105] Shea (1955), pp. 16–21.

[106] Shea (1955), pp. 16–21.

[107] Shea (1955), p. 19.

[108] Miles (2013), pp. 67–69.

throughout the nineteenth century. The establishment and functioning of the mixed claims commission is also an accurate example of how these forced agreements were imposed upon host states. The abysmal political and economic gap between such colonial powers and resource-rich, less developed countries had rendered it virtually impossible for host states to make a substantial contribution to the development of this particular field of international law, as colonial empires systematically and forcefully legitimised their intervention to protect and preserve their nationals' commercial interests abroad.[109] They have done so while enjoying, mostly through coercion and use of force, *de facto* universalisation of their rules, norms and values as Vitoria declared some centuries earlier.

This is why Calvo's doctrine and many of its subsequent variations were destined to fail. Expectedly, this Latin American counteraction to the development and exercise of the universal imposition of a Western system did not find the necessary support from Europe and the United States to develop into an internationally accepted doctrine.[110] This, however, is not to say that the doctrine has vanished completely today—in fact, its eventual legacy, namely the modern NT principle, is widely accepted not only in investment law, but also in trade law and commercial law proceedings and dispute settlement despite its significantly modified nature.[111] Beyond all, the Calvo Doctrine stands as among some of the first strings of doctrinal opposition to the allegedly biased development of international investment protection and treatment of foreigners; therefore its importance should not be understated and this initiative should not be seen primarily a failure. It acts as a reactionary movement against the then-growing tendency to, *inter alia*, stretch a global notion of what constituted fair treatment of foreigners, by emphasising on the contingent nature of what was could be regarded as fair treatment of a foreigner within a domestic context. Nonetheless, the doctrine continues to influence Latin America and beyond today, including the United States.[112]

2.6 Twentieth Century (I): Beginning of the Century Until the World War II

2.6.1 Prohibition of the Use of Force

The beginning of the twentieth century saw noteworthy efforts to adjust the position of capital-importing and capital-exporting states with regards to foreign claims and alien protection, notwithstanding the continuing use of force by European states and the United States to back up diplomatic claims in the territories of capital-importing

[109] Tzouvala (2020).

[110] Miles (2013), p. 50.

[111] Van Den Bossche (2008), p. 344 et seq.

[112] Escarcena (2014), p. 160.

states.[113] In 1899, upon the initiative of the Russian Czar Nicholas II, a peace conference was convened in The Hague, which included a convention for the "Pacific Settlement of International Disputes".[114] Article 1 of the Convention calls for the prevention of use of force to resolve disputes, and the signatory states agree to show their utmost efforts to ensure pacific settlement of disputes.[115]

Immediately after the Venezuelan blockade of 1902, Argentine minister of foreign affairs Luis Drago, in a diplomatic note to the United States, argued that states should not resort to use of force against Latin American states for debt collection. The Drago Doctrine, in different aspects, was built upon both Monroe[116] and Calvo doctrines. It enhanced the former in the sense that it concerns solely Latin American states; and the latter, for its opposition to the use of force to settle international disputes.

The doctrine was referred to the second conference in The Hague in 1907 after it was contended that the importance of the issue was global rather than regional.[117] Upon the proposal of the delegate of the United States, General Horace Porter, the Drago-Porter Convention was adopted; stating that:

> **Article 1:**
> The Contracting Powers agree not to have recourse to armed force for the recovery of contract debts claimed from the Government of one country by the Government of another country as being due to its nationals.
> This undertaking is, however, not applicable when the debtor State refuses or neglects to reply to an offer of arbitration, or, accepting the offer, prevents any compromise from being agreed on, or, after the arbitration, fails to submit the award.[118]

As is clear in the wording of the Article 1, the Drago-Porter Convention does not unconditionally prevent the use of force for the collection of debts, given the use of force was still a diplomatic tool, yet now only when a state refused to refer the dispute to arbitration, or prevented compromise after the arbitration. While the Drago-Porter Convention did not realise Drago's vision in its entirety, it was claimed that the provision softened the more radical approach adopted by the Calvo Doctrine.[119]

---

[113] Newcombe and Paradell (2009), pp. 8–9.

[114] Convention pour le règlement pacifique des conflits internationaux (The Hague Convention on the Pacific Settlement of International Disputes – the 'The Hague Convention 1899') (1899) The authentic (French) text: http://wetten.overheid.nl/BWBV0005494/geldigheidsdatum_23-05-2013.

[115] Article 1, The Hague Convention (1899): "En vue de prévenir *autant que possible le recours à la force* dans les rapports entre les Etats, les Puissances signataires conviennent d'employer tous leurs efforts pour assurer le règlement pacifique des différends internationaux." Emphasis added.

[116] Sexton (2011). Monroe Doctrine stated that further attempts to interfere with states in America by European powers would be considered as acts of aggression and it requires US intervention.

[117] Convention Respecting the Limitations of the Employment of Force for the Recovery of Contract Debts (the 'The Hague Convention 1907' or 'Drago-Porter Convention') (1907). http://avalon.law.yale.edu/20th_century/hague072.asp.

[118] Article 1, The Hague Convention 1907.

[119] Assessing that the Calvo Doctrine was "broader" than the alternative proposed by Drago; Hershey (1907), p. 27.

Eventually, despite expressed willingness by its parties to use and promote pacific means of settling disputes, The Hague Conventions of 1899 and 1907 were far from effectively preventing the use of force. Lipson provides for a striking illustration of the intensity of forceful intervention at the time: between the years 1820 and 1914, the British Empire intervened in Latin America "at least forty times" to enforce claims of their nationals.[120]

It was only in 1928 that the General Treaty for the Renunciation of War (Kellogg-Briand Pact) was signed to prohibit the use of force to settle international conflicts, albeit with a limited number of parties.[121] One of the main debates over the provisions of the Kellogg-Briand Pact was whether it also prevented use of force that did not "amount to war"—Newcombe argues that "[v]arious overt or covert interventions by Western states nevertheless continued, related in part to the protection of economic interests."[122] Nonetheless, representing the transitional period until the end of WWII[123] in terms of the prohibition of the threat and the use of force, it stands as an important stepping stone.

2.6.2 IMS of the Twentieth Century

Throughout the twentieth century, the corrosion of the traditional contingent approach which placed the treatment of foreigners fundamentally within the domestic legal system of the host state had continued. The growth, and growing systematisation, of international trade and investment; emergence of a variety of disputes, and the genesis of the international trade and investment law jurisprudence brought along new questions and political-legal problems to address. One of the persistent controversies was the heterogeneity of the national laws concerning the protection of foreigners around the globe. As was mentioned above, the consolidated arguments under the Calvo Doctrine, particularly with regards to the primacy of national sovereignty, were far from being satisfactory for Western investors and states. While Western, traditionally capital-exporting states had sustained the enjoyment of their terms, rules and laws beyond their borders, it was during the first half of twentieth century that the general idea among European and US legal scholars and lawyers had finally been shaped into an "international standard", which was to set a threshold for the minimum protection that any state should provide to foreigners in accordance with international law. The standard also brought along the consequence that any argument by states claiming that the treatment accorded to foreigners was consistent with the national provisions was insufficient *per se*. Indeed, the word 'treatment' itself means little, unless a state, through its national sovereignty and

[120] Lipson (1985), p. 54.

[121] General Treaty for the Renunciation of War (the 'Kellogg – Briand Pact') (1928).

[122] Newcombe and Paradell (2009), p. 10.

[123] Article 2(4), the Charter of the United Nations (1945).

regulatory powers, attaches to it a context. This context, it seemed, had to keep up with the new international standard which originated from the collection of rules adhered to by the 'civilised' nations.[124]

From different parts of the world arose different reactions to this 'exclusively Western and civilised'[125] concept of minimum standard. First, following the Bolshevik Revolution in 1917, the Soviet Union expropriated the property of national and foreign enterprises. The basis for this act was that there was equality—little was the difference between how much the national and foreign investor suffered damages.[126] Subsequent arbitral tribunals ruled that the Soviet Union must pay compensation due to, *inter alia*, unjust enrichment.[127]

Root, earlier during his famous 1910 address to the American Society of International Law, raised a crucial point: "If any country's system of law and administration does not conform to [IMS], although the people of the country may be content or compelled to live under it, no other country can be compelled to accept it as furnishing a satisfactory measure of treatment to its citizens."[128] In other words, the fact that people, locals and foreigners alike, are equal in poor conditions does not comply with the rationale of the existence of IMS. Its opposing idea, absolute equality, was unfair and unsatisfactory. This supremacy of international law over national laws, therefore, paved the way towards the establishment of a 'universal' fairness which aimed at guiding fragmented domestic rules.

While he referred to what *does not* determine the limits of the international standard, Root was mostly ambiguous about its framework. He drew attention to the "increase in facilities for transportation and communication" and how it "has set in motion vast armies of travellers who are making their way into the most remote corners of foreign countries".[129] He thereby stated that this situation had given rise to more mistreatment of these travellers, and this problem needed to be addressed "pursuant to fixed, definite, certain, and universally recognized rules of international action."[130] The speech, however, fails to sustain the assertive tone of its articulated objective. There are serious problems with the origin and content of this international standard. First, Root ambiguously referred to the "general acceptance by all civilized countries" as the source of MST relating to such citizens, without further elaboration on which countries and which rules were eligible in the making of this standard. Furthermore, as Paparinskis observes, Root does not address the contradiction that the acceptance of the standard is both a criterion for being a member of the said civilisation, and an obligation.[131]

[124] Root (1910), p. 21.

[125] Anghie (2004), p. 50 et seq.

[126] Dolzer and Schreuer (2012), pp. 28–36; Nussbaum (1950).

[127] Nussbaum (1950), p. 50.

[128] Root (1910), p. 21.

[129] Root (1910), p. 16.

[130] Root (1910), p. 19.

[131] Paparinskis (2013), p. 40.

This conclusion is consistent with the US-Mexico General Claims Commission's wording in its *Harry Roberts* decision, explicitly speaking of a 'test' to determine whether or not a state complies with this international standard. The Commission asserted that the way a state treated its nationals was not a determining factor on how foreigners should be treated, given that a state could grossly mistreat its nationals. This factor could not justify the equal mistreatment of foreigners. Should there be such a borderline, it is the "ordinary standards of civilization".[132] What these ordinary standards are, however, cannot be extracted from the decision.

IMS, as a threshold and a guiding notion originating from CIL, remains highly abstract to this day. While contemporary adjudicatory experience has revealed some constituent elements, it does not seem to have immediately identifiable, exhaustive content. During the early twentieth century, the criteria and the explanations provided, from a global perspective, did not suffice to tackle its inherent vagueness. What indeed were the ordinary standards of civilisation? More fundamentally, what was to be considered 'civilised'? What would be deemed unacceptable or ordinary in this context—and, what *is* the context? What is the most appropriate way to concretise such an arbitrary threshold? In the 1926 case *Neer*,[133] the Mixed Claims Commission ruled that for a state to violate the international standard, "the treatment of alien [...] should amount to an outrage, to bad faith, to wilful neglect of duty, or to an insufficiency of governmental action so far short of international standards that every reasonable and impartial man would readily recognize its insufficiency."[134] Later in mid-twentieth century, Roth attempted to further determine the extent of IMS within a more tangible framework. He argued that "the content of the fundamental idea must be determined by the principles which the civilized nations recognize in general in their municipal organization."[135] Despite these elaborations, the ambiguity persisted.

In August 1938, the Mexican government, after expropriating agricultural lands of *inter alia* American citizens, argued that foreign investors who voluntarily invest in another state with the expectation of enjoying the benefits of their investment should also be prepared for the risks their investments might entail.[136] The Mexican position also asserted that "[i]t would be unjust that [the investor] should aspire to a privileged position safe from any risk, but availing himself [...] of the effort of the nationals which must be to the benefit of the collectivity."[137] The Mexican position, revolving around a comparison between the rights and remedies enjoyed by the

---

[132] *Harry Roberts v. United Mexican States* (1926) *US-Mexico General Claims Commission Reports of International Arbitral Awards*, vol. IV pp. 77–81.

[133] *LFH Neer and Pauline Neer (U.S.A.) v. United Mexican States* (1926) IV RIAA, pp. 60–66. http://legal.un.org/riaa/cases/vol_IV/60-66.pdf. The case was brought before a Mixed Claims Commission following Mexico's failure to properly investigate the death of a US citizen.

[134] *Neer v. Mexico* (1926), p. 61.

[135] Roth (1949), p. 87.

[136] Borchard (1940), p. 447.

[137] Borchard (1940), p. 445.

nationals and foreigners, stemmed from a contingent understanding of what was deemed fair for foreigners—yet, it failed to succeed.

The US position, in contrast, originated from an overarching standard set by the international law and principles. The response to the Mexican position in this particular case reiterates the rationale behind the existence of an IMS:

> [The Mexican doctrine of risk] presupposes the maintenance of law and order **consistent with principles of international law**; that is to say, when aliens are admitted into a country, the country is obligated to accord them that degree of protection of life and property consistent with the standards of justice recognized by the law of nations.[138]

One fundamental difference is that whereas Mexican position perceived this (internationally) standardised protection as a privilege *vis-á-vis* nationals of the host state, the US position contended that it was far from being a privilege and that expropriation without compensation could not be justified on the grounds of equality.

While the twentieth century conceptualisations of international standard seem to revolve around a discourse promoting a threshold set by civilised nations, one historical tendency, maybe unintentionally, seems to have repeated itself: setting the limits by reference to relative qualifiers. It seems fairly evident that IMS aims at transcending beyond any treatment accorded to nationals as justification for the mistreatment of foreigners. However, as will be detailed in below Chapters, non-discrimination, a notion which injects an inescapable comparison of the treatment of the foreign and the national, is referred to among the few tangible constituent elements of this seemingly non-contingent, overarching meta-principle. This is particularly true for earlier IIAs encompassing the standard of treatment for foreigners.[139] How can the treatment accorded to the nationals both be a criterion, and be excluded as a justification at the same time? While it may be true that a foreigner might consider it fair to be accorded a treatment better than the nationals of the state in which he lives, what seems to further pose a flaw to the argument is, from a Calvonian perspective, the fact that it may now be the national not having the remedy—in other words, creating an unfair situation in reverse. To further elaborate on the controversy, one might also ask—if a treatment is unfair for a national, can it still be fair under the scheme of a non-contingent, objective, universally fair standard? Or is it the very nature of being a foreigner in another country that allegedly levels out this seeming inequality between a national, bound to seek a remedy through domestic means; and a foreigner, an inherently vulnerable subject in an alien environment who needs protection which stems from international law?

The twentieth century saw more attempts to define the standard more tangibly. There were some codification initiatives throughout 1920s and 30s. In 1924, a Committee of Experts for the Progressive Codification of International Law, which was to represent "the main forms of civilisation and the principal legal systems of

---

[138] Borchard (1940), p. 446.

[139] *See* Chap. 5.

the world" was established by the Assembly of the League of Nations.[140] Among several other topics such as nationality and territorial waters, the issue of state responsibility for damages done to foreigners was to be discussed and codified. In 1927, after consultations with governments, the Assembly decided to convene a diplomatic conference for this purpose. Despite high hopes, the 1930 Codification Conference, which convened in The Hague, was far from being effective,[141] as the conference was unable to adopt any conventions except one on territorial waters. One reason for the failure was the discrepancies on the issue of treatment standards. The draft included a provision which limited the state responsibility to suffered damages where the state fails to act where it would reasonably be expected to act "in order to prevent, redress or inflict punishment for the acts causing the damage."[142] The voting itself is a clear demonstration of how the majority of the capital-importing states, particularly Latin American states, upheld the idea that foreign nationals should be subject to equal treatment with nationals.[143] Consequently, the final draft was not adopted.

In 1929, the Convention on the Treatment of Foreigners was drafted with assertive provisions which equipped foreigners with an absolute equal treatment; particularly with regard to economic, civil, judicial and succession rights, following the International Conference on the Treatment of Foreigners which was held in Paris between 5 November to 4 December.[144] Over the course of three weeks, the draft was modified so much that most of the substance was completely changed or altered. Ultimately, most states refused to sign the draft.[145]

In 1933, the Seventh International Conference of American States took place in Montevideo, producing the 1933 Convention on the Rights and Duties of States.[146] This regional convention stands apart from the rest of the contemporary initiatives since its dominant ideas were inherited from the Latin American approach on standards of treatment. Many provisions revisited the Calvo Doctrine, as the convention clearly stated that "foreigners may not claim rights other or more extensive than those of the nationals."[147] The convention, despite major reservations by capital exporting states, was adopted.

---

140 League of Nations Official Journal, vol. 5, Special Supplement No. 21 (1924), p. 10.

141 Rosenne (1998), p. 3.

142 Borchard (1930), p. 535.

143 Borchard (1930), p. 536. From Borchard's account, it seems that this "well-known" point was initially raised by the Mexican delegation. He further remarked that this point had little relation to the subject matter.

144 Kuhn (1930); Deveze, Michel (President of the Conference) (1930) Work of the International Conference on the Treatment of Foreigners (C.10.1930.II).

145 Cutler (1933), p. 230.

146 Montevideo Convention on the Rights and Duties of States (the "Montevideo Convention") (1933). https://www.jus.uio.no/english/services/library/treaties/01/1-02/rights-duties-states.html.

147 Article 9, Montevideo Convention (1933).

IMS continued its development throughout twentieth century, as international law encompassed beyond what was then considered 'Western' or 'civilised' world—despite the complete absence of any fruitful substantial consensus or elaboration on where it began and ended.

2.7 Twentieth Century (II): The Cold War Era (1945–1990)

2.7.1 A Decolonising World

The WWII, notwithstanding its direct consequences such as the utmost destruction it had caused, has had countless indirect consequences in every aspect of the world history and global development. Likewise, the development of international investment and trade law was radically influenced by the war itself, as well as the subsequent events from 1945 onwards such as the peaceful settlement of disputes. The Charter of the United Nations, the foundational text of its titular organisation, reads that it is based on "the principle of the sovereign equality of all its Members", and it adds that "[a]ll Members shall settle their international disputes by peaceful means in such a manner that international peace and security, and justice, are not endangered." It also notes that "[a]ll Members shall refrain in their international relations from the threat or use of force against the territorial integrity or political independence of any state".[148]

After the war, a decolonisation process had begun. Many new states were founded in former colonial territories, and the shift in the global political environment had to be supplemented by global economic reforms. The formerly intra-colonial (or domestic) transactions and interrelations were now international relationships, established between independent states. This development intensified the number of international disputes on the protection of investments. Additionally, the process saw the modification and the development of the nature of investment disputes. The historical conflict between the 'civilised', developed world and the less developed world has taken a completely different form: the disputes between colonial empires, and colonies as well as quasi-colonies transformed themselves into fully-fledged clashes between capital-rich, industrialised states which needed raw material, natural resources and labour force on the one hand; developing, resource rich, underdeveloped, newly emerging agrarian states with infrastructural, political, civil, and economic issues.[149]

Following their independence, many former colonies adopted rather conservative and isolationist policies. Large-scale nationalisations took place in former colonial regions such as Latin America, Indonesia and Middle East.[150] In addition, other

[148] Article 2(1), (3) and (4), UN Charter (1945).

[149] For a comprehensive account, *see* James and Leake (2015).

[150] Newcombe and Paradell (2009), pp. 18–19.

regions such as Eastern Europe were influenced by the Soviet ideology, also leading them to isolation with regards to international political and economic relations. With the political polarisation and tension escalating throughout the Cold War, many new states closed themselves off to their former masters. As Muchlinski describes, "these states sought redress for past and […] continuing economic exploitation from the former […] colonial powers."[151]

For newly emerging states, "sovereignty [was] the hard-won prize of their long struggle for emancipation. It [was] the legal epitome of the fact that they [were now] masters in their own house."[152] This trend of isolation and nationalisation can be seen as a strong indication of distrust towards the Western world, and the desire to maintain true sovereignty free from foreign intervention, physical or diplomatic. In the wake of their independence, capital-importing states called for a "New International Economic Order",[153] with the primary aim of breaking what they perceived as their political and economic dependency on developed, industrialised nations. During 1970s, several resolutions in line with this objective were passed, targeting mainly "the remaining vestiges of alien and colonial domination, foreign occupation, racial discrimination, apartheid and neo-colonialism in all its forms."[154] This new order aimed to establish "[f]ull permanent sovereignty of every [s]tate over its natural resources and all economic activities", particularly the right "[t]o nationalize, expropriate or transfer ownership of foreign property, in which case **appropriate compensation** should be paid by the [s]tate adopting such measures […]."[155]

Another natural consequence of the decolonisation was that more nations emerged as subjects of international law, as the mandate of colonial empires collapsed. Hitherto overlooked parts of the globe were now *de jure* equals of the West, eligible to participate in the making of international law. Treatment of foreigners, and specifically the amount of compensation for the expropriation of property of a foreigner gave rise to intense and long-lasting disagreements. While newly emerging, mostly capital-importing states pushed for the principal application of their national laws and more favourable customary rules for such compensation, capital-exporting bloc insisted on the thresholds put in place through what they asserted to be the CIL: IMS on the treatment of aliens. Different positions upheld by capital importing and exporting states reignited the ambiguity and insecurity with regards to the customary international rules governing foreign investment and protection of

[151] Muchlinski (1996), p. 208.

[152] Abi-Saab (1962), p. 103.

[153] Lowenfeld (2008), p. 491.

[154] United Nations General Assembly, Declaration on the Establishment of a New International Economic Order (Resolution No. 3201 (S-VI), 1 May 1974). http://www.un-documents.net/s6r3201.htm.

[155] United Nations General Assembly, Charter of Economic Rights and Duties of States (Resolution No. 3281, 12 December 1974). https://undocs.org/a/res/3281(xxix). Emphasis added.

foreign investment.[156] With its *Barcelona Traction* case,[157] the ICJ concluded that there were no universally accepted rules on protection of foreign investors. According to the Court,

> [...] it may at first sight appear surprising that the evolution of law has not gone further and that no generally accepted rules in the matter have crystallized on the international plane. Nevertheless, a more thorough examination of the facts shows that the law on the subject has been formed in a period characterized by an intense conflict of systems and interests. [...] Here as elsewhere, a body of rules could only have developed with the consent of those concerned.[158]

The ICJ, however, was not alone in its assertion that the issue of an international standard was far from established. A decade earlier, Jennings, after refusing the *a priori* deduction of commercial rules and concessions from "the idea of an international standard",[159] concluded that:

> The international standard thus means little more in practice than the assertion of the primacy of international over municipal law. [...] [T]he time has probably come to concentrate on the development of specific rules of law for particular situations rather than to hark back to an obsolete controversy over the most general of principles.[160]

2.7.2 *Codification and Treaty-Making*

The discussions over the customary law governing foreign investment became an issue of global prominence. This political and economic environment, and particularly the lack of certainty with regards to the rules governing the international legal system, prompted ambitious attempts at establishing a comprehensive multilateral legal framework. The first post-WWII attempt on codification and consolidation of foreign investment protection was the Havana Charter of 24 March 1948.[161] A number of substantive provisions were included in the draft on matters such as regulation of foreign investment by corporations, security of foreign investments, "just and equitable"[162] treatment for foreign enterprise, skills, capital, arts and technology, and the right of capital-importing states to regulate the conditions of inward investment.[163]

---

[156] Kläger draws attention to the feasibility of bilateral negotiations due to this ambiguity and lack of consensus, Kläger (2013), p. 25.

[157] *The Barcelona Traction, Light and Power Company*, Limited (*Belgium v. Spain*), Second Phase (Judgment of 5 February 1970). https://www.icj-cij.org/sites/default/files/case-related/50/050-19700205-JUD-01-00-EN.pdf.

[158] *Barcelona Traction* (1970), par. 89.

[159] Jennings (1961), pp. 180–181.

[160] Jennings (1961), p. 181.

[161] Havana Charter for an International Trade Organization (1948, not in force). https://www.wto.org/english/docs_e/legal_e/havana_e.pdf.

[162] Article 11(2)(a)(i), Havana Charter (1948).

[163] Article 12, Havana Charter (1948).

The latter provision, along with the absence of an explicatory, definitive clause on how to compensate in case of an expropriation, generated a sound opposition to the Charter. It was eventually discarded when the United States Senate refused to approve the US ratification.[164] The failure was cemented as several other signatories also refused to ratify the Charter. Consequently, the Havana Charter never entered into force and the International Trade Organization, the international body to be created by the Charter, was never established.[165] Instead, the General Agreement on Tariffs and Trade (GATT)[166] replaced the ITO, yet with a less ambitious scope. GATT's exclusion of provisions on investment law and protection and exclusive focus on trade-related matters caused the segregation of two naturally inherent topics, namely international trade law and international investment law. From then on, these fields of international law have developed independently, with limited interaction.[167]

A second post-WWII attempt on multilateralisation was the Economic Agreement of Bogota, one of the agreements upon which the Organization of the American States[168] had agreed at the Bogota Conference. Like the Havana Charter, it never entered into force. The latter's failure is primarily attributed to the reluctance of the US Congress to ratify the draft—ironically, it is also credited for its remarkable influence on the subsequent US treaty practice.[169] Similarly, the Economic Agreement of Bogota seems to have fallen apart due to lack of ratification in the region.[170] Despite their demise, these treaties and their provisions had significant impact on future treaties concerning investment protection. It was hindered by disagreements between the capital-importing and capital-exporting states over the calculation of compensation in case of expropriation. The conflicting notions of 'full compensation' and 'appropriate compensation' played a significant role on the accumulation of discrepancies.

Until 1960s, there had been several non-governmental initiatives to achieve the multilateralisation of international investment protection. The first of those attempts, the *International Code of Fair Treatment for Foreign Investment* proposed by the ICC in 1949,[171] failed due to its expansive scope. In 1957, the ICC issued a similar call for a treaty, again, with little success.[172]

---

[164] Jackson (1997), p. 38.

[165] Newcombe and Paradell (2009), p. 20.

[166] The General Agreement on Tariffs and Trade ('GATT' - 1947). https://www.wto.org/english/docs_e/legal_e/gatt47.pdf.

[167] Newcombe and Paradell (2009), p. 20.

[168] The Economic Agreement of Bogota of the Organization of American States (1948). http://www.oas.org/juridico/english/treaties/A-43_Economic_Agreement_of_Bogota.pdf.

[169] Vandevelde (2010), p. 44.

[170] Nwogugu (1965), pp. 139–141.

[171] International Code of Fair Treatment for Foreign Investment (the 'ICC Code' - 1949), printed in: UNCTAD (2003) International Investment Instruments: A Compendium (Volume I – Multilateral Instruments), pp. 273–276, https://unctad.org/system/files/official-document/dtci30vol1_en.pdf.

[172] Newcombe and Paradell (2009), p. 21.

Despite its failure, several provisions of the ICC Code need mention. Articles 2 to 5 prohibit discrimination vis-à-vis nationals, ensure NT for foreigners, and guarantee due process and access to justice "under the same conditions as nationals".[173] Article 2 refers to "fair treatment".[174] Article 3 elaborates on what is meant by 'fair', and ties it down to contingent principles of non-discrimination and NT.

> The High Contracting Parties shall take no discriminatory political, legal or administrative measures designed to hamper investments in their territories by the nationals of the other High Contracting Parties. They shall give to investments originating with the other High Contracting Parties treatment no less favourable than to investments made by their own nationals. In the case, however, of investments immediately concerned with national defence, special conditions may, if necessary, be imposed.[175]

This contingent threshold aside, Article 5(4) sets an even higher, objective threshold as a 'safety belt':

> Should the nationals of one of the [parties] not enjoy the full benefit of the civil rights generally recognized by the [parties] or by international law, the nationals of the other [parties] shall be entitled to such rights and this protection shall not be denied to them on the ground that a preferential system would thus be established in their favour.[176]

The ICC Code Article 5(4) is one of the earliest, if not in fact the earliest, modern legal text drafted to include an obligation to accord fair treatment attached to a higher international standard with elaboration on its content and meaning. The limits are drawn by the civil rights enjoyed by the national of its parties, and it anchors the standard of treatment to international law. While the governing principles of international law are not further specified, non-discrimination, due process and access to justice are easily identified from a collective reading of the Code. All three are relevant sub-elements of the contemporary FET principle in investment arbitration.

In 1957 and 1958, two draft conventions were separately prepared: one by the German Society to Advance the Protection of Foreign Investments, and the other by a group of European lawyers led by Sir Hartley Shawcross.[177] These two drafts were later consolidated as the 1959 Draft Convention on Investments Abroad.[178] The draft contained a provision on MST which constitutes an early example of FET; protection against discrimination and "just and effective" compensation for expropriation; as well as a provision on ISDS.[179] The draft was the first instrument in investment law to include ISDS as a dispute settlement mechanism.

---

173 Articles 2, 3, 4, and 5, ICC Code (1949).

174 Article 2, ICC Code (1949).

175 Article 3, ICC Code (1949).

176 Article 5(4), ICC Code (1949).

177 Muchlinski (1996), p. 324.

178 Draft Convention on Investments Abroad (the 'Abs-Shawcross (Draft) Convention' - 1959), printed in UNCTAD (2003) *International Investment Instruments: A Compendium* –301 – 303. https://unctad.org/system/files/official-document/dite2vol5_en.pdf.

179 Article 6, Abs-Shawcross Draft Convention (1959).

In 1962, the Abs-Shawcross Convention eventually led to the OECD Draft Convention on the Protection of Foreign Property. The OECD Draft, however, was a text discussed by the members of the OECD, and did not reflect a global compromise between capital-importing and capital-exporting states (including non-members of the OECD) on the guiding principles of foreign investment law. As a consequence, several less developed members of the OECD (then OEEC, Organization for European Economic Cooperation) opposed to the adoption of the draft convention.[180] Instead of a convention, the rejected draft was adopted as a model for investment protection treaties in 1967 by the Council of the OECD.[181]

2.7.3 Regional and Bilateral Attempts at Consolidation

In the post-WWII period, many states signed bilateral treaties on commerce and navigation. From the end of the WWII to mid-1960s, the US alone signed twenty-one Treaties on Friendship, Commerce and Navigation ("FCN"). The twentieth century FCN treaties particularly concerned investment protection unlike its traditional predecessors—early FCN treaties were wider in scope as they addressed issues related to trade and commerce rather than investment protection. The shift in focus was caused mainly by the GATT and its designated scope.[182] Given that international trade was largely multilateralised, the FCN treaties assumed the role of filling in the gap left by the lack of investment protection provisions on a global scale. In that sense, mid-twentieth century FCN treaties are the late predecessors of the BITs,[183] which came into existence in late 1950s.

The gradual increase in references to international arbitration in IIAs brought along issues of practical and procedural significance. As is the case for many fields in international jurisprudence, the matters relating to the functioning and enforcement of arbitral awards were largely problematic, and most of the practical nuances were unvisited. It was not before 1958 that New York Convention on the Recognition of Foreign Arbitral Awards was ratified.[184] The Convention remains highly relevant

---

[180] Snyder (1963), p. 1113.

[181] The Draft Convention on the Protection of Foreign Property (the 'OECD Model') (1967). https://investmentpolicy.unctad.org/international-investment-agreements/treaty-files/2812/download. Another notable Draft Convention was simultaneously prepared in the United States, namely the Draft Convention on the International Responsibility of States for Injuries to Aliens ('the Harvard Draft Convention') (1961). This document has since been commonly referred as evidence that the so-called 'police powers doctrine' is a recognised rule in general international law. Sohn and Baxter (1961).

[182] Alschner (2013), p. 462.

[183] Alschner (2013), p. 462.

[184] New York Convention on the Recognition of Foreign Arbitral Awards (the "New York Convention" – 1958). https://www.newyorkconvention.org/english.

with regards to the current system of investment arbitration enforcement as well as international commercial arbitration.

The Convention on the Settlement of Investment Disputes between States and Nationals of Other States[185] was signed in 1965, establishing ICSID, the first forum to specifically target investor-state disputes arising from investments undertaken in a state other than the investor's home state.[186] It broke the mandate of diplomatic protection (or state-state dispute settlement) in investment disputes, abolishing the necessity of an investor relying on the action of a state against an alleged violation.

Within the context of international investment law, the twentieth century can be described, for the most part, by the subsequent failures outlined above. In early 1960s, after all these failed attempts at creating a multilateral framework for international investment protection, the World Bank took the initiative to pinpoint the trilateral relationship of economic development, international cooperation and international investment.[187] Aron Broches, the then-General Counsel of the World Bank, initiated the debates on the possible scope of a consolidated and multilateral instrument and institution on international investment protection.[188] His deduction was that despite seemingly irreconcilable differences on the issue of standards of protection, a procedural consensus regarding the rules on the settlement of disputes through arbitration was not as farfetched. The challenge was that this new concept, namely the '*procedure before substance*',[189] was initially considered to be very limited. Broches' vision was criticised on the grounds that without substantive rules, procedure would matter little, and that the results would be artificial.

This counter-argument has since been proven to be wrong. Indeed, given the high standards upheld by the capital-exporting states and the block of host states opposing to such international threshold, one possibility was naturally to push the consensus to its limits and attempt to achieve what was actually viable rather than aiming for something seemingly impossible. Another objective of such procedural institutionalisation was to 'depoliticise'[190] investment disputes, but as Miles argues, an irony is hidden in this rationale. First of all, this argument builds upon the historical perception that national courts are by default corrupt, biased, or politicised; and that the only reliable method to resolve investment disputes is international arbitration.[191] In this line of thought, such argument would superficially build upon an immense distrust towards the national legal systems of host states. Besides, given the intertwined relationship between law and politics, particularly with regards to

[185] The Convention on the Settlement of Investment Disputes between States and National of Other States (the 'ICSID Convention' – 1965). https://icsid.worldbank.org/sites/default/files/ICSID_Convention_EN.pdf.

[186] The International Centre for the Settlement of Investment Disputes ('ICSID'). https://icsid.worldbank.org.

[187] Dolzer and Schreuer (2012), p. 9.

[188] Dolzer and Schreuer (2012), p. 9.

[189] Dolzer and Schreuer (2012), p. 20. Also see, Broches (1965).

[190] Shihata (1986), p. 4.

[191] Miles (2013), p. 86.

the development of international investment protection framework, a fully depoliticised international investment protection system would require more than a consolidated agreement on the rules of procedure of international investment arbitration. Another corollary to the depoliticisation argument is that home states would be "disenfranchised from pursuing investment claims once they are lodged with ICSID."[192] As Schneiderman demonstrates, however, this is not necessarily true; as there are multiple instances where home states nonetheless tread the 'political' path to supplement arbitral claims brought by their investors.[193]

ICSID nonetheless maintains that it is a facilitator for investment disputes and an institution exclusively involved in the procedural aspects of investment arbitration. While the Centre has had little direct effect on the development of IMS and more specific substantial principles such as NT, MFN and FET, it was mainly through the ICSID tribunals that these rules assumed substance and relatively tangible context over the years. Arbitrators appointed to investment arbitration cases have no affiliation to the ICSID, and the ICSID has virtually no effect on the outcome of arbitral awards. This being said, the ICSID is one of the most significant advancements in international investment law, especially in terms of its well-organised facilitation of international investment dispute settlement.[194] Although ISDS predates the ICSID Convention,[195] unlike what is available pursuant to the New York Convention system, the ICSID framework is notably equipped with an 'automatic' enforcement mechanism.[196] Despite experiencing a wave of withdrawals of several of its member states in 2010s,[197] it currently stands as among the most acknowledged international conventions in existence, with an impressive number of signatories.[198]

Establishment of the Centre effectively complemented the newly emerging BIT-based international investment protection structure. The first BIT was signed a few

---

[192] Schneiderman (2011), p. 694.

[193] For a recent analysis on systemic bias entrenched in favour of 'global capital' in international investment and trade law, see Perrone and Schneiderman (2019).

[194] Schreuer (2013) International Centre for Settlement of Investment Disputes (ICSID). In: Peters A (ed) Max Planck Encyclopedia of Public International Law (MPEPIL). https://opil.ouplaw.com/display/10.1093/law:epil/9780199231690/law-9780199231690-e33.

[195] It is known that broadly speaking, ISDS existed since the nineteenth century. One of the first cases was between the Suez Canal Company (*Compagnie Universelle du Canal de Suez)* and Egypt, in 1864. Both parties consented to arbitration and, on an interesting note, appointed Napoleon III as the arbitrator. Yackee (2016).

[196] Articles 53 (on the finality of an award); and 54 (on automatic enforcement of an award), ICSID Convention (1965).

[197] Bolivia (May 2007), Ecuador (January 2010), Venezuela (January 2012), and more recently Honduras (February 2024) withdrew from the ICSID Convention. Ecuador eventually rejoined—twelve years after its denouncement. See, Manciaux (2007); Yalkin (2009); Ripinsky (2012); ICSID (2021) Ecuador Ratifies the ICSID Convention. https://icsid.worldbank.org/news-and-events/news-releases/ecuador-ratifies-icsid-convention#:~:text=On%20August%204th%2C%202021%2C%20the,State%20to%20the%20ICSID%20Convention.

[198] As of January 2025, ICSID has 165 Members. ICSID, Database of Member States. https://icsid.worldbank.org/about/member-states/database-of-member-states.

years earlier, in 1959, between Germany and Pakistan.[199] Given the discrepancies on substance, capital-exporting states sought to enter into individual agreements with developing (or rather, potential host) states to determine the standards of protection on a case-by-case basis. From then on, BITs were sporadically signed throughout the twentieth century.

Most of these instruments included rules on NT and MFN, as well as protection against (unlawful) expropriation and 'unfair' treatment. With the gradual establishment of substance of protection of foreigners on a bilateral basis, and the multilateral acknowledgement of the ICSID as the primary procedural guide, fundamental components of contemporary international investment dispute settlement system were now established. While the system had existed since early 60s, its creation and early existence was fairly uneventful and the caseload of ICSID had remained humble.[200] The breakthrough would not come before the last decade of the twentieth century, after the dissolution of the Soviet Union and its ideology. A new surge of economic and social liberalism engulfed the globe from then on, breaking the biggest political polarisation the world has seen since the end of the WWII. IMS, however, still lacked a consensus as to its content.

2.8 The 'Modern' Era: Proliferation and Reconstitution of IIAs (1990 -)

The collapse of the Soviet Union was not only the dissolution of a country; it was also the collapse of an ideology—an ideology that had influenced social and economic policies of a remarkable portion of the world for more than seventy years. After the end of the Cold War, the Soviet notion of collective administration of people's property and its concurrent isolationist doctrine lost much of its credibility. The global political shift from a world ready for imminent war to a world in relative peace required a massive reconfiguration in every aspect of life. This reconfiguration was costly for all—in Latin America, this trend of economic liberalisation caused a major financial crisis and consequently an urgent need for foreign capital arose.[201] After 1990, several Latin American states waived (or rather, had to waive) their traditional position stemming from the Calvo Doctrine.[202] In general, it is seems established that less developed states all around the world had started signing BITs to be able to participate in the global competition for attracting more FDI.[203]

[199] Germany – Pakistan BIT (1959).

[200] Between 1966 and 1986, only 21 disputes were registered by the ICSID Secretariat. For context, 66 disputes were registered in 2021 alone. Between January 2020 and June 2024, a total of 276 disputes were registered. ICSID – Caseload Statistics (Issue 2024-2), p. 3.

[201] Gomez (2011), pp. 196–197.

[202] Shan (2007), p. 633.

[203] Skovgaard Poulsen (2016), p. 31.

Given the global nature of this new economic liberalisation, many formerly isolated economies, rather than insisting on their former exclusionist and conservative methods, now showed utmost effort to adapt themselves to this new order. Many states included themselves in the BIT pool which had accumulated since mid-twentieth century. With this massive addition of states to the BIT network, the caseload of ICSID saw a rapid growth.[204] With this sudden growth of caseload and the instrumental bilateral basis of substance, consistency and coherence became a core discussion.[205]

Earlier in 1986, a very broad-scoped negotiation on trade related issues had begun in Punta del Este, Uruguay, among the GATT members. Known as the Uruguay Round of GATT negotiations, it would take seven and a half years to conclude—twice as long as the planned schedule. Its extent was simply unmatched—with a striking fifteen subjects on the agenda spanning from tropical products to subsidiaries and intellectual property rights,[206] WTO claimed it was the "largest trade negotiation ever, and most probably the largest negotiation of any kind in history."[207]

The Uruguay Round was the turning point for the international trade law as it eventually led to the creation of WTO,[208] but the negotiations on investment measures were not as fruitful. As any past attempt on multilateral investment protection framework, this initiative came to a halt after fierce opposition from the developing states, again, due to the lack of consensus with regards to protection standards. Despite the fact that several WTO agreements such as the GATS,[209] the TRIPS,[210] and the TRIMs[211] are related to investment in certain ways, the provisions contained in these agreements are far from achieving what a multilateral investment protection treaty would aim to achieve in terms of protection and promotion of investments.[212] This particular failure sustained the division between the development of trade and investment provisions at international level, and the segregation was sealed after the formation of WTO and the infamous Multilateral Agreement on Investment (MAI) let-down.

---

[204] ICSID – Caseload Statistics (Issue 2024-2).

[205] See generally, Schill (2009); Banifatemi (2013); Fiezzoni (2012).

[206] Fifteen topics on the agenda were as follows: Tariffs, non-tariff barriers, natural resource products, textiles and clothing, agriculture, tropical products, GATT articles, Tokyo Round codes, anti-dumping, subsidies, intellectual property, dispute settlement, the GATT system, services and investment measures.

[207] WTO Uruguay Round. http://www.wto.org/english/thewto_e/whatis_e/tif_e/fact5_e.htm.

[208] Hoekman and Mavroidis (2016), p. 13.

[209] The General Agreement on Trade in Services ('GATS' - 1994). https://www.wto.org/english/docs_e/legal_e/26-gats.pdf.

[210] Agreement on Trade-Related Aspects of Intellectual Property ('TRIPS' - 1994). https://www.wto.org/english/docs_e/legal_e/27-trips_01_e.htm.

[211] Agreement on Trade-Related Investment Measures ('TRIMS' - 1994). https://www.wto.org/english/docs_e/legal_e/18-trims.pdf.

[212] Van Harten (2008), p. 21.

The Multilateral Agreement on Investment (MAI) is an important attempt at creation of a multilateral investment framework. After the negotiations held between 1995 and 1998, a consolidated draft text was prepared by the OECD.[213] Van Harten believes that the content of the draft is the "culmination of decades of efforts by capital-exporting countries and international business to consolidate high level investor protection at the global level."[214] Almost all members of the OECD are developed and mostly capital-exporting states; therefore a consensus among the OECD members was by all means simpler than a consensus between GATT members. The failure of MAI clearly showed that even the so-called 'capital-exporting' bloc might have difficulties establishing a so-called "'fast track' liberalisation agreement"—an assertion one can still make, nearly three decades after Muchlinski had done it.[215] Beyond the dissent among the capital-exporting countries, MAI faced strong opposition from capital-importing states and NGOs in and outside the OECD member states.[216] Some who opposed MAI considered the agreement to be "a threat to the protection of human rights, labour rights, the environment, and lesser-developed nations."[217] The support for MAI gradually dropped, and the draft was completely abandoned after several OECD member states, including the host state France, withdrew from negotiations in late 1998. A North American legal counsel and arbitrator, with extensive experience in ISDS, noted during an interview that ultimately "[t]here was just no support from the business community [for the MAI]. They just did not think it was a big deal."[218]

The last decade of the twentieth century also saw the creation of the first and only global-multilateral instrument on trade *and* investment focusing on a specific industrial sector, namely energy. ECT was opened for signature in 1995, and after being ratified by the minimum required number of parties in 1998, it came into force.[219] As of 2021, 48 states, the EU, and the European Atomic Energy Community (EURATOM) were parties to ECT.[220] There are also several states that signed but have not ratified the treaty, such as Russia and Belarus. According to the Energy

[213] The Multilateral Agreement on Investment Draft Consolidated Text (1998), available at https://investmentpolicy.unctad.org/international-investment-agreements/treaty-files/2813/download.

[214] Van Harten (2008), p. 22.

[215] Muchlinski (2000), p. 1051.

[216] Van Harten (2008), p. 22.

[217] On general position of the opposition to the MAI, see Hopkins – Hayakawa, Sachie (2011) International Campaign Against the Multilateral Agreement on Investment (1996-98), Global Non-violent Action Database (Swathmore College, Pennsylvania). http://nvdatabase.swarthmore.edu/content/international-campaign-against-multilateral-agreement-investment-1996-98.

[218] Interview #8. Also see, Malanczuk (2000), p. 418.

[219] The Energy Charter Treaty (1998). http://www.italaw.com/sites/default/files/laws/italaw6101(20).pdf.

[220] ECT, Members and Observers. https://www.energycharter.org/process/energy-charter-treaty-1994/energy-charter-treaty/signatories-contracting-parties/.

Charter website, in 2009, Russia declared that "it did not intend to become a Contracting Party to the [ECT] […]".[221]

The ECT is a post-Cold War initiative, fuelled by the transitional economic environment of the early 90s. The then-Prime Minister of the Netherlands, Ruud Lubbers, proposed a joint energy cooperation project referred to as the 'European Energy Community', which would include the Member States of the European Communities (now the EU), the Soviet Union, and countries in Central and Eastern Europe.[222] The initiative primarily aimed at benefitting from the liberalising markets of the Eastern European and former Soviet countries. As state planning and monopoly gave way to a free market system, economic interaction and cooperation was now possible and highly beneficial for Europe. Russia and some former Soviet states in Central Asia[223] were known to be rich in oil and gas, and some other states were important for their strategic location as potential transit states, such as Ukraine and Belarus. Initially a European initiative, it transformed itself into a global instrument as many non-European states, particularly the United States, were included in the negotiations before they were completed by the end of 1994. It is a highly influential IIA—it is the most commonly invoked investment protection instrument in the world.

As of December 2023, 162 arbitration cases were filed under the ECT. Spain is by far the most oft-sued host state, with 51 cases. It is followed by Italy (14) and Romania (8).[224] In recent years, ECT has attracted significant criticism for the expansive protections it ostensibly extends to fossil fuel producers and posing risks to regulatory measures regarding the mitigation of global warming. To that end, the Energy Charter Conference initiated a process of 'modernisation' of the Treaty in 2017 and established a sub-group.[225]

Subsequent dissatisfaction with the extent of these modernisation efforts eventually resulted in what can be described as a *mass exodus*—many signatories, including the EU, EURATOM, the Netherlands, the United Kingdom, Spain, Portugal, Slovenia, Luxembourg, Poland, Germany, and France withdrew from the agreement. Despite the shortcomings, however, the Energy Charter Conference adopted

---

221 Mironova, Irina (2014) Russia and the Energy Charter Treaty. https://www.energycharter.org/what-we-do/knowledge-centre/occasional-papers/russia-and-the-energy-charter-treaty/.

222 Roe and Happold (2011), p. 8.

223 In this specific context, "Central Asia" also covers former Soviet states in the Caspian Sea region.

224 ECT, Statistics. https://www.energychartertreaty.org/cases/statistics. It must be noted that all arbitration cases brought against Spain concern incentives it had enacted in 2007 to attract foreign investment in the renewable energy sector. As of 2022, the claims lodged against Spain amount to 8 billion Euros. Keeley, Graham (2022) Spain Faces €8 billion in renewable legal claims over past solar boom (*Euronews*, 27 December 2022). https://www.euronews.com/my-europe/2022/12/27/spain-faces-8-billion-in-renewable-legal-claims-over-past-solar-boom.

225 ECT, Modernisation of the Treaty. https://www.energychartertreaty.org/modernisation-of-the-treaty/.

a series of decisions on the modernisation of the ECT, including a series of amendments, in December 2024.[226]

It is also necessary to make a few remarks on NAFTA. It was a trilateral FTA with provisions on investment and trade between the United States, Canada and Mexico. It had entered into force on 1 January 1994 and was eventually replaced by the USMCA, when this agreement entered into force in July 2020.[227] NAFTA is an overarching regional instrument and is notable for several features, such as the extent of the investment protection. Indeed, the North American model as reflected in the Chapter 11 of NAFTA defines an investor as "a Party or state enterprise thereof, or a national or an enterprise of such Party, that ***seeks to make***, is making or has made an investment",[228] extending the subjects covered by the agreement to those who have not yet made an investment but seeking to do so. In other words, NAFTA extends the protection of foreign investment to the pre-establishment phase, an extension that is largely non-existent in European BITs and other investment treaties, as they are usually limited to post-establishment protection.[229] Same inclination is also seen in other bilateral FTAs[230] of which the United States is a party, as well as the 2012 Model US and 2004 Model Canada BITs.[231]

---

[226] All withdrawal notifications can be found on the ECT website. See, for example, the written notification by the European Union and European Atomic Energy Community (EURATOM); and from the Kingdom of the Netherlands. https://www.energycharter.org/media/news/article/written-notification-of-withdrawal-from-the-energy-charter-treaty-5/?tx_news_pi1%5Bcontroller%5D=News&tx_news_pi1%5Baction%5D=detail&cHash=251bd2158111616d7f4e8729b4728d6a; ECT, Amendments to the ECT as set out in Conference decision CCDEC202412. https://www.energycharter.org/fileadmin/DocumentsMedia/CCDECS/2024/CCDEC202412_EN.pdf. Some of these amendments relating to Articles 10 and 13 are, in principle, relevant to Chaps. 4 and 5 of this book. These provisions, regulating fair and equitable treatment and expropriation respectively, have been extensively revised. Given most of the ECT signatories opting out of this modernisation process, this book will not address the modernised ECT provisions specifically.

[227] North American Free Trade Agreement (NAFTA) (1994). http://www.italaw.com/sites/default/files/laws/italaw6187(27).pdf; Agreement between the United States of America, the United Mexican States, and Canada (USMCA) (2020). https://investmentpolicy.unctad.org/international-investment-agreements/treaty-files/6008/download. As of 1 July 2023 and pursuant to the Annex 14-C of the USMCA, investors are no longer allowed to bring claims under the Chapter 11 of NAFTA.

[228] Article 1139, NAFTA (1994). Emphasis added.

[229] Bonnitcha (2014), p. 19.

[230] For instance, Article 11.17 of the Australia – US FTA (2005) has an almost identical provision on the definition of an investor. The same extension is commonly seen in other FTAs as well, such as Article 10.27 of the Chile – US FTA (2004). The Colombia – US FTA (2012), despite similar extension, articulates the pre-establishment phase in a different manner: an investor who is attempting to make an investment has to do so "through concrete action." This minor addition means that the FTA excludes merely planned investments with little or no progress. What is considered "concrete" is open to debate. Also, for a comprehensive list of the US FTAs, see https://ustr.gov/trade-agreements/free-trade-agreements.

[231] 2012 US Model BIT. http://www.italaw.com/sites/default/files/archive/ita1028.pdf; 2004 Canada Model BIT. https://edit.wti.org/document/show/d15e4f5d-0310-4db4-a1ed-85e5d19f8ee1.

NAFTA has a mixed legacy. While it can be credited for the global popularity of ISDS and the development of its case law, it has also been the target of consistent criticism for the same reason. This mostly refers to the larger scope of application and the consequent large number of investor claims brought against party states in accordance with Chapter 11 of NAFTA. Van Harten confirms that the popularity of early NAFTA experience "drew attention to the availability of investment treaty arbitration," and boosted the growth of claims under other investment treaties globally.[232] A lawyer, actively involved in NAFTA practice, recalled that

> [t]he NAFTA cases were getting a lot of coverage from nationalists and social democrats in Canada and the US. [...] There were various groups, such as the Council of Canadians, that really put a lot of emphasis on the early NAFTA cases, given there weren't any decisions [at the time]. [Some of the cases] were amenable to fearmongering, because you can say 'look at what they are doing, they want money for this.' [...] They really fed on Methanex for a long time until Methanex lost. Then they had to find another case.[233]

Another Canadian lawyer with extensive ISDS experience further elaborated on how NAFTA was received in 1990s:

> Backlash against the [ISDS] has existed as soon as the first [NAFTA] cases emerged. Canadian Institute for Sustainable Development and the Council of Canadians, as well as other public sector unions were all opposed to [ISDS] right from the beginning, as soon as the first cases came out. [...] Such local knowledge [in North America] certainly existed.[234]

NAFTA is particularly important as one of the main instruments representing the North American investment policies, partly because of its role in the shaping of modern investment law concepts such as FET and indirect expropriation. Both issues will be discussed in depth in subsequent Chapters.

The 1990s had been a prolific period in terms of treaty-making. The UNCTAD figures demonstrate that while by the end of 1989 there were 385 BITs, this number went up to 1857 only a decade later.[235] The vast majority of these BITs, as well as other IIAs such as the NAFTA and the ECT, include provisions that ensure fair treatment of foreign investors and protection against direct and indirect expropriation. Such increase in the number of IIAs, virtually all of which following the example of a template model originally inspired by the Abs-Shawcross Convention and the OECD Draft referred to above, invoked similar, and in most cases identical, provisions. In contrast and despite this unprecedented abundance, it is extremely rare, if at all possible, to find IIAs signed during 1990s which clarify the content of indirect expropriation or the sub-elements of the FET principle.

---

[232] Van Harten (2008), p. 27. Been and Beauvais also note that the 'regulatory takings' doctrine available under the US law had been extended beyond its domestic roots, and ended up being subject to excessive interpretations by arbitral tribunals. Been and Beauvais (2003), p. 128.

[233] Interview #7.

[234] Interview #8.

[235] UNCTAD (2000) Bilateral Investment Treaties 1959 – 1999 (UNCTAD/ITE/IIA/2). http://unctad.org/en/docs/poiteiiad2.en.pdf.

In certain cases, treaty negotiators seem to have taken for granted the interpretative consequences of these vague provisions. On the content of the MST provision under Article 1105 of NAFTA, Hugo Perezcano stated during an interview that:

> The standard [was] there. It is a single standard that should be equally applicable regardless of which country you are talking about [...] It is the same standard for everybody. There was some internal discussion about [whether it was] needed [in the treaty], [since] it is an international law standard. But of course, it was part of the [US Model BIT], and it had to be in, and it was accepted. [...] **We never debated which standard to include in the NAFTA.**[236]

Given the similar, vague drafting methods employed in their texts, the same rationale might have been valid for the IIAs signed up until the end of 90s particularly with regard to non-contingent principles. Essentially due to lack of jurisprudential experience up until late 90s, and the absence of similar provisions in trade and commercial disputes which may have been facilitated by way of analogy,[237] it may be argued that the applicatory extent of these principles were speculative at best prior to arbitral proceedings applying such principles. As Poulsen notes, "the vague terms of investment treaties have been used to raise broader complains about lacking transparency, stability, and predictability in government decisions affecting a large number of actors apart from claimants themselves,"[238] and these 'broader' complaints prompted states to reconsider and revise the scope and objectives of these treaties. These claims, and arbitral proceedings stemming from these claims, have invoked a surge of attempts to recalibrate policies on treaty-making in international investment law.

This process began more than twenty years ago, when the first NAFTA awards emerged.[239] A wide spectrum of issues, such as the inclusion of express references to sustainable development and climate change measures[240] and the establishment of investment courts[241] have been discussed in particular over the course of the last decade. One of the tools was undoubtedly the accumulated arbitral experience and jurisprudence. Such extensive arbitral practice effectively exposed the advantages and shortcomings of ISDS.

While states (and the EU) have been constructing and recalibrating their future IIAs in line with this arbitral experience and their revisited policy priorities, recent years have also seen global, multilateral efforts intensify. In 2017, UNCITRAL entrusted its Working Group III a broad mandate "to work on the possible reform of

[236] Interview #12; Hugo Perezcano Diaz. He further emphasised during the interview that Article 1105 was "not an FET provision, but rather an MST provision ... This is an important distinction and one that NAFTA Parties always emphasised".

[237] Whereas contingent principles, such as MFN and NT, exist in international law generally and international trade law specifically, protection against expropriation and the obligation to accord fair and equitable treatment are often associated with international investment law disputes.

[238] Skovgaard Poulsen (2016), p. 2.

[239] See Chaps. 4 and 5.

[240] Paine and Sheargold (2023), p. 291; Cotula (2016); Gordon et al. (2014).

[241] Damjanovic (2023), pp. 314–348; collection of articles in Ünüvar et al. (2020).

investor-State dispute settlement".[242] By its 49th session in September 2024, WGIII adopted two codes of conduct for arbitrators[243] and investment court judges;[244] the Statute of the Advisory Centre on International Investment Dispute Resolution;[245] as well as a set of guidelines on mediation for international investment disputes.[246] At the time of writing, the Working Group continues its work on procedural rules reform and 'cross-cutting' issues, a Multilateral Permanent Investment Court, an Appellate Mechanism, and a 'multilateral instrument' to implement the reforms agreed upon by the WGIII. The mandate of the WGIII is generally perceived to be procedural in nature. This being said, some of the 'cross-cutting' issues in question, such as damages, 'correctness' of arbitral decisions, and the right to regulate, certainly touch upon the substance of IIAs.[247]

In addition to the procedural reform of ISDS, OECD pursues a parallel reform process under two 'tracks', which focuses on the substantial principles in IIAs. Track 1, entitled "Investment Treaties, climate change and alignment with the Paris Agreement", is a multi-stakeholder effort to align climate change mitigation and prevention goals in line with the protections provided by IIAs.[248] Track 2, on "Reflections on whether and how to modernise existing investment treaties", focuses on the transformation of substantive protection principles such as indirect expropriation, MFN, and FET.[249]

As reform efforts intensify, arbitral case law follows suit. The accumulation of cases, since the first case back in 1972,[250] follows an uneven trend. As of September 2024, the UNCTAD database indicates that there have been a total of 1332

[242] UNCITRAL (2017) Report of Working Group III (Investor-State Dispute Settlement Reform) on the work of its thirty-fourth session – Part I (A/CN.9/931/Rev.1, p. 2; all documents relating to its ongoing mandate can be found here: UNCITRAL, Working Group III: Investor-State Dispute Settlement Reform. https://uncitral.un.org/en/working_groups/3/investor-state.

[243] UNCITRAL (2023) Code of Conduct for Arbitrators in International Investment Dispute Resolution and commentary. https://uncitral.un.org/sites/uncitral.un.org/files/media-documents/uncitral/en/2318824e-coc_arbitrators_ebook_11june.pdf.

[244] UNCITRAL Code of Conduct for Judges in International Investment Dispute Resolution and commentary (adopted in principle in 2023). https://uncitral.un.org/sites/uncitral.un.org/files/media-documents/uncitral/en/2318944e-coc_judges_ebook-11june.pdf.

[245] UNCITRAL (2024) Statute of the Advisory Centre on International Investment Dispute Resolution. https://uncitral.un.org/sites/uncitral.un.org/files/media-documents/uncitral/en/2413025e.pdf.

[246] UNCITRAL (2023) Guidelines on Mediation for International Investment Disputes. https://uncitral.un.org/sites/uncitral.un.org/files/media-documents/uncitral/en/2401497e_mediation_guidelines_-ebook_eng.pdf.

[247] Ünüvar (2023).

[248] OECD (2024) Future of Investment Treaties. https://web-archive.oecd.org/temp/2024-05-06/614572-investment-treaties.htm.

[249] OECD (2023) Considerations on means to improve outcomes of designs of "fair and equitable" treatment clauses in investment treaties. https://oecd.org/investment/investment-policy/research-note-fair-equitable-treatment.pdf.

[250] Holiday Inns S.A. and others v. Morocco, ICSID Case No. ARB/72/1.

cases—ICSID and non-ICSID combined.[251] The total number of ICSID cases registered between 1972 and 2000 stands at 69. This number is currently over 1000 (993 as of June 2024).[252]

There are at least two takeaways from this upsurge in case count. The first, and perhaps obvious, takeaway is that the accumulation of case law over the last two and a half decades clearly shows the growing popularity (and, according to some, infamy) of ISDS. Secondly, this upsurge attests to the temporal and substantive development of rules and principles in international investment law through arbitral interpretations. It was particularly during the last one and a half decade that arbitral practice has sculpted this elaborate set of discussions as to the scope and extent of many principles—including MST and the benchmark of modern 'fairness' in investment law. In other words, vague and unclear protection principles and international standards mired by centuries-long disagreements examined above were granted a more tangible meaning through this jurisprudential knowledge only in the last few decades. In the absence of any elaboration on their meaning by the treaty-makers, these principles have instead developed over time and through experience—ultimately finding their way back in newer generation IIAs.

A North American lawyer, involved in investment and trade disputes, underlined the importance of jurisprudence:

> Precedence emphasises that the only way you can get clarification [on what certain provisions mean] is through litigation. You have cases, and they give guidance to the parties. [...] You are in a situation that, because of certain deficiencies in the [treaty] text[s], you are inevitably driven to the case law.[253]

Further elaboration will be made on specific jurisprudential development of these treaties under Chaps. 4 and 5, showing how, and upon which basis, the leap from referencing vague principles (such as the MST) to specific articulation of constituent elements was made. In the following Chapters, the relevant provisions enshrining the non-contingent standards essentially guiding treatment to be accorded to foreign investors will be put under scrutiny.

2.9 Final Remarks

As this Chapter demonstrated, 'fairness', embedded within the standard of treatment accorded to foreigners, has developed as a relative concept. The recurring question of whether or not a situation, interference, act or omission, verdict or

[251] UNCTAD Investment Dispute Settlement Database. https://investmentpolicy.unctad.org/investment-dispute-settlement.

[252] ICSID Caseload – Statistics (Issue 2024-2). https://icsid.worldbank.org/resources/publications/icsid-caseload-statistics. ICSID Case Database indicates that there are 1053 cases. https://icsid.worldbank.org/cases/case-database. ICSID notably celebrated its 1000th registered case as a 'milestone' on 8 August 2024: ICSID Caseload Milestones. https://icsid.worldbank.org/resources/multimedia/icsid-caseload-milestones.

[253] Interview #1.

measure is fair has been answered in accordance with a number of variables. Reciprocity; fairness assessed in reference to treatment of own subjects, among others, had been prevalent determinants in the absence of any systematised global interaction among nations and states of the world.

Intensified cross-cultural and political interaction brought about a new age of clashing domestic orders, all of which abode by their own norms and concepts—the underlying objective of fairness being among them. It is no coincidence that the emergence of the idea of an IMS coincided with the colonial expansion and conception of European sovereignty, through which stronger, wealthier states have enjoyed universal application of their norms and values. The notion of fairness has been continuously redesigned as to fit the transforming international context outside the domestic scope. It has bolstered the understanding that a meta-principle had existed, which pointed towards a higher and overarching standard of treatment that reflected the understanding of what was fair, and with which all states were expected to comply. The question of what this standard was, however, have never been satisfactorily answered.

This 'standard' assumed a more specific, yet derivative role under modern IIAs: it was embedded within the rules governing the treatment of foreigners, it served as a rationale for indirect expropriation also as to cover measures affecting property, and the fair amount of compensation to be made to foreign investors who lost their investments. Its historical, contingent features were encapsulated under traditional rules of NT and MFN—strictly assessed vis-à-vis the treatment accorded to nationals, and nationals of other states, respectively. What was "fair treatment", or "minimum" treatment, what qualified as indirect expropriation, have been persistently left vague, and they have ever since been attached to a meta-principle. Despite their vagueness, they remain as principles with which states are expected to comply. Through new treaties and adjudicatory experience, traditionally vague notions have started to take shape, answering the question of what would be considered fair within the specialised context of international investment law.

This Chapter further argued that, especially since the fifteenth century, it had been the unchanging tendency of states and legal scholars to point towards the direction of a non-contingent standard of treatment for foreigners without actually articulating its content, and leaving it deliberately vague. This is now clearly changing. The following Chapters will demonstrate how this change is taking place within the context of international investment law, which now enjoys (or suffers from) an ever-growing collection of arbitral awards. These awards have assigned meaning and context to these traditionally vague principles. This Chapter set the stage for the subsequent elaborations of how adjudication helped develop this context, and how it availed treaty-makers to capture these developments in their new generation IIAs.

Building upon this historical-legal background, the book will, in subsequent Chapters, turn its focus towards the contemporary answers to the question of whether fairness succeeds in aspiring to be an objective norm from an international investment law perspective. It will scrutinise the most common and the most controversial manifestations of treating foreign investors fairly: namely the FET and indirect expropriation in modern IIAs, their most recent form and most importantly, their future. Before going into the specific principles, however, the book now turns to state sovereignty and the clash of paradigms in this legal field to concretise its theoretical foundations, and explain the interaction between a state's sovereignty and the IIAs as an exercise of this sovereignty.

References

Abi-Saab G (1962) The newly independent states and the rules of international law: an outline. Howard Int Law 8:95–121

Alschner W (2013) Americanization of the BIT universe: the influence of Friendship, Commerce and Navigation (FCN) treaties on modern investment treaty law. Göttingen J Int Law 5:455–486

Alvarez JE (2011) The public international law regime governing international investment. Brill, The Hague

Anderson C (2009) Law essentials: Roman law. Dundee University Press, Dundee

Anghie A (2004) Imperialism, sovereignty and the making of international law. Cambridge University Press, Cambridge

Anzola JE (2008) From gunboats to arbitration. Transnational Dispute Management (TDM) 5. https://www.transnational-dispute-management.com/article.asp?key=1223

Aristotle (1998) Politics. English translation: Reeve CDC. Hackett, Indianapolis/Cambridge

Armstrong D (1993) Revolution and world order: the revolutionary state in international society. Oxford University Press, Oxford

Banifatemi Y (2009) The emerging jurisprudence on the most-favoured-nation treatment in investment arbitration. In: Bjorklund A, Laird I, Ripinsky S (eds) Investment treaty law: current issues III. British Institute of International and Comparative Law, pp 241–273

Banifatemi Y (2013) Consistency in the interpretation of substantive investment rules: is it achievable? In: Echandi R, Sauve P (eds) Prospects in international investment law and policy. Cambridge University Press, Cambridge

Been V, Beauvais JC (2003) The Global Fifth Amendment? NAFTA's investment protections and the misguided quest for an international "regulatory takings" doctrine. NYU Law Rev 78(1):30–143. https://nyulawreview.org/issues/volume-78-number-1/the-global-fifth-amendment-naftas-investment-protections-and-the-misguided-quest-for-an-international-regulatory-takings-doctrine/

Bjorklund AK (2008) National treatment. In: Reinisch A (ed) Standards of investment protection. Oxford University Press, Oxford, pp 29–58

Black's Law Dictionary (2019), 11th edn. Thomson Reuters, St Paul

Bonnitcha J (2014) Substantive protection under investment treaties: a legal and economic analysis. Cambridge University Press, Cambridge

Borchard E (1913) The diplomatic protection of citizens abroad. Am J Int Law 7:497–520

Borchard E (1930) "Responsibility of States" at The Hague Codification Conference. Am J Int Law 24:517–540

Borchard E (1940) Minimum standard of the treatment of aliens. Mich Law Rev 38:445–461

Broches A (1965) The convention on the settlement of investment disputes. Sect Int Comp Law Bull 9:11–15

Brown C (2013) Introduction: the development and importance of the model bilateral investment treaty. In: Brown C (ed) Commentaries on selected model investment treaties. Oxford University Press, Oxford, pp 1–15

Cantor L (ed) (1982) The English Medieval Landscape. Croom Helm, London

Chaudhary S (2008) Foreigners and foreign languages in India: a sociolinguistic history. Foundation Books, Delhi

Choukroune L (2014) National treatment in international investment law and arbitration: a relative standard for autonomous public regulation and sovereign development. In: Sanders AK (ed) The principle of national treatment in international economic law: trade, investment and intellectual property. Edward Elgar, Cheltenham, pp 183–222
Chung O (2007) The Lopsided international investment law regime and its effect on the future of investor-state arbitration. Va J Int Law 47:953–976
Cotula L (2016) Foreign investment, law and sustainable development. IIED, London
Crawford J (2012) Brownlie's principles of public international law, 8th edn. Oxford University Press, Oxford
Cutler JW (1933) The treatment of foreigners in relation to the Draft Convention and Conference of 1929. Am J Int Law 27:225–246
Damjanovic I (2023) The European Union and international investment law reform. Cambridge University Press, Cambridge
De Vattel E (1758) The law of nations or, principles of the law of nature, applied to the conduct and affairs of nations and sovereigns. Reprinted version: Chitty J (ed) (2011) Cambridge University Press, Cambridge
De Vitoria F (2009) De Indis et de Ivre Belli Relectiones (Latin Edition, reprint). University of Michigan Library, Ann Arbor
Di Biase-Dyson C (2013) Foreigners and Egyptians in the Late Egyptian Stories. Brill, Leiden
Dimopoulou-Piliouni A (2008) Apeleutheroi: Metics or Foreigners? DIKE Rivista di storia del diritto Greco ed ellenistico 11:27–50
Dolzer R, Schreuer C (2012) Principles of international investment law, 2nd edn. Oxford University Press, Oxford
Endicott T (2000) Vagueness in law. Oxford University Press, Oxford
Escarcena SL (2014) Indirect expropriation in international law (Leuven Global Governance Series). Edward Elgar Publishing, Northampton
Ferguson N (2011) Civilization: the west and the rest. Penguin Books, New York
Fiezzoni KS (2012) Striking consistency and predictability in international investment law from the perspective of developing countries. Front Law China 7:521–552
Frank J (2004) Citizens, slaves, and foreigners: Aristotle on human nature. Am Polit Sci Rev 98:91–104
Gallagher J, Robinson R (1953) The imperialism of free trade. Econ Hist Rev 6:1–15
Geyikdağı N (2008) Osmanlı Devleti'nde Yabancı Sermaye 1854 - 1914. Hil Yayın, Istanbul
Gilbert F (1970) To the farewell address: ideas of early American foreign policy. Princeton University Press, Princeton
Gomez KF (2011) Latin America and ICSID: David versus Goliath? Law Bus Rev Am 17:195–230
Gordon K, Pohl J, Bouchard M (2014) Investment treaty law, sustainable development and responsible business conduct: a fact finding survey (OECD Working Papers on International Investment 2014/1). https://doi.org/10.1787/5jz0xvgx1zlt-en
Hagan KJ (1973) American Gunboat Diplomacy and the Old Navy 1877 – 1889. Greenwood Press, Westport and London
Hamilton A (1795) The Defence No. XIX. In: Syrett HC (ed) The Papers of Alexander Hamilton, vol 19 (July 1795-December 1795), pp 318–324. https://founders.archives.gov/documents/Hamilton/01-19-02-0056
Herdegen M (2013) Principles of international economic law. Oxford University Press, Oxford
Hernandez R (1991) The internationalization of Francisco de Vitoria and Domingo de Soto. Fordham Int Law J 15:1031–1059
Hershey AS (1907) The Calvo and Drago Doctrines. Am J Int Law 1:26–45
Hoekman BM, Mavroidis PC (2016) World Trade Organization: law, economics, and politics. Routledge, London and New York
Hood M (1975) Gunboat Diplomacy 1895 – 1905: great power pressure in Venezuela. George W & J Mackay Limited, Chatham
Jackson JH (1997) The world trading system, 2nd edn. MIT University Press, Cambridge

James L, Leake E (eds) (2015) Decolonization and the cold war: negotiating independence. Bloomsburg Academic, London

Jennings RY (1961) State contracts in international law. In: Waldock H, Jennings RY (eds) The British Yearbook of International Law 1961. Oxford University Press, Oxford, pp 156–182

Kamen D (2013) Status in classical Athens. Princeton University Press, Princeton

Karadeniz Çelebican Ö (2014) Roma Hukuku, 17th edn. Turhan Kitabevi, Ankara

Keene D (2002) Emperor of Japan: Meiji and his world 1852 – 1912. Columbia University Press, New York

Kim K (2001) Aliens in Medieval law: the origins of modern citizenship. Cambridge University Press, Cambridge

Kläger R (2013) 'Fair and equitable treatment' in international investment law. Cambridge University Press, Cambridge

Kuhn AK (1930) The International Conference on the Treatment of Foreigners. Am J Int Law 24:570–573

Lesaffer R (2015) Too much history: from war as sanction to the sanctioning of war. In: Weller M, Solomou A (eds) The Oxford handbook of the use of force in international law. Oxford University Press, Oxford, pp 35–55

Lipson C (1985) Standing guard: protecting foreign capital in the nineteenth and twentieth centuries. University of California Press, Berkeley

Lowenfeld AF (2008) International economic law, 2nd edn. Oxford University Press, Oxford

Magna Carta (1215) National Archives and Records Administration (trans: Vincent N). https://www.archives.gov/press/press-kits/magna-carta/magna-carta-translation.pdf

Malanczuk P (2000) State-state and investor-state dispute settlement in the OECD Draft Multilateral Investment Agreement. J Int Econ Law 3:417–439

Manciaux S (2007) Bolivia's withdrawal from ICSID. TDM 5. https://www.transnational-dispute-management.com/article.asp?key=1076

Mathijsen PSRF (2007) A guide to European Union law, 9th edn. Sweet and Maxwell, London

McLean D (1976) Finance and "Informal Empire" before the First World War. Econ Hist Rev 29:291–305

Miles K (2013) The origins of international investment law: empire, environment and the safeguarding of capital. Cambridge University Press, Cambridge

Miller S, Hicks GN (2015) Investor-State Dispute Settlement: a reality check (A Report of the CSIS Scholl Chair in International Relations). Rowman & Littlefield, Lanham

Milward AS (2005) Politics and economics in the history of the European Union. Routledge, London

Mitchell N (1999) The danger of dreams: German and American imperialism in Latin America. The University of North Carolina Press, Chapel Hill and London

Moore JB (1906) A digest of international law, vol 4. Government Printing Office, Washington D.C

Muchlinski P (1996) The Energy Charter Treaty: towards a new international order for trade and investment or a case of history repeating itself? In: Wälde T (ed) The energy charter treaty: an east-west gateway for investment & trade. Kluwer Law International, London, pp 205–225

Muchlinski P (2000) The rise and fall of the multilateral agreement on investment: where now? Int Lawyer 34(3):1033–1053

Murase S (1976) The most-favored-nation treatment in Japan's treaty practice during the period 1854 – 1905. Am J Int Law 70:273–297

Newcombe A, Paradell L (2009) Law and practice of investment treaties. Wolters Kluwer, Alphen aan den Rijn

Nicholson FJ (1965) The protection of foreign property under customary international law. Boston Coll Law Rev 6:391–415

Nikièma SH (2017) The most-favoured-nation clause in investment treaties. IISD Best Practices Series. mfn-most-favoured-nation-clause-best-practices-en.pdf

Nussbaum A (1950) Arbitration between the Lena Goldfields Ltd and the Soviet Government. Cornell Law Rev 36:31–53

Nwogugu EI (1965) The legal problems of foreign investment in developing countries. Manchester University Press, Manchester

O'Brien H (1833) Phoenician Ireland. R. M. Timms, M. Keene & Son and F. W. Wakeman, Dublin

OECD (2004) "Indirect expropriation" and the "right to regulate" in international investment law (OECD Working Papers on International Investment 2004/4)

Paine J, Sheargold E (2023) A climate change carve-out for investment treaties. J Int Econ Law 26(2):285–304

Paparinskis M (2013) The international minimum standard and fair and equitable treatment. Oxford University Press, Oxford

Perrone NM, Schneiderman D (2019) Chapter 24: International Economic Law's Wreckage: depoliticization, inequality, precarity. In: Christodoulidis E, Dukes R, Goldoni M (eds) Research handbook on critical legal theory. Edward Elgar, Chelthenham, pp 446–472

Philpott D (2001) Revolutions in sovereignty: how ideas shaped modern international relations. Princeton University Press, Princeton

Plato (2008) Menexenus. English translation: Jowett B. The Project Gutenberg. http://www.gutenberg.org/files/1682/1682-h/1682-h.htm

Poscher R (2011) Ambiguity and vagueness in legal interpretation. In: Solan L, Tiersma P (eds) Oxford handbook on language and law. Oxford University Press, Oxford

Rawls J (1971) A theory of justice. Harvard University Press, Cambridge

Richter DS (2011) Cosmopolis: imagining community in late classical Athens and the Early Roman Empire. Oxford University Press, Oxford

Ripinsky S (2012) Venezuela's withdrawal from ICSID: what is does and does not achieve. Investment Treaty News. https://www.iisd.org/itn/2012/04/13/venezuelas-withdrawal-from-icsid-what-it-does-and-does-not-achieve/

Roe T, Happold M (2011) Settlement of Investment Disputes under the Energy Charter Treaty. Cambridge University Press, Cambridge

Root E (1910) The basis of protection to citizens residing abroad. Proc Am Soc Int Law Annu Meeting (1907 – 1917) 4, 16 -27

Rosenne S (1998) Codification revisited after 50 years. In: Frowein J, Wolfrum R (eds) Max Planck Yearbook of United Nations Law, vol 2. Kluwer Law International, London, pp 1–22

Roth AH (1949) The minimum standard of international law applied to Aliens. A. W. Sijthoff, Leiden

Schill SW (2009) The multilateralization of international investment law. Cambridge University Press, Cambridge

Schmidt S (2011) To order the minds of scholars: the discourse of the peace of Westphalia in international relations. Int Stud Q 55:601–623

Schneiderman D (2011) Revisiting the depolicization of investment disputes. In: Sauvant KP (ed) Yearbook on International Investment Law & Policy 2010-2011. Oxford University Press, Oxford, pp 693–714

Schreuer C (2013) International Centre for Settlement of Investment Disputes (ICSID). In: Peters A (ed) Max Planck Encyclopedia of Public International Law (MPEPIL)

Schrijver N (1997) Sovereignty over natural resources. Cambridge University Press, Cambridge

Scott JB (1934) The Spanish origin of international law: Francisco de Vitoria and His Law of Nations. Clarendon Press, Oxford

Sexton J (2011) The Monroe Doctrine: empire and nation in nineteenth- century America. Hill and Wang, New York

Shan W (2007) From north – south divide to private – public debate: revival of the Calvo Doctrine and the changing landscape in international investment law. Northwest J Int Law Bus 27:631–664

Shea DR (1955) The Calvo Clause: a problem of Inter-American and international law and diplomacy. University of Minnesota Press, Minneapolis

Shihata IFI (1986) Towards greater depoliticization of investment disputes: the roles of ICSID and MIGA. ICSID Rev 1(1):1–25

Skovgaard Poulsen L (2016) Bounded rationality and economic diplomacy: the politics of investment treaties in developing countries. Cambridge University Press, Cambridge

Snyder E (1963) Foreign investment protection: a reasoned approach. Mich Law Rev 61:1087–1124

Sohn LB, Baxter RR (1961) Responsibility of states for injuries to the economic interests of Aliens: II. Draft convention on the international responsibility of states for injuries to Aliens. AJIL 55(3):548–584. https://icsid.worldbank.org/sites/default/files/parties_publications/C8394/Claimants%27%20documents/CL%20-%20Exhibits/CL-0250%20%28with%20OCR%29.pdf

Thatcher OJ (ed) (1901) The library of original sources, Vol. III – The Roman World. University Research Extension Co, Milwaukee

Thucydides (1914) The History of the Peloponnesian War. English translation: Crawley R. The Internet Classics Archive, Massachusetts Institute of Technology), J. M. Dent & Sons Ltd, London. http://classics.mit.edu/Thucydides/pelopwar.1.first.html

Tzouvala N (2020) Capitalism as civilisation: a history of international law. Cambridge University Press, Cambridge

UNCTAD (2010) Most-Favored-Nation Treatment (UNCTAD Series on Issues in International Investment Agreements II)

Ünüvar G (2023) The Mandate Conundrum: Reflections on the 46th Session of the UNCITRAL Working Group III on ISDS Reform. EJIL: Talk!. https://www.ejiltalk.org/the-mandate-conundrum-reflections-on-the-46th-session-of-the-uncitral-working-group-iii-on-isds-reform/

Ünüvar G, Lam J, Dothan S (eds) (2020) Permanent investment courts: the European experiment. Springer, Cham

Vadi V (2015) Analogies in international investment law and arbitration. Cambridge University Press, Cambridge

Van Den Bossche P (2008) The law and policy of the World Trade Organization. Cambridge University Press, Cambridge

Van Harten G (2008) Investment treaty arbitration and public law. Oxford University Press, Oxford

Vandevelde KJ (2010) A unified theory of fair and equitable treatment. Int Law Polit 43:43–106

Wandahl Mouyal L (2015) International investment law and the right to regulate: a human rights perspective. Routledge, London and New York

Whitaker AP (1948) The United States of America and South America: The Northern Republics. Harvard University Press, Cambridge

Whitehead D (1977) The Ideology of the Athenian Metic. Cambridge University Press, Cambridge

Wierzbicka A (2006) English: meaning and culture. Oxford University Press, New York

Yackee JW (2016) The First Investor-State Arbitration: The Suez Canal Company v Egypt (1864). J World Invest Trade 17(3):401–462

Yalkin T (2009) Ecuador Denounces ICSID: Much Ado About Nothing? EJIL: Talk! Blog. http://www.ejiltalk.org/ecuador-denounces-icsid-much-ado-about-nothing/

Yarrow D (2011) Law's infidelity to its past: the failure to recognize indigenous jurisdiction in Australia and Canada. In: Knafla LA, Westra H (eds) Aboriginal title and indigenous peoples: Canada, Australia, and New Zealand. UBC Press, Vancouver

Chapter 3
State as a Sovereign and a (Respondent) Party in Investment Treaty Disputes

Abstract This Chapter, building upon the framework established by Chap. 2, explores the evolving role of state sovereignty within the framework of international investment agreements (IIAs), emphasizing the dual capacity of states as treaty-makers and potential respondents in disputes. It argues that sovereignty inherently includes the power to self-limit through international agreements, enabling states to pursue policy goals while balancing domestic and international obligations. Traditionally, international investment agreements (IIAs) have focused on promoting and protecting investments, but the Chapter highlights and reiterates well-explored risks hidden in their vaguely drafted provisions if left solely to arbitral interpretation. The Chapter underscores the importance of clarity in IIA provisions, and argues for the inclusion of *ex ante* clarifications during the negotiation phase to ensure predictable legal regimes. This approach, the Chapter argues, aligns with the ongoing process of normative clarification and concretisation within international investment law informed by decades of arbitral practice, alluding to the case studies and the emergence of new-generation IIAs examined in Chaps. 4 and 5. The Chapter concludes that clarity is not merely desirable, but an essential progression in fostering a reliable and equitable framework for future IIAs.

G. Ünüvar, *The Transformation of International Investment Law and Its Principles*, European Yearbook of International Economic Law 44,
https://doi.org/10.1007/978-3-032-01110-7_3

3.1 Introduction

International investment law is a hybrid legal field, a peculiar domain within international law—or, as some assert, a "conceptual mess".[1] It borrows both from public and private international law:[2] the involvement of private parties, as well as host and home states, is crucial to the functioning of the current structure. International instruments, such as BITs, are negotiated between states. At the dispute settlement phase however, private parties, namely *foreign* investors, submit claims against their host states at an *ad hoc* arbitral tribunal if they suffer damages due to a state act or measure.[3] There are essentially two bases for a foreign investor to use arbitration. An investor might initiate a (1) contract-based claim at an arbitral tribunal; or (2) might rely on an *ex ante*, treaty-based consent of the host and home states.[4] Foreign investors are entitled to full compensation if the said breach amounts to certain classifications of 'acts'. These acts may manifest themselves as general, regulatory measures; or they could take the shape of more specific, targeted measures.[5] Whether or not these acts amount to compensable acts is determined with reference to their effects on the foreign investment *vis-à-vis* their purpose.[6]

On the macro level, scrutiny of policies, and regulatory restrictions of a state's investment regime play a naturally significant role in the interpretation of the legal implications of a particular state act. It is important to note, however, that not every state act which causes hindrance to foreign investors necessarily violates a contract or a treaty provision, or implies a general lack of promotion or protection of—or an inhospitable environment for—foreign investment in that particular state. States' sphere of interests, given their multiple roles and objectives as sovereigns, go beyond the protection of foreigners and their property. Therefore, it is possible that states may prioritise a public concern at the expense of promoting or protecting foreign investment or, as a result of a regulatory measure aimed at addressing a particular public concern, foreign investors may consequentially have to deal with

---

[1] Roberts (2013), p. 48.

[2] Public and private law characteristics of international investment law have been discussed in depth by a number of scholars. For instance, Arato generally criticised the structural deficiencies and the one-size-fits-all approach adopted in IIAs, as well as their negative effects on private law institutions in domestic systems. Arato (2019), p. 50; also see, Douglas (2003).

[3] At this point, it is important to note that I use the term "private international law" as Catharine Titi described: it "does not refer to the system that governs conflict of laws but rather to international law administrated in cross-border disputes between individuals or private entities." Titi (2024), p. 445.

[4] Paulsson (1995), p. 233.

[5] Nikièma (2012), pp. 3–11.

[6] Kriebaum (2007), pp. 719–721. This balancing between the effects and purpose of a state measure vis-à-vis foreign investment is a fundamental debate in international investment law scholarship, and a key component of this book's case studies in Chaps. 4 and 5.

undesirable effects on their investment.[7] In other cases, a state's conduct may be targeted specifically towards the investor as the former discharges its regulatory or administrative authority. Common examples are cancellations of permits or licenses of specific investment activities and operations subject to authorisation.[8] Within the context of protection of foreign investment, these indispensable roles, functions and responsibilities of states as sovereign entities put their activities at odds with the economic interests by foreign investors. This conundrum, namely how to balance the state and investor interests, have attracted remarkable attention over the years.[9]

This Chapter scrutinises the attraction and friction between the two roles of a state: a sovereign treaty-maker, and a potential (respondent) party to disputes arising out of an IIA. A host state's interaction with foreign investors and their activities and interests within the former's territory is central in this context. The Chapter will further look into the clash of *paradigms*, which represents different approaches (namely public international, private international, and public law)[10] adopted to understand the dynamics within the system, given its complex inter-state and investor-state interaction.

The objective here is not to position investment law exclusively within the branch of public or private law, as I believe this is not a helpful, or even a relevant, pursuit.[11] The emphasis will be on fleshing out how international investment law (and investment arbitration) borrows from all different paradigms that feed its creation and structure. This analysis is complemented by a contextualised deep dive into state sovereignty, and how it can be used by states themselves to limit their own conduct through international (investment) agreements. The purpose of the Chapter is, therefore, to reinforce the theoretical framework that has been established in Chap. 2 above, in further maintaining that the pursuit of objective 'fairness' necessitates an interplay between state prerogatives on the one hand, and conceptual clarity at an international level on the other. This is an important prerequisite to examine specific treaty provisions in IIAs, and what they mean or *should* mean: ultimately, this Chapter will set the stage for the preposition furthered in Chaps. 4 and 5 that (a) it is less about the precise content of these provisions and its specifics, and more about the importance of *having* a clear and distinguishable content in line with the 'object and purpose' of an IIA and the policy objectives of the states in question; and (b) states are still, and will continue to be, the decision makers going forward—regardless of the shape and form international investment law may take in the years to come. This search for clarity is not a shot in the dark, however. Arbitral practice is an important guide in establishing and maintaining this clarity—both on what to do, and on what to avoid.

---

[7] Markert (2011), pp. 148–151.

[8] Coe and Rubins (2005), pp. 607–608.

[9] Titi (2024).

[10] Roberts (2013), pp. 58–64; Wälde (2010).

[11] Titi (2024), p. 446.

3.2 State Sovereignty, Foreign Investors and IIAs

3.2.1 How to Limit Sovereignty

Jean Bodin, a sixteenth century jurist and political theorist, asked a critical question which reverberates through centuries: "But is the prince not subject to those laws of the land that he has sworn to keep?" He saw a distinction between the sovereign's own laws, and promises he makes to other princes. For the former, Bodin asserted that "he is not bound by that law any more than an oath made to himself." For the latter, however, he is not as absolute: "[the sovereign] is obligated to keep [his promises] if the prince to whom he gave its word has an interest in his so doing—even if he did not take an oath."[12] He elaborates on the distinction as follows:

> It is not that the prince is bound by his own or his predecessors' laws, but rather by the just contracts and promises that he has made, whether with or without an oath, as is any private individual.[13]

This distinction between domestic laws and 'promises' made to 'other princes' is noteworthy. Bodin equates the said promises to that of private contracts, and while he maintains that such promises should be kept, he notes that "[he is only subject] to his just and reasonable contracts in the observation of which his subjects in general or particular subjects have an interest."[14]

Sovereignty (and particularly its boundaries) has always been a controversial subject matter. Since the clashes between Hobbes' absolutism conveyed through his *Leviathan,*[15] and Locke's liberal ideas on its origins and nature,[16] jurists and political scientists have immensely contributed to a vast collection of thoughts and writings on the matter. First and foremost, sovereignty is the legal, political and social fabric of governance, primarily of discretionary nature, driven by the "bundle of rights, powers and privileges" held by the state.[17] According to Krasner, who described sovereignty as "organized hypocrisy",[18] the oldest usage of sovereignty referred to domestic sovereignty, or "the organisation of authority within a given state and its effectiveness."[19] In a classical sense, Downes reflected that "[sovereignty] cannot be partial; the sovereign shares nothing; the sovereign is a singular and self-justifying force beholden to no law or obligation but his own."[20]

---

[12] Bodin (1992), p. 13.

[13] Bodin (1992), pp. 13–14.

[14] Bodin (1992), p. 14.

[15] Hobbes (1651).

[16] Locke (1690).

[17] Koskenniemi (2010), p. 62.

[18] Krasner (1999).

[19] Krasner (2012), p. 7.

[20] Downes (2015), p. 26.

Koskenniemi noted that international lawyers have been critical of sovereignty because of how it was perceived to be "a narrow, ethnocentric way to think about the relations of human beings."[21] Its failure to address actual economic and social realities of the globe—global warming and refugee crises being among the most recent issues—has also been repeatedly expressed. Others have targeted what they saw as the holy grail of its inadequate origins, namely, "an archaic tradition of theologically based royal or state privilege".[22]

However, this primarily domestic understanding of sovereignty, particularly over a territory, has changed notably over the years. The domestic, unilateral perspective which focuses on a sovereign's authority in a positive manner gave way to an international, multilateral perspective, which has added the *auto-restrictive* aspects of sovereignty within the equation—perhaps parallel to the prevalent 'supremacy' of international law and standards over domestic laws, as mentioned in Chap. 2. In a sense, this echoes from Bodin's take on a sovereign prince's promise to another prince. The domestic sphere highlights the relationship between the sovereign and the people with an emphasis on the former's supremacy; whereas the international sphere, at least within a strictly public international law context, alludes to the relationship *between* sovereigns. On an inter-state level, states co-exist in a dimension where they agree, disagree, and compromise with each other.

The emergence of universal human rights, particularly since the mid-twentieth century, goes hand in hand with such self-limitation. Benhabib, to this end, argued that

> [this] is the uniqueness of the many human rights covenants concluded since WWII: sovereign states through them undertake the self-limitation of their own prerogatives, thus initiating a new regime of sovereignty. Sovereignty can no longer be understood as the supreme power of a single political authority over all that is living and dead on its territory.[23]

The states' capability of limiting their own sphere of competences has increasingly come under scrutiny. International law and relations have fostered a broader understanding of state sovereignty, encapsulated by a narrative establishing that states "do not relinquish, but rather, exercise their sovereignty when they enter into a treaty."[24] It is a sovereign's right to make promises—in a sense, similar to that of an individual, entering into a private contract which incurs obligations. Such obligations usually entail a projected benefit from the other party.

Any delegation of sovereignty is, then, considered to be an exercise of sovereignty by definition; because only a sovereign can delegate its sovereignty in the first place.[25] The EU is the epitome of such delegation: It exists as a supranational organisation not because of its own right, but because a group of sovereigns have willingly conferred part of their sovereignty to create it in pursuance of a series of

[21] Koskenniemi (2010), p. 61.

[22] Berlant (2007), p. 755.

[23] Benhabib (2016), p. 113.

[24] Alvarez (2011), p. 223.

[25] Klabbers (1998), p. 347.

collective benefits and objectives. By way of analogy, a private project, made up of a number of partners, exists because of their collective intent. While each individual partner may be able to solely undertake tasks and achieve the objectives intended under the project, each individual may see benefit in sharing in the costs and scaling up their objectives and aspirations. This, of course, would come at the expense of the capability of deciding alone on a number of issues, including those which would have otherwise been within their exclusive sphere of influence.

3.2.2 IIAs as Self-Limiting Instruments for States

IIAs are international agreements; and they do exactly what is outlined above: through them, states delegate parts of their sovereignty and impose self-limitations, in this case with regard to treatment of foreign investors. States, in pursuance of short or long-term objectives and projected benefits, engage in trade-offs through such international agreements. In case of IIAs (and particularly those with arbitration clauses), the trade-off can concern a multitude of considerations. For its respective parties, one could argue that a BIT with an ISDS mechanism principally aims at, *inter alia*, decreasing political risk[26] and the substitution or alternation of jurisdiction of domestic courts by arbitral tribunals (or other forms of mutually agreed dispute settlement methods) with regard to foreign investment-related disputes on the one hand; and an anticipated increase in inbound FDI flow on the other.[27] A state's willingness to attract foreign capital and investment can have multiple reasons, such as more employment, increased tax revenues, sustainable development through sustainable investment, cleaner energy production, infrastructural development, and so on.

Earlier in the twentieth century and before the proliferation of IIAs, many states had reservations about such trade-offs. Particularly from the perspective of newly-independent former colonies during the ultimate dissolution of colonial powers in 1950s and 1960s, the focus was mostly on benefits to be extracted from certain degrees of economic protectionism, especially with regard to natural resources. Concerns related to the energy security and resource management were highly relevant to this tendency. The issue of sovereignty aspired to a new height of political volatility. For these newly independent developing states, the priority was ascertaining autonomy and to tackle immediate socio-economic problems. The UN Commission of Human Rights concluded that the right of peoples and nations to

[26] Yackee (2014), pp. 491–497; Rubins and Kinsella (2005).

[27] Elkins et al. (2008), p. 297. They argue that "BITs are significantly more likely to be signed during years in which signatory states appear to be benefiting (in terms of FDI) from the treaties than when they are not."; Skovgaard Poulsen (2016).

permanent sovereignty over their natural wealth and resources amounted nothing less than "a basic constituent of the right to self-determination." This trail of ideas eventually led to the Resolution no. 1803 (XVII) on Permanent Sovereignty over Natural Resources.[28] This declaration emphasised on the sovereignty rights of every state and, in that regard, acknowledged the "right of all States freely to dispose of their natural wealth and resources in accordance with their national interests, and on respect for the economic independence of States".[29] Sornarajah linked its significance to the fact that "it received the support of the capital exporting states" and that "[i]t represents a compromise between the interests of developing countries in the protection of their rights over their resources and those of the developed countries in securing adequate guarantees for foreign investors."[30] In *Texaco v. Libya*[31] case, Professor René-Jean Dupuy, who served as the sole arbitrator, contended that "the right of a State to nationalize is unquestionable today. It results from international customary law, established as the result of general practices considered by the international community as being the law".[32]

This recognition notwithstanding, Resolution 1803 underlined that "[t]he rights of peoples and nations to permanent sovereignty over their natural wealth and resources must be exercised **in the interests of their national development and of the well-being of the people of the State concerned**".[33] Furthermore, it is stated that the rules and conditions on authorisation, restriction or prohibition that apply to the "exploration, development and disposition of such resources, as well as the import of the foreign capital required for these purposes" should be *freely* considered to be necessary or desirable. In other words, the provision aims to maintain that governments are not to impose upon people what was *supposed to be* necessary or desirable—the free will of the people is the key to legitimate exploitation and utilisation of natural resources.

In short, despite the explicit recognition of the sovereignty over domestic natural resources, the Resolution 1803 reserved certain situations and brings conditions to the exercise of this sovereignty. This is largely parallel to the position of developed,

---

[28] UN General Assembly, Resolution 1803 (XVII) Permanent Sovereignty over Natural Resources, 14 December 1962, p. 15. https://undocs.org/a/res/1803(xvii).

[29] UN General Assembly, Resolution 1803 (XVII), p. 15. Also see, regarding the debates on whether this Resolution constitutes *jus cogens*, Hossain (2005), p. 84.

[30] Sornarajah (1986), p. 121.

[31] *Texaco Overseas Petroleum Company v. The Government of the Libyan Arab Republic* (*Texaco v Libya*), ad hoc (Award of 19 January 1977). Excerpts of the award are available at https://www.trans-lex.org/261700/_/texaco-overseas-petroleum-company-v-the-government-of-the-libyan-arab-republic-yca-1979-at-177-et-seq-/.

[32] *Texaco v. Libya* (1977), p. 183. Also see, Kerwin (1983), p. 883.

[33] UN General Assembly, Resolution 1803 (XVII), p. 15. Emphasis added.

capital-exporting states that (may) have concerns over arbitrary (and often ideologically-driven) acts which might risk the activities of their investors within a host state.

Another provision, Article 2 of the UN Charter of Economic Rights and Duties of States (CERDS) of 1974,[34] reads "[e]very state has and shall freely exercise full permanent sovereignty [...] including possession, use and disposal, over all its wealth, natural resources and economic activities"; but it does not provide any condition as to whether or not national development or the well-being of the people should be observed. The wording excludes the above-mentioned conditions related to public security or national interest, therefore seems to favour the position of many developing states which, in principle, rejected treatment standardisation on an international level. A number of arbitral tribunals[35] cautiously refrained from adopting this unconditional wording.

The United States, the UK, Germany, Luxembourg, Belgium and Denmark voted against the CERDS, and another ten (developed, capital-exporting) states abstained due to its extensive interpretation of sovereign discretion. Wälde noted that the less developed states gradually adopted more lenient policies during the 90s, which significantly departed from the principles reflected in the CERDS in general.[36]

By the 1990s, this conceptualisation of national sovereignty was moderated by liberalisation and privatisation programmes of many developing states, aimed at attracting foreign investment. This trend is supported by the increase in the number of short, vaguely-drafted IIAs signed between capital-exporting and capital-importing companies with substantive promises and strong enforcement mechanisms throughout the decade.[37] While it is true that majority of the earlier IIAs are modelled on drafts prepared by the OECD states and other developed countries, it was through arbitral practice that the true extent of implications, and the potential, of these IIAs became apparent.[38] The premise that foreign investors are entitled to protection, in that sense, urged, and still urges, the question: *Protection at what cost?*

Sections below will explore this delicate balance, why it exists, and how it may be maintained.

---

[34] United Nations General Assembly, Resolution no. 3281 (XXIX) Charter of Economic Rights and Duties of States, 12 December 1974. https://investmentpolicy.unctad.org/international-investment-agreements/treaty-files/2778/download.

[35] *Texaco v. Libya* (1977); *American Independent Oil Co. v. Government of Kuwait* (Aminoil v. Kuwait) (1982) 21 ILM 976; *Amoco International Finance Corp. v Iran (Amoco v. Iran)* (1987), 15 Iran-US CTR 189.

[36] Wälde (1998), p. 771 et seq.

[37] Newcombe (2013), p. 18. Van Harten and Loughlin claim that IIAs could protect foreign investors against "virtually any sovereign act of the state", Van Harten and Loughlin (2006), p. 130.

[38] Van Harten and Loughlin (2006), pp. 124–125.

3.2.3 *Promotion and Protection of Foreign Investment*

Debates on whether IIAs exist only for the benefit of foreign investment, or they should have the dual role of promoting public good while protecting and promoting these investments are well-known. Arguably, however, the most explicit objectives of these treaties are the promotion and protection of foreign investment,[39] as a vast majority are officially called so.[40] Before delving further into discussions originating from this dual role, the Chapter will elaborate on these two traditional objectives of these treaties.

3.2.3.1 Promotion

Promotion of foreign investment usually relates to *attracting* foreign investment in a particular country. Research conducted on whether IIAs have a positive effect on Foreign Direct Investment (FDI) has yielded differing and controversial results over the years,[41] particularly with regards to their methodology and how they evaluated their data.[42] Furthermore, Brazil, the largest FDI recipient in Latin America, has no BIT in force as of 2025.[43] A Southeast Asian academic involved in the preparation of a national Model BIT noted that they

> could not find the justification that signing […] BITs actually directly influenced the capital inflow to [X]. We have come to the conclusion that given [we are] a resource-rich country, even if we do not have these BITs, investors will still come to [X].[44]

---

[39] However, see, Stone Sweet (2010), p. 75 (noting that the consideration of protection and promotion of foreign investments as the central objectives of IIAs is, from a proportionality perspective, 'suicidal').

[40] For instance, the Albania – Czech Republic BIT (1995) is officially called 'Agreement between the Czech Republic and the Republic of Albania for the Promotion and Reciprocal Promotion of Investments'.

[41] Egger et al. (2022); Sauvant and Sachs (2009); Yackee (2008); Salacuse and Sullivan (2005). In arbitral jurisprudence, some tribunals have referred to the objective of the ICSID Convention in this context, for instance see *Amco Asia Corporation and others v. Indonesia* (1984) ICSID Case No. ARB/81/1, Decision on Jurisdiction, 25 September 1983: "the [ICSID] Convention is aimed to protect, to the same extent and with the same vigour the investor and the host State, not forgetting that to protect investments is to protect the general interest of development and of developing countries".

[42] Egger et al. (2022), pp. 1560–1561; Skovgaard Poulsen et al. (2013), p. 2.

[43] UNCTAD IIA Navigator counts 28 Brazilian investment agreements as of January 2025, 14 of which are BITs, signed between 1994 and 1999. From 2015 onwards, Brazil started signing the so-called "Investment Cooperation and Facilitation Agreements" (ICFA). These agreements differ markedly from a common BIT. Except for two ICFAs signed in 2015 with Mexico and Angola and one ICFA signed in 2019 with the United Arab Emirates, none of the agreements mentioned above (BITs or ICFAs) are in force. https://investmentpolicy.unctad.org/international-investment-agreements/countries/27/brazil. Also see, Bellak and Liebrecht (2024); Perrone and de Cerqueira Cesar (2015).

[44] Interview #16.

Similarly, a North American legal counsel, when asked about whether he believed that the existence of an IIA has any role in promoting FDI inflow in a country, replied that "the existence, or the absence, or an [IIA] to protect investment may be a consideration [for investors], but not necessarily the driving consideration, or even an important one."[45]

IIAs can also usually be viewed as guarantees of states to uphold the rule of law within the domestic sphere. Another North American counsel noted the following:

> I don't think that anyone is going to be able to track investment flows based on treaty with any kind of certainty. That's not what I think that the [IIAs] are for. I think the treaties are for establishing or re-establishing the rule of international law, and by extension, the rule of law in that country.[46]

Providing sustainable economic growth is considered among the chief concerns and responsibilities for any government, and it is one of the fundamental components of social development as a whole.[47] Incentives and progress towards market liberalisation and strengthened rule of law are given generous credit on their role towards achieving sustainable welfare and attracting foreign capital. Promotion of inbound FDI is one of the tools of market liberalisation[48] and is considered among one of the major catalysts of developing domestic markets seeking further integration into the global market.

Their importance notwithstanding, domestic liberal economic policies do not necessarily mean a definite increase in FDI inflows. Recent trends in some emerging markets, such as India and China, present a vibrant comparison as to how open market policies and domestic regulations affect domestic markets. While both states have enjoyed "extraordinary inflows of foreign capital [...] due to a measured, yet profound, liberalisation of foreign investment restrictions",[49] interesting data with regards to the level of liberalisation and the corresponding FDI inflow shows that China managed to attract more foreign investment, despite more state control towards foreign capital.[50] Recent figures indicate that China, despite the slowing growth in the past decade, is the second largest target economy in the world (after

---

[45] Interview #7.

[46] Interview #8.

[47] See generally, Sweeney (2010), p. 207.

[48] "Liberalization of Inward Foreign Direct Investment" was included in John Williamson's "Consensus", which came to be known as the "Washington Consensus", written in 1989 as a list of conditions for successful economic growth, following a decade of economic stagnation in regions like Africa and Latin America. Williamson (2009), p. 7. Dolzer and Scheuer maintain that this recession was mostly due to "inward-looking, non-competitive economic policies and a lack of domestic reforms." Dolzer and Schreuer (2012), p. 87.

[49] Sweeney, (2010), p. 209.

[50] Between 1990 and 2004, India "absorbed a total of $33.9 billion in FDI, while China secured almost $550 billion." See, Sachdev (2006), p. 174.

the United States) in terms of FDI inflow with $163 billion in 2023 (and $189 billion in 2022),[51] whereas India had about $28 billion in 2023 ($49 billion in 2022).[52]

There are numerous factors taken into account by foreign investors before they bring investment into a host country, and this comparison underlines the multi-faceted nature and variety of these considerations. While they may differ depending on the target country, relevant sector and the size of the foreign investment; it is still possible to discern certain general features to which every investment, foreign and domestic, will be exposed. The rule of law in a particular state is almost always important for foreign investors to decide whether or not a potential target country is eligible for investment.[53] Access to justice, judicial due process and impartiality of courts in a particular country are generally very important. This being said, it is not necessarily directly proportionate to the FDI inflow of a state. Factors such as "large local markets, natural resource endowments, good infrastructure, low inflation [...], [and] good investment framework" are important considerations.[54] One oil and gas lawyer practicing in Türkiye also noted during an interview that "bureaucracy needs to be manageable [for investors]".[55] In host countries with political and/or economic instability, faltering judiciary or little regard to due process, claims relating to arbitrary conduct are not uncommon.[56]

Particularly with regard to economic and political instability, an energy lawyer interviewed for this book noted the following:

> Investors seek stability, true, but they also know that higher profits come from less stable and emerging markets. Investors somewhat compensate the disadvantages of economic instability and they know that such [economic] instability is the reality of emerging markets. The real problem is the political instability.[57]

The examples of India and China clearly show that merely opening up markets, signing IIAs, and giving access to foreign capital are not sufficient to attract investors—other factors, such as political stability or targeted sectors may prevail over

---

[51] This number goes up to $276 billion in 2023 (and $299 billion in 2022) if China and Hong Kong are taken collectively. UNCTAD, World Investment Report 2024. available at https://unctad.org/publication/world-investment-report-2024, p. 9.

[52] UNCTAD, Work Investment Report 2024, p. 9.

[53] See, for an article on Latin American states in this regard, Staats and Biglaiser (2011) (suggesting, through their aggregate analysis, that "countries in the region with greater judicial strength and rule of law tend to receive higher levels of FDI.") In addition, all lawyers from *inter alia* Sweden, Türkiye, Singapore, Korea and Canada, who were interviewed for the this book, unanimously counted rule of law as a decisive element for their clients to invest in a country.

[54] Asiedu (2006), p. 74. Also see, UNCTAD, World Investment Report 2024, p. 138 (noting that while "improvements in governance and institutions take time to affect investor perceptions, [...] other fundamental FDI determinants – ranging from macroeconomic and political stability to market size and income levels, labour costs and the quality of physical infrastructure – are ultimately more important.").

[55] Interview #2.

[56] See Chap. 5.

[57] Interview #3.

liberal policies. The example of Brazil shows, on the other hand, that IIAs may not equal to, or even be needed for, attracting FDI. It is clear that economic liberalisation and consequent promotion of foreign capital into a particular state need to be facilitated through social, political, and institutional reforms. A free market economy may still be relatively undesirable by the investors, particularly if the said country suffers from administrative, economic or bureaucratic inefficiency. In that sense, IIAs should function as indicators that the domestic framework is palpable, investor-friendly and easy to navigate. They should "endorse rule of law standards for the treatment of foreign investors by states."[58] When built upon a shaky foundation, promises embodied in an IIA will fall short of becoming reality.

3.2.3.2 Protection

Notwithstanding the effect of IIAs on FDI, the relationship they maintain particularly between an *established* foreign investor and the host state is essential to the functioning of the international investment law regime. The *protection* of foreign investment is a more directly observable effect of these treaties, as evidenced by the ever-growing use of the ISDS mechanism over the years—not only against developing countries, but also against some of the most developed ones.[59] They usually provide for an alternative adjudicatory remedy for foreign investors, namely, international arbitration, against potential interventions by home states. As international investment law and ISDS develop, it is by consequence that IIAs are more widely known than they were twenty years ago.

As noted above, for many foreign investors, IIAs mitigate political risks. They may be more inclined to pay attention to whether a target country has an IIA with their home country, especially if the target country is perceived to pose political risks to the investment. The relevance, at least from a foreign investor's perspective, is higher in countries where the investor feels more vulnerable.[60] A Western European arbitrator and lawyer argued the following:

> It is safe to say that generally the North American investors trust the legal systems in […] most Western European countries. […] [In Eastern Europe], the situation is a bit different, because even though the European Commission doesn't believe it, we are still different. To invest in Slovakia is not the same with investing in Sweden or Norway. So I think if you are

[58] Schill (2011), p. 59.

[59] Out of 92 known cases filed under NAFTA Chapter 11 as of 2023, 39 were filed against Mexico, 33 were filed against Canada, and 20 were filed against the United States. https://investmentpolicy.unctad.org/investment-dispute-settlement.

[60] De Mestral (2015), p. 7: "The fears, often quite legitimate, that a court in a developing country may not offer the same guarantees of neutrality, fairness and impartiality that may be expected in a developed democracy, are allayed by recourse to arbitration before judges chosen by the parties who apply procedures and substantive rules known in advance to both sides."

> a North American investor and you are looking to invest in, say, [Czechia], or Bulgaria, or Romania; I think they would probably take into account whether there are BITs in force.[61]

The importance of this protection is naturally more important for an investor already established in a country. One significant risk facing established investors would be a drastic change in the political environment. After many years of economic and political cooperation between Iran and the United States, Iran's Islamic Revolution substantially discarded Western foreign investment.[62] Among other issues, as a relevant form of arbitrariness, the temporal aspects of managerial intervention were in length discussed by the US – Iran Claims Tribunal,[63] which was established pursuant to the 1981 Algiers Accords.[64] *Indefinite* hindrance of the operation and management of an investment has ever since been a prevalent issue in arbitral practice and academia.[65] Although the (then-new) Islamic Republic of Iran claimed that the government-appointed managers were put in place temporarily or provisionally, the Tribunal had realised that by late 1983, the intervention had been going on for at least three years in cases of some claimants. The Tribunal contended that there was little reason to believe that such interference would soon end.[66] While the US – Iran Claims Tribunal was not established as a result of an IIA, the setting of dispute settlement fora and the nature of some claims (expropriation) resemble the investment treaty disputes.

As another form of potential political risk, some (host) states might be inclined to adopt wider interpretations of public purpose to extend and justify their regulatory reach. In 2007 and 2010, two laws were approved in Venezuela called the *Leyes Habilitantes*.[67] This kind of law gives the President the power to legislate via decrees, particularly to speed up the legislation process in key issues such as transport, state institutions and property. It is to consolidate the power under the executive branch temporarily to avoid bureaucratic delays the legislative mechanisms otherwise may entail. For instance, in 2011, a law was passed which allowed the taking of underutilised land for the benefit of victims who had suffered during heavy torrential rains.[68] Similarly, in 2010, the government assumed direct responsibility for producing and distributing the food by prohibiting owning large amount of land by law. Even though this law stems from the idea that the land belongs to those who work on and with it, as Timmers points out, there has been no known transfer of title

[61] Interview #6.

[62] Escarcena (2013), p. 192.

[63] The Iran – US Claims Tribunal. http://www.iusct.net/.

[64] Algiers Accords (19 January 1981). http://www.parstimes.com/history/algiers_accords.pdf.

[65] *Starrett Housing Corporation, Starrett Systems, Inc., Starrett Housing International, Inc. v. Iran, Bank Markazi Iran, Bank Omran, Bank Mellat* (1987). Case No. 24, Award No. 314-24-1.

[66] *International Technical Products Corporation v. Iran* (1985). Award No. 196-302-2.

[67] Timmers (2013), p. 135.

[68] Timmers (2013), p. 135.

to any 'tiller' that works on these lands, and only a little portion of this land actually produces food.[69] The consequence is that these expropriated lands are leased by the state (instead of private landlords) to the farmers. Although there is no uniform or globally consensual definition of 'public purpose', such discretion could be considered to be in excess of what is intended by the limitation of public purpose in CIL, particularly in line with acknowledged sets of principles such as the Resolution 1803.[70] In other words, the realised measure (*leyes habilitantes*) and its projected purpose (the benefit of the people of Venezuela) have failed to correlate on a proportionate and efficient causality. Venezuela's rationale stems from its government's ideological standpoint. However, the execution may not necessarily meet the expectations if public purpose is not genuine. In line with the arguments conveyed throughout Chap. 2 on why treatment accorded to nationals may fall short of an international threshold for treatment of foreigners, and why the maintenance of a non-contingent, objective fairness protecting foreign investors from such potential arbitrary conduct may be necessary, this national threshold is instructive.

3.3 Rising Anti-ISDS Sentiment

3.3.1 Examples of Vattenfall, Philip Morris, Eco Oro, *and* Rockhopper

While IIAs are, by definition, promises made by states to each other, they have direct effects, characterised as either benefits or rights,[71] on certain groups of private individuals and legal persons. This may be identified as the primary peculiarity of the international investment law regime: states promise that they would protect each other's nationals and their economic activities within each other's territory, with actionable consequences vis-à-vis private persons. At the same time, claims originating from these treaties may have profound effects on a wide array of public issues: among them are public security, health, and environment of the host country. If the said foreign investor operates within a relevant sector such as energy production and distribution, waterworks, waste disposal, or resource extraction, these effects are even more prominent. IIAs, therefore, kick-start an intricate and highly complex relationship between states, citizens, and foreign investors.

Several recent examples would shed light to this elaborate interaction between investor-state disputes and public, and the influence the former is claimed to have on governance, as well as regulatory acts benefiting the latter. This interaction is highly illustrative of the need to have a workable balance between different interests.

---

[69] Timmers (2013), p. 135, p. 136.

[70] UN General Assembly, Resolution 1803 (XVII).

[71] Roberts (2013), p. 60, discussing whether foreign investors gain enforceable rights, or mere benefits, from IIAs.

The first example, namely the *Vattenfall v. Germany (II)*[72] case, concerns the well-known dispute between a Swedish energy company and Germany regarding the former's nuclear energy production in the latter. Following the nuclear power plant disaster which followed the 2011 earthquake and tsunami in Fukushima, Japan quickly suspended its nuclear power production activities. Several other countries followed Japan's example, such as Switzerland, which had decided not to build any new reactors and initiated a nuclear phase-out by 2034.[73] Germany, a country which had held extensive public debates on the issue, "immediately shut down eight of its oldest reactors"[74] (two of which were operated by Vattenfall) and undertook an even more assertive nuclear phase-out to be completed by 2022.[75] The shutdown allegedly resulted in a loss of expected revenue of USD 1.5 billion for Vattenfall in 2011 alone.[76] The company filed a complaint to ICSID earlier in 2012, demanding USD 6 billion in compensation.[77]

The case, and its perceived impact on the phase-out act motivated by general health and safety concerns of the public, have resulted in increased (and often negative) publicity of the entire investment law regime.[78] In 2014, Vattenfall's General

---

[72] *Vattenfall AB and others v. Germany (II)*, ICSID Case No. ARB/12/12 (Settled) (*Vattenfall v. Germany (II)*).

[73] Kanter J, Switzerland Decides on Nuclear Phase-Out (*The New York Times*, 25 May 2011). http://www.nytimes.com/2011/05/26/business/global/26nuclear.html?_r=0. In August 2024, the Swiss Energy Minister Albert Rösti announced that the government would "submit a proposal to amend nuclear legislation by the end of 2024" to overturn the ban on building new power plants. Reuters, Switzerland to scrap ban on building nuclear power stations (*Reuters*, 28 August 2024). https://www.reuters.com/world/europe/switzerland-scrap-ban-building-nuclear-power-stations-2024-08-28/.

[74] Sapsted D, Europe split over future of nuclear energy (*The National*, 15 March 2012). https://www.thenationalnews.com/world/europe/europe-split-over-future-of-nuclear-energy-1.584645.

[75] Steitz C and Copley C, Exit now, pay later: Germany's rushed farewell to nuclear power (*Reuters*, 1 November 2015). http://www.reuters.com/article/us-germany-nuclear-idUSKCN0SQ1G520151101; Bernasconi-Osterwalder and Hoffman (2013); According to the Federal Office for the Safety of Nuclear Waste Management, "[t]he last three nuclear power plants in Germany were shut down on 15 April 2023: Isar 2, Emsland and Neckarwestheim 2. Their shutdown had been planned for 31 December 2022. Due to the energy crisis, the three nuclear power plants continued operation in stretch-out mode until 15 April 2023 at the latest." Bundesamt für die Sicherheit der nuklearen Entsorgung, The Nuclear Phase-out in Germany. https://www.base.bund.de/en/nuclear-safety/nuclear-phase-out/nuclear-phase-out_content.html.

[76] Hessler U, German nuclear phase-out causes Vattenfall profits to slump (*Deutsche Welle*, 9 February 2012). http://www.dw.com/en/german-nuclear-phase-out-causes-vattenfall-profits-to-slump/a-15732588.

[77] IAReporter, Arbitrators Selected to Hear Billion-Dollar Treaty Claim by Vattenfall Arising Out of Germany's Phase-Out of Nuclear Power Generation (*IAReporter*, 2 January 2013). https://www.iareporter.com/articles/arbitrators-selected-to-hear-billion-dollar-treaty-claim-by-vattenfall-arising-out-of-germanys-phase-out-of-nuclear-power-generation/.

[78] Provost C and Kennard M, The obscure legal system that lets corporations sue countries (*The Guardian*, 10 June 2015). https://www.theguardian.com/business/2015/jun/10/obscure-legal-system-lets-corportations-sue-states-ttip-icsid.

Counsel Anne Gynnerstedt said in a written statement that "[Vattenfall was not] questioning the decision to phase out nuclear power in Germany […] [It] insists on being compensated for the financial loss resulting from this decision."[79] In November 2021, Vattenfall formally requested the discontinuance of the proceedings.[80]

This is not the first case brought by Vattenfall against Germany. In 2009, the energy company had brought an earlier arbitral claim over the permits relating to a coal-fired power plant to be built in Hamburg.[81] According to the Request for Arbitration dated 30 March 2009, Vattenfall had engaged in lengthy negotiations with regard to issuance of construction permits for the power plant with the Hamburg Government, through the Authority for Urban Development and Environment (BSU).[82] In 2007, the parties had reached an agreement on the issuance of those permits after lengthy negotiations particularly on issues relating to the cooling water to be released to the Elbe river, construction of a carbon capture and storage plant, and the increased output of district heating.[83] According to the claimants, Vattenfall had agreed to all of these demands put forth by the government. BSU, upon the agreement, had initiated the procedure to issue the construction permits, and stated that "there [were] no obstacles that cannot be removed by covenants that stand in the way of the approval."[84]

Following the 2008 state parliament elections, Christian Democrats (CDU) had lost their absolute majority and began coalition negotiations with the Green Party, who, according to Vattenfall, had heavily relied on promises relating to the suspension of the construction for their election campaign. After several months of delays, final permits promised by BSU had been issued, albeit with "severe limitations".[85] Claimants argued that

> the amount of cooling water which could be used by the power plant was severely limited, and made dependent on the amount of surface water, i.e water flowing downriver in the Elbe notwithstanding the fact that the Elbe, where the plant is located, is heavily influenced by the tide […] The effects of these limitations would be so severe that the plant would have to be shut down for days or weeks during summertime. Restrictions of this magnitude had not even been remotely mentioned, discussed or proposed during the administrative procedure.[86]

---

[79] Why Vattenfall is taking Germany to court (9 December 2012). https://corporate.vattenfall.com/press-and-media/news/2014/why-vattenfall-is-taking-germany-to-court/.

[80] *Vattenfall v. Germany (II)*, Discontinuance Order (9 November 2021); Bohmer L, Vattenfall Asks for Discontinuance of ICSID Arbitration against Germany, After Settlement Enters into Force (*IAReporter*, 2 November 2021). https://www.iareporter.com/articles/vattenfall-asks-for-discontinuance-of-icsid-arbitration-against-germany-after-settlement-enters-into-force/; The Settlement Agreement (in German) can be accessed here: https://www.italaw.com/sites/default/files/case-documents/italaw181399.pdf.

[81] *Vattenfall AB, Vattenfall Europe AG, Vattenfall Europe Generation AG (I) v. Germany*, ICSID Case No. ARB/09/6, Award (11 March 2011) (*Vattenfall v. Germany (I)*).

[82] *Vattenfall v. Germany (I)*, Request for Arbitration, (30 March 2009).

[83] *Vattenfall v. Germany (I)*, par. 20.

[84] *Vattenfall v. Germany (I)*, par. 21.

[85] *Vattenfall v. Germany (I)*, par. 36.

[86] *Vattenfall v. Germany (I)*, par. 37.

In 2010, the parties settled the claim. A new set of permits were issued in the second half of 2010, and the ICSID tribunal recognised the settlement by a formal award in March 2011.[87] According to a briefing note by Verheyen, the new permits have "considerably lowered the environmental standards".[88] This being said, she cautiously remarks that "[the challenged permit] was indeed stricter than others in many respects, and even the [new permit issued after the settlement] is still a better example of the water permits issued around the country in the past years", while acknowledging the need for verification of such comparison through case-by-case analysis for each power plant.[89]

Another popular example is the *Philip Morris v. Australia* and *Philip Morris v. Uruguay* cases.[90] Philip Morris, a tobacco company, filed a complaint against Uruguay in 2010 and Australia in 2011, in relation to the standard packaging laws these countries had enacted, which aimed at eliminating or limiting the use of branding, and prescribing uniform packaging for tobacco products. The regulation in Australia, which had not been adopted at the time of Philip Morris' initiation of arbitration, further prohibited

> the use of trade marks, symbols, graphics or images on or in relation to tobacco products and packaging other than the brand, business or company name and variant name [as defined in the regulations] [...] [The legislation] also prescribes the appearance of cigarette sticks [...] colour of the wrapping paper and tip, and [precludes] the use of brand and variant names on individual cigarette sticks.[91]

In Uruguay, two regulations were enacted: The Single Presentation Requirement (SPR) (through the Ordinance 514) in 2008, and the so-called 80/80 Regulation (through a Presidential Decree) in 2009.[92] The former required each cigarette brand to have a 'single presentation' for different variants of tobacco products, whereas the latter prescribed an increased size for health warnings on the packages (from 50% to 80%), leaving 20% for the branding.

Australia eventually triumphed as the arbitral tribunal declined its jurisdiction because Philip Morris, due to not being admitted into Australia properly, fell outside the scope of the Hong Kong – Australia BIT as a covered investor.[93] In *Philip Morris v. Uruguay*, the Arbitral Tribunal ruled that "a limitation to 20% of the space avail-

[87] *Vattenfall* v. Germany (I), Award (11 March 2011).

[88] Verheyen (2012), p. 8.

[89] Verheyen (2012), pp. 10–11.

[90] *Philip Morris Asia Limited v. Australia*, UNCITRAL, PCA Case No. 2012-12, Award on Jurisdiction and Admissibility (17 December 2015) and Final Award Regarding Costs (8 July 2017) (*Philip Morris v. Australia*); *Philip Morris Brands Sàrl, Philip Morris Products S.A. and Abal Hermanos S.A. v. Oriental Republic of Uruguay*, ICSID Case No. ARB/10/7, Award (8 July 2016) (*Philip Morris v. Uruguay*).

[91] *Philip Morris v. Australia*, par. 4.12–4.13.

[92] *Philip Morris v. Uruguay* (2016), par. 9–11.

[93] Hurst, Daniel; Australia wins international legal battle with Philip Morris over plain packaging (*The Guardian,* 18 December 2015). https://www.theguardian.com/australia-news/2015/dec/18/australia-wins-international-legal-battle-with-philip-morris-over-plain-packaging.

able [for the brand and other distinctive elements to appear] could not have a substantial effect on the Claimants' business" and disagreed with the Claimant's contention that the investment was expropriated.[94] It further contended that "the effects of the SPR were far from depriving [the Claimant] of the value of its business or even causing 'substantial deprivation' of the value, use or enjoyment of the Claimants' investments".[95] Furthermore, it contended that the Claimant was not treated unfairly, as neither the SPR nor the 80/80 Regulation were "arbitrary, grossly unfair, unjust, discriminatory or … disproportionate".[96] It also concluded that the Claimant had no legitimate expectations that "such or similar measures would not be adopted".[97] The Tribunal's notable deference to Uruguay's prerogatives to protect public health, reinforced by the relatively minor effects on the investment, is noteworthy.

Finally, two recent cases in relation to environmental protection and resource extraction, namely *Eco Oro v. Colombia*[98] and *Rockhopper v. Italy*,[99] deserve mention. In the former, the Claimant, Eco Oro Minerals Corporation, brought a claim against Colombia in 2016 arguing that its investment was harmed due to legislative and administrative measures aimed at protecting high-mountain ecosystems called *páramos*, known for their unique capacity to absorb and restore water. Eco Oro claimed that its mining exploration and extraction activities were critically affected, particularly by Colombia's measures hindering mining activities in certain areas that fell within the *páramos*, arguing that they were unfair and expropriatory. The infamy of this case, and in particular the 2021 Award on Jurisdiction, Liability and Directions on Quantum, stems primarily from the Tribunal's take on the application of the general exceptions clause under Article 2201 of the Canada-Colombia FTA.[100] After finding that Colombia's measures did not amount to expropriation but violated the MST provision in the FTA, the Tribunal further contended that even if the general exceptions clause applied, this did not preclude the Claimant from seeking and being entitled to compensation.[101] As a result, this reading could lead to a situation where a measure that is captured by a general exceptions clause still compel a

[94] *Philip Morris v. Uruguay*, Award (8 July 2016), par. 276.

[95] *Philip Morris v. Uruguay*, Award (8 July 2016), par. 283.

[96] *Philip Morris v. Uruguay*, Award (8 July 2016), pars. 410 and 420.

[97] *Philip Morris v. Uruguay*, Award (8 July 2016), par. 434.

[98] *Eco Oro Minerals Corp. v. Republic of Colombia*, ICSID Case No. ARB/16/41, Decision on Jurisdiction, Liability and Directions on Quantum (9 September 2021) and Award on Damages (15 July 2024) (*Eco Oro v. Colombia*).

[99] *Rockhopper Italia S.p.A., Rockhopper Mediterranean Ltd, and Rockhopper Exploration Plc v. Italian Republic*, ICSID Case No. ARB/17/14, Final Award (23 August 2022) (*Rockhopper v. Italy*).

[100] *Eco Oro v. Colombia* (2021), par. 837.

[101] *Eco Oro v. Colombia* (2021), par. 830.

Respondent state to pay compensation, as opposed to the clause having the effect of wiping out a violation and rendering restitution or compensation impossible.[102] However, in the July 2024 Award on Damages, the Tribunal ultimately decided that “the only identifiable loss which does flow from the finding of the breach of [the MST] is the inability of Eco Oro to apply for an environmental license”,[103] but “Eco Oro has offered the Tribunal no basis on which to value the loss it has suffered, and as a consequences the majority of the Tribunal has concluded that it has no basis on which to justify awarding damages to the Claimant.”[104]

In *Rockhopper v. Italy*, Rockhopper Italia brought a claim against Italy for the latter’s denial of a production permit to operate Ombrina Mare oil field pursuant to the Law No. 208 of 2015. This law prohibited research, prospection and exploitation in waters within a 12-mile limit of the Italian Peninsula.[105] The case was filed pursuant to the ECT, and the Claimant argued that the denial of this permit amounted to expropriation. The Tribunal ultimately delivered an award in favour of the Claimant, deciding that Italy’s denial was a direct expropriation of Rockhopper’s investment.[106]

The case garnered immediate and widespread public attention.[107] It also came at a time when ECT had already faced criticism for being incompatible with climate change mitigation efforts of states, and the fact that Rockhopper benefited from the ECT’s sunset clause to bring a claim against Italy, which had withdrawn from the ECT in 2014 (effective 2016), exacerbated the backlash.[108]

One of the key controversies was the Tribunal’s efforts to bifurcate a ‘civic and political’ reality on the one hand, and a ‘legal’ one on the other.[109] According to some commentators, the arbitrators thus argued “that environmental norms and considerations are irrelevant to determining, from a strictly ‘legal’ point of view, first whether an expropriation took place, and second the amount of compensation owed to the investor.”[110] Given this strong environmental undercurrent and the Tribunal’s

[102] Ünüvar (2023a), p. 532; Heath (2021).

[103] *Eco Oro v. Colombia* (2024), par. 303.

[104] *Eco Oro v. Colombia* (2024), par. 304.

[105] *Rockhopper v. Italy* (2022), par. 97.

[106] *Rockhopper v. Italy* (2022), par. 198–199.

[107] Neslen, A. Oil firm Rockhopper wins £210m payout after being banned from drilling (*The Guardian*, 24 August 2022). https://www.theguardian.com/business/2022/aug/24/oil-firm-rockhopper-wins-210m-payout-after-being-banned-from-drilling; Arcuri et al. (2024); some commentators also criticised Italy for not adequately constructing a defence around policy priorities such as environment and climate change mitigation—see, Mazzotti (2022).

[108] Italy, Energy Charter Treaty website. https://www.energycharter.org/who-we-are/members-observers/countries/italy/.

[109] Rockhopper v. Italy (2022), par. 10.

[110] Marzal (2023).

apparent and persistent efforts to distance itself from this context,[111] the decision remains controversial.

The examples above stand as prominent illustrations on how private economic interests are facilitated to trample regulatory prerogatives of states as sovereigns, particularly those who stem from democratic, legitimate acts aimed at realising *inter alia* health and environment objectives.

3.3.2 The Fear of Regulatory Chill: Negative Effects of the Risk of Arbitration on States' Regulatory Incentives

As a result of a broader discourse constructed upon the concept of *regulatory chill*,[112] which focuses on the chill effect on acts claimed to pursue public benefit. ISDS has been criticised for causing states to tone down their regulatory objectives regarding these policy spheres or to refrain from regulating and legislating for public good altogether in certain cases.[113] These effects can be particularly harmful in the context of public health and environmental regulations, as the examples above indicate. In line with this narrative (and understandably so), regulatory chill has been used almost always with a negative, restrictive subtext. In a sense, it represents an exogenous limitation with regard to a state's sovereign prerogatives, rather than one that is self-imposed.

When liability is more than likely or certain as a result, states may, one could argue, be less inclined to adopt a certain measure.[114] Bonnitcha, likewise, maintained that "[i]t remains reasonable to assume that states are less likely to maintain measures that give rise to liability than to maintain measures that do not."[115] While this may be part of the story, it is far from being representative of the whole picture.

Indeed, there are several examples of states refraining from adopting measures and enacting regulations to pursue public goals due to risk of facing investment claims. One of the clearest examples of such direct chilling effect of potential liability relates to New Zealand's planned tobacco plain packaging. Earlier in 2013, Associate Minister of Health Tariana Turia issued a press release which strongly endorsed the plain packaging legislation. However, she pointed out that the

[111] However see, Opinion of Pierre-Marie Dupuy (23 August 2022). https://jusmundi.com/en/document/opinion/pdf/en-rockhopper-exploration-plc-rockhopper-italia-s-p-a-and-rockhopper-mediterranean-ltd-v-italian-republic-opinion-of-pierre-marie-dupuy-wednesday-24th-august-2022.

[112] UNCTAD (2005) Investor – State Disputes Arising from Investment Treaties: A Review (UNCTAD Series on International Investment Policies for Development), p. 43; for an empirical study on environmental regulation, see Laudal Berge and Berger (2021).

[113] Brown (2013), p. 19.

[114] Tienhaara calls this the 'threat chill'. Tienhaara (2017), p. 235.

[115] Bonnitcha (2014), p. 121.

enactment would be delayed until the arbitral claim by Philip Morris against Australia is decided.[116] Besides the *Philip Morris* claim, New Zealand had been monitoring the WTO claims brought against Australia by Honduras, Dominican Republic, Cuba, Indonesia, and Ukraine on the same set of laws.[117]

It seems however, at the end of the day, the outcome of *Philip Morris v. Australia* had lost its relevance. Before the decision on *Philip Morris* in December 2015, New Zealand's then Prime Minister John Key, in reference to the then-newly negotiated TPP, asserted during an interview that "[w]hat will be carved out of TPP will be any restrictions when it comes to public health, so we'll be quite free to have plain packaging if we want".[118] In February 2016, the government had iterated its goal to pass the plain packaging laws "by the end of [2016]."[119] This indicates that the outcome of this particular case may have had a limited effect on whether New Zealand would be liable due to a similar legislation, as the TPP was not in force. When taken into account collectively, the regulatory chill inflicted upon the New Zealand government due to the risk of an arbitral claim seems to have been addressed by *another prospective IIA*: one which contains clear public purpose exceptions and carve-outs put in place.[120] This illustration shows why the criticism towards the system is better placed if it primarily (and not exclusively) targets the vague, broad, and unqualified instruments that do not have due regard to public goals. If the risk of regulatory chill indeed exists, this example illustrates, its potential threat may be mitigated by the policy space recognised within an IIA. If such policy space is recognised, the adjudicatory and discretionary leeway will be limited in a similar fashion, regardless of the dispute settlement body—be it an international investment court, or an arbitral tribunal.

Another issue is that regulatory chill claims bear the risk of being highly presumptive, as it is difficult to establish an unconditional, causal link between international investment law and arbitral claims, and a holistic, systemic regulatory

116 Turia, Tariana, Government moves forward with plain packaging of tobacco products (*Beehive NZ*, 19 February 2013). https://www.beehive.govt.nz/release/government-moves-forward-plain-packaging-tobacco-products.

117 *Australia – Tobacco Plain Packaging (Cuba v. Australia)*, 3 May 2013, DS458; *Australia – Tobacco Plain Packaging (Honduras v. Australia)*, 4 April 2012, DS435; *Australia – Tobacco Plain Packaging (Dominican Republic v. Australia)*, 18 July 2012, DS441; *Australia – Tobacco Plain Packaging (Indonesia v. Australia)*, 20 September 2013, DS467; *Australia – Tobacco Plain Packaging (Ukraine v. Australia)*, 13 March 2012, DS434.

118 Hickey B (2015) Trans Pacific Partnership Agreement near completion; Drug patents and auto parts access deals said done; dairy access for NZ still in the air; New conference delayed to 1 pm NZT. (Interest, 15 October 2015). https://www.interest.co.nz/rural-news/77946/trans-pacific-partnership-agreement-near-completion-drug-patents-and-auto-parts.

119 Kirk S (2016) Tobacco plain packaging likely to be law by end of year – John Key (*Stuff*, 15 February 2016). https://www.stuff.co.nz/national/politics/76917027/tobacco-plain-packaging-likely-to-be-law-by-end-of-year%E2%80%93john-key; Smoke-free Environments (Tobacco Standardised Packaging) Amendment Act 2016 No 43, 14 September 2016. https://www.legislation.govt.nz/act/public/2016/0043/latest/DLM5821008.html.

120 According to Article 29.5 of the TPP text, "[a] party may elect to deny the benefits of Section B of Chapter 9 (Investment) with respect to claims challenging a tobacco control measure of the Party." For a detailed analysis of the tobacco carve-out, see, Puig and Shaffer (2016).

drawback. There are many methodological challenges with regards to establishing such causal link. Many spontaneous events could play a role in any regulatory drawback, from domestic politics to other economic considerations. While the assumption that ISDS causes states to think twice before legislating may be true, same can be said for impending WTO claims, as was the case for New Zealand example above. Arbitral proceedings between investors and states do not take place in a vacuum, and a plethora of elements possibly play part in such regulatory decisions and related risk assessments. Coupled with challenges with regards to internal dynamics and confidential nature of state affairs, to pinpoint the exact role of each element is challenging, if at all possible.

Some of the more classic examples of regulatory chill rely on (temporal) correlation. *Ethyl Corporation v. Canada*,[121] an early NAFTA case, has been frequently cited as evidence that Canada was coerced to revoke the ban on the gasoline additive MMT.[122] In the meanwhile, a Canadian court ruled against the legislation and deemed it invalid, since it regarded the legislation to be an illegitimate restraint on interprovincial trade. The settlement between Ethyl Corporation and Canada came only after this ruling.[123] Bonnitcha, however, pointed out that "the fact that Canada choose to make settlement [...] rather than scrap the measure and contest the arbitral claim on the merits suggests that investment treaty protections did play some role in the government's decision."[124]

Another way to look at regulatory chill is to consider the classic approach on why IIAs exist, namely, the protection of foreign investments. Can this goal be achieved by way of self-imposed limitations? Would IIAs bear the potential to prevent states from enacting hazardous, arbitrary laws that would unjustifiably impede economic activities, as much as they are claimed to prevent states from enacting public objectives? According to Brower and Blanchard, "if the spectre of investor challenges risks 'chilling' anything, it is the misuse of regulatory authority".[125] From this perspective, the regulatory chill phenomenon may well embody the very purpose of IIAs—a sovereign prerogative to self-limit. Hugo Perezcano stated during an interview that

> Mexico enacted legislation in breach of our international obligations [...] On the other hand, [...] we wanted an instrument [which we could] use to talk to [the legislature or other government agencies], and say, "Look, you cannot enact [this] law, because we will be in breach of our [international] obligations. [...] In terms of the [domestic] legal context, [an IIA] is an international treaty and it is above federal and state laws [...] [an IIA] will prevail ultimately." It did work to a large extent. So, when you talk about regulatory chill, that's when I say, **we wanted the regulatory chill**. We did not want the [legislator] to enact cer-

[121] *Ethyl Corporation v. Canada*, UNCITRAL, ad hoc, Award on Jurisdiction (24 June 1998).

[122] Footer (2009); Beharry and Kuritzky (2015).

[123] Brower and Blanchard (2014), p. 752.

[124] Bonnitcha (2014), p. 123.

[125] Brower and Blanchard (2014), p. 753.

> tain laws, or [local authorities] to adopt certain decrees. We know what we are capable of, **and we wanted to tie our hands.**[126]

The above remarks do not intend to absolve regulatory chill of its adverse effects in its entirety or to disconnect any possible causal link between concerns about any impending litigation on the one hand, and a state refraining from enacting a certain legitimate regulatory act for public welfare on the other. However, they highlight the importance of concretely pinpointing within which context a state may refrain from enacting a law or regulation.

3.4 Actors and the Scope of International Investment Law: Exploring the Paradigms

The above analysis strives to demonstrate that there exists an unavoidable, undeniable and highly impactful interaction between the stakeholders involved within the international investment law system. This multi-faceted system first and foremost flows from public international law as based upon treaties signed between states.[127] However, the principal beneficiary of the system is the foreign investor, who can bring arbitral claims against host states through procedural and enforcement rules "developed largely in the context of international commercial arbitration and investor-state contracts."[128] This friction between a public international law foundation and an essentially private international law procedure and enforcement is supplemented with the consequential effects in terms of its above-analysed sphere of influence within the trilateral relationship of state (as sovereign), foreign investor (as governed), and the public (as affected). International investment law has undeniable domestic public law characteristics. According to some, it presents one of the clearest examples of a global administrative law regime.[129] This intricate and mutual effect inevitably calls for the better understanding of the relationship between these sovereigns and those they govern, as well as the rules pursuant to which this relationship is maintained.

Anthea Roberts outlined three common paradigms facilitated by actors and through their respective interests in the system which effectuate this complex interaction. According to Roberts, the first paradigm, public international law, focuses on the foundations of the system as brought together by international treaties. This, she argued, put "the treaty parties in a position of relative superiority to both

[126] Interview #12, Hugo Perezcano Diaz.

[127] Van Harten (2008), p. 131.

[128] Roberts (2013), p. 45.

[129] Peat (2019), s. 107–139; Van Harten and Loughlin (2006).

investors [...] and investment tribunals".[130] The second paradigm stems from 'private international law' (or rather, international commercial arbitration), which underlines the equality of arms between investors and states as parties to disputes, placing investors on a relatively higher pedestal, equal to host states.[131] Third paradigm, she maintained, was the public law paradigm; according to which the interests of the public are emphasised and underlined. In other words, according to this last and relatively new approach, the emphasis is on states' duties towards their people.

One frontline for the clash of different paradigms is treaty interpretation. Given the large number of vaguely drafted, short IIAs dominating the IIA regime, many treaties have remained silent or vague on a number of matters: as briefly mentioned above, the question whether IIAs existed solely for the protection of investors or they inherently called for the balancing of regulatory authority for public good and the economic rights of investors, even in the absence of clear language, has occupied much of the arbitral decisions rendered especially during the first decade of the twenty-first century.[132] While incomplete or vague instruments are by no means exclusive to international investment law,[133] the hybridity of the regime makes it particularly susceptible to this clash of different approaches and perspectives put forth by different stakeholders. Two issues stand out in particular: the interpretation of treaty provisions, and determination of interpretative authority.

3.4.1 Interpretation of Treaty Provisions

As constructs of (*inter alia*) public international law, IIAs must be interpreted in accordance with VCLT.[134] Its Article 31 lays forth the general rules for interpretation. Its first paragraph reads that "A treaty shall be interpreted in good faith in accordance with the ordinary meaning to be given to the terms of the treaty in their context and in the light of its object and purpose."[135] The interpretation of an international agreement, therefore, requires the assessment of (1) the ordinary meaning of its text, (2) its context, as well as (3) its object and purpose. The subsequent paragraph elaborates on what the "context of a treaty" means. After noting that the principle reference would be to "the text, including its preamble and annexes" of the treaty, the paragraph adds "[a]ny agreement relating to the treaty which was made between all the parties in connexion with the conclusion of the treaty", and "[a]ny

---

[130] Roberts (2013), p. 54.

[131] Titi (2024), p. 445.

[132] *See* case law analyses conducted in Chaps. 4 and 5.

[133] Van Aaken (2009) (largely drawing an analogy between WTO law and international investment law on treaty interpretation).

[134] Article 1, VCLT (1969), states that "The present Convention applies to treaties between States", which also covers IIAs.

[135] Article 31(1), VCLT (1969).

instrument which was made by one or more parties in connexion with the conclusion of the treaty and accepted by the other parties as an instrument related to the treaty."[136]

Since a reference to VCLT inevitably calls for further scrutiny of the object and purpose of an IIA, how the IIAs are articulated is extremely important.[137] Earlier treaties are usually silent on the matter of public goals of states, and how it weighs against the protection of investment protection and promotion. Many of these treaties simply refer to "[creating] and [maintaining] favourable conditions for investments by investors" while recognising "the need to promote and protect foreign investments with the aim to foster economic prosperity of both states".[138] The consequence was, therefore, an overall tendency among arbitral tribunals to lean towards favouring investors while interpreting the provisions of an IIA at the expense of an inherent consideration of public policy goals of states. The *SGS v. Philippines*[139] tribunal succinctly articulates this approach:

> [...] The object and purpose of the BIT supports an effective interpretation of Article X (2). The BIT is a treaty for the promotion and reciprocal protection of investments. According to the preamble it is intended 'to create and maintain favourable conditions for investments by investors of one Contracting Party in the territory of the other'. It is legitimate to resolve uncertainties in its interpretation so as to favour the protection of covered investments.[140]

In the case, the preamble of the applicable BIT explicitly mentions the creation and maintenance of "favourable conditions by investors".[141] Similarly, the *Noble Ventures v. Romania* tribunal adopts an interpretation "exclusively in favour of investors",[142] since the object and purpose as included in the US – Romania BIT of 1992, arguing that this interpretation is justified. According to the preamble of the BIT, the parties have "resolved to conclude a Treaty concerning the reciprocal encouragement and protection of investment".[143] Parties also acknowledge the importance of "[maintaining] a stable framework for investment".[144] None of these agreements recognise, or in any way refer to, any counter-balance *vis-à-vis* promotion and protection of foreign investment.[145] In accordance with VCLT and the

---

136 Article 31(2), VCLT (1969).

137 Ünüvar (2023b), p. 382.

138 Croatia – Switzerland BIT (1996).

139 *SGS Société Générale de Surveillance S.A. v. Republic of the Philippines*, ICSID Case No. ARB/02/6, Decision of the Tribunal on Objections to Jurisdiction (29 January 2004) (*SGS v. Philippines*).

140 *SGS v Philippines* (2004), par. 116.

141 Preamble, Philippines – Switzerland BIT (1997).

142 Noble Ventures, Inc. v. Romania, ICSID Case No. ARB/01/11, Award (12 October 2005), par. 52.

143 Preamble, Romania – US BIT (1992).

144 Preamble, Romania – US BIT (1992).

145 One exception could be that in the US – Romania BIT (1992), the parties refer to "well-being of workers in both Parties" and the promotion of "respect for internationally recognized worker rights".

respective provisions in relevant IIAs, arbitral tribunals 'simply' apply the rules at their disposal. As was seen above, more recent tribunals, such as Rockhopper, also rely on similar discourse regarding an ostensibly 'legal' reading, and subsequent application, of treaty provisions.

Arbitral practice also shows that different preambles in other BITs yielded different interpretative results. In *Saluka v. Czech Republic*,[146] the arbitral tribunal interpreted the preamble of the Netherlands – Czech Republic BIT,[147] which refers to parties' desire "to extend and intensify the economic relations between them particularly with respect to investments [...]", and their recognition that "[this] agreement upon the treatment to be accorded to such investments will stimulate the flow of capital and technology and the economic development of the [parties] [...]".[148] According to the Tribunal,

> This is a more subtle and balanced statement of the Treaty's aims than is sometimes appreciated. The protection of foreign investments **is not the sole aim of the Treaty**, but rather **a necessary element** alongside **the overall aim of encouraging foreign investment** and extending and intensifying the parties' economic relations. That in turn calls for **a balanced approach** to the interpretation of the Treaty's substantive provisions for the protection of investments, since an interpretation which exaggerates the protection to be accorded to foreign investments may serve to dissuade host States from admitting foreign investments and so undermine the overall aim of extending and intensifying the parties' mutual economic relations.[149]

The divergence in *Saluka* award is unsurprising. When compared to previous examples, the Netherlands – Czech Republic BIT stands out. It neither includes a reference to creating and maintaining favourable conditions for investors nor reiterates the promotion and protection of investments in its preamble. This, according to the Tribunal, alludes to a more balanced approach as the Tribunal sees the promotion and protection of investment as a tool towards the bigger objective embedded within the treaty, namely, extension and intensification of the parties' economic relations.

It should be immediately noted here that the comparison above *per se* does not intend, nor does it suffice, to maintain a universal and definite pattern in interpretative divergence with regards to how preambles are formulated and how tribunals interpret them. However, it surely hints at how preambles may affect interpretation and how tribunals, when preambles or treaty texts allow them, may lean towards more balanced approaches with regards to investors' and states' interests.[150] It illustrates how important it is to adopt an express method in drafting IIAs in line with intended objectives—therefore, it should not be surprising that the arbitral tribunal

---

[146] *Saluka Investments B.V. v. Czech Republic*, UNCITRAL, ad hoc, Partial Award (17 March 2006) (*Saluka v. Czech Republic*).

[147] Preamble, Czech Republic - Netherlands BIT (1991).

[148] Preamble, Czech Republic - Netherlands BIT (1991).

[149] *Saluka v. Czech Republic* (2006), par. 299–300.

[150] Ünüvar (2023b), pp. 383–384.

can 'favour' investors if the IIA at hand comes with a preamble referring to the creation and maintenance of favourable conditions for investments without any explicit or implicit reference to how such objective relates to states' regulatory authority.[151] As Alvarez wrote, as the IIAs have proliferated, "many of the states that established the regime [were] having second thoughts about the amount of sovereign 'police space' they have ceded."[152] One could also argue that since they were almost entirely mute with regard to the limits of this policy space, adjudicators have seized the interpretative authority to assume that states had intended to adopt a broad approach.

Systemic analyses and debates over whether the international investment law regime should favour foreign investors over state prerogatives, or establish a balance between foreign investors' interests and public goals and objectives of states should begin with the very text of each and every individual IIA examined in arbitral cases. Notwithstanding the importance of their background, personal beliefs or convictions, and their respective appointees which may or may not drive their interests, it is first and foremost the enabling divergences in texts that cause the perceived inconsistencies and guide arbitrators as interpreters. Biased adjudicatory approaches, if they exist, may be better identified within the context and practice of better-framed treaties with more clear-cut objectives.

3.4.2 *Determination of Interpretative Authority*

The second issue with regard to the clashing paradigms is the role of states, as treaty-makers and parties to arbitral disputes, in determining the interpretation of IIA provisions. In other words, and pursuant to Roberts' paradigmatic analysis, a conundrum arises as the result of the friction between public international law and private international law approaches on states' interpretative authority.[153] In this context, the former maintains that states, as treaty-makers, may intervene and establish guidance on how to interpret treaty provisions, before and after a foreign investor invokes an arbitral claim based on the said treaty. Private international law approach, to the contrary, considers such intervention by states as manipulation of the adjudicatory process by way of imposing retroactive amendments to the IIA.

One popular illustration is the Free Trade Commission (FTC)'s "Notes of Interpretation" dated 31 July 2001 (hereinafter the "Notes"). The Notes was issued "in order to clarify and reaffirm the meaning of certain of its provisions".[154] The

[151] It, however, does not mean that IIAs should be rigidly drafted. *See*, Van Aaken (2009).

[152] Alvarez (2011), p. 234.

[153] Roberts (2013), p. 59.

[154] NAFTA Free Trade Commission (FTC), North American Free Trade Agreement (NAFTA) Notes of Interpretation of Certain Chapter 11 Provisions (FTC Notes (31 July 2001).

reference made to 'certain' provisions principally relate to NAFTA's Article 1105 titled "Minimum Standard of Treatment", which prescribes "treatment in accordance with international law, including fair and equitable treatment" to foreign investors.[155] Following a number of arbitral awards (namely *Metalclad*, *S.D. Myers* and *Pope & Talbot*)[156] and broad interpretations adopting various reference points facilitated in their reasoning by their respective tribunals, the NAFTA parties have issued the Notes to pre-empt further unanticipated claims by investors.[157]

From the perspective of the clash of paradigms discourse, the issue at hand primarily concerns states' authority to direct, or manipulate, interpretation of treaty provisions by issuing clarifications. One could claim that states should be able to issue guidelines, such as the Notes, which aimed at clarifying treaty provisions. One could also argue that they should be barred from intervening in such a manner which may motive them to 'overrule' arbitral decisions in cases which they may be deemed liable. The latter perspective mainly focuses on states' role as respondents and emphasises on the equality of arms as parties to an international arbitration dispute. It draws attention to how states may unfairly dominate the proceedings and arbitrarily change a prospective arbitral decision by imposing an interpretation in their favour. Similar criticisms were also directed at the Notes. Brower II described the Notes as a "crude and self-interested form of political intervention designated to influence the outcome of pending disputes."[158] Jennings, in his expert opinion for the *Methanex* case, referred to the "impropriety" of the Notes and deemed it "against the most elementary rules of the due process of justice".[159]

The former approach, according to Roberts, "provides a counterbalance because it focuses attention on the role of the states as treaty parties with a legitimate and ongoing interest in interpreting their own treaty obligations."[160] However, she added that if it was accepted that the "investors have been granted enforceable rights, or the treaties were intended to induce them to rely upon the obligations in order to invest, there is a stronger case for providing some constraints on the ability of treaty parties to reinterpret those rights or obligations at will."[161] In can also be claimed that this counterbalance and the constraints Roberts speaks of are crucial for the states' effective and meaningful use of their own sovereignty to self-restrict. Similar *ex post* clarifications, therefore, represent an excessive reach of this very power, rendering any self-restriction compromised and perfunctory.

155 Article 1105, NAFTA (1994).

156 *Metalclad Corporation v. The United Mexican States*, ICSID Case No. ARB(AF)/97/1, Award (30 August 2000) (*Metalclad v. Mexico*); *S.D. Myers, Inc. v. Canada* (2002) UNCITRAL, ad hoc; *Pope & Talbot Inc. v. The Government of Canada*, UNCITRAL, Award on the Merits of Phase 2 (10 April 2001) (*Pope & Talbot v. Canada*).

157 Brower II (2006), p. 353.

158 Brower II (2006), pp. 355–356.

159 *Methanex Corporation v. United States of America*, UNCITRAL, ad hoc, Second Opinion of Professor Sir Robert Jennings, QC (6 September 2001), pp. 6–7.

160 Roberts (2013), p. 60.

161 Roberts (2013), p. 60.

The topic of what these constraints could be may have curious implications. In the FTC example, the content of the Notes is a crucial aspect of this discussion, which directly alludes to the extent which the NAFTA parties clarified the Article 1105. This extent also would be helpful in appraising whether the Notes could be considered as an amendment of NAFTA, rather than an interpretative clarification. This distinction is important, because it is claimed that an amendment, which would require constitutional processes of the NAFTA parties, would exceed FTC's interpretative competence.[162]

The Notes reads that "Article 1105(1) prescribes the customary international law minimum standard of treatment of aliens as the minimum standard of treatment [...]",[163] which limits the treaty language "in accordance with international law"[164] to "customary international law".[165] It has been suggested that the Notes, provided that it excludes free-standing treaty obligations but not the general principles of law, may pass as an interpretation. This is because of the limited nature of the consent the NAFTA parties have given to investor-state arbitration pursuant to Article 1116. Pursuant to this article, "[a]n investor [...] may submit to arbitration [...] a claim that [a NAFTA] party has breached an obligation under (a) Section A [Investment] [...]".[166] This effectively excludes other treaty obligations within the NAFTA, and therefore the reading of "international law" under Article 1105 would automatically carve-out any other free-standing obligation under any other treaty, except for those included under NAFTA's aforementioned Section on investment. In that sense, the limitation of "international law" as to exclude international treaties would not amend the treaty but instead would work as a clarification. However, same cannot be said for a possible exclusion of the general principles of law, which is considered among the sources of international law in accordance with Article 38 of SICJ.[167]

In international investment law, states' *ex post* interpretative interjections are highly controversial, arguably due to the sphere of influence of the IIAs which includes the treaty parties, private actors (foreign investors), and, by consequence, the public. While it is rather unrealistic to abandon the public international law paradigm and expect states to waive their authority to amend treaties they have signed with other states, one is unavoidably provoked by the multi-faceted influence on inter-state, investor-state, and investor-public relationships. In this sense, while any method of drafting may eventually need clarifications from a previously unanticipated perspective, a compromising way to address any lack of clarity could be pushing for further *ex ante* clarification within treaty texts. This is particularly important with regards to provisions aiming at setting thresholds for obligations and responsibilities.

[162] Brower II (2006), p. 350.

[163] FTC Notes (2001).

[164] Article 1105, NAFTA (1994).

[165] FTC Notes (2001).

[166] Article 1116, NAFTA (1994).

[167] Article 38, SICJ (1945).

3.5 Final Remarks

The need for clarity sits at the core of this book, and thus below Chapters will strive to demonstrate two very important case studies. As briefly referred to above, state acts may give rise to a dispute between a foreign investor and the host state. The said dispute may arise from a general regulatory act (hereinafter referred to as *regulatory measures*), or a measure (sometimes a series of measures) directed specifically at the foreign investor (*specific measures*) involved in the dispute.[168] Judicial decisions can also be counted among these measures.[169] As a result of such act, a foreign investor may be able to claim compensation from the host state for the deprivation caused by such measure(s). In another scenario, the host state could take the ownership of the investment usually via a decree, which would normally constitute a direct, formal expropriation. In the current global structure, most investment disputes are handled via investment arbitration, often under the auspices of, *inter alia*, the ICSID, PCA or SCC.[170]

When taken collectively, these considerations indicate that IIAs can be viewed from a variety of perspectives. First of all, they embody a state undertaking to protect foreign investments by accepting international remedies, alongside with domestic judicial avenues already available—which may or may not show signs of partiality. This relationship is chiefly shaped in accordance with the intent of a particular state to promote or protect foreign investment, and authorise foreign capital into its domestic market. While such intent is embodied by domestic concessions, laws and regulations; the manner in which an IIA is drafted is also crucial. The existence of an IIA is only as significant as the way specific protection principles are framed as to determine the extent of international protection granted to the foreign investors.

Secondly, while protection of foreign investment may be an important foreign policy goal for states, international investment law is a multi-faceted regime. It concerns not only an inter-state or investor-state interaction, but also other sensitive interactions between the public and the state, as well as the dialogue between the foreign investor and the public. On this relationship, a Southeast Asian government official and academic, talking about the increased popularity and backlash against the BITs and ISDS, further remarked that "[our] government has the goal of protecting natural resources and national interest [...] and [people] see it on the newspapers that **many investments do not benefit the society**."[171]

Paragraphs above attempted to illustrate these clashing interests of different stakeholders while demonstrating the intricate nature undergirding this legal field, and why it calls for further clarity. In short, how (and at what cost) the protection of foreign investors weighs against other sovereign considerations and responsibilities, such as health, environmental protection, human rights, public security, and more generally regulatory authority attached therewith should be well-framed in IIAs.

---

[168] See Chap. 4.

[169] See, for instance, Demirkol (2018).

[170] Arbitration Institute of the Stockholm Chamber of Commerce. http://www.sccinstitute.com/.

[171] Interview #17.

While it is true that IIAs are self-limiting prerogatives, the fact that they *limit* the leeway of a sovereign should not be considered to be inherently negative. After all, this is what international law generally does: it limits domestic sphere of sovereignty. Rather than focusing on the fact that IIAs limit sovereign prerogatives, it is more important to address how this limitation is framed, and how different paradigms, often characterised as 'clashing', can 'complement' one another. If the IIAs expressly pursue a balance between promotion and protection of investments on the one hand, and uphold other sovereign concerns which relate to public interest on the other; their overarching purpose would better capture the needs and concerns of its stakeholders.

The subsequent Chapters explore how some of the most controversial principles in IIAs, through adjudicative processes, address this need for clarity and balance.

References

Alvarez JE (2011) The return of the state. Minn J In Law 20:223–264

Arato J (2019) The private law critique of international investment law. AJIL 113(1):1–53

Arcuri A, Tienhaara K, Pellegrini L (2024) Investment law v. Supply-side climate policies: insights from Rockhopper v. Italy and Lone Pine v. Canada. Int Environ Agreements: Polit Law Econ 24:193–216

Asiedu E (2006) Foreign direct investment in Africa: the role of natural resources, market size, government policy, institutions and political instability. World Econ 29:63–77

Beharry CL, Kuritzky ME (2015) Going green: managing the environment through international investment arbitration. Am Univ Int Law Rev 30:383–429

Bellak C, Liebrecht M (2024) Do the new Brazilian Agreements on cooperation and facilitation of investment promote outward foreign direct investment? J World Invest Trade 25(4):535–563

Benhabib S (2016) The new sovereigntism and transnational law: legal utopianism, democratic scepticism and statist realism. Global Const 5:109–144

Berlant L (2007) Slow death (sovereignty, obesity, lateral agency). Crit Inq 33:754–780

Bernasconi-Osterwalder N, Hoffman RT (2013) The German nuclear phase-out put to the test in international investment arbitration? Background to the new dispute Vattenfall v. Germany (II). https://www.tni.org/files/download/vattenfall-icsid-case_oct2013.pdf

Bodin J (1992) On sovereignty: four chapters from the six books of the commonwealth (Julian H Franklin (editor and translator), *Cambridge texts in the history of political thought*). Cambridge University Press, Cambridge

Bonnitcha J (2014) Substantive protection under investment treaties: a legal and economic analysis. Cambridge University Press, Cambridge

Brower CN, Blanchard S (2014) What's in a Meme? The truth about investor-state arbitration: why it need not, and must not, be repossessed by states. Columbia J Transnatl Law 52:689–779

Brower CH II (2006) Why the FTC notes of interpretation constitute a partial amendment of NAFTA Article 1105. Va J Int Law 46:347–363

Brown JG (2013) International investment agreements: regulatory chill in the face of litigious heat? West J Leg Stud 3(1):1–25

Coe J, Rubins N (2005) Regulatory expropriation and the Tecmed Case: context and contributions. In: Weiler T (ed) International investment law and arbitration: leading cases from the ICSID, NAFTA, bilateral treaties and customary international law. Cameron May, London, pp 597–668

De Mestral A (2015) Investor-state arbitration between developed democratic countries. Investor-State Arbitration Series, Paper no. 1

Demirkol B (2018) Judicial acts and investment treaty arbitration. Cambridge University Press, Cambridge

Dolzer R, Schreuer C (2012) Principles of international investment law, 2nd edn. Oxford University Press, Oxford

Douglas Z (2003) The hybrid foundations of investment arbitration. Br Yearb Int Law 74:151–289

Downes P (2015) Hobbes, sovereignty, and early American literature. Cambridge University Press, Cambridge

Egger P, Pirotte A, Titi C (2022) International investment agreements and foreign direct investment: a survey. World Econ 46:1524–1565

Elkins Z, Guzman AT, Simmons B (2008) Competing for capital: the diffusion of bilateral investment treaties, 1960 – 2000. Univ Ill Law Rev 2008(1):265–304

Escarcena S (2013) Expropriations and other measures affecting property rights in the case law of the Iran – United States Claims Tribunal. Wisconsin Int Law J 31:177–207

Footer ME (2009) BITs and pieces: social and environmental protection in the regulation of foreign investment. Mich State J Int Law 18:33–64

Heath B (2021) Eco Oro and the twilight of policy exceptionalism (Investment Treaty News, 20 December 2021). https://www.iisd.org/itn/en/2021/12/20/eco-oro-and-the-twilight-of-policy-exceptionalism/

Hobbes T (1651) Leviathan (reprinted in 1985). Penguin Books, London

Hossain K (2005) Jus Cogens and obligations under the UN Charter. Santa Clara J Int Law 3:72–98

Kerwin GJ (1983) The role of United Nations General Assembly Resolutions in determining principles of international law in United States Courts. Duke Law J 1983:876–899

Klabbers J (1998) Clinching the concept of sovereignty: Wimbledon Redux. Aust Rev Int Eur Law 3:345–367

Koskenniemi M (2010) What use for sovereignty today? Asian J Int Law 1:61–70

Krasner SD (1999) Sovereignty: organized hypocrisy. Princeton University Press, Princeton

Krasner SD (2012) Problematic sovereignty. In: Krasner SD (ed) Problematic sovereignty: contested rules and political possibilities. Columbia University Press, New York, pp 1–23

Kriebaum U (2007) Regulatory takings: balancing the interests of the investor and the state. J World Invest Trade 8:717–744

Laudal Berge T, Berger A (2021) Do investor-state dispute settlement cases influence domestic environmental regulation? The role of respondent state bureaucratic capacity. J Int Dispute Settlement 12(1):1–41

Locke J (1690) Second treatise of government (Macpherson CB (ed), reprinted in 1980). Hackett Publishing, Indianapolis and Cambridge

Markert L (2011) The crucial question of future investment treaties: balancing investors' rights and regulatory interests of host states. In: Bungenberg M, Griebel J, Hindelang S (eds) European yearbook of international economic law, special issue: international investment law and EU law. Springer, Heidelberg, pp 145–171

Marzal T (2023) Polluter Doesn't Pay: The Rockhopper v Italy Award (EJIL: Talk! 19 January 2023). https://www.ejiltalk.org/polluter-doesnt-pay-the-rockhopper-v-italy-award/

Mazzotti P (2022) Rockhopper v. Italy and the Tension between ISDS and Climate Policy (Völkerrechtsblog, 21 December 2022). https://voelkerrechtsblog.org/de/rockhopper-v-italy-and-the-tension-between-isds-and-climate-policy/

Newcombe A (2013) Developments in IIA treaty-making. In: de Mestral A, Levesque C (eds) Improving international investment agreements. Routledge, London and New York, pp 15–24

Nikièma SH (2012) Best Practices Indirect Expropriation (IISD Best Practices Series). https://www.iisd.org/publications/guide/best-practices-indirect-expropriation

Paulsson J (1995) Arbitration without privity. ICSID Rev – Foreign Invest Law J 10:232–257

Peat D (2019) Comparative reasoning in international courts and tribunals. Cambridge University Press, Cambridge

Perrone NM, de Cerqueira Cesar GR (2015) Brazil's bilateral investment treaties: More than a new investment treaty model? (Columbia FDI Perspective, No. 159) available at https://ccsi.columbia.edu/content/no-159-brazils-bilateral-investment-treaties-more-new-investment-treaty-model-nicolas-m

Puig S, Shaffer G (2016) A breakthrough with the TPP: The Tobacco Carve-Out. Yale J Health Policy Law Ethics 16(2):327–333

Roberts A (2013) Clash of paradigms: actors and analogies shaping the investment treaty system. AJIL 107:45–94

Rubins N, Kinsella NS (2005) International investment, political risk and dispute resolution. Oceana Publications, Dobbs Ferry

Sachdev R (2006) Comparing the legal foundations of foreign direct investment in India and China: law and the rule of law in the Indian Foreign Direct Investment Context. Columbia Bus Law Rev 2006:167–214

Salacuse JW, Sullivan NP (2005) Do BITs really work? An evaluation of bilateral investment treaties and their grand bargain. Harv Int Law J 46:67–130

Sauvant KP, Sachs L (eds) (2009) The effect of treaties on foreign direct investments. Oxford University Press, New York

Schill SW (2011) Enhancing international law's legitimacy: conceptual and methodological foundations of a new public law approach. Virginia JIL 52:57–102

Skovgaard Poulsen L (2016) Bounded rationality and economic diplomacy: the politics of investment treaties in developing countries. Cambridge University Press, Cambridge

Skovgaard Poulsen L; Bonnitcha J, Yackee JW (2013) Analytical framework for assessing costs and benefits of investment protection treaties (LSE Enterprise)

Sornarajah M (1986) The pursuit of nationalized property (Developments in International Law, No. 8). Martinus Nijhoff Publishers, Leiden

Staats JL, Biglaiser G (2011) Foreign direct investment in Latin America: the importance of judicial strength and rule of law. Int Stud Q 56:193–202

Stone Sweet A (2010) Investor-state arbitration: proportionality's new frontier. Law Ethics Hum Rights 4:47–76

Sweeney M (2010) Foreign direct investment in India and China: the creation of a balanced regime in globalized economy. Cornell Int Law J 43:207–248

Tienhaara K (2017) Regulatory chill in a warming world: the threat to climate policy posed by investor-state dispute settlement. Transnatl Environ Law 7(2):229–250

Timmers L (2013) The protection against expropriations in Venezuela: a right to property in theory? In: Baetens F (ed) Investment law within international law. Cambridge University Press, Cambridge, pp 129–163

Titi C (2024) Investment treaty arbitration caught in the public-private law divide. Mich J Int Law 45(3):441–486

Ünüvar G (2023a) A tale of policy carve-outs and general exceptions: Eco Oro v Colombia as a case study. J Int Dispute Settlement 14(4):517–533

Ünüvar G (2023b) The 'object and purpose' and incrementalism of investment treaties: can international investment law reinvent its identity? In: Egan M, Raube K, Wouters J, Chaisse J (eds) Contestation and polarization in global governance. Elgar, Cheltenham

Van Aaken A (2009) International investment law between commitment and flexibility: a contract theory analysis. J Int Econ Law 12:507–538

Van Harten G (2008) Investment treaty arbitration and public law. Oxford University Press, Oxford

Van Harten G, Loughlin M (2006) Investment treaty arbitration as a species of global administrative law. Eur J Int Law 17:121–150

Verheyen R (2012) The Coal-fired Power Plant Hamburg-Moorburg, ICSID Proceedings by Vattenfall under the Energy Charter Treaty and the result for environmental standards

Wälde T (1998) A Requiem for the "New International Economic Order" the rise and fall of paradigms in international economic law and a post-mortem with timeless significance. In: Rest A, Hafner G, Loibl G, Zemanek K, Sucharipa-Behrmann L (eds) Liber Amicorum Professor Ignaz Seidl-Hohenveldern. Brill, Leiden, pp 771–803

Wälde T (2010) Procedural challenges in investment arbitration under the shadow of the dual role of the state – asymmetries and tribunals' duty to ensure, pro-actively, the equality of arms. Arbitr Int 26:2–42

Williamson J (2009) A short history of the Washington consensus. Law Bus Rev Am 15(1):7–24

Yackee JW (2008) Bilateral investment treaties, credible commitment, and the rule of (international) law: do BITs promote foreign direct investment? Law Soc Rev 42:805–832

Yackee JW (2014) Political risk and international investment law. Duke J Comp Int Law 24:477–500

Chapter 4
(Indirect) Expropriation as a Sovereign Act: A Case for Balance

Abstract This Chapter examines the evolving legal and political dynamics surrounding subsequent generations of expropriation provisions in international investment agreements (IIAs), highlighting the tension between states' sovereign rights and the protection of foreign investors against expropriatory measures. It analyzes how modern expropriation provisions attempt to balance these interests by incorporating clearer and more specific provisions in an attempt to guide adjudicators. Qualitatively engaging with a broad selection of case law, the Chapter presents a new framework for the analysis of effects and police powers doctrines, situating their application within a so-called 'effect-intent scale'. Based upon this framework, the Chapter concretely demonstrates inconsistencies stemming from varying emphases on the effects of state measures versus their intent or regulatory prerogatives, resulting in unpredictable outcomes for both states and investors. Drawing on case law and new-generation IIAs, the Chapter illustrates how states have responded to these challenges by adopting provisions aimed at safeguarding their legitimate, non-discriminatory regulatory measures. Examples from agreements such as the CPTPP, RCEP, and EU IIAs demonstrate a global trend toward greater clarity and recalibration of expropriation provisions, minimizing liability for actions taken in pursuit of public policy goals such as health and environmental protection. It argues that this global shift, driven by accumulated arbitral experience, has led to increased coherence and predictability in investment arbitration, although challenges remain, as evidenced by cases like *Bear Creek v. Peru*. The Chapter concludes by noting that the convergence of interests between capital-importing and exporting states creates a unique opportunity for collective recalibration of international investment law.

4.1 Introduction

Virtually all IIAs provide protection against certain acts, decisions, or omissions of the state within the context of the treatment of foreign investment. Some of these acts, decisions or omissions, depending on their severity, may amount to

G. Ünüvar, *The Transformation of International Investment Law and Its Principles*, European Yearbook of International Economic Law 44,
https://doi.org/10.1007/978-3-032-01110-7_4

expropriatory acts. This Chapter concerns expropriation as a state act, and it principally scrutinises indirect expropriation as a case study. It is a sovereign act which forms the backbone of one of the most commonly invoked, free-standing, *non-contingent* protection principles included in the IIAs in force today.[1]

Definition and scope of expropriation, as embodied within thousands of IIAs and developed through arbitral interpretations, have provided for an elaborate case study for practitioners, scholars and policy-makers on how the efforts on establishing a balance between sovereign discretion, protection of foreign investments, and pursuance of public goals may play out and how, from a state's perspective, their international obligations and prerogatives to self-limit should be framed.[2] Particularly the normative and contextual development of the latter sub-category is the result of a largely spontaneous sequence of legal, political, and socio-economic developments.

The next two Chapters build their case studies, as well as subsequent analyses of a selection of new generation IIAs conducted pursuant to these case studies, upon the following 4-step argument: Especially since the advent of modern IIAs, the development of expropriation and FET provisions, not unlike the IIAs in general, follow the recurrent series of events which consists of (a) vague formulation,[3] (b) subsequent application,[4] (c) unanticipated or divergent adjudicatory consequences,[5] and (d) reformulation of provisions in newer IIAs.[6] I suggest that international investment law is, yet again, undergoing the phase (d) on reformulation, and the contours are becoming ever clearer as more and more new generation treaties resemble one another, albeit with exceptions, in terms of their wording, scope and reflected concerns.[7]

This Chapter will first look into different types of expropriations—*lawful* and *unlawful*, as well as *direct* and *indirect* expropriation, to provide the background for the subsequent case law and analysis of the newer IIAs. It will highlight their differences, and their adjudicatory structure and transformation. Indirect expropriation, this Chapter's primary focus, stands out as one of the most controversial, vague, and open-ended principle within the sphere of expropriatory measures, in particular with regard to older generation IIAs that rarely elaborate on its determinative elements.[8] The vast majority of IIAs in force today define indirect expropriation simply

[1] A plethora of scholarly works focus on expropriation. See, for instance, Rajput (2018); Kriebaum (2018); De Luca (2014); Vandevelde (2010).

[2] Recently, a comprehensive policy-making effort is ongoing under the auspices of the OECD. See, OECD (2022) and OECD (2021); OECD (2004); Coe and Rubins (2005).

[3] Reinisch (2012), p. 422 (referring to broad references to indirect expropriation in IIAs).

[4] Kriebaum (2007) (on different approaches in regard to what 'indirect' expropriation means).

[5] Dumberry (2001) (an account of the pre-2001 case law on NAFTA Article 1110, pointing out different approaches).

[6] See UNCTAD's policy suggestions in this regard: UNCTAD (2012) Expropriation (UNCTAD Series on Issues in International Investment Agreements II), pp. 125–135.

[7] Some scholars already believe that these newer treaties are nonetheless poised to deliver the same, undesirable outcomes. See, for example, Alschner (2022).

[8] Dolzer and Schreuer (2012), p. 89.

as measures having equivalent effect to that of direct expropriation.[9] However, this elaboration is not sufficient to accurately delimit which state acts (or omissions) amount to indirect expropriation.[10] In order to demonstrate the decades-long interaction between treaty-making and adjudicatory experience and how they have affected one another, this Chapter will scrutinise the arbitral case law, including some of the most recent awards at the time of the writing of this book, to establish a clear and up-to-date definition and scope particularly for indirect expropriation, as it stems from adjudicatory experience in the absence of clearer rules. One preliminary suggestion, which will be put to test, is that the current, unspecified expropriation provisions in IIAs in fact do not prevent arbitrators to disregard (or give less weight to) certain considerations, given virtually none until mid-2000s included any references and carve-outs for legitimate regulatory measures. On top of that, most have emphasised the active protection of foreign investors in their preambles, or other operative provisions.

Once the conceptual vagueness surrounding the (indirect) expropriation is demonstrated, the Chapter will focus on the incremental adjudicatory clarifications which have been accumulating since the first NAFTA[11] cases in early 2000s. Following the identification of this emergent framework, the Chapter will focus on new generation IIAs and their provisions on expropriation to understand how the adjudicatory process continues to influence these new provisions. The focus will be on whether these new provisions inject further clarity with regard to identifying expropriatory acts. It is also crucial to assess whether these new provisions bear the potential to accommodate, sequence, and effectively embed the multitude of paradigms (public law, international private law, international public law) examined in Chap. 3 within their transformative configuration.

4.2 What Is Expropriation?

Under international law, states have "a sovereign right [...] to take property held by nationals or aliens through nationalisation or expropriation for economic, political, social or other reasons."[12] It is considered as the most "severe form of interference with property".[13] It was also common practice prior to twentieth century—as Harris describes, a "typical nineteenth century case was the occasional taking of property of a single foreigner in the context of a particular project or dispute".[14] In the

[9] Some treaties instead refer to "measures of similar effects" which, arguably, sets a different threshold. See, for example, Article 4, Bahrain – Türkiye BIT (2006).

[10] Dolzer and Schreuer (2012), p. 89.

[11] North American Free Trade Agreement (NAFTA) (1994).

[12] UNCTAD Expropriation (2012), p. 1.

[13] Dolzer and Schreuer (2012), p. 89.

[14] Harris (2010), p. 474.

contemporary context, nationalisation is conceived as a sub-group within expropriation. Notwithstanding the traditional conceptualisation, nationalisation mainly refers to sector-wide expropriations by states usually with regards to their public policy and national interests.[15] Recent oil and gas nationalisations in Bolivia during the last decade,[16] as well as earlier nationalisations in Iran and Libya,[17] could serve as examples.

4.2.1 Lawful–Unlawful Expropriation

Expropriation is not prohibited in international law subject to certain conditions. The protection of individuals *vis-à-vis* the state's conduct, in this case foreign investors, limits the authority of the sovereign. Above mentioned Resolution 1803,[18] besides recognising expropriation as a legitimate state act, provides for a list of conditions upon which the state act shall be based; such as public utility, security or national interest.[19]

Conditions for *lawful* expropriation generally include public interest, principle of non-discrimination, due process and "prompt, adequate, and effective compensation", reflecting the generally accepted CIL on the matter.[20] The main significance of an expropriation being lawful or unlawful essentially relates to the nature and amount of compensation to be paid.[21] Majority of IIAs explicitly articulate the conditions of lawfulness of expropriation. IIAs have fairly similar provisions on the requirements of a lawful expropriation. This being said, as will be shown, there can

---

[15] Harris (2010), p. 474.

[16] Nationalising utilities in Bolivia: From tap to socket (*The Economist,* 19 January 2013). http://www.economist.com/news/americas/21569707-can-government-do-better-job-private-sector-tap-socket; Prada P (2006) Bolivia Nationalizes the Oil and Gas Sector (*The New York Times,* 2 May 2006). http://www.nytimes.com/2006/05/02/world/americas/02bolivia.html?_r=1.

[17] See, for instance, the award of *Libyan American Oil Company (LIAMCO) v. Libya,* ad hoc, Award (12 April 1977) (*LIAMCO v. Libya*). The claim challenged measures in the aftermath of the 1973 coup d'etat in Libya by Muammar Gaddafi.

[18] UN General Assembly, Resolution 1803 (XVII) Permanent Sovereignty over Natural Resources, 14 December 1962, p. 15. https://undocs.org/a/res/1803(xvii).

[19] UN General Assembly, Resolution 1803 (XVII). It is also an interesting detail that the Resolution clearly considers such public concerns to be "recognized as overriding purely individual or private interests, both domestic and foreign".

[20] Resolution 1803 can be said to reflect the CIL in this respect. Visser further contended that "the principle of permanent sovereignty over natural resources, as embodied in resolution 1803 (XVII), still reflects the current position in public international law", and that it "forms part of the general principles of public international law". Visser (1988), pp. 90–91. Furthermore, see, Article 20(8), Investment Agreement for the COMESA Common Investment Area (2007) which reads: "...[c]onsistent with the right of states to regulate and the customary international law principles on police powers".

[21] Kriebaum (2007), pp. 742–743.

be certain differences in some IIAs.[22] It is crucial to underline that an arbitral tribunal will go into the analysis of lawfulness only after maintaining that expropriation has actually occurred—it is therefore very important not to confuse the indirect expropriation analysis and the lawfulness of the said expropriation.

4.2.1.1 Conditions for Lawful Expropriation

Public interest is one of the requirements of a lawful expropriation, found virtually in all IIAs which regulate expropriation.[23]

Article 13(1) of the ECT provides that investments shall not be expropriated unless such expropriation is, *inter alia*, "for a purpose which is in the public interest".[24] The 2012 US Model BIT, under its Article 6, refers to "public purpose".[25] Although the necessity of the host state to act in accordance with such a purpose is beyond doubt; the determination of what is considered to be for a public purpose may prove to be challenging. Several arbitral tribunals, in order to set this limit, asserted that the public purpose claim has to be genuine. As the *ADC v. Hungary* Tribunal stated, "a treaty requirement for 'public interest' requires some genuine interest of the public. If mere reference to 'public interest' can magically put such interest into existence and therefore satisfy this requirement, then this requirement would be rendered meaningless".[26]

Arbitral tribunals also seem to be interested when, and under what circumstances, the expropriation actually starts serving the allegedly upheld public purpose. Six years after a land expropriation, the Egyptian government transferred the expropriated assets to a state-owned company for the installation of a pipeline. Even though the eventual use might have benefited the public, "[t]he [t]ribunal [did not] accept that because an investment was eventually put to public use, the expropriation of that investment must necessarily be said to have been 'for' a public purpose."[27] Similarly, the character and the manner in which a legitimate public purpose is pursued might also affect the outcome. According to the *Siemens v. Argentina* tribunal, "[…] while the public purpose of the [relevant domestic law] is evident, its application through [a decree] to the specific case of Siemens' investment and the public purpose of the same are questionable", essentially because the realisation of the

[22] UNCTAD Expropriation (2012), pp. 41–42.

[23] Article VI, Lithuania – Norway BIT (1992); Article 6, Iran – Kazakhstan BIT (1996); Article 13, ECT (1998). For a recent work on how these conditions (i.e. public purpose, non-discrimination, due process, and compensation) reflect elements related to the concept of rule of law, see Bungenberg (2023).

[24] Article 13(1), The Energy Charter Treaty (ECT) (1998).

[25] Article 6, 2012 US Model BIT.

[26] *ADC Affiliate Limited and ADC & ADMC Management Limited v. Hungary*, ICSID Case No. ARB/03/16, Award (2 October 2006), par. 432 (*ADC v. Hungary*).

[27] *Waguih Elie George Soag and Clorinda Vecchi v. Egypt*, ICSID Case No. ARB/05/15, Award (1 June 2009), par. 432 (*Vecchi v. Egypt*).

reflected public purpose was actually done "as part of a change of policy by a new [a]dministration eager to distance itself from its predecessor."[28]

Due process is another requirement by international law for an expropriation to be lawful.

According to the UNCTAD, due process requires (a) compliance of the expropriation with procedures established in domestic legislation *and* "fundamental internationally recognised rules in this regard"; and (b) the availability of an independent and impartial body to review the case brought by the deprived investor.[29] Furthermore, due process "must be free from arbitrariness", which emphasises the duty of pursuing justice and not ideological goals particularly for host states. In its famous *ELSI* case, the ICJ defined arbitrariness as "a wilful disregard of due process of law, an act which shocks, or at least surprises, a sense of juridical propriety."[30] According to the *Lauder v. Czech Republic* tribunal, arbitrariness stems from "[…] individual discretion; […] founded on prejudice or preference rather than on reason or fact".[31]

Many BITs include a due process requirement for lawful expropriation. Many IIAs, such as Denmark – Turkey BIT[32] and the new Pakistan – Germany BIT refer to "due process of law."[33] Many other BITs follow this example, albeit with minor, possibly unsubstantial, wording differences.

Other states, however, diverge from the principle of due process and its compliance with domestic, as well as internationally recognised rules. China, for instance, has persistently excluded the international aspect of the principle of due process. An illustration is Argentina – China BIT of 1992,[34] which provides "due domestic legal procedure" as a condition for lawful expropriation under its Article 4. This means that the lawfulness of an expropriation, pursuant to this particular BIT, will be scrutinised in accordance with the legality as prescribed by (or pursuant to) the domestic procedure, regardless of its compliance (or lack thereof) with internationally recognised rules. This exclusive domestic perspective of due process had not changed in subsequent Chinese BITs, such as Germany – China BIT of 2009.[35] Under Article 4 titled "Expropriation and Compensation", there is no explicit mention of due process.[36] However, the last sentence of Article 4(2) allude to the second UNCTAD requirement for due process: "At the request of the investor the legality of any such

[28] *Siemens A.G. v. Argentina*, ICSID Case No. ARB/02/8, Award (17 January 2007), par. 273 (*Siemens v. Argentina*).

[29] UNCTAD Expropriation (2012), p. 27 et seq.

[30] *Elettronica Sicula S.p.A. (United States of America v. Italy)*, Judgment (20 July 1989). https://www.icj-cij.org/sites/default/files/case-related/76/076-19890720-JUD-01-00-EN.pdf, par. 128.

[31] *Ronald S. Lauder v. Czech Republic*, UNCITRAL, ad hoc. Award (3 September 2001), par. 221 (*Lauder v. Czech Republic*). Tribunal adopted the dictionary meaning of 'arbitrary'.

[32] Article 4, Denmark – Türkiye BIT (1990).

[33] Article 4, Germany – Pakistan BIT (2009).

[34] Article 4, Argentina – China BIT (1992).

[35] Germany – China BIT (2009).

[36] Article 4, Germany – China BIT (2009).

expropriation and the amount of compensation shall be subject to review by national courts [...]".[37] In the last two BITs signed by China, this domestic perspective has been gradually abandoned. According to Article 5 of the BIT signed with Turkey in 2015 states that the assessment of lawfulness is subject to the measure in question being conducted "in accordance with domestic law and due process of law in accordance with the general principles of treatment provided for in Article 3 [on Treatment of Investors]".[38] According to the wording of the Treaty, it is not clear whether this 'due process' requirement is only in accordance with domestic law, or whether a more general due process requirement is sought. Finally, in the Angola-China BIT signed in 2023, the domestic law reference was completely abandoned. According to its Article 7, the 'due process' requirement, which is listed among the conditions for lawful expropriation, is not limited by a domestic benchmark in any way.[39]

Due process has been perused by many arbitral tribunals. In *ADC v. Hungary*, a case concerning the renovation and construction of an airport terminal, the Tribunal found that several basic legal mechanisms were expected to be available within the context of due process, such as reasonable advance notice, fair and unbiased hearing and adjudication.[40] It is further maintained that an investor should have the possibility to claim its legitimate rights within a reasonable time.[41]

Depending on the facts of each particular case, it has been argued, prior notice of the expropriation may not necessarily constitute an intrinsic part of the due process requirement[42] particularly when the circumstances require an imminent taking.

Non-discrimination is the third requirement for the lawfulness of an expropriatory measure. Although the exact scope of non-discrimination principle is not without controversy,[43] it has been maintained that most tribunals have consistently scrutinised this principle within the context of discrimination based on nationality. According to Rubins and Kinsella, a "discriminatory taking is one that singles out a particular person or a group of people with a reasonable basis".[44] Therefore, the core (and the most common) feature of non-discrimination from an ISDS perspective is nationality.

In *Alpha v. Ukraine*,[45] said the Tribunal contended that discrimination "could arise *de jure* if there is a government measure such as a law or regulation that explicitly discriminates between domestic and foreign investors, or *de facto* if the measure is not explicitly or inherently discriminatory but discriminates between domestic

[37] Article 4, Germany – China BIT (2009).

[38] Article 5, China – Türkiye BIT (2015).

[39] Article 7, Angola – China BIT (2023).

[40] *ADC v. Hungary* (2006), par. 435.

[41] *ADC v. Hungary* (2006), par. 435.

[42] UNCTAD Expropriation (2012), p. 40.

[43] Reinisch (2008), p. 186.

[44] Rubins and Kinsella (2005), p. 177.

[45] *Alpha Projektholding GmbH v. Ukraine*, ICSID Case No. ARB/07/16, Award (8 November 2010) (*Alpha v.Ukraine*).

and foreign investors in the way in which it is applied."[46] This being said, the arbitral tribunals have been paying close attention to the legitimacy of the government measure and policy while examining whether or not the taking had been discriminatory. This also means that not every measure or realisation of a particular policy goal targeting foreign investors is discriminatory.[47]

GAMI Investments v. Mexico[48] is a fine illustration. Following the expropriation of several sugar mills owned by a partially foreign-owned Mexican company, Mexico maintained that the takings were not conducted because of the nationality of some of the shareholders. In the Tribunal's words,

> [...] a reason exists for the measure which was not itself discriminatory. That the measure plausibly connected with a legitimate goal of policy (ensuring that the sugar industry was in the hands of solvent enterprises) and was applied neither in a discriminatory manner nor as a disguised barrier to equal opportunity.[49]

Coupled by the failure of the claimant to demonstrate that the measure resulted from the foreign participation in the Mexican company GAM,[50] the Tribunal decided that the measure was not discriminatory.

The Tribunal at *LIAMCO v. Libya*[51] focused on the radius of impact of the nationalisation and the intent of the respondent state simultaneously: "[...] LIAMCO was not the first company to be nationalised, nor was it the only company nor the only American company to be nationalised [...]. Other companies were nationalised before it, other American and non-American companies were nationalised with it and after it, and other American companies are still operating in Libya."[52] The Tribunal then went on to assert that the political motive was not the "predominant motive" for the taking, therefore the motive *per se* did not ascertain that the measure was discriminatory.

Last but not least, *compensation* is crucial for an expropriatory act to be deemed lawful. CIL recognises that the deprivation resulting from a taking of foreign property must be compensated.[53] *Norwegian Shipowners' Claims* (Norway v. USA),[54] a well-known and commonly cited early arbitral award, reads that

---

[46] *Alpha v. Ukraine* (2010), par. 426.

[47] Reinisch (2008), p. 186.

[48] *Gami Investments Inc. v. Mexico*, UNCITRAL, ad hoc. Award (15 November 2004) (*GAMI v. Mexico*).

[49] *GAMI v. Mexico*, par. 114.

[50] *GAMI v. Mexico*, par. 115.

[51] *Liamco v. Libya* (1977), p. 117.

[52] *Liamco v. Libya* (1977), p. 118.

[53] Nicholson, (1965), p. 400.

[54] *Norwegian Shipowners' Claims* (*Norway v. USA*) (1922). http://legal.un.org/riaa/cases/vol_I/307-346.pdf. Emphasis added.

> No State can exercise towards the citizens of another civilized State the 'power of eminent domain' without respecting the property of such foreign citizens or without paying **just** compensation as determined by an impartial tribunal, if necessary.[55]

However, what *is* just compensation?

This question also has historic significance in relation to the development of international investment law. In 1928, the PCIJ ruled in *Chorzów Factory* case[56] that the damage suffered must be repaired by way of "fair compensation", and further maintained that "reparation must, as far as possible, wipe out all consequences of the illegal act and re-establish the situation which would, in all probability, have existed if that act had not been committed."[57]

There is a difference between compensation for *damages* and the compensation to be paid for expropriation to be deemed lawful. The principle pertaining to compensation for expropriation was reformulated more tangibly by Cordell Hull, the Secretary of State of the US at the time, in the aftermath of the Mexican agrarian reforms through which Mexico had expropriated American agricultural assets during late 1920s.[58] In 1938, on a letter addressed to the Mexican Government, Secretary Hull asserted that the taking of the alien property must be accompanied by "adequate, effective, and prompt payment."[59]

According to this formulation, three elements need to be present in order to claim legitimate compensation: payment has to have a reasonable relationship with the *market value* of the investment or property concerned (adequacy); it should be paid without delay (promptness); and it has to be paid in convertible or freely useable currency (effectiveness).[60]

The Hull Formula has been incorporated in thousands of IIAs. The 1959 Germany – Pakistan BIT,[61] the first BIT ever signed, included the following provision under its Article 3:

> Nationals or companies of either [p]arty shall not be subjected to expropriation except for [...] compensation, which shall represent the equivalent of the investments affected. Such compensation shall be actually realizable and freely transferable in the currency of the other [p]arty without undue delay.[62]

Despite its general acceptance and continued application to this day, the Hull Formula has seen some pushback. Mid-twentieth century saw economic and political developments which challenged the predominance of this approach. Reinisch

[55] *Norway v. USA*, p. 338; Corey (2012), p. 1007 et seq.

[56] *Case Concerning the Factory at Chorzow (Germany v. Poland)*. Judgment (13 September 1928), PCIJ Series A. No 17, p. 55.

[57] *Germany v. Poland* (1928), p. 47.

[58] U.S. Department of State, Office of the Historian, Mexican Expropriation of Foreign Oil, 1938. https://history.state.gov/milestones/1937-1945/mexican-oil.

[59] Nicholson (1965), p. 400.

[60] UNCTAD Expropriation (2012), pp. 135–136.

[61] Germany – Pakistan BIT (1959).

[62] Article 3, Germany – Pakistan BIT (1959).

counts expropriations by Eastern Bloc states in Europe, large-scale nationalisations in developing countries and the attempts to establish a New International Economic Order (NIEO) among these developments.[63] Today's IIAs usually specify what is meant by 'just compensation', 'appropriate compensation', 'fair' or 'fair and equitable compensation' by articulating its components. Despite the common association of 'fair market value' with 'adequate' or 'just' compensation; and 'real value' with 'appropriate' compensation, individual scrutiny of the applicable agreement is necessary to clearly pinpoint what exactly is meant by these terms used.

Today, IIAs contain varying provisions. The Australia – Argentina BIT of 1997 includes a provision which reads that "the expropriation [shall be] accompanied by the payment of prompt, adequate and effective compensation."[64] Identical or legally equivalent provisions can be found in a vast number of BITs in force. As a more recent example, Turkey – Azerbaijan BIT of 2014 prescribes the same criteria for compensation.[65] Article 13 of the ECT, similarly, prescribes "prompt, adequate and effective compensation" which amounts to the "fair market value of the [i]nvestment expropriated".[66] The 2003 India Model BIT requires "fair and equitable" compensation for lawful expropriation, which is expressed to be the "genuine value of the investment".[67] The 2015 India Model BIT, on the other hand, refers to "adequate" compensation,[68] which refers to the "fair market value of the investment".[69] The 2003 Model, in line with the Hull Formula, asserts that payment shall be done with unreasonable delay; it shall be effectively realisable and freely transferable.[70] Such elaboration does not exist in the 2015 Model.[71] 2004 Canada Model BIT maintains that "prompt, adequate and effective compensation" is necessary.[72] It has been clarified that compensation shall amount to the fair market value of the investment. 2004[73] and 2012[74] US Model BITs include identical provisions. 2021 Canada Model BIT contains a much more detailed provision on this matter, and states that compensation shall "be paid without delay in a freely convertible currency", and "be equivalent to the fair market value".[75] It further specifies that "[a]ppropriate valuation criteria includes going concern value, asset value including the declared tax value of

[63] Reinisch (2008), p. 194.

[64] Article 7, Argentina- Australia BIT (1997).

[65] Article 6, Azerbaijan – Turkey BIT (2014).

[66] Article 13, ECT (1998).

[67] Article 5, India Model BIT (2003).

[68] Article 5.1, India Model BIT (2015).

[69] Article 5.1, India Model BIT (2015).

[70] India Model BIT (2003).

[71] Article 5, India Model BIT (2015).

[72] Article 13, 2004 Canada Model FIPA.

[73] Article 6, 2004 US Model BIT.

[74] Article 6, 2012 US Model BIT.

[75] Article 9(5)(a) and (b), 2021 Canada Model FIPA.

tangible property, and other criteria, which may be appropriate or relevant under the circumstances, to determine fair market value".[76]

The 2008 Model Germany BIT states that 'compensation' shall be 'equivalent to the value of the investment'.[77] Adequacy, effectiveness and promptness are also underlined. The 2019 Netherlands Model BIT prescribes "fair market value", noting that this method also applies to compensation in cases of unlawful expropriation. Similar to 2021 Canada Model BIT, it counts "going concern value, asset value including the declared tax value of tangible property, and other criteria, as appropriate".[78] This provision notably contains a clause which allows judicial review "of [the investors'] claim and of the valuation of its investment".[79] The EU Model BIT, released in 2023 (and updated in January 2024) to serve as the Model BIT for all EU Member States vis-à-vis third countries, includes a provision similar to the 2019 Netherlands Model BIT, and refers to the same valuation methods.[80]

The now-shelved 2007 Norway Model BIT[81] had included one of the broadest and the most ambiguous compensation provisions among model investment agreements. Compensation against expropriation was not explicitly stated. Only a reference to the "conditions provided by law and general principles of law" is made. Despite the lack of an explicit mention of compensation, the reference made to the general principles of law renders it unlikely that the application of the provision would have excluded compensation against expropriation as a CIL principle.

The 2015 Norway Model BIT, unlike the 2007 Model, includes a lengthy expropriation clause under its Article 6.[82] The Model refers to "payment of prompt, adequate and effective compensation".[83] Article 6(3), (4), and (5) give specific guidelines on how the compensation shall be calculated.[84] After designating 'market value' as the relevant benchmark, the provision further notes that compensation on the market value shall be "determined on the basis of the amount that it is likely that ordinary buyers would have offered for the investment in a voluntary sale process."[85]

---

[76] Article 9(5)(b), 2021 Canada Model FIPA.

[77] Article 4, 2008 Germany Model BIT.

[78] Article 12(5), 2019 Netherlands Model BIT.

[79] Article 12(7), 2019 Netherlands Model BIT.

[80] Annotations to the Model Clauses for Negotiation or Re-negotiation of Member States' Bilateral Investment Agreements with third countries (EU Model BIT, 31 January 2024). https://circabc.europa.eu/ui/group/be8b568f-73f3-409c-b4a4-30acfcec5283/library/9a3525b5-a8cb-47e7-a96a-fe1e7d378809/details?download=true.

[81] Article 6, 2007 Norway Model BIT.

[82] Article 6, 2015 Norway Model BIT.

[83] Article 6(1)(iv), 2015 Norway Model BIT.

[84] Article 6(3), (4), and (5), 2015 Norway Model BIT.

[85] Article 6(3), 2015 Norway Model BIT.

4.2.1.2 Consequences of Lawfulness or Unlawfulness of Expropriation

It is accepted that compensation is a feature that is supposed to accompany expropriation, regardless of its lawfulness.[86] If the state fails to compensate the investor before arbitral case, the state may have to compensate the foreign investor in *damages*, as the expropriation would be unlawful. As was explained above, public purpose, due process, non-discrimination and compensation are required for a lawful compensation, and a proposal of payment by the host state, as far as the adjudication is concerned, suffices to render the expropriation lawful.[87]

In either case, many IIAs assert that the indemnification has to be paid in full. Depending on their lawfulness, however, their base value will differ.[88] The reparation (which can either be pecuniary or restitution in kind) or compensation paid operate under a different legal context in each case.

This formulation requires the state to restore the investor to a position in which they would have been; had the expropriation not occurred. If such *restitution in kind* is not possible, monetary alternatives would take effect. An unlawful expropriation constitutes a breach of contract; and unlike a lawful expropriation, its indemnification will be for damages.

In case of lawful compensation, the *lex specialis* under expropriation provisions will take effect and the compensation will be based on provisions defining compensation against expropriation. Depending on the provision, it can be based on the fair market value or any other predetermined framework incorporated in the relevant investment agreement.

In *SPP v. Egypt*,[89] the distinction and its consequences are explained as follows:

> [...] the [c]laimants are seeking 'compensation' for a lawful expropriation, and not 'reparation' for an injury caused by an illegal act such as a breach of contract. The cardinal point [...] in determining the appropriate compensation is that [...] [c]laimants are entitled to receive fair compensation for what was expropriated rather than damages for breach of contract.[90]

As briefly mentioned above, lawfulness of an expropriatory measure will be scrutinised only after the existence of an expropriation is maintained. Therefore, an arbitral tribunal will first ask the question of whether an expropriation exists. Direct and indirect expropriation dichotomy sits at the core of this question. What is particularly important with regard to the lawfulness of expropriation vis-à-vis direct-indirect expropriation dichotomy is that while public purpose is almost always included as the subset of lawfulness (and is always taken into account by arbitral tribunals) by states as treaty-makers, the identification of indirect expropriation

---

[86] Kriebaum (2007), p. 719.

[87] Reinisch (2008), p. 200.

[88] Based on the difference between the real value and the fair market value. Kriebaum (2007), p. 719.

[89] *Southern Pacific Properties v. Egypt*, ICSID Case No. ARB/84/3, Award on the Merits (20 May 1992) (*SPP v. Egypt*).

[90] *SPP v. Egypt* (1992), par. 183.

does not necessarily entail such scrutiny by arbitral tribunals with regard to intentions of a state—unless, of course, such policy space is recognised for states in the IIA in question.

4.2.2 Direct–Indirect Expropriation

Direct expropriation can be defined as "a mandatory legal transfer of the title to the property or its outright physical seizure", while such transfer is to "[benefit] the state itself or a state-mandated third party". Indirect expropriation, on the other hand, requires "total or near-total deprivation of an investment but without a formal transfer of title or outright seizure."[91] What makes an expropriatory act indirect is the lack of formal seizure and express intent to expropriate.[92] This difference between a direct and indirect expropriation is generally found under expropriation clauses.[93] For instance, the (now unilaterally denounced) 1991 Netherlands – Venezuela BIT, under its Article 6, stated that:

> Neither Contracting Party shall take any measures to expropriation or nationalize investments of nationals of the other Contracting Party **or take measures having an effect equivalent to nationalization or expropriation** with regard to such investments [...][94]

A direct expropriation is often undisputed, given its formal, physical, and explicit nature. Its existence is usually easily identifiable. A transfer of ownership from the foreign investor to host state is required for a taking to qualify as direct expropriation.

While the direct expropriation provisions have not changed dramatically since the advent of IIAs, some of the newer IIAs define 'direct expropriation' more expressly. For instance, Annex 4 of the EUVIPA states that "direct expropriation occurs if an investment is nationalised or otherwise directly expropriated through formal transfer of title or outright seizure".[95] This provision does not redefine direct expropriation but rather clarifies the definition that is already widely accepted in case law and scholarship.

The answer to the question of what constitutes *indirect expropriation*, is less clear. The foreign investor typically formally retains the ownership of its investment, but is deprived of the use and benefits of the investment to such an extent that the effects are equivalent (or similar) to that of a direct taking. In other words,

---

[91] UNCTAD Expropriation (2012), p. 6.

[92] UNCTAD Expropriation (2012), p. 7; Dolzer (2003), p. 66.

[93] Article 13, ECT (1998). The ECT provision on expropriation reflects the wording in the majority of investment treaties currently in force.

[94] Article 6, the Netherlands – Venezuela BIT (1993). Emphasis added.

[95] Annex 4, EUVIPA, Signed in 2019, not in force as of January 2025). https://policy.trade.ec.europa.eu/eu-trade-relationships-country-and-region/countries-and-regions/vietnam/eu-vietnam-agreement/texts-agreements_en.

despite the absence of a formal or outright taking, this particular type is considered an expropriation due to its similar or identical consequences of a direct taking. Indirect expropriation can appear under different names, such as *de facto* or *creeping* expropriation.[96] Its definition and extent, as will be thoroughly demonstrated below, have been gradually crystallising through adjudicatory experience primarily driven by the efforts to establish a balance between what is usually referred to as a state's right to regulate, and the economic interests of a foreign investor.[97]

One key feature of expropriation is the attributability of the measure to the host state: When attributability is absent, it would not possible to argue in favour of an expropriatory measure.[98] An investor may suffer significant damage to (or total destruction of) his investment due to actions attributable to himself or a third party (or factor) other than the state. A relevant example of what is *not* expropriation in this regard would be the *Paraguay Navigation Company Claim*,[99] concerning the events (including the subsequent establishment of a claims tribunal) in the aftermath of an alleged government confiscation of the property owned by a US company. After continuous frictions between the company management and the Paraguayan government, a land dispute resulted in the repossession of property, and subsequent failures to comply with certain licensing requirements caused infrastructural takings.[100] The commission tasked with resolving the dispute came to the conclusion that the acts conducted by the government were not compensable, the property had not been expropriated and/or the business of the company had not been damaged due to any state act. The taking of the property was pursuant to the mortgage agreement the parties had between them, therefore fell outside the scope of expropriation. Furthermore, it was the neglect of the company management that had caused the damage as the required licenses had not been acquired from the government, the infrastructure had been abandoned and the government debts had been unpaid for long periods.[101] This criterion of attributability of investors' losses to a state act or a series of acts is inherently attached to the principle of compensation, and this remains a critical feature for arbitral tribunals when determining whether an act amounts to expropriation or nationalisation.[102]

---

[96] Cox (2019), pp. 142–151 (defining creeping expropriation as "a form of indirect expropriation which often manifests itself in cases of regulatory, contractual and judicial expropriation); Schill (2007), p. 107 (referring to both *de facto* and creeping expropriation).

[97] Titi (2014); Subedi (2008), pp. 3 and 75.

[98] Mouri (1994), p. 213. Along with the discussion on the duration of an expropriatory measure, the attributability had been a prevalent issue for the Iran - U.S. Claims Tribunal.

[99] Miles (2013), pp. 56–58.

[100] Johnson C (1860) Opinion and Award of the United States and Paraguay Commission; Interesting History of the Claim (*The New York Times*, 28 August 1860). A digital version is available at https://www.nytimes.com/1860/08/28/archives/opinion-and-award-of-the-united-states-and-paraguay-commission.html; Miles (2013), p. 56.

[101] Miles (2013), p. 58.

[102] See, *J.I. Case Company v. The Islamic Republic of Iran* (1983) Award No. 57-244-1, reprinted in 3 Iran-US Cl. Trib. Rep. 62 - 65; *Otis Elevator Company v. Iran* (1987) Award No. 304-284-2, reprinted in 12 Iran-US Cl. Trib. Rep. 335. *In J. I. Case Company*, the tribunal considered the pos-

Liman Caspian Oil BV v. Kazakhstan,[103] and ECT claim, provides for a fine illustration of the possible extent of challenged state acts and measures in terms of determining attributability. An undisclosed company had transferred its Kazakh exploration rights and obligations to Liman. The company's minority shareholders, upon learning about the transaction, brought a claim before the Kazakh court. The transfer had been subsequently cancelled since the consent by the minority shareholders was absent. The Court decision further compelled Liman to re-transfer its newly acquired rights and obligations. Following the court decision, Liman brought an arbitral claim against Kazakhstan, arguing that the decision of the Kazakh court amounted to indirect expropriation by rendering the investment worthless.

The Tribunal scrutinised the attributability of a domestic court decision to the state of Kazakhstan:

> [T]he Tribunal acknowledges that the domestic courts of Kazakhstan are [...] organs of the Republic of Kazakhstan. Therefore, their decisions are attributable to [Kazakhstan] and could be measures falling under ECT Article 13 [...] [I]t is also clear and undisputed that [Liman] were subject to the jurisdiction of the Kazakh courts. The mere fact that decisions of the Kazakh court declared that [c]laimants [...] were not holder of rights they claimed to have [...] is not sufficient to find an expropriatory measure falling under ECT Article 13.

The *Liman* Tribunal explicitly included domestic court decisions within the scope of expropriation, and accepted their potential to cause deprivation if certain conditions are present.[104] The Tribunal contended that the "court decisions were not arbitrary, grossly unfair, unjust, idiosyncratic, discriminatory or lacking due process, even if they might have been incorrect as a matter of [domestic] law, and that correspondingly they have to be accepted from the perspective of [the ECT]."[105] Therefore, expropriation or the attributability analysis is not necessarily limited to the acts or omissions of legislative and executive organs and extends to judicial decisions if conditions are met.

As briefly noted above, while direct expropriations are less common international investment adjudication, one of the biggest controversies in the legal field has arguably been indirect expropriation and its exact framework. It is not possible to claim that all state measures and acts which have adverse effects on foreign investments will amount to indirect expropriation. Therefore, especially for arbitral tribunals, it is important to be able to differentiate between a *non-compensable state act*

sibility of other factors such as civil unrest, strikes or disruptions of the sort which accompany the [Islamic] revolution which might have contributed to the deprivation. The Tribunal in *Otis Elevator* stated that the infringement would have to be caused by a conduct attributable to the government of Iran. For an analysis and digest of like cases, see Helgeson (2001).

[103] *Liman Caspian Oil BV and NCL Dutch Investment BV v. Kazakhstan*, ICSID Case no. ARB/07/14, Award (22 June 2010) (*Liman v. Kazakhstan*).

[104] Demirkol (2018), p. 55.

[105] *Liman v. Kazakhstan (2010)*, par. 285; citing *Waste Management, Inc. v. Mexico*, ICSID Case No. ARB (AF)/00/3, Award (30 April 2004) (*Waste Management v. Mexico*).

and a *compensable expropriatory measure*.[106] Case law has occasionally pointed towards various approaches to determine whether or not a specific state act is expropriation. Thus, there are different interpretations and applications as to what qualifies as a non-compensable regulatory measure, and which measures amount to indirect expropriation. The following paragraphs will look into these approaches used by tribunals handling expropriation claims and further investigate how they differ in terms of interpretation and application.

4.3 Different Approaches to Indirect Expropriation Analysis: The *Effect-Intent* Scale

For host states and foreign investors, to be able to pinpoint the difference between an expropriatory act and a non-compensable state act is of great importance. Clarity and coherence are increasingly popular subjects under international investment law with a growing number of scholarly work and substantive regulatory initiatives by international political and legal institutions, due to increasing numbers of arbitral cases.[107] It has become more and more apparent that for the sake of jurisprudential consistency and predictability, at least a certain degree of coherence, or the availability of recurring patterns in behaviour and interpretation, is beneficial.[108] This necessity is particularly visible in the recent treaty-making practice—as will be argued below, treaty-makers, through a growing number of regional trade and investment deals, have diverged from broader drafting methods in favour of further clarity as legal, political and pecuniary consequences of IIAs have become more evident.

---

[106] Some scholars argue that this distinction must be made on the basis of "the impact of the act, taking into account inter alia the costs for the investor, welfare gains, and socio-economic benefits". Gazzini (2010), p. 37.

[107] In addition to the proposals concerning the investment court system (ICS) and a multilateral investment court (MIC) in recent European Union FTA/IPA texts, discussions on the establishment of an appellate mechanism and earlier suggestions concerning a preliminary ruling mechanism are two of the proposed solutions to the perceived lack of coherence and consistency in ISDS. Some of these alternatives, namely a multilateral instrument for ISDS, a permanent court and an appellate mechanism, are being actively discussed under the auspices of the Working Group III (WGIII) of the UN Commission on International Trade Law (UNCITRAL), as of January 2025. *See*, UNCITRAL, Appellate Mechanism. https://uncitral.un.org/en/appellatemechanism; Kucik and Puig (2023), pp. 566 and 576 (entertaining the possibility that an Appellate Mechanism might provide further consistency, coherence, or correctness of decisions); Giannakopoulos (2023) (specifically on the connection between reform and coherence in ISDS). For earlier works on the establishment of an appellate structure, see the collection of papers in Sauvant and Chiswick-Patterson (2008); UNCTAD, Reform of Investor-State Dispute Settlement: In Search of a Roadmap (IIA Issues Note Series, June 2013, No.2). http://unctad.org/en/PublicationsLibrary/webdiaepcb2013d4_en.pdf. Specifically on the proposal that a preliminary rulings system could benefit ISDS, see Schreuer (2008).

[108] Giannakopoulos (2023); Zarra (2018), p. 141.

This assessment is highly consistent with growing number and the content of arbitral awards, which are primarily responsible for this policy shift towards further clarity in the first place. Given the lack of binding precedence and the typical broad formulation of expropriation provisions in investment treaties, *ad hoc* tribunals have exercised interpretative discretion, too generously according to some,[109] on determining whether or not an act falls within the scope of compensable expropriation. Different tests, determined by different constituent doctrines, have been employed over the years.

From another perspective, it could be said that arbitral tribunals have served as 'laboratories' for the sustainability, desirability, and accuracy of drafting methods of expropriation provisions in IIAs in force at any given period. Echoing from the *supra* discussed clash of paradigms,[110] some arbitral tribunals leaned towards the effects of a state act on a foreign investor's investment, while others used their discretion to give more weight to the intent and purpose of the challenged state act. Different tests applied by arbitral tribunals usually reflect the degree of importance attached to the character of the measure, the public purpose and state intent behind it; and the severity of the deprivation suffered by the foreign investor.

With regards to the determining factors of an (indirect) expropriation, two well-known main doctrinal ends exist in scholarship: the *effects* and *police powers doctrines*. While the effects doctrine regards the effects of a measure on foreign investment to be the more important (or the exclusive) point of reference, the police powers approach prioritises the intent of the measure enacted to realise a legitimate public objective, and considers it as a possible way to absolve state responsibility even if a foreign investor suffers harm as a result of an act or measure.

Several terminological clarifications are necessary. As will be shown below, one could refer to two extreme and largely hypothetical theoretical end points, where one consideration is unconditionally and absolutely dominant over the other: I will call them *absolute (sole) effects* (where the adverse effects of a measure are the exclusive point of reference, regardless of the legitimacy of the measure in question); and *absolute police powers*, (where all regulatory measures, regardless of their harmful effects, are excluded from being expropriatory, tribunals do not apply these approaches in such a strict and uncompromising way. In other words, while these doctrinal end points are important to understand the doctrinal tendencies and identify their extreme ends, arbitral tribunals have adopted these approaches with varying levels of intensity. As a result, a more proportionate and fluid middle playing ground has emerged, according to which the intent and effects of a measure has been counter-weighed and the result has been applied to a particular case. I will refer to this middle ground as the *proportionality margin*.

In addition, it is crucial to clarify and differentiate the usage of terms *regulatory carve-out* and *absolute police powers*: I will use the former to refer to the treaty practice which embodies the principle which carves out *non-discriminatory* state

109 Harbine (2002) (a contemporary analysis of the *Metalclad* case and the Tribunal's analysis).

110 Chapter 3.

measures explicitly, as will be detailed below. In contrast, as noted above, the latter refers to the (hypothetical) position according to which *all* state measures are excluded from the scope of expropriation, even when such carve-out does not exist in a treaty.

Below, I will scrutinise the degrees of arbitral inclination towards any of the approaches mentioned above with regard to expropriation claims. In order to do so, I will first outline each doctrinal approach, and delve into relevant case law for each doctrine applied. In the following selection of cases embedded in the doctrinal analysis, geographical and sectoral distribution, as well as IIA variety were key considerations. Arguably the most important consideration was to include awards published in the recent years (as of 2025) to accurately identify the most up-to-date adjudicatory tendencies. Ultimately, I will conclude that the analyses conducted by arbitral tribunals, despite several exceptions, avoid extreme interpretations of the doctrines under which they are usually examined. In other words, although policy carve-outs or explicit public purpose exclusions in IIAs applicable to available case law so far remain limited, the general tendency is far from completely ignoring public policies *vis-à-vis* the protection of investors. Furthermore, in most cases where the public policy considerations were clearly outweighed by the protection of foreign investors, the general argument is that they are in compliance with the rules of interpretation of VCLT, as well as the extremely vague content and context of the IIAs interpreted (as *lex lata*).[111] In addition, I will argue that when it is the case, the tendency towards *de facto* consideration of public concerns and purpose, as bolstered by the guidance provided by preceding arbitral decisions, has now begun to find its way into the new generation IIAs; and the current legal framework is slowly but surely giving way to articulations which explicitly allow public considerations as opposed to investors' interests (as *lex ferenda*)—even superseding *prima facie* findings of expropriation where, absent a regulatory carve-out, tribunals would have maintained the existence of expropriation and ruled in favour of a foreign investor.[112] As will be shown further in the next Chapter, a parallel development is the case for the FET provisions.

---

[111] Vienna Convention (1969).

[112] Despite the infamy of the case, as will be shown below, the *Eco Oro v. Colombia* (2021) Tribunal's expropriation analysis is noteworthy in how regulatory carve-outs affect expropriation provisions. This analysis is often overshadowed by the Tribunal's erroneous interpretation of the general exceptions clause. Ünüvar (2023).

4.3.1 The (Sole) Effects Doctrine

The effects doctrine attaches less (or no) weight to the intent of a host state while determining whether or not expropriation occurred or, in other words "the focus on the effect will be the only exclusive relevant criterion".[113] The most important determinant in this test is the effects the act has on the foreign investment—therefore, if the challenged act exceeds a certain level of intensity, such interference will qualify as indirect expropriation, regardless of the intent or purpose of the said act.[114] Below, several cases which are often designated as manifestations of the sole effects doctrine are critically analysed—primarily by fleshing out whether the arbitral tribunals in question actually disregarded public purpose (as a particular award's association with the doctrine would typically imply); or indeed considered it and deemed in insufficient to justify the alleged violation in light of the effects of the measure.

Iran – United States Claims Tribunals (IUSCT)[115] has been hailed as the "modern pioneer of the international takings jurisprudence",[116] and its influence on the contemporary practice is evident. Particularly the ***Tippetts***[117] case is well-known with regard to, *inter alia*, its analysis of the effects of an expropriatory measures and the government intent behind it. The claimant, TAMS, an American engineering and architecture consulting company, created the Iranian joint entity called TAMS-AFFA with AFFA, an Iranian engineering company, to conduct engineering and architecture services for the construction of the Tehran International Airport. Following the Islamic Revolution, however, the work at the airport stopped entirely. Shortly after, the new government appointed a manager for TAMS-AFFA with extensive competences. From early 1980, TAMS, the American partner for TAMS-AFFA, lost contact with the joint entity. The case was eventually brought before the IUSCT.

While the United States and Iran had signed a Treaty of Amity earlier in 1955[118] with provisions on expropriation and FET,[119] the Tribunal contended that the applicable law was "international law and general principles of law".[120] On how the

[113] Dolzer (2003), p. 79. Prof. Dolzer possibly coined the term "sole effect doctrine", and he had noted that this was the case on multiple occasions in international conferences (some of which were personally attended by the author of this book).

[114] Kriebaum (2007), p. 724.

[115] The Iran – United States Claims Tribunals. https://iusct.com/.

[116] Heiskanen (2007), p. 218.

[117] *Tippetts, Abbett, McCarthy, Stratton (TAMS) v. TAMS-AFFA Consulting Engineers of Iran*, Award No. 141-7-2 (29 June 1984) (*Tippetts*). https://iusct.com/cases/final-award-no-141-29-june-1984/.

[118] Treaty of Amity, Economic Relations, and Consular Rights between the United States of America and Iran (1955), p. 110. https://www.state.gov/wp-content/uploads/2019/05/Treaty-of-Amity-Economic-Relations-and-Consular-Rights-between-the-United-States-of-America-and-Iran-Aug.-15-1955.pdf ('Treaty of Amity').

[119] Article IV(1) and (2), Treaty of Amity (1955).

[120] *Tippetts* (1984), p. 10.

intent of the government weighed *vis-à-vis* the effects of a governmental measure that caused the deprivation, the Tribunal contended that

> While assumption of control over property by a government does not automatically and immediately justify a conclusion that the property has been taken by the government, thus requiring compensation under international law, such a conclusion is warranted whenever events demonstrate that the owner was deprived of fundamental rights of ownership and it appears that this deprivation is not merely ephemeral. **The intent of the government is less important than the effects of the measures on the owner, and the form of the measures of control or interference is less important than the reality of the impact.**[121]

A factor which may have prompted the Tribunal to base its decision on 'international law and general principles of law', and not the Treaty of Amity *per se*, could be that "[t]he parties in this case have not argued the question of the relevance of the investment protection provisions of Article IV, paragraph 2 of the Treaty of Amity of 15 August 1955 between Iran and the United States."[122] Article IV(2) of the Treaty of Amity notes that "[s]uch property shall not be taken except for a public purpose, nor shall it be taken without the prompt payment of just compensation … such compensation … shall represent the full equivalent of the property taken".[123] On the basis of the Tribunal's note, had the parties invoked this provision (which refers to public purpose), it could plausibly be argued that the Tribunal may have engaged with a public purpose discourse more directly, possibly altering its seemingly effects-centric analysis.

This being said, in the ***Sea-Land*** *award* rendered a week prior on 22 June 1984, the Tribunal dealt with a case where the claimant made "extensive reference in its pleadings to the [Treaty of Amity] which, it says, lays down the standards which apply to the taking of property".[124] Against the claim that the Treaty sets a "particularly high standard for protection", the Tribunal concluded that "[t]he concept of taking is the same in the Treaty as in international law".[125] Upon this background, the Tribunal had a strikingly different take on the role of intent in a government measure. The Tribunal stated that

> A finding of expropriation would require, at the very least, that the Tribunal be satisfied that there was deliberate governmental interference with the conduct of Sea-Land's operation, the effect of which was to deprive Sea-Land of the use and benefit of its investment.[126]

Whereas the *Sea-Land* Tribunal, in its analysis, emphasised on the argument that the governmental interference should be intentional, the *Tippetts* award's sequencing of effects and intent of a measure, giving express primacy to the former over the latter, poses a stark contrast to this position. This being said, it should be noted that the

[121] Tippetts (1984), p. 11. Emphasis added.

[122] Tippetts (1984), p. 11.

[123] Article IV(2), Treaty of Amity (1955).

[124] *Sea-Land Service, Inc. v Iran,* Award No. 135-33-1 (22 June 1984) (*Sea-Land*), p. 26. https://iusct.com/cases/final-award-no-112-22-june-1984/.

[125] *Sea-Land* (1984), p. 27.

[126] *Sea-Land* (1984), p. 24.

Tippetts award does not, by any means, disregard the intent entirely. The intent of a government being less important than the effects of a measure does not preclude the possibility that, provided the effects do not raise above a certain gravity, the intent and execution of a measure might still justify the said effects—or at least affect the amount of compensation. In that sense, the *Tippetts* Tribunal's framing of this doctrine differs from that which was defined by Prof. Dolzer, who attached a certain exclusivity (and thus a more predominant power) to the effect of a measure vis-à-vis other considerations such as intent.[127]

The *Tippetts* Tribunal's position has influenced a number of subsequent IUSCT awards, as well as subsequent IIA practice.[128] Heiskanen notes that the Tribunal's "endorsement of the effects doctrine is often seen as [its] principal contribution to the doctrine of indirect expropriation in international law."[129]

Another important issue is the difference between the *intention of harming the investment*, i.e. the question of whether a government act was a deliberate attack on the investment (which seems to be the meaning of intent that the *Sea-Land* Tribunal had scrutinised), and the question of whether the state had other, broader motivations behind the act, i.e. whether the -consequentially- harmful act *intended to realise a public goal*. For the latter case, the ***Phelps Dodge*** Tribunal, citing the *Tippetts* award, stated that "the Tribunal understands the financial, economic and social concerns that inspired the law pursuant to which it acted, but those reasons and concerns cannot relieve the Respondent of the obligation to compensate Phelps Dodge for its loss."[130]

Notwithstanding the *Sea-Land* example, one might inquire why such a seemingly strong effects doctrine prevailed in the IUSCT practice. The foremost justification possibly stems from the common factual background of all cases, namely the Islamic Revolution. Heiskanen, within the context of how the Tribunals often refrained from scrutinising the legality of expropriation, wrote that

> [g]iven that almost all of the expropriation claims brought before the Tribunal arose out of the extraordinary circumstances that prevailed in Iran during the Islamic Revolution and its aftermath, the Tribunal appears to have taken the view [...] that it was not necessary to address the legality issue on a case-by-case basis [...] if the effect of the measure was to deprive the foreign investor of its property right, failure to comply with the requirements of legality [...] could be presumed.[131]

It should finally be noted that this tendency is more prevalent in cases in which Iran was a respondent. In other claims brought by Iranian investors against the United

---

[127] In that sense, it might also be plausible to draw a conceptual distinction between what one might call the "*sole* effects doctrine", and the "effects doctrine"—the difference being that in the former case effects do carry an exclusive weight, whereas for the latter, effects are simply prioritised.

[128] Brunetti (2001), pp. 206–207.

[129] Heiskanen (2007), p. 227.

[130] *Phelps Dodge International Corp. v. Iran*, Award No. 217-99-2 (19 March 1986) (*Phelps Dodge*), par. 22 (p. 14). https://iusct.com/cases/final-award-no-217-19-march-1986/.

[131] Heiskanen (2007), pp. 221–222.

States, such as ***Emanuel Too***, an almost entirely opposite approach dominates the Tribunal's analysis. The Tribunal stated that

> a State is not responsible for loss of property or for other economic disadvantage resulting from bona fide general taxation or any other action that is **commonly accepted as within the police power of States**, provided it is not discriminatory and is not designed to cause the alien to abandon the property to the State or sell it at a distress price.[132]

In this case, unlike the others analysed above, the mere fact that the investor had lost its investment *per se* did not suffice for the Tribunal to conclude that compensation had to be paid. This aside, the Tribunal contended that the harmful consequence, namely the imposition of a tax levy, was the claimant's own doing; because he failed "to pay taxes withheld by him on his employee's salaries."[133]

Beyond the IUSCT claims, the sole effects doctrine has appeared under different fora—albeit rarely. ***Biloune v. Ghana***[134] is an oft-cited, classic example. The dispute arose between Antoine Biloune, a Syrian national and principal shareholder for MDCL, a Ghanaian corporation; and Ghana Tourist Development Company (GTDC), a state-owned entity. MDCL and GTDC entered into a lease agreement for the renovation and operation of a restaurant complex. At a later stage of the project, MDCL applied GTDC for the expansion of the project and the transformation of the mere renovation and operation work into the construction of a four-star hotel. Ghana Investment Centre (GIC) approved the project with necessary concessions and concluded an agreement (GIC Agreement) with MDCL, which contained, *inter alia*, an arbitration clause and an expropriation provision.

Within the framework of the new project, MDCL applied for a construction permit, however proceeded with the construction without obtaining it—claiming that Ghanaian authorities gave the company assurance that the permit would follow. Shortly, however, a stop work notice was issued due to the absence of a construction permit. A demolition order followed despite Mr. Biloune's efforts. He was eventually arrested and deported from Ghana.

According to the claimant, the Government of Ghana interfered with his investment in MDCL and that by various means, including Mr. Biloune's arrest and deportation from Ghana, the respondent effectively expropriated the assets of MDCL.[135]

The Tribunal reached the following conclusion on the expropriation issue:

---

[132] *Emanuel Too v. United States of America,* (1989) Award No. 460-880-2 (29 December 1989) (*Emmanuel Too*), par. 26 (pp. 13–14). https://iusct.com/cases/final-award-no-460-29-december-1989/.

[133] *Emmanuel Too* (1989), par. 27 (p. 14).

[134] *Antoine Biloune (Syria) and Marine Drive Complex Ltd. v. Ghana Investments Centre and the Government of Ghana*. Award on Jurisdiction and Liability (27 October 1989) and Award on Compensation and Costs (30 June 1990) (*Biloune v. Ghana*). Reprinted (with commentary) in Lauterpacht and Greenwood (1994). https://icsidfiles.worldbank.org/icsid/ICSIDBLOBS/OnlineAwards/C3004/CLA-056_Eng.pdf.

[135] Lauterpacht and Greenwood (1994), p. 187.

> This Tribunal must determine whether the above facts constitute, as the claimants charge, a constructive expropriation of MDCL's assets and Mr. Biloune's interest in MDCL. The motivations and omissions of Ghanaian governmental authorities are not clear. **But the Tribunal need not establish those motivations to come to a conclusion in the case.**[136]

The application of the sole effects doctrine to *Biloune* should not be read in isolation and separately from the facts of the case and the positions of its parties. The subsequent paragraphs of the award may be read as though the Tribunal implicitly considered, or at least referred to, other possible elements that may have balanced out the said effects. The Tribunal contended that expropriation existed, but added that it was "unless the respondents can establish by persuasive evidence sufficient for these events."[137] Expropriation was reaffirmed following the failure of Ghanaian authorities to provide for convincing evidence. The tribunal made it very clear that the intent of the state was not tantamount to expropriation analysis at hand, but the subject-matter of the case (the construction work related to a restaurant), the content of the applicable law (the absence of public purpose exceptions in the GIC Agreement, which could have provided a relatively clear-cut guidance for the arbitral tribunal); as well as the failure of Ghana to justify its actions against Mr. Biloune, prompted this outcome. *Biloune v. Ghana*, often used to demonstrate the application of the sole effects approach, therefore, does not concern a dispute where public benefit had driven the government to act against the interests of an investor. The respondent does not seem to have claimed that there existed a public benefit which was at odds with the operations of MDCL. Despite the lack of these arguments, the tribunal's reasoning did not necessarily ignore public interest and state purpose.

As a result, *Biloune* case and its consistent association with the sole effects doctrine in academia demonstrates that (a) the applicable legal instrument (in this case the GIC Agreement) should provide leeway for public purpose considerations to be used in disputes where the facts and the context of a case is relevant; and (b) in general, there exists a major difference between acts intrinsically attached to public purpose, and those which do not necessarily relate to issues that might affect the public.

Some scholars[138] also contend that the sole effects doctrine applies to the expropriation analysis in ***Vivendi II***.[139] The Tribunal addressed a dispute concerning the expropriation and mistreatment claims by Vivendi and its Argentine subsidiary. Vivendi had been granted a concession to undertake water and sewage services in Tucuman, Argentina for thirty years in 1995. However, it was during the successor government's term that Vivendi's concession was denounced, the tariff rates were reduced despite the concession and a re-negotiation of the concession agreement

[136] *Biloune v. Ghana* (1989), par. 26 (p. 209).

[137] *Biloune v. Ghana* (1989), par. 26 (p. 209).

[138] Kriebaum (2007), p. 724; Hoffmann (2008), p. 161.

[139] *Compania de Aguas del Aconquija S.A. and Vivendi Universal S.A. v. Argentina,* ICSID Case No. ARB/97/3, Second Award (20 August 2007) (*Vivendi II*).

was imposed, which failed and resulted in termination of the concessions three years later.

The Tribunal, weighing the effects of a measure against the intent of a state to expropriate, clearly stated that "the *effect* of the measure on the investor, not the state's intent, is the critical factor."[140] It is important to emphasise here that the 'intent' referred to here is not about the intent to regulate for a public purpose, but rather the determinative factor which denotes whether a measure is directly or indirectly expropriatory.

As noted above, the lawfulness criteria, namely public purpose, non-discrimination, due process, and compensation will be engaged only after a measure is ascertained to be expropriatory. The Tribunal also takes note of this fact. Therefore, the weighing of a public purpose while assessing whether a measure is expropriatory or not is different from engaging this very same question when deciding whether expropriation is lawful. Against Argentina's position that "regulatory measures that are for a public purpose, are non-discriminatory and are enacted in accordance with due process do not amount, under international law, to expropriation",[141] the Tribunal noted that "[i]f public purpose automatically immunises the measure from being found to be expropriatory, then there would never be a compensable taking for a public purpose."[142]

There a few critical observations to be made here. First of all, keeping in mind the different stages of the expropriation analysis referred to above (ascertaining the existence of expropriation and the subsequent analysis of the *lawfulness* of expropriation), there appears to be a conflation of arguments. While Argentina argued against the very existence of expropriation using the police powers doctrine, the Tribunal seems to have countered this argument with the lawfulness criteria, presuming that compensation is not required once expropriatory nature of a measure is maintained. Admittedly, given Argentina's use of the exact same sequence of subset found in the expropriation provision, it could be that the Respondent itself conflated the lawfulness criteria and read it as the police powers doctrine enshrined in the BIT in question. It is indeed true that, once a measure is deemed to be expropriatory (and *only* once it is deemed as such), compensation must be paid; as a lawful expropriation is still expropriation. A measure, even if ultimately considered to be expropriatory, must *still* be for a public purpose, non-discriminatory, and in accordance with due process for it to be lawful. Absent these elements, an unlawful expropriation will have taken place, and damages would be paid.

The conflation and confusion is also evident in the way that the Tribunal engages with the public purpose argument in an absolute way: "If public purpose automatically immunises the measure from being found to be expropriatory, then there would never be a compensable taking for a public purpose."[143] Having engaged with

[140] *Vivendi II* (2007), par. 7.5.20.

[141] *Vivendi II* (2007), par. 6.11.5.

[142] *Vivendi II* (2007), par. 7.5.21.

[143] Vivendi II (2007), par. 7.5.21.

Argentina's argument within the framework of the lawfulness criteria, the Tribunal abruptly falls back to the assessment of whether expropriation exists. Either way, Argentina does not suggest that any and all measures pursuing public purpose are excluded—they must also be non-discriminatory and comply with due process.

Finally, in its conclusions, the Tribunal pointed out that "the provincial authorities mounted an illegitimate campaign against the concession"[144] granted to Vivendi, and then went on to analyse whether or not the activities of the claimant company under the concession agreement was harmful to the public. The Tribunal noted that "[the red turbidity] affected only a relatively small part of the population [...] for short periods and occurred over only one or two months [...] [the manganese turbidity] [...] was unquestionably unpleasant but it only lasted about two weeks, posed no health risks and [the claimant]'s response to an unforeseeable event was highly professional."[145] It is further remarked that the government reaction had the effect of pressuring the company and aimed to destroy its base of paying customers.[146]

The application of the effects doctrine in this particular case is evident, but it was not absolute, given the above-mentioned elaboration on the effects of concession activities on public health. It is true that the Tribunal failed to find a legitimate public purpose; however, outright rejection of public benefit as an element of consideration was not the case. Whether or not the finding of a legitimate public purpose enacted by Argentina would alter the Tribunal's analysis (and if so, to what degree) is, however, unclear.

A similar conflation of public purpose as a *police powers* argument on the one hand, and a lawfulness criterion on the other, is arguably present in the ***Santa Elena v. Costa Rica*** award.[147] The Tribunal famously noted that

> [w]hile an expropriation or taking for environmental reasons may be classified as a taking for a public purpose, and thus be legitimate, the fact that property was taken for this reason does not affect either the nature or the measure of the compensation to be paid for the taking. That is, the purpose of protecting environment for which the Property was taken does not alter the legal character of the taking for which adequate compensation must be paid.
>
> [...]
>
> Expropriatory environmental measures- no matter how laudable and beneficial to society as a whole- are, in this respect, similar to any other expropriatory measures that a state may take in order to implement its policies: where property is expropriated, **even for environmental purposes**, whether domestic or international, **the state's obligation to pay compensation remains.**[148]

The paragraph above, which has been particularly popular among commentators, indicates that the Tribunal, in its analysis, appears to have disregarded public benefit

[144] *Vivendi II* (2007), par. 7.4.19.

[145] *Vivendi II* (2007), par. 7.6.2.

[146] *Vivendi II* (2007), par. 7.6.2.

[147] *Compania del Desarrollo de Santa Elena, S.A. v. Costa Rica*, ICSID Case No. ARB/96/1, Award (17 February 2000) (*Santa Elena v. Costa Rica*).

[148] *Santa Elena v. Costa Rica* (2000), par. 72.

and interest, while maintaining that a severe hindrance on the investment alone was sufficient for compensation. In academia, likewise, the *Santa Elena* case has been referred in order to illustrate the lack of public purpose as an element while determining the existence of expropriation—for instance, Fauchald notes that "[e]xamples of cases that primarily follow a sole effects doctrine include [Santa Elena]"[149]

One important point, however, is that Santa Elena case concerns a *direct* expropriation; therefore, in this particular instance, this absolute exclusion of the public purpose was not utilised in order to determine whether a governmental measure would amount to expropriation, but merely to pinpoint the impact that the authority intent had on compensation in a situation where expropriation is undisputed. The paragraph does not, unlike what has been argued, indicate that public purpose is completely irrelevant to the discussion of whether or not a compensable, expropriatory act has arisen. It establishes the fact that once expropriation is determined (in this case direct and undisputed), public purpose does not play a pivotal role while assessing whether or not compensation is to be paid. It is further important to emphasise that the case concerned the amount of compensation to be paid after a mutually acknowledged expropriation. Therefore, the case illustrates what elements are taken into consideration while determining the compensation due—it does not concern the elements of the indirect expropriation analysis.[150]

Nykomb v. Latvia[151] is the first known public award[152] delivered under the ECT, and an apt illustration of the consequences of the sole effects doctrine. The dispute arose from the Latvian foreign investment concessions in electricity sector. The concessions included an undertaking of the electricity purchase from private energy companies at a price of double the average tariff rate. Nykomb was the sole shareholder of SIA Windau, a Latvian energy company. When SIA Windau requested the purchase at the double tariff rate, Latvia initially refused; however eventually applied a 75% rate instead of double (200%). The failure to fulfil the undertaking resulted in the arbitral claim.

The Tribunal first determined which one of the factors taken into account will prevail over the rest: "[t]he decisive factor for drawing the border line towards

[149] Fauchald (2006), p. 21.

[150] Another notable paragraph from the *Santa Elena v. Costa Rica* award, sometimes used to demonstrate the sole effects approach, is par. 77, which reads as follows: "There is ample opportunity for the proposition that a property has been expropriated when the effect of the measures taken by the state has been to deprive the owner of title, possession or access to the benefit and economic use of his property", citing the abovementioned *Tippetts* case. Besides the necessary reiteration that the taking has been direct, explicit, and uncontested; it should also be noted that this paragraph relates chiefly to the assessment of the date as at which the property must be valued and not to the existence of expropriation itself.

[151] *Nykomb Synergetics Technology Holding AB v. Latvia,* SCC Case No. 118/2001, Award (16 December 2003) (*Nykomb v. Latvia*).

[152] First known submitted case is *AES Summit Generation v. Hungary (AES I),* ICSID Case No. ARB/01/4. The case was amicably settled, thus did not produce an award. It differs from the case, *AES Summit Generation Limited and AES-Tisza Eromu Kft v. Hungary,* ICSID Case No. ARB/07/22, Award (23 September 2010) *(AES II).*

expropriation **must primarily be the degree of possession taking or control over the enterprise that disputed measures entail.**"[153] Therefore, the primary element inspected by the tribunal is the severity of the measure. Latvia maintained that a decrease from 200% to 75% does not substantially affect the value of the investment, and therefore does not reach to the level of a severe interference. The Tribunal acknowledged the adverse effect, however contended that an adverse effect *per se* does not constitute expropriation. Indeed, the lower percentage did not amount to an expropriatory measure, given the company continued doing business and was in no way deprived of the benefits, control and the enjoyment of the investment.[154]

Given that the analysis had not gone beyond the failure to find substantial deprivation of the investment, it is not granted how (or if) the tribunal would include state intent and public interest from a value balancing perspective. Nonetheless, given that the Tribunal had seen the deprivation of the investor as the *decisive* factor, Nykomb tribunal had adopted an approach more proximate to the effects doctrine.

Nykomb case is a fitting illustration to dispel the common misconception that sole effects doctrine always leads to an award in favour of foreign investors. While the sole effects doctrine may bear the risk of underplaying the importance of public interest, it is important to note that the fact that just because *some form* of deprivation took place will not make the challenged act expropriatory *per se*. While it attaches primacy on the effects, these effects are not to be taken into account free from their degree of severity.

Another similar award borne out of the ECT, which explicitly recognised the prevalent importance of effects, yet failed to find sufficient deprivation to determine the existence of expropriation, was ***Mohammad Ammar Al-Bahloul v. Tajikistan***.[155] The case concerned a dispute that had arisen out of the failure of Tajik authorities to issue exploration licenses in relation to four agreements. According to the claimant, this failure resulted in an indirect expropriation.

The *Al-Bahloul* Tribunal cited the *Tecmed* award[156] in relation to the permanency and severity of the deprivation. It was also pointed out that the government intention should be deemed less important than the effects.

The Tribunal continued by analysing whether or not "the conduct of the [s]tate [resulted] in an irreversible and permanent taking or destruction of [c]laimant's rights."[157] In the light of the facts, the Tribunal reached the conclusion that the inactivity on the state's end was a "temporary non-fulfilment"; and given the lack of a permanency element, the deprivation had not risen to the level of expropriation. The Tribunal also reflected on what it would consider to be an indirect expropriation within the scope of the facts of the case: "[t]he [s]tate must terminate the contract or

[153] *Nykomb v. Latvia* (2003), p. 33. Emphasis added.

[154] *Nykomb v. Latvia* (2003), p. 33.

[155] *Mohammad Ammar Al-Bahloul v. Tajikistan*, SCC Case No. 064/2008, Partial Award on Jurisdiction and Liability (2 September 2009) and Award (8 June 2010) (*Al-Bahloul v. Tajikistan*).

[156] *Al-Bahloul v. Tajikistan* (2009), par. 279. *Técnicas Medioambientales Tecmed, S.A. v. The United Mexican States*, ICSID Case No. ARB (AF)/00/2, Award (29 May 2003) (*Tecmed v. Mexico*).

[157] *Al-Bahloul v. Tajikistan* (2009), par. 278–288.

at least definitively refuse to perform its obligation under it."[158] Despite the inactivity, the Tribunal found no evidence that the licenses would not be issued, albeit with a delay.

This case has particular importance especially with regards to the act (or the inaction) in question. In fact, it illustrates that *inactivity* on the state's end might amount to expropriation, as long as the deprivation caused by such inactivity is permanent and sufficiently severe.

Metalclad v. Mexico[159] is an early NAFTA case. Metalclad, a US company, claimed that Mexico, through its administrative organs in the state of San Luis Potosí (SLP) and Guadalcázar (municipality), interfered with the establishment and operation of a hazardous landfill area.[160] Metalclad argued that its investment was expropriated in violation of Article 1110 of NAFTA.

COTERIN, a state-owned company, had obtained a construction and operation authorisation for a hazardous landfill in Guadalcázar in 1990. Three years later, the National Ecological Institute (NEI), an independent agency of the federal Mexican government, granted the subsidiary a federal permit to construct a hazardous waste landfill.[161] A few months into its operation, Metalclad bought COTERIN with its landfill permits in order to build and operate the landfill. According to Metalclad officials, the company had had the support of the governor of SLP who had praised the fact that the landfill project complied with the Mexican health and environment standards.[162]

Metalclad claimed that following the acquisition of the state-owned COTERIN, the governor of SLP had initiated a campaign against the operation of the landfill. This being said, government officials were known to have visited the site during this period to inspect the progress. On the grounds of the absence of a construction permit, progress was eventually stopped by the authorities. A second independent environmental impact report which reaffirmed the earlier report was also produced. The second report indicated that with proper engineering and operation, the landfill was in fact suitable and did not pose any health risks or substantial environmental impact.

However, the campaign against the landfill continued. During the opening of the landfill area, protesters blocked the entry and exit of buses carrying guests and workers, and "employed tactics of intimidation against Metalclad."[163] Ultimately, the construction permit application was denied; and a few years later (and after the submission of the dispute to arbitration)[164] the landfill area was declared as a natural area for the protection of a rare cactus species via an Ecological Decree.

[158] *Al-Bahloul v. Tajikistan* (2009), par. 278–288.

[159] *Metalclad Corporation v. The United Mexican States,* ICSID Case No. ARB(AF)/97/1, Award (20 August 2000) (*Metalclad v. Mexico*).

[160] *Metalclad v. Mexico (2000)*, par. 1.

[161] *Metalclad v. Mexico* (2000), par. 31.

[162] *Metalclad v. Mexico* (2000), par. 33.

[163] *Metalclad v. Mexico* (2000), par. 46.

[164] *Metalclad v. Mexico* (2000), par. 59.

The *Metalclad* tribunal's expropriation analysis is usually considered to reflect a landmark 'sole effects' approach,[165] due to the following paragraph:

> [...] expropriation [...] includes not only open, deliberate and acknowledged takings of property, such as outright seizure or formal or obligatory transfer of title in favour of the host state, but also covert or incidental interference with the use of property which has the effect of depriving the owner, in whole or in significant part, of the use or reasonably-to-be-expected economic benefit of property **even if not necessarily to the obvious benefit of the host state.**[166]

This paragraph arguably does not extend the application of indirect expropriation—neither does it imply the application of any particular interest balancing doctrine such as sole effects or *ad hoc* regulatory carve-out. The paragraph instead seems to reflect the division between "open, deliberate and acknowledged takings of property, such as seizure or formal or obligatory transfer of title" (direct expropriation) and "covert or incidental interference with the use of property which has the effect of depriving the owner, in who or in significant part, of the use or reasonably-to-be-expected economic benefit of property" (indirect expropriation); a principle that is adopted and accepted in virtually all investment treaties. But why, then, has this seemingly straightforward paragraph caused such controversy as to its true meaning?

A possible answer is that the ambiguity is caused by the last phrase mentioning the "*obvious benefit of the host state*". The last sentence could be (and probably has been) interpreted to mean the damage suffered by the investor will prevail *vis-à-vis* state (public) benefit. This might imply that damaging and depriving acts, despite their public benefit, are expropriatory.

It could be argued that the paragraph does not deal in absolutes, and its wording does not necessarily bring about broad approach on whether effects of a measure prevail over its intent. On the contrary, such interpretation would possibly stretch the meaning. A more plausible interpretation of this paragraph is that not every act deemed as indirect expropriation *has to benefit the state*, i.e. the state does not have to obtain or appropriate any economic value as a result. A direct or formal expropriation, by its definition, has to include a transfer of title from an investor to

---

[165] Dolzer and Bloch (2003), pp. 161–163. According to Dolzer and Bloch, what they call the "*Tippetts – Biloune – Metalclad Line*" represents a series of arbitral decisions that are "unequivocal pronouncement[s]" of the sole effects doctrine. The *Metalclad* award's inclusion to the *Line* seemingly stems from the contention of the Supreme Court of British Columbia that "the Tribunal gave an extremely broad definition of expropriation for the purposes of Article 1110", because the definition included "covert or incidental interference with the use of property which has the effect of depriving the owner, in whole or in significant part, of the use or reasonably-to-be-expected economic benefit of property" in addition to a (direct) taking of property. See, *The United Mexican States v. Metalclad Corporation* (2001) BCSC 664. B.C.J. No. 950 (Q.L.), par. 99. https://www.italaw.com/sites/default/files/case-documents/ita0512.pdf. The broadening of this definition stems from the inclusion of the concept of *indirect* expropriation. Likewise, as Newcombe points out, in some Commonwealth countries such as Canada, compensation is only required for expropriation when there is deprivation *as well as* a corresponding appropriation of economic value, which is not always required for indirect expropriation in international investment law. See, Newcombe (1999); Mostafa (2008), p. 286 (noting that the effects are the 'relevant' factor, as opposed to the intent).

[166] *Metalclad v. Mexico* (2000), par. 103.

state, which entails a benefit for the state by way of acquisition of property. Since indirect expropriation does not concern formal title transfers, host state's subsequent benefit is not necessarily one of the constituent requirements or consequences of indirect expropriation.[167]

An indirectly expropriated investment can be lost without anyone else obtaining the lost investment, or its value. The neutralisation and destruction of an investment through an act without a formal transfer of title may well amount to indirect expropriation even if the taking and damage suffered by the investor is not accompanied with a benefit for the host state.[168] Nonetheless, subsequent (unjust) enrichment or the eventual acquisition of the destroyed investment's assets could be considered as 'anticipatable' benefits with potential aggravating effects in terms of state intent. In other words, although strictly subject to other supplementary facts pointing towards the genuineness of public purpose, host states might have an argumentative upper hand if there is no subsequent enrichment on their end.

As also pointed out by Brower and Blanchard, the *Metalclad* analysis is usually conducted solely (and therefore erroneously) based on the above-mentioned paragraph.[169] However, the following paragraph is one of several which demonstrates the consideration of public purpose—in this case, the public purpose of the alleged expropriation by the denial of the permit.[170] Such consideration would be largely absent in an award with actual sole effects application.

> By permitting or tolerating the conduct of Guadalcázar [authorities] in relation to Metalclad which the Tribunal has already held amounts to unfair and inequitable treatment [...] and by thus participating or acquiescing in the denial of Metalclad of the right to operate the landfill, notwithstanding the fact that the project was fully approved and endorsed by the federal government, Mexico must be held to have taken a measure tantamount to expropriation in violation of NAFTA Article 1110(1).[171]

Tribunal delved further into host state's actions and their consistency. Hindering the operation of the landfill after Metalclad's acquisition, yet having tolerated Guadalcázar's conduct during state operation of the same landfill was ultimately deemed unjustified. This argument was bolstered with a number of expert reports, which had indicated that the landfill was as harmless as it had been during the state operation.[172]

This analysis directly stems from the FET evaluation of the tribunal, according to which elements such as legitimate expectations and the proportionality of the measures had been scrutinised. The Tribunal underlined the issued permits and

[167] Newcombe (2005) 7, p. 15. The appropriation of expropriation and unjust enrichment is reflected as an 'unorthodox approach'

[168] This view can also be found in more recent awards. See, for example, UAB Garsų Pasaulis v. Kyrgyzstan, PCA Case No. 2020-59, Award (8 April 2024), par. 290 (*UAB v. Kyrgyzistan*).

[169] For an in-depth analysis of this award by the author of this book, as well as other earlier NAFTA awards, see Howse and Ünüvar (2022).

[170] Brower and Blanchard (2014), p. 734.

[171] *Metalclad v. Mexico* (2000), par. 104.

[172] *Metalclad v. Mexico* (2000), par. 104.

approvals. No genuine public interest was present to supersede the investor's damage. Likewise, no additional public purpose justified the failure to realise Metalclad's legitimate expectations arising from the issuance or promise of relevant permits, as well as correspondence with state authorities.[173]

Other scholars cite the *Metalclad* award's paragraph 111 to justify the sole effects approach,[174] which reads that

> [t]he Tribunal need not decide or consider the motivation or intent of the adoption of the Ecological Decree [declaring a Natural Area for the protection of rare cactus]. Indeed, a finding of expropriation on the basis of the Ecological Decree was not essential to the Tribunal's finding of a violation of NAFTA Article 1110. However, the Tribunal considered that the implementation of the Ecological Decree would, in and of itself, constitute an act tantamount to expropriation.[175]

This paragraph should be read and analysed within its proper context. When read in conjunction with the preceding and succeeding paragraphs, it establishes that the intent of the decree (which is not part of the central claim) did not relate to the analysis conducted by the Tribunal which asserted the existence of expropriation. While one could reach to the conclusion that such paragraph undeniably establishes an outright rejection of the consideration of public purpose of a regulatory measure in any given situation, one could also argue that the facts of the case and the conduct of the government and the municipality hindered a plausible argument which could justify the protection of the rare cactus species. In another paragraph, the Tribunal emphasises the "investor's justified reliance on the government's representations regarding the permit, the fact that government authorities knew of the construction for more than one year before issuing the stop work order, the fact that permits had not been required for other projects and the fact that no procedure was in place for dealing with building permit applications."[176] In light of these representations and the misconduct of the government, the Tribunal simply noted that whether such misconduct was carried by the refusal of the permit (as was the case in *Metalclad*) or by the issuance of an Ecological Decree (the Tribunal did not further decide on this additional, latter claim), would not suffice to justify the government's conduct on the grounds of public purpose.[177]

This aside, an argument can be formulated against the *Metalclad* Tribunal's reasoning so as to suggest that the government intent to protect environment as embodied by the Ecological Decree, even in the given circumstances of the case, should have sufficed for justification. However, this is a different subject matter from the assertion that *Metalclad* Tribunal had not considered any public intent *vis-à-vis* the government's misconduct and misrepresentation. In any case, this analysis does not intend to analyse the relevant standard of review in the Tribunal's decision. Instead,

---

[173] *Metalclad v. Mexico* (2000), par. 108.

[174] Viñuales (2012), p. 125; Firger and Gerrard (2012), p. 542.

[175] *Metalclad v. Mexico* (2000), par. 111.

[176] *Metalclad v. Mexico* (2000), par. 108.

[177] *Metalclad v. Mexico* (2000), par. 111.

the emphasis should be on the fact that *Metalclad* is a stark illustration of why further clarification on the definition of indirect expropriation in any given IIA is essential.

While *Metalclad* award may be one of the oldest illustrations, it is certainly not the only example as to why newer generation IIAs warranted further clarification on what constitutes (direct or indirect) expropriation, and what does not—and how this determination is made. Mischaracterisation of an expropriatory measure, coupled with superficial applications of the effects doctrine lacking any rigorous analysis, pose an actual, contemporary problem. Heiskanen argued that "[t]here is nothing 'indirect' about a physical seizure or appropriation of property. Taking is a direct and immediate object of such measures, and the informal nature of the act, or the mere absence of a statutory justification, is not an adequate reason to describe them as 'indirect'."[178] In other words, according to his analysis, the line between the direct and indirect expropriation would in fact be better marked by the *de facto* taking which entails acquired benefit, rather than the existence of a formal transfer. This being said, a formal transfer is a solid indication that such expropriation, a direct one at that—may have taken place. Without either *de facto* taking or a formal transfer, however, it is difficult to argue that a direct expropriation has occurred.

A fitting, recent example is ***Rockhopper v. Italy***.[179] The case stems from Rockhopper's claim that its investment was expropriated as a result of an Italian law which prohibited the operation of an off-shore oil rig within 12 miles of the Italian coast.[180] After ascertaining that the claimant had "the right to be granted the production concession", the Tribunal considered this right to be capable of being expropriated. Interestingly, the Tribunal characterised the violation as direct expropriation: "There were no indirect actions, whether described as creeping or otherwise, cumulatively leading to such deprivation, but rather a specific act on the part of the Respondent which brought about this circumstance".[181]

There are a myriad of problems in this conclusion. Even putting aside the Tribunal's designation of a 'right to be granted' a concession as an investment capable of being expropriated, its designation of the expropriation as 'direct' warrants further scrutiny. As discussed above, a formal or physical taking of property can result in direct expropriation. However, no such taking took place in this case. The Tribunal seems resolute that 'indirect actions, whether described as creeping or otherwise, cumulatively' leading to some deprivation is the only way that indirect expropriation can exist; as opposed to a single act which creates the expropriation or similar consequences. Indirect expropriation can be the result of a *single* expropriatory act as opposed to a *creeping* expropriation, and does not have to be

[178] Heiskanen (2007), p. 219.

[179] *Rockhopper Italia S.p.A., Rockhopper Mediterranean Ltd, and Rockhopper Exploration Plc v. Italian Republic*, ICSID Case No. ARB/17/14, Award (23 August 2022) (*Rockhopper v. Italy*).

[180] See, Chap. 3, where the facts of the case were laid out more in detail.

[181] *Rockhopper v. Italy* (2022), par. 194.

cumulative.[182] An indirect act, such as the one in question rendering an investment unable to operate, is not the same as a transfer of title of the said investment, or its physical take-over.

The Tribunal, in addition to its problematic identification of a 'direct' expropriation, also summarily rejected the police powers argument of the Respondent state. In response to Italy's argument that "reasonable regulatory measures that a State passes to pursue societal policies without discriminating among its addresses [sic] constitute the legitimate exercise of police powers and, therefore, any economic impact that they might cause on investors is not compensable",[183] the Tribunal contended that, in light of its finding of a direct expropriation, the Respondent's invocation of police powers is unconvincing. It further noted that, "for a sovereign to avoid the consequences of unlawful expropriation it must cumulatively satisfy all of the requirements [referring to public purpose, non-discrimination, due process, and compensation] of Art. 13(1) of the ECT."[184]

While the Tribunal does not overtly align itself with any reiteration of the effects doctrine, it does appear to build its assertion that the measure was expropriatory solely on the perceived effects of the measure (inability to acquire the concession). It arguably confuses Italy's argument that the measure was not expropriatory (therefore not compensable) with an argument that the expropriation was lawful pursuant to the elements articulated under Article 13 of the ECT.

The *Rockhopper v. Italy* award is certainly a testament to the consequences of erroneous arbitral reasoning, conflation of legal arguments, and misconstruing different segments of even the most commonly invoked principles after decades of arbitral elaborations and practice in light of vague and imprecise provisions in IIAs.

Above, some arbitral awards that are often associated with the sole effects doctrine were scrutinised. This section demonstrates that a blanket, general application of the sole effects doctrine is challenging to ascertain: it is often qualified, does not negate the high severity required from the 'effects' in question, and is confined generally to earlier awards.[185] For instance, in *Nykomb* and *al-Bahloul* awards, the Tribunals had set high thresholds for the severity of damages suffered, and despite its explicit recognition of the effects of a measure as the primary determinant of whether expropriation occurred, they found that the harm was not severe enough. Some of the awards mentioned above also appear to conflate the *lawfulness* of expropriation with the *existence* of expropriation, rendering the effects—public purpose analysis muddled and, in some cases, outright confused.

Several common examples for sole effects, such as *Metalclad* and *Santa Elena* awards, are usually partially read and analysed: while the former concerns whether states need to benefit from expropriation (for instance, by acquiring the ownership or control of the investment targeted), the core matter of the latter award is a direct

---

[182] Nascimbene (2024).

[183] *Rockhopper v. Italy* (2022), par. 195.

[184] *Rockhopper v. Italy* (2022), par. 195.

[185] Brower and Blanchard (2014).

expropriation—and the question relates to the amount of compensation. While other awards, such as *Nykomb v. Latvia* which concern specific acts and not general regulatory acts, explicitly prioritise the effects over other elements, it is not granted this comparison would have extended to a general regulatory measure with the intent of realising a public purpose. In short, a strict sole effects approach in arbitral practice, prioritising *any degree* of harm to an investor and disregarding completely any legitimate public purpose embedded within a general regulatory measure, is far from being the norm.

4.3.2 The Police Powers Doctrine and the Regulatory Carve-out

4.3.2.1 The Reformulation of Expropriation Provisions

According to the *police powers* doctrine, "a measure that falls within the state's police powers resulting in loss of property does not constitute an indirect expropriation, and, accordingly, does not give rise to an obligation to compensate."[186] In other words, an arbitral tribunal adopting the police powers doctrine will attach more importance to the intent and nature of a measure *vis-à-vis* the adverse effects this measure may have on a foreign investor.[187] *Regulatory carve-out* forms an explicit, written manifestation of the police powers doctrine, pursuant to which an IIA explicitly excludes non-discriminatory and legitimate regulatory measures from the scope of indirect expropriation.[188] In other words, if the alleged expropriation concerns a general regulatory act that is 'legitimate' and 'non-discriminatory', regardless of the damage suffered by the investor as a result of the said act, there will be no expropriation (and therefore, no compensation based on expropriation). This, however, does not mean that such regulation will also be excluded from the scope of another treaty provision, such as the FET obligation of the host state, provided that the IIA includes such provision.[189]

It is debated whether the police powers doctrine forms part of CIL today. While some tribunals famously declared it so,[190] some scholars argue that its designation

[186] Titi (2018), p. 323.

[187] Kriebaum (2007), pp. 725–729; Dolzer and Bloch (2003), p. 163 (implicitly referring to this doctrine by noting that "[a] second strand is not identical to the 'sole effect doctrine', giving weight to the purpose and the circumstances of the respective governmental action.").

[188] As will be shown below in this Chapter, many newer generation IIAs include regulatory carve-out provisions to ensure that the police powers of the respondent states are respected. See, for instance, Annex 9-B on Expropriation, TPP. https://ustr.gov/sites/default/files/TPP-Final-Text-Investment.pdf.

[189] For example, *see*, *Al-Bahloul v. Tajikistan* (2009) (rejecting expropriation claim but ruling that the host state breached its FET obligation).

[190] *Saluka Investments B.V. v. The Czech Republic*, UNCITRAL, Partial Award (17 March 2006) (*Saluka v. Czech Republic*), par. 262; also see *Emmanuel Too* (1989), par. 26 (pp. 13–14).

as a CIL rule is not a given.[191] Others point at its recognition "in international law" and argue that a *narrow* reading of the doctrine, which stipulates that "only measure relating to the maintenance of health, moral and police order, such as tax and crime prevention, fall within the police powers doctrine" can be said to have attained this designation, seeking guidance from secondary sources such as the Restatement (Third) of the Foreign Relations Law of the United States of 1987.[192] Citing Brownlie[193] and Sornajarah,[194] the OECD Report of 2004 declared that "not all state measure interfering with property are expropriation", and that "[i]t is an accepted principle of customary international law that where economic injury results from a bona fide non-discriminatory regulation within the police powers of the State, compensation is not required."[195]

The police powers doctrine came to the adjudicatory forefront following several arbitral claims filed pursuant to NAFTA. This FTA remains as one of the most important initiatives during the proliferation of IIAs throughout the 90s, particularly for its future impact on the interpretation of substantive protection principles, including expropriation provisions. Both adjudicatory and treaty-making practice have been influenced by arbitral claims initiated under NAFTA during late 90s and early 2000s.

Similar to the vast majority of other BITs signed during the 90s by North American states[196] as well as other states around the globe,[197] which generally contain brief and vague expropriation provisions, NAFTA's investment chapter included a short, unqualified provision under its Article 1110, to protect foreign investors from expropriation without compensation:

> No [p]arty may directly or indirectly nationalise or expropriate an investment of an investor of another [p]arty in its territory or take a measure tantamount to nationalisation or expropriation of such investment [...].[198]

---

[191] Titi (2018), p. 341; Bulut (2022), p. 584.

[192] American Law Institute, Restatement (Third) Foreign Relations of the United States (1987), vol. 1, par. 712 (Third Restatement of 1987).

[193] Brownlie (2003), p. 509. "state measures, prima facie a lawful exercise of powers of governments, may affect foreign interests considerably without amounting to expropriation. Thus, foreign assets and their use may be subjected to taxation, trade restrictions involving licenses and quotas, or measures of devaluation. While special facts may alter cases, in principle such measures are not unlawful and do not constitute expropriation".

[194] Sornarajah (1994), p. 283.

[195] OECD (2004), pp. 4–5.

[196] Article VI, Canada -USSR (Russia) BIT (1991); Article III, Egypt - US BIT (1992); Congo – US BIT (1994); Romania – US BIT (1994); Article VIII; Canada – Ukraine BIT (1995); Georgia – US BIT (1995); Article V, Mexico – Spain BIT (1995); Mongolia – US BIT (1995); Canada – Thailand BIT (1998), Canada – Costa Rica BIT (1999).

[197] Article 4, Denmark – Sri Lanka BIT (1985); Article 5, Bolivia – UK BIT (1990); Article 5, Finland – Latvia BIT (1992); Article III, Kazakhstan – Türkiye BIT (1995); Article 5, Cuba – South Africa BIT (1997); Article IV, Indonesia – Singapore BIT (2006); Escarcena (2014), pp. 112–118; 165–172.

[198] Article 1110, NAFTA (1994).

This provision provides for the default division between a direct and indirect expropriation. However, like many IIAs currently in force, the NAFTA does not define, or attempt to delimit, the scope of indirect expropriation. While the United States is yet to lose an arbitral case as of January 2025,[199] it has faced a number of unanticipated claims under, *inter alia*, Article 1110 of NAFTA.[200]

To retain the regulatory autonomy *vis-à-vis* foreign investor claims and ensure that their legitimate and non-discriminatory regulatory measures are not targeted merely for their adverse effects on investments, the US and Canada[201] reformulated their future investment treaties by including annexes, exceptions, and guidelines to treaties which, to a certain extent, outlined the framework of the expropriation test that the arbitral tribunals would apply. While the base provisions differ little from the classical formulation of expropriation provisions, the North American model aims at clarifying these provisions through annexes.[202]

See, for instance, the Australia – US FTA:

> Neither [p]arty may expropriate or nationalise a covered investment either directly or indirectly through measures equivalent to expropriation or nationalisation ("expropriation"), except:
>
> a- For a public purpose;
> b- In a non-discriminatory manner;
> c- On payment of prompt, adequate, and effective compensation; and
> d- In accordance with due process of law.

However, this particular provision includes a footnote, which reads that "Article 11.7 shall be interpreted in accordance with Annexes 11-A and 11-B".[203]

Annex 11-A concerns the definition of CIL as agreed by the parties. It is stated that CIL "results from a general and consistent practice of [s]tates that they follow from a sense of legal obligation".[204] On the other hand, Annex 11-B titled 'Expropriation' contains the actual interpretative substance for Article 11.7. After clarifying that expropriation concerns only "a tangible or intangible property right

---

[199] UNCTAD ISDS Database. https://investmentpolicy.unctad.org/investment-dispute-settlement/country/223/united-states-of-america. The United States has thus far acted as Respondent in a total of 24 cases. 10 of these cases resulted in favour of the state, and 5 are still pending. The remainder of the cases were either discontinued, or settled out of court.

[200] ITALAW remains to be one of the most comprehensive, publicly available databases on investment arbitration cases. See, ITALaw.com, http://www.italaw.com.

[201] In addition to the rather unexpected wave of NAFTA Chap. 11 claims against Canada and the US, Alschner explains that "the traditional investment treaty paradigm of Northern countries being capital exporters, and Southern States being capital importers, began to wane." Alschner (2013), p. 477.

[202] Edsall (2006), p. 937.

[203] Article 11.7, Australia – US FTA (2005); other examples include Article 10.7 and Annex 10-C, Dominican Republic – Central America FTA (CAFTA-DR) (2006); Article 6 and Annex B, Uruguay – US BIT (2006); Article 11.6 and Annex 11-B, Korea – US FTA (2012); Article 10.7 and Annex 10-B, Panama – US FTA (2012).

[204] Annex 11-A, Australia – US FTA (2005).

or property interest in an investment", it goes on to articulate the difference between direct and indirect expropriation.[205]

Following paragraph concerns the indirect expropriation test:

> The determination of whether an action or series of actions by a [p]arty, in a specific fact situation, constitutes an indirect expropriation, requires a case-by-case, fact-based inquiry that considers, among other factors: (a) the economic impact of the government action, although the fact that an action or series of actions by a [p]arty has an adverse effect on the economic value of an investment, standing alone, does not establish that an indirect expropriation has occurred; (b) the extent to which the government action interferes with distinct, reasonable investment-backed expectations; and (c) the character of the government action.[206]

Sub-paragraph 4 concerns indirect expropriation and it lays forth the factors that shall be considered while determining whether or not the act amounts to indirect expropriation. These factors, which are contained in both the US and Canadian Model BITs as well as many recent IIAs of Canada and the US, are developed by the US Supreme Court in the case *Penn Central Station v. New York City* in 1978.[207] These considerations are not exhaustive; therefore, other relevant factors or considerations might come into play.

The first listed factor is *the economic impact of the measure on the investment*.[208] It is followed by a clarification that deprivation alone will not amount to expropriation. This very factor might be the central element in the expropriation annex, as it introduces the subsequent qualifications (analysed below), and indicates a subtle but powerful delimitation of the tribunal's discretion on factor-balancing. The UNCTAD report on expropriation puts forth three relevant questions to be answered while considering whether a deprivation has occurred: (a) Has the measure caused total or near-total destruction of the economic value attached to the investment? (b) Has there been a deprivation of the control over the investment? (c) What are the temporal aspects of the deprivation—are they temporary, or permanent?[209] The consideration of the economic impact is, without a doubt, crucial to ascertaining that an expropriatory measure took place. However, this provision and its variations across other IIAs clearly bars a *sole* effects reading.

The second factor specifies that *legitimate investment-related expectations* play a role in the expropriation analysis. It is not clarified what is exactly meant by "distinct" and "reasonable" in this particular FTA, however there are examples of such provisions in other investment agreements[210] specifying that the representations and undertakings giving rise to such expectations should be formal and written. The determination of what is a distinct and reasonable expectation (for instance, whether or not unwritten representations or informal promises would possibly give rise to

---

[205] Annex 11-B, Australia – US FTA (2005).

[206] Annex 11-B, Australia – US FTA (2005).

[207] *Penn Central Transportation Co. v. New York City* (1978) 438 US 104.

[208] Kriebaum (2014).

[209] UNCTAD Expropriation (2012), pp. 62–63.

[210] Annex 2 (3)(b), ASEAN Comprehensive Investment Agreement (2009) (ASEANIA).

legitimate expectations as specified by the agreement), therefore, is left to the tribunal's discretion.

The third factor adds the regulatory perspective into the equation: *the character of the measure*, particularly with regards to its context and underlying intent, shall be taken into consideration. The relevance of the context and intent is that this particular factor scrutinises whether or not the public purpose is genuine in the process of identifying whether a measure is expropriatory. This is also followed by a number of additional considerations: proximity of the measure and the consequences and whether or not the measure is proportionate is among the most important.[211]

These listed facts hint at the weight of importance these elements would have in such an analysis. In clarifying and affirming which factors are to be taken into consideration while determining whether or not an act amounts to expropriation, the North American annexes assist arbitral tribunals. One could argue that the true function of these annexes is not merely to curb arbitral discretion but to give a certain argumentative weight to those factors and, based on facts, strike a balance between the regulatory concerns of a state and the deprivation suffered by the investor.

These considerations are consolidated under the final paragraph of the Annex as follows:

> Except in rare circumstances, **non-discriminatory regulatory actions** by a [p]arty that are **designed and applied to achieve legitimate public welfare objectives**, such as the protection of public health, safety, and the environment, **do not constitute indirect expropriations.**[212]

If a regulatory measure is non-discriminatory and is taken in order to apply a legitimate public purpose, regardless of the severity of the deprivation suffered by the foreign investor, that measure will not constitute indirect expropriation. If, however, a measure (specific or general regulatory) destroys or severely affects an investment, deprives the investor of the control of their investment with no genuine public purpose and in a discriminatory manner, this particular act is likely to be an indirect expropriation—therefore, it will be subject to compensation. The Annex does not go as far as to suggest that the mere fact that a measure is of general and regulatory nature excludes it from the scope of expropriation.

In light of the conflations, confusions, and in some cases wilful disregard of the public purpose in some of the awards mentioned above (and will be mentioned below) in this Chapter, the clarity injected by the North American reformulation is a step towards ensuring coherent interpretation by way of regulating the interpretative processes without entirely abolishing arbitral discretion. Instead of delving into lengthy discussions as to which considerations shall prevail over others and with *ex ante* guidance of party states as sovereign treaty-makers, arbitral tribunals are instead expected to apply a relatively streamlined expropriation analysis, which adjusts the balance between the effects and the intent beforehand. Such clarifications, particularly those regarding the scope and extent of vague principles such as

[211] UNCTAD Expropriation (2012), p. 78.

[212] Annex 11-B(4)(b), Australia – US FTA (2005).

indirect expropriation, would also work towards minimising *ex post* interferences by states (for instance, an interpretative note regarding a provision relevant in an ongoing arbitral dispute) and controversial paradigm clashes between states as treaty-makers and states as dispute parties.[213]

This, however, is not to say that prioritising regulatory sovereignty over protection of foreign investors is the better option in every case. Some states intentionally leave expropriation provisions vague to grant arbitral tribunals more interpretative discretion. This may have various reasons, but arguably the most relevant reason is that such broad articulation usually allows tribunals to use discretion on which interest shall prevail. Even though this has begun to change in North America as evident by the newer Canadian and American FTA and IIAs, many European states (such as the Netherlands)[214] still have many IIAs in force containing some variety of the base expropriation provision, without any clarification annexes. The 2004 Netherlands Model BIT[215] had been seen as a feature of the '*gold standard*' model for investor protection.[216] It broadly spoke of "measures depriving, directly or indirectly, nationals of the other Contracting Part of their investments".[217] This type of leeway gives the arbitral tribunal a choice: if the facts allow the tribunal to give more weight to investors' interests, given the absence of any regulatory carve-out, the tribunals are under no obligation to apply any particular doctrine. It could, therefore, mean a wider area of protection for foreign investors against harmful state measures regardless of their general regulatory nature, or any legitimate purpose they may seek to pursue. With a North American regulatory carve-out, this is not possible; as legitimate and non-discriminatory measures will be automatically excluded from the scope regardless of the deprivation suffered by the investor. As the carve-out excludes legitimate and non-discriminatory measures, the arbitral tribunal will still retain discretion to determine whether an act is discriminatory or legitimate.[218]

While many EU Member States had adopted this broader framework for expropriation following the Dutch 'gold standard' principally stemming from the OECD Model;[219] the EU, led by the European Commission, entirely overhauled this policy. This regionwide departure is apparent when one examines the shift from the 2004 Model BIT 'gold standard' to the new Netherlands Model BIT from 2019.[220] The new model contains an expropriation provision that defines direct and indirect expropriation; refers to the aforementioned factors such as the economic impact, the

---

[213] Chapter 3.

[214] Lavranos (2013), p. 1.

[215] 2004 Netherlands Model BIT.

[216] Hoffmeister and Ünüvar (2013), p. 57.

[217] Article 6, 2004 Netherlands Model BIT.

[218] Kriebaum (2014), p. 468 (noting that the 'regulation exceptions in the draft texts allow for a balancing of the investor's interest [...] and the State's interest [...] is possible within certain limits.').

[219] Draft Convention on the Protection of Foreign Property (the 'OECD Model' - 1967). https://investmentpolicy.unctad.org/international-investment-agreements/treaty-files/2812/download.

[220] Article 12, 2019 Netherlands Model BIT.

duration of the measure, as well as the character of the measure; and includes a regulatory carve-out.[221] As will be detailed below, the new generation EU FTAs and IPAs, such as CETA,[222] EUVIPA,[223] EUSIPA,[224] EUMA,[225] and EUCAFA,[226] as well as previous negotiation drafts of TTIP[227] released by the European Commission indicate an evolving yet consistent policy spill-over unfolding in the past decade and a half.[228] On top of that, the EU released the so-called 'Annotations to the Model Clauses for negotiation and re-negotiation of Member States' Bilateral Investment Agreements with third countries' in 2023, largely following the same blueprint.[229] All of these treaties mentioned include an explanatory annex with a regulatory carve-out—largely absent in Member State BITs as of yet.[230] I will return to these IIAs mentioned above at the end of this Chapter.

Like the regulatory carve-out, the implementation of a standard, broad expropriation clause is a foreign trade policy choice for states (and, as far as its Member States are concerned, the EU). At the advent of the EU common commercial policy and a slowly emerging EU BIT framework in the aftermath of the Lisbon Treaty, several arguments were made in favour of the Member State-driven gold standard provisions.[231] If a state believes that attracting foreign investment and capital to its domestic market could benefit from such broad reading, evidently, this is by all means possible. By leaving the definition of expropriation rather unframed, they may choose to delegate more interpretative discretion to adjudicators. This might lead to more favourable interpretations for foreign investors, as arbitral experience indicates. When Latin American states started signing investment treaties with capital-exporting countries during the 90s, at a time when virtually all investment treaties accepted the gold standard with no explicit regulatory carve-out to declare

---

[221] Article 12 (2), (3), (4), and (8), 2019 Netherlands Model BIT.

[222] Comprehensive and Economic Trade Agreement between Canada and the European Union (CETA) (2017). https://policy.trade.ec.europa.eu/eu-trade-relationships-country-and-region/countries-and-regions/canada/eu-canada-agreement_en.

[223] EUVIPA (2019).

[224] EUSIPA (Signed in 2018; not in force as of January 2025). https://policy.trade.ec.europa.eu/eu-trade-relationships-country-and-region/countries-and-regions/singapore/eu-singapore-agreements/texts-agreements_en.

[225] EUMA, Agreement reached in principle, published in 2018. https://circabc.europa.eu/ui/group/09242a36-a438-40fd-a7af-fe32e36cbd0e/library/0cc57f29-63bc-476f-80f9-4516a0b0b739/details.

[226] EUCAFA. Signed in February 2023; the European Parliament gave its consent in February 2024. https://circabc.europa.eu/rest/download/6a47b636-0dbd-4537-8544-cdb01b6e80a3?

[227] TTIP Negotiating Directives. https://circabc.europa.eu/ui/group/09242a36-a438-40fd-a7af-fe32e36cbd0e/library/8c193123-2084-4231-9e71-bed0d034bb9c/details?download=true.

[228] Fontanelli and Bianco (2014) (suggesting that the (then-leaked) CETA text indicates a shift towards what they describe as the 'NAFTA' model).

[229] European Union (EU) Model BIT Clauses (2023). https://edit.wti.org/document/show/74fa928b-21bd-4ff6-b80d-e21dda7e13c7.

[230] Kriebaum (2014), p. 467.

[231] Lavranos (2013), p. 13.

their intentions of curbing investment protection in favour of regulatory sovereignty, this was likewise perceived as a waiver from their centuries-long anti-foreign investment position.[232] Taking note of the far-reaching economic, societal, and cultural consequences of investor-State disputes, this Chapter argues that substantive principles should be specified to the extent possible, with proper regulatory pathways secured.[233] However, while many states indeed find such broad formulations undesirable in light of the accumulating arbitral practice and their own experience (as respondents), it is important to point out that those states which see higher benefits in vague language rather than regulatory exceptions may, and will, nonetheless consider them.

4.3.2.2 The Police Powers Doctrine and Regulatory Carve-out in Arbitral Practice

Below is a selection of cases either employing some form of the police powers doctrine (without an explicit carve-out in the applicable IIA), or applying a direct regulatory carve-out in accordance with the provisions in an IIA. The cases below demonstrate how arbitral awards may choose to apply police powers doctrine to vague expropriation provisions, as well as how regulatory carve-out annexes and provisions allow for a more streamlined, less divergent approach as to how indirect expropriation is perceived. While police powers in general has broader temporal relevance, regulatory carve-outs in IIAs are relatively recent phenomenon, therefore it has limited, yet a growing and highly illustrative, adjudicatory implications.[234]

Methanex v. United States[235] is a classic and highly influential case, particularly for its elaborate evaluation of a general legislative measure and its interrelation with the foreign investment affected by its consequences. It also presents a remarkable example of discretionary (and broad) use of the police powers approach.

The dispute was between Methanex, a Canadian company and world's leading methanol producer; and the United States. It concerned a state-wide ban on MTBE in California, a substance used in unleaded gasoline for octane enhancement, of which methanol is a key component.[236] Methanex had argued that the ban was tantamount to an expropriation of the company's investment, therefore it constituted a

---

[232] Shan (2007); Cremades (2004).

[233] Perrone (2022), p. 839 ("When the laws of extractivism enter into tension with environmental protection or local rights, and states give in to the pressure of activists or local communities, ISDS becomes foreign investors' weapon of last resort.").

[234] At the time of the publication of this book, numerous arbitral awards analysing qualified expropriation provisions, have been rendered. Four cases filed by Canadian investors, three against Colombia and one against Peru respectively, are particularly noteworthy. They will be analysed below.

[235] *Methanex Corporation v. United States of America, UNCITRAL*, Final Award on Jurisdiction and Merits (3 August 2005) (*Methanex v. United States*).

[236] *Methanex v. United States* (2005), Part I, p. 2.

violation of NAFTA Article 1110. Curiously, Methanex, in its amended statement of claim, acknowledges from the outset that "international law does give some deference to a State's ability to carry out its regulatory powers"[237] and, instead, argues that the issue at hand was that the regulation was discriminatory. The United States, in response, argued that the ban had a public purpose and necessity due to its serious health risks, as it contaminated drinking water supplies.[238] It is noteworthy that the Respondent claimed that "[i]t is a principle of customary international law that, where economic injury results from a *bona fide* regulation within the police powers of a State, compensation is not required."[239] Methanex argued that the ban was in fact not necessary, since the contamination was not the producers' fault but was a result of several Californian and federal acts and laws. Further corruption allegations about the California Governor of the time, Gray Davis, were also part of Methanex's claims.[240]

The Tribunal, in its decision, stated the following:

> [...] as a matter of general international law, **a non-discriminatory regulation for a public purpose, which is enacted in accordance with due process and, which affects [...] a foreign investor or investment is not deemed expropriatory** and compensable unless specific commitments had been given by the regulating government to the then putative foreign investor contemplating investment that the government would refrain from such regulation.[241]

Accepting the Respondent's arguments, the Tribunal, on its own discretion, acknowledged the police powers of the state and carved it out of the scope of expropriation under Article 1110, where no such regulatory carve-out exists in writing. The language of the Tribunal is also notable in hindsight, as it is very similar to the current carve-out language adopted in newer generation IIAs.[242] Here, the Tribunal chose to exclude from the scope of expropriation the legitimate, non-discriminatory regulatory measures. This being said, the Tribunal foresaw an exception: this rule is applicable unless investors' legitimate, investor-backed expectations are invoked. One example given by the Tribunal is the case where the state specifically undertook the task of refraining from a particular regulation, yet nonetheless proceeds with it

---

[237] *Methanex v. United States*, Amended Statement of Claim (12 February 2001), p. 67.

[238] *Methanex v. United States,* Statement of Defence (9 August 2000), par. 152: "Moreover, the challenged actions were environmental measures taken to protect the public health by safeguarding the public's drinking water supply. Customary international law recognizes that, absent extraordinary circumstances, States are not liable to compensate aliens for economic loss incurred as a result of a nondiscriminatory action to protect public health. This rule of customary international law encompasses environmental measures, such as those at issue here, that are taken to protect the public health."

[239] *Methanex v. United States,* Amended Statement of Defense of Respondent United States of America (5 December 2003), par. 410. Compared to its initial position that CIL recognised the absence of liability in case of "nondiscriminatory action to protect public health", the United States appears to have broadened the scope of what it considers to be within the ambit of CIL.

[240] *Methanex v. United States* (2005), Part I, p. 4.

[241] *Methanex v. United States* (2005), Part IV, Chapter D, p. 4. Emphasis added.

[242] Annex 11-B(4)(b), Australia – US FTA (2005).

at the expense of the investor's legitimate expectations.[243] On the matter, the Tribunal cited two decisions, namely *Revere Copper & Brass, Inc. v. Overseas Private Investment Corporation*[244] and *Waste Management v. Mexico.*[245]

The Tribunal refused that such commitments and representations were given to Methanex, and underlined the fact that Methanex was well aware of the political and economic risks of investing in the US particularly with regards to future health and environment amendments to relevant legislation. It was also contended that Methanex did not enter the United States market "because of special representations made to it".[246]

"[T]he California ban was made for a public purpose," ruled the Tribunal, "[it] was non-discriminatory and was accomplished with due process. [...] From the standpoint of international law, the California ban was a lawful regulation and not an expropriation."[247] In addition to being one of the earlier examples of a clear-cut acknowledgement of the police powers doctrine, Methanex is also noteworthy with regard to its parties essentially agreeing that the police powers doctrine indeed existed in international law. This mutual contention may have also prompted the Tribunal to accept this doctrine, given its application does not appear to be contentious—albeit with differences in its scope.

The ***Saluka v. Czech Republic***[248] case included an expropriation claim, and the Claimant challenged the conduct of the Czech National Bank (CNB). The facts followed the privatisation of a number of state-owned commercial banks at the beginning of the 90s. One of these banks, IPB, was acquired by a UK subsidiary of a Japanese company called Nomura Europe. By late 90s, Czech government, in order to tackle several macroeconomic problems, provided aid to newly privatised banks. Initially IPB received little assistance, and was eventually completely excluded from the aid programme. This was followed by its forced administration, suspension of its shares and eventually the cancellation of its banking license.[249]

The case is significant particularly due to the Tribunal's analysis of the interrelation between the applied doctrine (police powers) and the substance of the applicable instrument. The Tribunal, through the Dutch – Czech Republic BIT,[250] applied

---

[243] *Methanex v. United States* (2005), Part IV, Chapter D, pp. 4–5.

[244] *Revere Copper and Brass Incorporated v. Overseas Private Investment Cooperation,* AAA Case No. 1610013776, Award (24 August 1978), par. 37. https://jusmundi.com/en/document/decision/en-revere-copper-and-brass-inc-v-overseas-private-investment-corporation-award-thursday-24th-august-1978/.

[245] *Waste Management v. Mexico* (2004). It should however be noted that this paragraph of the *Waste Management* award concerns the violation of the minimum standard of treatment, and not expropriation.

[246] *Methanex v. United States* (2005), Part IV, Chapter D, p. 5.

[247] *Methanex v. United States* (2005), Part IV, Chapter D, p. 5.

[248] *Saluka v. Czech Republic* (2006).

[249] *Saluka v. Czech Republic* (2006), par. 140 et seq.

[250] Czech Republic - Netherlands BIT (1991). As noted above, the Dutch BITs signed during the 90s typically include very broad provisions and do not contain any exception clauses, including on expropriation.

the police powers doctrine on its own initiative: "[i]t is now established in international law that [s]tates are not liable to pay compensation to a foreign investor when, in the normal exercise of their regulatory powers, they adopt in a non-discriminatory manner bona fide regulations that are aimed at the general welfare."[251] Despite this general rule, it was explicitly stated that the police powers principle was not absolute and in fact had certain limitations. *Bona fide* regulations, as well as other acts commonly accepted as within the police power of a state were counted among permitted acts.[252]

After citing the *Methanex* award with regards to the exclusion of *bona fide* regulatory measures from compensable acts, the Tribunal added:

> That being said, **international law has yet to identify** in a comprehensive and definitive fashion **precisely what regulations are considered 'permissible' and 'commonly accepted'** as falling within the police or regulatory power of [s]tates and, thus, non-compensable [...] **It thus inevitably falls to the adjudicator to determine whether particular conduct by a state 'crosses the line'** that separates valid regulatory activity from expropriation.[253]

With the permissibility of *bona fide* and non-discriminatory measures, the Tribunal eventually maintained the deprivation of the investment; however, it ultimately designated the measure to fall within the scope of permissible regulatory actions.

4.3.2.3 Case Law on New Expropriation Provisions with Regulatory Carve-outs

In light of the emergent regulatory carve-outs and detailed expropriation provisions included in new generation IIAs, it is important to examine some of the arbitral awards where these provisions are interpreted and applied. Below, I look at five arbitral cases: namely *Al Tamimi v. Oman,*[254] *RDC v. Guatemala*;[255] as well as four recent cases concerning environmental regulatory measures, challenged by

---

[251] *Saluka v. Czech Republic* (2006), par. 255.

[252] *Saluka v. Czech Republic* (2006), par. 260 and 262. The tribunal cited *Methanex v. United States* (2005); *Emmanuel Too* (1989); *S.D. Myers, Inc. v. Government of Canada,* UNCITRAL, Partial Award (13 November 2000) (*S.D. Myers v. Canada*); *Ronald S. Lauder v. The Czech Republic,* UNCITRAL, Final Award (3 September 2001) (*Lauder v. Czech Republic*); and *Tecmed v. Mexico* (2003).

[253] *Saluka v. Czech Republic* (2006), par. 263.

[254] *Adel A Hamadi Al Tamimi v. Sultanate of Oman*, ICSID Case No. ARB/11/33, Award (3 November 2015) (*Al Tamimi v. Oman*).

[255] *Railroad Development Corporation v. Republic of Guatemala*, ICSID Case No. ARB/07/23, Award (29 June 2012) (*RDC v. Guatemala*).

investors active in extractive industries: *Bear Creek v. Peru*,[256] *Eco Oro v. Colombia*,[257] *Red Eagle v. Colombia*,[258] and *Montauk v. Colombia*.[259]

Al Tamimi v. Oman concerns a case between Mr. Adel A Hamadi Al Tamimi, a US citizen and civil engineer, and the Sultanate of Oman.[260] The subject matter of the dispute is the development and operation of a limestone quarry in Mahda, Oman. Having established two companies in order to operate a quarry in the region, the Claimant entered into two separate lease agreements, subject to the claimant obtaining necessary permits and licenses in 2007. After obtaining the initial environmental permits and upon approval of the authorities, Mr. Al Tamimi's companies had begun operations. Following a plethora of allegations by the Omani government which included, *inter alia*, unauthorised use of equipment and excavation of material, operating outside the permit, as well as an alleged failure on the claimant's side to register one of his companies in accordance with the Omani laws, the lease agreements were deemed null and void. Subsequently, Mr. Al Tamimi was arrested in May 2009.[261] The claimant alleged that the Omani police had intervened repeatedly, seizing property and hindering the operations. Later that year, Mr. Al Tamimi was convicted by an Omani court on the counts of stealing sands and stones, and violating Omani environmental law by engaging in excessive operational activities at the quarry. His sentence of three-month imprisonment was later suspended.[262]

Article 10.6 of the US – Oman FTA, the applicable IIA to the dispute, identifies direct and indirect expropriation, and further notes the requirements for their lawfulness (public purpose, due process, compensation, and non-discrimination). It further points at Annex 10-B, which carves out non-discriminatory regulatory measures taken by its parties.[263] Pursuant to this Article and its Annex, Oman argued that "the application of existing environmental laws lies at the core of a State's police power, and that any application of those laws that leads to the loss of property constitutes a non-compensable regulatory action as opposed to a compensable taking."[264] It further contended that the actions of its police and prosecutors "were *bona fide* and taken for a legitimate purpose."[265] The Claimant, on the other hand, contested

[256] *Bear Creek Mining Corporation v. Republic of Peru*, ICSID Case No. ARB/14/21, Award (30 November 2017) (*Bear Creek v. Peru*).

[257] *Eco Oro Minerals Corp. v. Republic of Colombia*, ICSID Case No. ARB/16/41, Decision on Jurisdiction, Liability and Directions on Quantum (9 September 2021) and Award on Damages (15 July 2024) (*Eco Oro v. Colombia*).

[258] *Red Eagle Exploration Limited v. Republic of Colombia*, ICSID Case No. ARB/18/12, Award (28 February 2024) (*Red Eagle v. Colombia*).

[259] Montauk Metals Inc. (formerly known as Galway Gold Inc.) v. Republic of Colombia, ICSID Case No. ARB/18/13, Award (7 June 2024) (*Montauk v. Colombia*).

[260] *Al Tamimi v. Oman* (2015).

[261] *Al Tamimi v. Oman* (2015), par. 63.

[262] *Al Tamimi v. Oman* (2015), par. 78.

[263] Article 10.6 and Annex 10-B, Oman – US FTA (2009).

[264] *Al Tamimi v. Oman* (2015), par. 177.

[265] *Al Tamimi v. Oman* (2015), par. 178.

this position and argued that the measures could not be deemed within the scope of the Annex, as they "were not designed and applied for legitimate purposes and were discriminatory."[266] Given the language contained within the Annex and unlike the cases discussed above, the contention between the disputing parties was not about whether the police powers doctrine was applicable—this was already clear. The disagreement was on whether the actions in question were covered by the regulatory carve-out.

The Tribunal agreed with the police powers argument put forth by the Respondent, and acknowledged that upon the termination of the lease agreement, Mr. Al Tamimi had no right to remain at the quarry. In line with this contention, the Tribunal went on to note that the measures which had forced Mr. Al Tamimi's company to abandon the quarry site "[are] entirely consistent with [Oman]'s exercise of its police powers to act against those who by this time must in law have been trespassers."[267]

While a substantial portion of the Claimant's arguments have been dismissed either on jurisdictional grounds or because the challenged measures were not deemed to be attributable to Oman,[268] the impact of the explicit articulation of the police powers doctrine in the US – Oman FTA is visible when applied to the facts of the case. Ultimately, the Tribunal dismissed the entirety of the Claimant's expropriation claims, including those relating to police activities in the quarry and allegations of looting and vandalism, deeming presented evidence to be "insubstantial".[269]

Railroad Development Corporation (RDC) v. Guatemala is another tribunal which applied a qualified, annexed expropriation provision.[270] RDC, a railway investment company, had won the right to use the railroad infrastructure to provide railway services in Guatemala through FVG, its subsidiary. FVG and the state-owned Ferrocarriles de Guatemala (FEGUA) entered into a usufruct contract which consisted of a 50-year right to rebuild and operate the Guatemalan railway system.[271] The contract was ratified by the Guatemalan Congress, and it came into force in May 1998. An additional contract for the onerous usufruct of the FEGUA rail equipment was also signed in early 1999, which granted FVG "the use, enjoyment, repair and maintenance of railway equipment owned by FEGUA for the purposes of rendering railway transportation services."[272] It never went into force, and in 2003, another contract was signed which intended to replace the 1999 agreement.

After several operational activities, FVG brought two domestic arbitration cases against FEGUA alleging breach of contract due to, *inter alia*, non-payment. Shortly after, the Attorney-General issued an opinion, recommending Guatemala to declare the 2003 contract void, since the agreement was not executed "in due form and with

[266] *Al Tamimi v. Oman* (2015), par. 172.

[267] *Al Tamimi v. Oman* (2015), par. 372.

[268] *Al Tamimi v. Oman* (2015), par. 353–354.

[269] *Al Tamimi v. Oman* (2015), par. 373–374.

[270] *RDC v. Guatemala* (2012).

[271] *RDC v. Guatemala* (2012), par. 30 et seq.

[272] *RDC v. Guatemala* (2012), par. 32.

legal validity",[273] and that it was "not in the interest of the country."[274] Following the Attorney-General's opinion, FEGUA issued another opinion declaring that the 2003 agreement had not been reached following a public bid.[275] Although the parties had tried to find common ground, the talks were suspended, which eventually lead to the arbitral proceedings.

The applicable IIA is CAFTA-DR, and the relevant expropriation clause is Article 10.7 (along with Annex 10-C).[276] Just like the US – Oman FTA mentioned above, it is inspired by the 2012 Model US BIT and contains virtually the same provision on expropriation. In the award, the Tribunal succinctly explained the relevant method and the prescribed considerations for its expropriation analysis in the light of the guidance provided by the Annex as follows:

> The Tribunal will first consider Respondent's argument that Claimant cannot claim expropriation of usufruct rights that FVG does not own [due to the fact that the agreement was not in force]. It will then proceed to analyse **the nature** of the [Government's resolution that declared the usufruct to be injurious to the interests of Guatemala], **its public purpose**, whether the Government **interfered with reasonable investment backed expectations** and **their economic impact** on Claimant's investment.[277]

The Tribunal then engaged in a detailed analysis of the nature of the measure, and concluded that the declaration, *inter alia*, "leaves the rights of the parties unaffected".[278] On the purpose of the measure, the Tribunal examined the Claimant's assertion that the objective of the alleged expropriation was not the alleged injury of the usufruct to national interest, but rather to grant the right to a third party.[279] The Tribunal deemed the Claimant's evidence insufficient and rejected the argument that there was no public purpose.[280] As for the investment-backed legitimate expectations, the Tribunal highlighted the fact that

> [...] The Tribunal has not been given any explanation for the absence of ratification of [the 1999 contract] by the Respondent. Absent such an explanation, in its view, in a situation where three contracts are let that relate to the same operation, an investor who had won all three, two of which had been approved by the Respondent or its agencies, could reasonably expect that the third contract would also be ratified [...] This factual context shows that both parties moved to implement the rehabilitation of the railroad and restoration of service once the contracts were awarded and signed.[281]

---

[273] *RDC v. Guatemala* (2012), par. 35.

[274] *RDC v. Guatemala* (2012), par. 35.

[275] *RDC v. Guatemala* (2012), par. 35–37.

[276] Article 10.7 and Annex 10-C, CAFTA-DR (2009).

[277] *RDC v. Guatemala* (2012), par. 81. Emphasis added.

[278] *RDC v. Guatemala* (2012), par. 91.

[279] *RDC v. Guatemala* (2012), par. 93.

[280] *RDC v. Guatemala* (2012), p. 110.

[281] *RDC v. Guatemala* (2012), par. 120.

In light of these facts, the Tribunal concluded that "the expectation of Claimant to have a legally valid contract was not misplaced."[282]

The final examination concerned the economic impact of the measure—in other words, whether the effects of the measure reached a certain threshold that would render it expropriatory.[283] The Tribunal noted that, given the drop in the volume of freight carried by the railroad after the declaration, the refusal of suppliers to accept FVG credit, as well as the reluctance of customers entering into long-term arrangements with FVG, the effect of the declaration was "evident".[284] However, the Tribunal drew attention to the fact that the relevant question was whether the measure was expropriatory, i.e., whether the claimant was "deprived substantially of the use and benefits of the investment."[285] Since the Claimant continued its operations under the contracts for more than five years *after* the declaration, that the Claimant continued to receive rents in relation to its real estate rights, which constituted the substantial portion of FVG's revenue, the Tribunal rejected the expropriation claim, failing to find any substantial deprivation.

The *RDC v. Guatemala* award was one of the first examples of how the qualified expropriation provisions contained in newer IIAs are interpreted, and the argumentative sequence it prompted the Tribunal to follow is noteworthy. The Tribunal's analysis highlights the explicit elements of consideration that aim at guiding the arbitral discretion. The Annex and the clarifications contained therewith elevates and exposes the contours of the interpretative framework of the Tribunal. In other words, the Tribunal, instead of solely using its jurisprudential discretion to decide whether public purpose is relevant in determining the existence of an expropriatory act, instead directly proceeded with the 'checklist' of considerations put in place by the IIA parties. Likewise, it refers to the nature,[286] public purpose,[287] reasonable investment-backed expectations[288] (Annex 10-C (4)(a)(ii)), and the economic impact (Annex 10-C (4)(a)(i)) and analyses these elements in detail.[289] Whereas the first two elements capture the police powers considerations, the final element captures importance of the *effect* of the given measure—a key determinant of whether expropriation exists, regardless of the doctrine utilised to identify expropriation. Given the explicit reference to the public purpose and the nature (the text refers to *character*) of the measure on the one hand, and the economic impact on the other; it could be argued that the Annex prompts a relatively balanced consideration of the effects, as well as the intent and objectives of the challenged governmental act.

[282] *RDC v. Guatemala* (2012), p. 123.

[283] *RDC v. Guatemala* (2012), par. 124–152.

[284] *RDC v. Guatemala* (2012), par. 150.

[285] *RDC v. Guatemala* (2012), par. 150.

[286] Annex 10-C (4)(a)(iii), CAFTA-DR (2009).

[287] Annex 10-C (4)(b), CAFTA-DR (2009).

[288] Annex 10-C (4)(a)(ii), CAFTA-DR (2009).

[289] Annex 10-C (4)(a)(i), CAFTA-DR (2009).

More recently, four awards, all concerning mining operations and subsequent environmental regulations hindering their operations were rendered. All four cases were filed by Canadian mining companies against Latin American countries, and the two relevant FTAs (Canada – Peru FTA[290] and Canada – Colombia FTA[291]) contain similar, qualified expropriation provisions.

The first of these cases is ***Bear Creek v. Peru***.[292] It concerns the alleged violations against the legal and contractual rights of Bear Creek in relation to a silver mine. Bear Creek endeavoured to obtain mining exploration and operation licenses and submitted a series of mining petitions in the Puno region by the Peruvian-Bolivian border—at first, through a Peruvian employee, and then on its own behalf for the Santa Ana Mining Exploration Project.[293] Eventually in November 2007, the "Supreme Decree 083" was enacted, "declaring that the Santa Ana Project was a public necessity and authorizing Claimant to acquire, own, and operate the corresponding mining concessions and to exercise any rights derived from the ownership."[294] Bear Creek subsequently acquired title to the mining concessions over the Project and commenced exploration activities in the area amidst increasing public backlash from the communities in the area. From 2009 through 2011, Bear Creek conducted community building efforts to explain the local communities, including the Kelluyo and Ancomarca peoples, the benefits of the project, and subsequently presented an environmental and social impact assessment to the Peruvian government. In 2011, widespread protests against mining activities in the Puno region, reaching tens of thousands of people by May, resurfaced; resulting in lootings and severe unrest in the region.[295] While the Peruvian government initially pushed back against the protests, in June 2011, it adopted the Supreme Decree 032, revoking Supreme Decree 083 "and the Peruvian executive's finding of a public necessity, thereby eliminating the legal prerequisite for Claimant's ownership of mineral concessions in the border region."[296]

Bear Creek claimed that the Supreme Decree 032 constituted indirect expropriation, pursuant to the Annex 812.1 of the Canada – Peru FTA.[297] The Tribunal declared that the Decree constituted an indirect expropriation and that it was "so

---

[290] Canada – Peru FTA (2008).

[291] Canada – Colombia FTA (2008).

[292] *Bear Creek v. Peru* (2017).

[293] Pursuant to Article 71(2) of the Peruvian Constitution, "within a distance of fifty kilometers from the borders, foreigners may not acquire or possess under any title, directly or indirect, mines, lands, woods, water, fuel, or energy sources, whether individually or in partnership, under penalty of losing that so acquired right to the State. The sole exception involves cases of public need expressly determined by the executive decree and approved by the Cabinet, in accordance with the law." Peruvian Constitution (1993). https://www.constituteproject.org/constitution/Peru_2021.pdf?lang=en.

[294] *Bear Creek v. Peru* (2017), par. 149.

[295] *Bear Creek v. Peru* (2017), par. 189.

[296] *Bear Creek v. Peru* (2017), par. 202.

[297] Annex 812.1, Canada – Peru FTA (2009).

severe in light of its purpose that it cannot be reasonably viewed as having been adopted and applied in good faith"[298]

Article 812.1 of the FTA, as well as the aforementioned Annex 812.1, are expropriation provisions near-identical to the North American model outlined above. It prescribes the method of determination for an indirect expropriation, and first counts the economic impact of the measure as an important consideration, with the caveat that the "sole fact that a measure or series of measures of a Party has an adverse effect on the economic value of an investment does not establish that an indirect expropriation has occurred".[299] It then counts "distinct, reasonable investment-backed expectations", as well as the "character of the measure" to be taken into account.[300]

Annex 812.1(c) provides a typical regulatory carve-out clause, noting that

> Except in rare circumstances, such as when a measure or series of measures is so severe in the light of its purpose that it cannot be reasonably viewed as having been adopted and applied in good faith, non discriminatory measures of a Party that are designed and applied to protect legitimate public welfare objectives, such as health, safety and the environment, do not constitute indirect expropriation.[301]

The Tribunal applied the abovementioned three-factor test. Highlighting the fact that the Claimant was deprived "of all the major legal rights it had obtained and needed for the realization of its mining Project," it maintained that there was an obvious economic impact. Secondly, by way of relying on an express governmental authorisation under the Decree 083, Bear Creek was found to have distinct, reasonable expectations.[302] Finally, the Tribunal conducted an extensive analysis of the character of the measure, ultimately dismissing that the reasons given for the Decree 032, namely the involvement of a Peruvian citizen in the process of acquiring concessions, as well as "the purpose of safeguarding the environmental and social conditions", were not satisfactory.[303] Notably, the Tribunal allocated the responsibility of the alleged social unrest to the Respondent, noting that "[w]hile Claimant could have gone further in its outreach activities, the relevant question for the Tribunal is whether Respondent can claim that such further outreach was legally required and its absence caused or contributed to social unrest, so as to justify Supreme Decree 032."[304]

After examining the lawfulness elements (public purpose, due process, non-discrimination, and compensation), the Tribunal also contended that the indirect expropriation was unlawful.[305] Subsequently, the Tribunal tackled the question of

---

[298] *Bear Creek v. Peru* (2017), par. 341.

[299] Annex 812.1(b)(i), Canada – Peru FTA (2009).

[300] Annex 812.1(b)(ii) and (iii), Canada – Peru FTA (2009).

[301] Annex 812.1(c), Canada – Peru FTA (2009).

[302] *Bear Creek v. Peru* (2017), par. 375–376.

[303] *Bear Creek v. Peru* (2017), par. 414.

[304] *Bear Creek v. Peru* (2017), par. 408.

[305] *Bear Creek v. Peru* (2017), par. 449.

whether the police powers doctrine applied to the case. Curiously, despite the clear language of the Annex 812.1(c), the Claimant declared in its arguments that "the Tribunal must interpret and apply the FTA, which does not excuse expropriations resulting from the exercise of police powers."[306] Conflating the *existence* analysis with the *lawfulness* analysis with regard to expropriation, it instead harks back to the lawfulness criteria, noting that "regulatory actions are not excluded from the definition. Absent this express carve-out, the legality of Respondent's expropriation of Claimant's investment can only be assessed against these four elements."[307]

Even more curiously, Peru, in its lengthy assertion that the police powers doctrine applies to the Decree in question regardless of whether the treaty in question expressly so states, does not bring up the express carve-out under the Annex either. Instead, it points towards a myriad of case law, and the general exception clause under Article 2201(3)(a) of the FTA, which states that "nothing in this Agreement shall be construed to prevent a Party from adopting or enforcing measures necessary … to protect human, animal or plant life or health, which the Parties understand to include environmental measures necessary to protect human, animal or plant life or health".[308]

The Tribunal also takes note of the non-disputing party submission by Canada, which notes that "[a] State is not required to compensate an investment for any loss sustained by the imposition of a non-discriminatory, regulatory measure designed and applied to protect legitimate public welfare objectives."[309] Canada does not appear to have referred to the Annex 812.1(c) carve-out, either. In its reading of the non-disputing party submission, the Tribunal noted that "it does not disagree with this general evaluation, but considers that it must be taken in the context of the specific provisions provided in the FTA", all the while inexplicably ignoring the very specific provision regulating this precise situation. It ultimately confirms its finding that the Decree 032 constitutes unlawful expropriation.

The *Bear Creek* award is problematic on multiple levels. All parties and actors involved in the adjudication, including the Respondent and ultimately the Tribunal, disregard the express regulatory carve-out and refrain from building a police powers doctrine case around it. Despite the Tribunal's persistent emphasis on reading the case in line with the specific language of the FTA, ironically, no reference is made to the actual carve-out itself. While the Decree may have ultimately fallen short of satisfying the carve-out given the preceding analysis and the Tribunal's assertion that the public purpose of the Decree was not genuine, the abject disregard of the carve-out is nonetheless difficult to explain.

---

[306] *Bear Creek v. Peru* (2017), par. 452.

[307] *Bear Creek v. Peru* (2017), par. 452.

[308] Article 2201(3)(a), Canada – Peru FTA (2009).

[309] *Bear Creek v. Peru,* Submission of Canada Pursuant to Article 832 of the Canada – Peru Free Trade Agreement (9 June 2016), par. 5.

The ***Eco Oro v. Colombia*** award is another recent example,[310] and it includes a claim on indirect expropriation.[311] The applicable provisions are Article 811 and Annex 811 of the Canada – Colombia FTA,[312] which are virtually the same as the ones discussed under Canada – Peru FTA above. Eco Oro argued that Colombia had indirectly expropriated its investment under the concession contract in question, and that Eco Oro was deprived of the value, use and enjoyment of its rights.[313]

Eco Oro argued that the delimitation of the paramos was conducted in an arbitrary manner, and the lack of uncertainties in the legal regime prevented Eco Oro from conducting its mining activities.[314] In line with the Annex 811's language specifying the relevance of "the extent to which the measure or the series of measures interfere with distinct, reasonable investment-based expectations", Eco Oro argued that the measure was not adopted in good faith and frustrated the said expectations.[315] Pointing at the alleged arbitrariness and disproportionality in how the delimitation resolution was implemented, Eco Oro argued that the measure affected its own project, as it overlapped with a designated Transition Zone that was not even within the allegedly protected ecosystem.[316] Finally, Eco Oro argued that the measure was implemented in an opaque manner, given there were no scientific field studies confirming the appropriateness of the delimitation.

In February 2020, Canada filed a non-disputing party submission to the case—one that is much more detailed and expressly linked to the provisions of the FTA in question than the one submitted for the *Bear Creek* case.[317] It is clearly noted that "the police powers of the State are expressly reflected in Annex 811."[318] The Tribunal took note of this observation, and emphasised the intertwined relationship between the Annex 811.2(a) elements such as economic impact, investment-backed expectations, and the character of the measure; and subparagraph (b), where the regulatory carve-out is found.

Despite its finding that Eco Oro had suffered a complete deprivation of its potential right to exploit due to the measures in question, concluded that Colombia's actions *prima facie* amounted to expropriation, the Tribunal categorically applied the Annex 811(2)(b) against this preliminary finding. It noted that the measures were undertaken as a welfare measure for the protection of a valuable ecosystem, which are considered to be under threat from human interference and climate

[310] Facts of the case were provided in supra Chap. 3. *Eco Oro v. Colombia* (2021).

[311] Ünüvar (2023), p. 521.

[312] Canada – Colombia FTA (2008).

[313] *Eco Oro v. Colombia* (2021), par. 502.

[314] *Eco Oro v. Colombia* (2021), par. 529.

[315] *Eco Oro v. Colombia* (2021), par. 544.

[316] *Eco Oro v. Colombia* (2021), par. 570.

[317] *Eco Oro v. Colombia,* Non-Disputing Party Submission of Canada (27 February 2020).

[318] *Eco Oro v. Colombia* (2020), pp. 9 and 11: "a non-discriminatory measure that is designed and applied to protect legitimate public welfare objectives such as health, safety and the protection of the environment, does not constitute indirect expropriation, except in rare circumstances. This conclusion is set out in Annex 811.2(b) …".

change. Given their general application to all mining operators, it was found to be non-discriminatory.[319] The Tribunal, pointing out that the paramos are well-known to be in need of protection, Eco Oro, as a mining operator, ought to have known this. Despite certain shortcomings in its implementation, the Tribunal ultimately did not find any lack of good faith.[320]

Satisfied with the application of the regulatory carve-out found in the Annex, the Tribunal noted that despite the *prima facie* finding of deprivation, the challenged measures were not expropriatory, pursuant to Annex 811(2).[321]

The *Eco Oro* award is heavily criticised for its decision that the applicability of a general exceptions clause (in this case to an FET violation) does not prevent a state from having to compensate an investor.[322] However, its expropriation analysis is certainly a silver lining. It presents a clear example of how the expropriation annexes and regulatory carve-outs enshrining the police powers doctrine affect Tribunals' findings with regards to expropriation. The Tribunal is clear in its language that the measures have in fact, as far as their effects are concerned, reached a sufficient level of deprivation for a *prima facie* finding of expropriation. In reference to cases examined above, where unqualified expropriation provisions were applied and the effects were given primacy over regulatory prerogatives, many Tribunals had stopped their analyses. As such, the importance of such an express carve-out is difficult to overstate. The Tribunal, absent such regulatory carve-out, would have possibly ended its analysis and decided that in light of the complete deprivation suffered, the measures were expropriatory. This was not the case in Eco Oro, largely thanks to the Annex 811.

The ***Red Eagle v. Colombia*** award also warrants a brief mention.[323] The facts of the dispute are very similar to those of the Eco Oro case, as the dispute stems from the delimitation of the Santurbán páramo which also gave rise to the claim by Eco Oro. The applicable provision is likewise Article 811 and Annex 811 of the Canada – Colombia FTA, referred to above. Despite extensive party submissions by both disputing parties pertaining to the existence of an investment that is capable of being expropriated, on whether the measures allegedly deprived Red Eagle of its investment, and ultimately whether these measures were within the meaning of Article and Annex 811, the Tribunal dismissed the expropriation claim on the basis that Red Eagle had not obtained necessary environmental licenses to possess the right to carry out mining activities. However, the Tribunal, "for the sake of completeness", still notes that the measures "do fall within the scope of the Respondent's police powers. As can be seen from the extensive documentary evidence, [...] the

[319] *Eco Oro v. Colombia* (2021), par. 640–644.

[320] *Eco Oro v. Colombia* (2021), par. 678.

[321] *Eco Oro v. Colombia* (2021), par. 699.

[322] Ünüvar (2023), pp. 532–533.

[323] *Red Eagle v. Colombia* (2024).

measures were plainly designed and applied to protect the public policy goal of environmental protection."[324]

In addition to the *Eco Oro* and *Red Eagle* awards, another notable award, stemming from a case filed against Colombia by a Canadian mining company in relation to the *páramos* delimitation measures, is ***Montauk v. Colombia***.[325] Similar to the awards examined above, the Tribunal engaged in an analysis broken down in three parts, namely "the economic impact of the measures", "whether the measures interfered with the expectations of the Claimant", "and the legitimate exercise of Respondent's police powers".[326] As for the economic impact, the Tribunal noted that "the value was lost" after Colombia's measures came into force.[327] As for the legitimate expectations, the Tribunal observed that the "Claimant never received any 'clear and explicit representation' that the paramo delimitation would not overlap with the Concession area."[328] As for the police powers, the Tribunal clearly noted that "the measures issues by Respondent pursued the objective of protecting the environment."[329] Taking guidance from the language of the carve-out under Annex 811, which qualifies the carve-out so as to apply only when the measure in question is not "so severe in the light of its purpose that it cannot be reasonably viewed as having been adopted in good faith", the Tribunal adopts identical language to demonstrate that despite having severe consequences, the measures were nonetheless justified.[330]

The Tribunal finally decided that there was no expropriation:

> In consideration of the above, the Tribunal finds that there are no elements that could support an argument that the measures (Resolution 2090 and Judgment C-035) were adopted by Respondent in a manner other than in good faith, and in a non-discriminatory manner. They were designed and applied to protect the páramo ecosystems, which constitutes a legitimate public welfare objective. Thus, it cannot qualify as an indirect expropriation in the "rare circumstances" terms of Annex 811 of the FTA.[331]

Similar to the *Eco Oro* award, the Montauk Tribunal, despite its contention that the investment was devoid of its value, carved out the challenged measure from the scope of expropriation. This is arguably a direct consequence of the express carve-out, and the award lays forth a forceful example of the regulatory carve-out clause in action, in spite of the total destruction of an investment.

[324] *Red Eagle v. Colombia* (2024), par. 400.

[325] *Montauk v. Colombia* (2024).

[326] *Montauk v. Colombia* (2024), par. 762.

[327] *Montauk v. Colombia* (2024), par. 775.

[328] *Montauk v. Colombia* (2024), par. 780.

[329] *Montauk v. Colombia* (2024), par. 785.

[330] *Montauk v. Colombia* (2024), par. 795.

[331] *Montauk v. Colombia* (2024), par. 826; The Tribunal, in the subsequent paragraph 827, drew a parallel between the present award and the Eco Oro award rendered three years prior, noting that "these conclusions do not depart from the Eco Oro tribunal".

4.3.3 The Proportionality Margin

Beyond the distinct cases demonstrating various applications of the sole effects doctrine and the police powers doctrine (including regulatory carve-out), third quasi-category roughly covers the *proportionality margin*, according to which the above-analysed two ends are counter-weighed at varying degrees. In its core sits the proportionality analysis, a "judicial technique or analytical structure for adjudicating disputes concerning measures intruding on protected rights or interests but pursuing a public objective or communal aim."[332] This margin, *inter alia*, includes the so-called proportionality approach of the European Court of Human Rights (ECtHR),[333] but captures all awards attempting to balance, particularly in the absence of any guidance by the applicable IIA, the economic interests of the foreign investor on the one hand, and the regulatory prerogatives of states on the other. As will be demonstrated below, several arbitral tribunals conducted analogous analyses on how to balance the intent and the effects of a challenged measure or a sequence of measures with reference to ECtHR jurisprudence.[334]

This being said, any balancing effort, arguably including those which are conducted as a result of the language contained within the annexes mentioned above, could theoretically fall within this margin. This also includes some of the cases already examined above. Given the absence of a singular or analogous methodology adopted across different awards (perhaps with the exception of the ECtHR-inspired elaborations), it should not be understood as a stand-alone 'third' category in the sense that the doctrines above are understood.

The ***Tecmed v. Mexico***[335] award is arguably one of the most cited, and equally criticised, awards in the history of ISDS. The case is based on Tecmed's allegations that national authorities in Mexico did not renew the operation permit for a landfill under Tecmed's operation, and this absence of conduct amounted to a measure equivalent to expropriation.[336] Since the landfill activity is only possible under relevant permits, the refusal to renew such permit effectively disabled the investment.

"Without such permit," the Claimant argued, "the personal and real property had no individual or aggregate market value and that the existence of the Landfill as an ongoing business, as well as its value as such, were completely destroyed due to such [measure] which, in addition, ordered the closing of the Landfill."[337]

---

[332] Henckels (2012), p. 226.

[333] Ruoppo (2022), p. 348; Dupuy and Viñuales (2015), p. 1740.

[334] Henckels (2012), p. 226. Besides the ECtHR jurisprudence, an analogy can be drawn from the General Exceptions clause, Article XX of the GATT. In addition, Hirsch explains the possible 'reluctance' of investment tribunals to accord significant weight to human rights treaties with reference to 'a considerable sociocultural distance between these branches of international law'. See, Hirsch (2013), p. 104.

[335] *Tecmed v. Mexico* (2003).

[336] *Tecmed v. Mexico* (2003), par. 38–41.

[337] *Tecmed v. Mexico* (2003), par. 96.

Mexico claimed that a state "had the discretionary powers required to grant and deny permits, and that such issues, except in special cases, are exclusively governed by domestic and not international law."[338] The government refused the fact that the denial of the permit was arbitrary or discriminatory, and further objected to the assertion that it entailed a legislative change that "could have destroyed the *status quo*".[339] An argument based on the states' discretion within the context of the police powers doctrine was emphasised, given the landfill was within "the highly regulated and extremely sensitive framework of environmental protection and public health".[340]

Tecmed countered the Mexican argument, on the basis that the justifications specified by Mexico were "not proportional" to the denial of license.[341] This is backed by an audit report which states that "the infringements committed by the company involved are not sufficient to immediately cancel, suspend or revoke the permit for carrying out hazardous material and/or waste management activities, nor do they have an impact on public health or generate an ecological imbalance."[342]

The Spain – Mexico BIT of 1995[343] neither defines expropriation, nor indicates which measures or acts amount to indirect expropriation. With this in mind, the *Tecmed* tribunal's expropriation analysis is as follows.

The first point to consider was whether or not the measure radically deprived the investor of the economical use and enjoyment of its investments, similar to a situation in which such rights no longer exist. Deprivation is listed as "one of the main elements to distinguish [...] between a regulatory measure [...] and a *de facto* expropriation".[344] The Tribunal defined *de facto* expropriation as indirect state takings through acts and measures that adversely affect assets or rights of the investment to such an extent that they would be considered neutralised or destroyed—provided that the measure's consequences are permanent.

Concerning the government's motivation and pursued public purpose and the investor's suffered deprivation, The Tribunal stated that "[t]he government's intention is less important than the effects of the measures on the owner of the assets or on the benefits arising from such assets affected by the measures; and the form of the deprivation measure is less important than its actual effects."[345] In the absence of any guidance from the Spain – Mexico BIT itself, the Tribunal attempted to devise a method to distinguish compensable and non-compensable acts. Following the abovementioned sequencing of importance between economic deprivation and

[338] *Tecmed v. Mexico* (2003), par. 97.

[339] *Tecmed v. Mexico* (2003), par. 97.

[340] *Tecmed v. Mexico* (2003), par. 97.

[341] *Tecmed v. Mexico* (2003), par. 98.

[342] *Tecmed v. Mexico* (2003), par. 100 (citing PROFEPA's (Federal Attorney of Environmental Protection of Mexico) official communication).

[343] Mexico – Spain BIT (1995). This BIT has since been replaced by the Mexico – Spain BIT (2006).

[344] *Tecmed v. Mexico* (2003), par. 115.

[345] *Tecmed v. Mexico* (2003), par. 116; citing, *inter alia*, Tippetts (1984).

public intent echoing the effects doctrine the Tribunal nonetheless delved into the character of the measure. On the question whether or not regulatory measures are excluded from the scope of expropriation *per se*, the Tribunal reached to the conclusion that Article 5(1) of the BIT contains no clarification as to how expropriation is to be defined:

> After reading Article 5(1) of the [BIT] and interpreting its terms according to the ordinary meaning to be given to them (Article 31(1) of VCLT), we find no principle stating that **regulatory administrative actions are per se** excluded from the scope of the [BIT], even if they are beneficial to society as a whole – such as environmental protection -, particularly if the negative economic impact of such actions on the financial position of the investor is sufficient to neutralize in full the value, or economic or commercial use of its investment without receiving any compensation whatsoever.[346]

The Tribunal then proceeded to examine "whether such actions or measures are proportional to the public interest presumably protected thereby and to the protection legally granted to investments, taking into account that the significance of such impact has a key role upon deciding the proportionality."[347] The *Tecmed* tribunal cited several ECtHR cases,[348] particularly with regards to its inclusion of the proportionality analysis to the question whether expropriation existed in this case. Suggesting that the imposition of burden on foreign investors and nationals should be proportionate, the Tribunal further argued that foreign investors, who have limited or no political rights which eventually affect them, may benefit from a reasonably higher protection. On that point, the Tribunal cited the ECtHR case *James and Others*:[349]

> Not only must a measure depriving a person of his property pursue, on the facts as well as in principle, a legitimate aim "in the public interest", but there must also be a reasonable relationship of proportionality between the means employed and the aim sought to be realised [...] The requisite balance will not be found if the person concerned has had to bear "and individual and excessive burden" [...] The Court considers that a measure must be both appropriate for achieving its aim and not disproportionate thereto. [...][350]
>
> [...] non-nationals are more vulnerable to domestic legislation: unlike nationals, they will generally have played no part in the election or designation of its authors nor have been consulted on its adoption. Secondly, although a taking of property must always be effected in the public interest, different considerations may apply to nationals and non-nationals and there may well be legitimate reason for requiring nationals to bear a greater burden in the public interest than non-nationals.[351]

---

[346] *Tecmed v. Mexico* (*2003*), par. 121.

[347] *Tecmed v. Mexico* (2003), par. 122.

[348] *Mellacher and Others v. Austria,* 10522/83; 11011/84; 11070/84, Judgment (19 December 1989), 48, p. 24 (cited in par. 122); *Pressos Compania Naviera S.A. and Others v. Belgium,* 17849/91, Judgment (20 November 1995), 38, p. 19, (cited in par. 122).

[349] *James and Others v. United Kingdom,* 8793/79, Judgment (21 February 1986) cited in par 122).

[350] *James and Others v. United Kingdom* (1986), 50, pp. 19–20 (cited in par. 122).

[351] *James and Others v. United Kingdom* (1986), 63, p. 24 (cited in par. 122).

The reasons that eventually led to denial of the renewal of the license, as the Tribunal saw it, were "related to the social or political circumstances and the pressure exerted on municipal and state authorities [...]"—a reference to the community backlash and subsequent demonstrations and protests related to the landfill.

Ultimately, in the guidance of the prescribed proportionality test, the *Tecmed* tribunal had to tackle the question of whether or not such circumstances which caused the state to reject the renewal of the license were sufficient to justify such deprivation. The conclusion was that "there [is no] emergency, no serious social situation, nor any urgency related to such situations, in addition to the fact that the Mexican courts have not identified any crisis."[352] Even though the measures were to address socio-political concerns, the Tribunal contended that these problems posed no public hardship, or wide-ranging, serious consequences. Additionally, this socio-political pressure did not arise from Tecmed's misconduct—it related to the location of the landfill as determined by the state. Furthermore, the Tribunal remarked that the activities never compromised the ecological balance, as proven by a number of reports and audits on different periods. The Tribunal eventually reached to the conclusion that the denial amounted to indirect expropriation.

Despite its seemingly clear preference for the sole effects doctrine, Tecmed Tribunal's engagement with the nature of the measure, and particularly its examination of whether the means were proportionate to the ends, is noteworthy.

The ***Azurix v. Argentina***[353] award concerns the claim against Argentina of an American company undertaking potable water and sewerage services in Buenos Aires. The claimant argued that *inter alia* pursuant to the (unqualified) expropriation provision under the Argentina - US BIT,[354] the concession agreement which granted operational rights to Azurix was expropriated: "the [Buenos Aires] Province took away Azurix's rights under the tariff regime of the Concession [Agreement], compromised the ability of [Azurix's subsidiary] to obtain financing, saddled [the subsidiary] with unexpected expenses by not finishing the promised infrastructure".[355] The respondent argued that Azurix gradually violated the agreement and attempted to "renegotiate the Concession Agreement under more convenient terms to its own satisfaction and has failed to meet its obligations".[356]

The Respondent cited *Lauder v. Czech Republic* award, a decision often cited in support of the police powers doctrine, to emphasise that the "[d]etrimental effect on the economic value of property is not sufficient, Parties to the [BIT] are not liable for economic injury that is the consequence of bona fide regulation within the accepted police powers of the state."[357] The Respondent further relied on the

[352] *Tecmed v. Mexico* (2003), par. 147.

[353] *Azurix Corp. v. Argentina*, ICSID Case No. ARB/01/12, Award (14 July 2006) (*Azurix v. Argentina*).

[354] Argentina – US BIT (1991).

[355] *Azurix v. Argentina* (2006), par. 277.

[356] *Azurix v. Argentina* (2006), par. 278.

[357] *Azurix v. Argentina* (2006), par. 278; citing *Lauder v. Czech Republic* (2001), par. 198.

contention that "[a Tribunal] must look at the real interests involved and the purpose and effect of the government measure" as noted by the *S.D. Myers v. Canada* Tribunal.[358]

The Tribunal began its analysis by stating that "the BIT should not be interpreted in favour or against the investor. The BIT is an international treaty and should be interpreted in accordance with [...] [VCLT]", according to which a BIT should be "interpreted in good faith in accordance with the ordinary meaning to be given to the terms of the treaty in their context and in light of its object and purpose."[359]

The Tribunal's effect-intent analysis is noteworthy, particularly given the absence of any substantial internal interpretative guidance from the BIT itself as to how to balance the effects and the intent of an allegedly expropriatory measure. After noting that "governments take all sorts of measures that may affect the economic value of investments without such measures giving rise to a need to compensate", it disagreed with the *S.D. Myers* Tribunal's argument that the purpose of a regulatory measure is a sufficient determinant to distinguish measures according to which the state would be liable. However, it did not deem this analysis "wrong", but rather "insufficient"; citing Judge R. Higgins who asked: "Is not the State in both cases (that is, either by a taking for a public purpose, or by regulating) purporting to act in the common good?"[360]

After its contention that public purpose by itself may not be sufficient, the Tribunal contended that "additional elements" were needed. It went on to analyse the *Tecmed* tribunal's reference to *James and Others*,[361] which emphasised on the proportionality between a public purpose and the means employed to realise this purpose. It further noted that such proportionality would be deemed non-existent if the foreign individual was found to bear an "excessive burden".[362]

Finally, the Tribunal delved into the legitimate expectations analysis, and noted that it would determine whether such expectations were "in conflict with the normative system of the [Concession Agreement] and they have been frustrated to the extent of depriving the investor of the benefits of the investment".[363] It acknowledged the "unhelpful attitude" of the Argentine authorities, but concluded that

> the impact on the investment attributable to the [Buenos Aires] Province's actions was not to the extent required to find that [...] these actions amounted to an expropriation; Azurix did not lose the attributes of ownership, at all times continued to control [its subsidiary] and its ownership of 90% of the shares was unaffected. No doubt the management of [the subsidiary] was affected by the Province's actions, but not sufficiently for [expropriation].[364]

[358] *Azurix v. Argentina* (2006), par. 278; citing *S.D. Myers v. Canada* (2000), par. 285.

[359] Article 31(1), Vienna Convention (1969); cited in par. 307.

[360] *Azurix v. Argentina* (2006), par. 310.

[361] *James and Others v. United Kingdom* (1986).

[362] *Azurix v. Argentina* (2006), par. 311–312.

[363] *Azurix v. Argentina* (2006), par. 318.

[364] *Azurix v. Argentina* (2006), par. 321–322.

In short, the *Azurix* Tribunal interpreted the expropriation provision in the BIT as to require a consideration of both the effects, the public purpose; and the proportional relationship between the two. Ultimately, the decisive factor was that the damage had not reached the sufficient threshold for a measure to be deemed expropriatory. Its approach is nonetheless more nuanced than a straightforward effects doctrine - while it was cautious to grant the purpose of a measure the absolute power to absolve a state from potential liability, it clearly saw merit in contextualising any ascertainment of harm of the investor with the ability of states to be able to regulate without having to pay compensation.

The ***Yukos v. Russia*** cases,[365] which resulted in the highest arbitral award in history 50 Billion USD),[366] stand as a remarkable example with regards to the overall analysis of whether or not a state measure (or a series of measures) amounts to expropriation; particularly in terms of consequential severity of state measures ostensibly stemming from public interest. The arbitral cases were filed after a number of abusive and punitive measures by Russia, primarily due to alleged tax evasion tactics employed by Yukos. Yukos, fully privatised by 1996, became the biggest oil company in terms of daily crude oil production in Russia by 2002. To benefit from a tax reduction scheme in place at the time, the company relocated to other jurisdictions within the Russian Federation with lower tax rates. From July 2003 onwards, a series of criminal and civil proceedings were launched against the company officials and employees mostly on grounds of tax evasion. At the verge of its anticipated merger with another oil company, Sibneft, Yukos faced what it alleged to be politically and economically motivated harassment. It is also noted several times that some of the key figures of the company were known to be in close contact with the opposition party.[367]

Other alleged interventions included the auctioning off of one of the company's subsidiaries at a price dramatically lower than its actual market value; seizure of shares in subsidiaries; preventing the merger with Sibneft and "allowing Gazprom [the state-owned gas company] to acquire Sibneft instead"; freezing and seizing various assets of the company and preventing day-to-day management of the company. By the end of 2004, the projected merger was frustrated, and by August 2006,

[365] There are three cases submitted to PCA by three shareholders of Yukos against the Russian Federation: *Hulley Enterprises Limited (Cyprus) v. Russian Federation*, UNCITRAL, PCA Case No. AA 226, Final Award (18 July 2014) (*Yukos I*); *Yukos Universal Limited (Isle of Man) v. Russian Federation* UNCITRAL, PCA Case No. AA 227, Final Award (18 July 2014) (*Yukos II*); Veteran Petroleum Limited (Cyprus) v. Russian Federation, UNCITRAL, PCA Case No. 228, Final Award (18 July 2014) (*Yukos III*). *Yukos v. Russia* collectively refers to all three arbitral awards.

[366] Simkin S (2015) The Yukos Settlement: An Insider's View into the Largest Arbitration Award in History. https://hls.harvard.edu/today/the-yukos-settlement-an-insiders-view-into-the-largest-arbitration-award-in-history/#:~:text='97%2C%20head%20of%20international%20arbitration,Cooperative%20against%20the%20Russian%20Federation.

[367] *Yukos v. Russia* (2014); par. 73 (the three awards are virtually identical).

Yukos filed for bankruptcy. The *coup de grâce* was the liquidation of the company in 2007. The claimed reparation amounted approximately to 114 billion USD.[368]

The Tribunal conducted a two-tier examination of the challenged measures. First, the question of whether the measures amounted to expropriation was addressed. According to the claimant, the investment was completely taken from the investor by a series of acts, as illustrated above. Russia challenged the claims by asserting that the deprivation was not linked to acts attributable to the state, since the measures were related to tax collection—an undisputed power bestowed upon a state due to its sovereign position. Further, it was claimed that the company summoned the consequences upon itself by deciding "to siphon off billions of dollars" to further personal financial gains. The Tribunal eventually maintained that Yukos itself was doubtful of its *modus operandi*, however added the following:

> The Tribunal has not overlooked or discounted the [...] weaknesses in the contentions of Claimants. But are they sufficient to support what the Tribunal understands to be central contention of Respondent, namely, that Claimants should have expected that the Russian Federation would react as it did to what it claims were violations of Russian tax law and practice as its courts had interpreted that law and practice to be?[369]

The Tribunal, at this point, expressed that Yukos should or could have expected an adverse reaction from the Russian Federation; however, the intensity and severity of the reaction went far beyond what was anticipatable. According to the Tribunal - and even when Yukos' apparent perplexity regarding their activities in the low-tax regions is taken into account - the Russian reaction to the alleged tax evasion scheme had been so dire that it was simply impossible for Yukos officials to expect the utmost destruction of their investment and the eventual liquidation of the company.[370] The Tribunal was of the opinion that "the primary objective of the Russian Federation was not to collect taxes but rather to bankrupt Yukos and appropriate its valuable assets"—a clear indication that the state, by initiating this series of measures which eventually destroyed Yukos, did not have a genuine public purpose.

In this particular case, it is apparent that the Tribunal departed from the sole effects doctrine and mostly relied on some form of a proportionality analysis. If the Tribunal had applied the sole effects approach, it is safe to assume that there would be virtually no reason to continue the analysis by looking into the public intent in such a manifest example of absolute and permanent deprivation. By consequence, the *Yukos* tribunal attached equivalent, or at least comparable, degrees of importance to the severity of deprivation on the one hand (the effects of the measure), and the nature of the measure and the undergirding public purpose on the other; and in this particular case, it simply fails to find evidence to maintain that the latter in fact exists. Even though the Tribunal does not engage openly with the police powers doctrine, the foregoing analysis demonstrates a methodology that is strikingly similar to one that could be the case under an annexed expropriation provision, laying

[368] *Yukos v. Russia* (2014), par. 4.

[369] *Yukos v. Russia* (2014), par. 1577.

[370] *Ibid*, par. 1578.

out the effects and the nature of a measure to determine whether an act is expropriatory.

Generation Ukraine v. Ukraine[371] concerns allegations of state intervention and an alleged deprivation of a construction project in Kiev undertaken by Generation Ukraine. The claimant was a US corporate vehicle, and it contended that the interference by the state over the course of six years amounted to a measure tantamount to expropriation. The arbitral claim was submitted pursuant to the Ukraine – US BIT.[372]

According to the claimant, Kiev City State Administration (KCSA) failed "to produce revised land lease agreements with valid site drawings" at the early stages of the establishment of the investment. It was further claimed that the absence of the revised lease agreements and site drawings "created an insurmountable obstacle for any construction work to lawfully proceed."[373]

According to the Tribunal, at the time of submission of the dispute, "the Claimant had a very limited bundle of rights [...] Thus, if the [KCSA]'s omission [...] did not constitute an expropriation, it could only have deprived the Claimant of these legal interests and them alone."[374]

The Claimant's limited bundle of rights was mostly due to the fact that the transfer of the project had not taken place at the time of alleged expropriation. Additionally, the Tribunal considered the intent of the state act, stating that the measure "did not have the express intention of depriving the Claimant of the legal basis of this right to proceed to construction."[375]

The following paragraph, reflecting the perceived lack of clarity with regard to the scope of indirect expropriation in the early 2000s, expressed the need for clarity:

> [...] It would be useful if it were absolutely clear in advance whether particular events fall within the definition of an 'indirect' expropriation. It would enhance the sentiment of respect for legitimate expectations if it were perfectly obvious why [...] an arbitral tribunal found that a governmental action or inaction crossed the line that defines acts amount to an indirect expropriation. But there is no checklist, no mechanical test to achieve that purpose. The decisive considerations vary from case to case, depending not only on the specific facts of a grievance but also on the way the evidence is presented, and the legal bases pleaded. The outcome is a judgment, i.e. the product of discernment, and not the printout of a computer programme.[376]

In the absence of any interpretative guideline or any form of checklist according to which arbitral tribunals could pinpoint the acts that qualify as indirect expropriation, the *Generation Ukraine* tribunal prescribed how the tribunals decide on the matter and evaluate the data. The observations of the Tribunal are particularly

---

[371] *Generation Ukraine, Inc. v. Ukraine,* ICSID Case No. ARB/00/9, Award (16 September 2003) (*Generation Ukraine v. Ukraine*).

[372] Ukraine – US BIT (1994).

[373] *Generation Ukraine v. Ukraine* (2003), par. 20.6.

[374] *Generation Ukraine v. Ukraine* (2003), par. 20.8.

[375] *Generation Ukraine v. Ukraine* (2003), par. 20.28.

[376] *Generation Ukraine v. Ukraine* (2003), par. 20.29.

interesting in the light of the arbitral analyses examined above, pursuant to annexed expropriation provisions. Such clarifications may not be *absolutely* clear on which measures amount to expropriation, but they provide arbitral tribunals the necessary tools to identify the interests to be weighed against each other, as well as the relative weight these interests bear when compared to one another.

Returning to the award, the Tribunal elaborated on what, in its view, would *not* amount to indirect expropriation. First, the mere fact that an investment had become worthless does not necessarily mean that an expropriation occurred. The reasons and the nature of deprivation or neutralisation are also equally relevant to the consequences—investor protection agreements do not protect foreign investors from *business* risks.[377] Therefore, a "disappointed investor" pointing towards a government initiative that might have contributed to the adverse effects that the foreign investor had suffered will not be sufficient to successfully claim expropriation. IPAs and provisions primarily protect the investors against *political* risks and ideologically-motivated acts that have no legitimate or genuine public goal.

Seeking redress through local courts or authorities has been considered as an indication of showing efforts towards resolving the dispute, and it stands aside from the hard law requirement of exhaustion of local remedies. Judicial interaction between the foreign investor and the domestic courts or authorities was used to assess whether the investor had acted with good faith in order to save its investment from failure, neutralisation or destruction.[378] In the words of the Tribunal:

> [...] an international tribunal may deem that the failure to seek redress from national authorities disqualifies the international claim, not because there is a requirement of exhaustion of local remedies but because the very reality of conduct tantamount to expropriation is doubtful in the absence of a reasonable -not necessarily exhaustive- effort by the investor to obtain correction.[379]

The Tribunal eventually failed to find the element of attributability between the deprivation and a state act or a series of acts (by one or multiple state organs), even if it had been accepted that the rights claimed to have been expropriated had actually existed. The Tribunal, in its award, contended that the challenged act and its consequences "[do] not come close to creating a persistent or irreparable obstacle to the Claimant's use, enjoyment or disposal of its investment."[380] The fact that the Claimant had not sought redress through domestic channels had been underlined

---

[377] *Generation Ukraine v. Ukraine (2003)*, par. 20.30. *Emilio Augustin Maffezini v. The Kingdom of Spain*, ICSID Case No. ARB/97/7, Award (13 November 2000) (*Maffezini v. Spain*) is a particularly well-known case in this regard: "[...] the Tribunal must emphasize that [BITs] are not insurance policies against **bad business judgments**. While it is probably true that there were shortcomings in the policies [of the state], they cannot be deemed to relieve investors of the business risks inherent in any investment." (par. 64, emphasis added). For an earlier case reaching the same conclusion, see, *Robert Azinian, Kenneth Davitian & Ellen Baca v. The United Mexican States*, ICSID Case No. ARB(AF)/97/2, Award (1 November 1999) (*Azinian v. Mexico*).

[378] *Generation Ukraine v. Ukraine* (2003), par. 20.30.

[379] *Generation Ukraine v. Ukraine* (2003), par. 20.30.

[380] *Generation Ukraine v. Ukraine* (2003), par. 20.32.

and how such initiative would point towards a *bona fide* attempt to resolve the dispute had been acknowledged. The Tribunal went on to draw a parallel between the present case and the *Feldman v. Mexico* award,[381] in which four situations are considered to be out of the scope of the indirect expropriation analysis: (a) deprivation arising from *business problems per se*; (b) situations in which the state had *no particular obligation* to permit the kind of activity that was prohibited by a regulation; (c) situations in which the local (domestic) law had not created *the right to engage* in such activity; and (d) deprivation *not resulting in the loss of control* of the investment by the investor will not, under normal circumstances, amount to expropriation.[382]

The Tribunal also cited *Feldman* on failure to seek "formal, binding rulings" particularly with regards to claims related to tax issues. It should be once again noted that seeking redress in domestic courts might indicate good faith towards the resolution of arbitral disputes. Furthermore, it might be advantageous to foreign investors eventually seeking international redress through arbitral tribunals. Looking at a state's reaction towards a foreign investor initially seeking to resolve the dispute domestically will also provide additional data with regards to that state's intent concerning an expropriation claim.

Despite the relative clarity the newer annexed provisions may have provided in more recent case law, as the *Generation Ukraine* Tribunal accurately observed, there should be no illusions about the fact that each indirect expropriation analysis is a case-by-case scrutiny, often confined to the pleadings of the parties. The Tribunal's observations, in that regard, foreshadow cases such as *Bear Creek v. Peru*, where the parties inexplicably refrained from using tangible, directly applicable provisions, possibly prompting the Tribunals to disregard relevant legal instruments at hand. As such, no case and no analysis is independent from the specific facts undergirding them, and the manner in which legal arguments and the evidence have been presented. Today, this *ad hoc* nature of the indirect expropriation analysis is expressly included under many explanation annexes aimed at clarifying the scope of indirect expropriation.[383] *ADC v. Hungary*[384] concerns an alleged expropriation against the investments of two Cypriot companies, ADC Affiliate Ltd., and ADC & ADMC Management Ltd.

The Claimants were subsidiaries established in Hungary in order to realise an airport project in Budapest. To accommodate future passenger requirements, the Air Traffic and Airport Administration of Hungary (ATAA), a then-government agency, initiated a tender to renovate (and partially reconstruct) Terminal 2 of the Budapest

[381] *Marvin Roy Feldman Karpa v. United Mexican States*, ICSID Case No. ARB(AF)/99/1, Award (16 December 2002) (*Feldman v. Mexico*), par. 109 cited in *Generation Ukraine v. Ukraine* (2003), par. 20.34.

[382] *Feldman v. Mexico* (2002), par. 111; also citing *Azinian v. Mexico* (1999) (*supra* note 702).

[383] Colombia – US FTA (2012), under its Annex 10-B(3)(a), notes that "the determination of whether an action [...] constitutes an indirect expropriation requires a case-by-case, fact-based inquiry". As will be shown below, identical language exists across many new generation IIAs.

[384] *ADC v. Hungary* (2006).

Airport. ADC had been selected for the renovation and construction, and within a few years (1994 to 1998) the renovation was completed. Until late 2001, ADC had also operated the terminals—however, the operation was disrupted by a decree from the Hungarian Parliament. The eventual result was the takeover of all operation and management of the airport from the Claimant subsidiaries.[385]

The Tribunal confirmed that the taking constituted unlawful expropriation, as the actions of the state were not "merely an exercise of its right under international law to regulate its domestic economic and legal affairs."[386] It asserted that a sovereign state's "inherent right to regulate its domestic affairs" were not 'limitless'. Those limits to right to regulate were, according to the Tribunal, usually drawn by international treaties and the rule of law; and that the BIT upon which the claim is based served as a direct example to such limitation.[387]

On the issue of risk, the Tribunal pointed towards the crucial difference between (a) the inherent risk of operating in another country in accordance with domestic laws and regulations (economic or commercial risks), and (b) the subsequent political 'risk' of the arbitrary measures of a state.[388] Indeed, the Tribunal was of the opinion that it was unacceptable to claim that an investor should bear however the host state treats them—and that such an expectation would clearly contradict the very purpose of an IIA.[389] The Tribunal further asserted that the facts at hand pointed towards such a. It was impossible to miss expropriation in such a substantial taking with no real public purpose, contrary to what Hungary had claimed.

While the wording in Hungary – Cyprus BIT entailed the possibility of a broad interpretation disregarding public purpose vis-à-vis effects, the Tribunal took the public purpose into account to assess whether it balanced out the effects.[390] The Tribunal further rejected Hungary's assessment that the "deprivation" articulated under Article 4 of the BIT on expropriation should be interpreted in accordance with Hungarian domestic laws.

The Tribunal pointed out that Hungary had failed disclosing the genuine public purpose that was claimed to have been pursued. Only a vague "strategic interest of the state"[391] had been mentioned, but no elaboration on to what this referred was given. Therefore, the genuineness of public interest was speculative as far as the Tribunal was concerned.

Finally, ***Pope & Talbot Inc v. Canada***,[392] both in terms of its parties' arguments and the Tribunal's conclusions, is another popular arbitral award with notable impli-

[385] *ADC v. Hungary* (2006), par. 264–266.

[386] *ADC v. Hungary* (2006), par. 423.

[387] Cyprus – Hungary BIT (1989).

[388] *ADC v. Hungary* (2006), p. 424.

[389] *ADC v. Hungary* (2006), p. 424.

[390] Article 4, Cyprus – Hungary BIT (1989).

[391] *ADC v. Hungary* (2006), par. 431.

[392] *Pope & Talbot Inc. v. The Government of Canada,* UNCITRAL, Interim Award (26 June 2000) (*Pope & Talbot v. Canada*).

cations in light of the newer expropriation provisions. The case concerned a dispute between Pope & Talbot, an American softwood lumber company active in British Columbia; and Canada. The dispute arose after the allegations of Pope & Talbot with regards to Canada's implementation of the Softwood Lumber Agreement ("SLA"), a bilateral agreement between Canada and the United States, on the limitation of softwood lumber exports from British Columbia, Alberta, Ontario and Quebec. In brief, Canada was entitled to issuing licenses and collecting fees with regards to softwood lumber exports first manufactured in the above-mentioned Canadian states based on a number of fixed thresholds. The Claimant (which had remained below its allocated export quota for the relevant year), had claimed for a breach of Article 1110 of NAFTA.

According to the investor, Article 1110 on expropriation "provides the broadest protection for the investments of foreign investors who may suffer harm by being deprived of their fundamental investment rights."[393] It noted that the phrase "measure tantamount to expropriation" covers not only outright taking, but "*even non-discriminatory measures of general application* which have the effect of substantially interfering with the investments of investors of NAFTA Parties."[394]

Against these contentions, Canada argued that international law requires an "actual interference with fundamental ownership rights."[395] It emphasised on the degree of severity and asserted that "mere interference is not expropriation: rather, a significant degree of deprivation of fundamental rights of ownership is required."[396]

For the purposes of this Chapter, the disagreement over the meaning of the term "tantamount to expropriation", which essentially covers indirect expropriations, is highly relevant. Canada argued that the word 'tantamount' did not extend the meaning of expropriation. According to the Respondent, the challenged quota regime was "an exercise of regulatory power".[397] It furthered its argument by stating that in international law, states are not "required to compensate an investment for any loss sustained by the imposition of a non-discriminatory, regulatory measure" and that "liability is possible only if the measure is discriminatory."[398]

The Tribunal rejected the Claimant's argument that the word 'tantamount' extended the concept of expropriation. It noted that measures affecting property interests cannot be deemed compensable independent from the degree of severity they inflict upon investments. Furthermore, the Tribunal maintained that "creeping expropriation could be conducted by regulation, and a blanket exception for regulatory measures would create a gaping loophole in international protections against expropriation."[399]

---

[393] *Pope & Talbot* (2000), par. 83.
[394] *Pope & Talbot* (2000), par. 84.
[395] *Pope & Talbot* (2000), par. 88.
[396] *Pope & Talbot* (2000), par. 88.
[397] *Pope & Talbot* (2000), par. 90.
[398] *Pope & Talbot* (2000), par. 90.
[399] *Pope & Talbot* (2000), par. 99.

The Tribunal, therefore, rejected both assertions that (a) a governmental measure is expropriatory if it has *any* degree of impact on the investment, even if it is non-discriminatory (Claimant); and that (b) if such a measure is regulatory and non-discriminatory, it is excluded from the scope of Article 1110 (Respondent). It then moved on to assess the severity of the challenged measure, and noted the following:

> [...] the investor remains in control of the Investment, it directs day-to-day operations of the Investment, and no officers or employees of the Investment have been detained by virtue of the [quota regime]. Canada does not supervise the work [...], does not take any of the proceeds of company sales [...], does not interfere with management or shareholders' activities [...], does not interfere with the appointment of directors or management and does not take any other actions ousting the Investor from full ownership and control of the Investment.[400]

The Tribunal finalised its analysis by explicitly stating that the claimed "loss of profits" does not constitute a degree of interference so severe that the measure would amount to expropriation.

Despite being one of the earliest cases (award rendered in 2000) examined under this Chapter, the contemporaneity and persistent relevance of the analysis conducted by the Tribunal is noteworthy. It is also illustrative of the degree of clarity thus far reached with regard to the expropriatory takings doctrine in international investment law. As will be demonstrated per treaty below; the discussion relating to what kinds of measures would be excluded from the scope of expropriation provisions remains one of the most topical issues within the context of the new generation IIAs, and the arbitral awards rendered pursuant to some of the newer IIAs already reveal the direction the case law has taken since the days of the *Pope & Talbot*. Canadian position in *Pope & Talbot*, as well as a few other NAFTA disputes, played a pivotal role in the revision of expropriation provisions in Canadian, as well as American Model BITs. As noted above, since early 2000s, virtually all North American treaties have contained language that non-discriminatory measures are excluded from the scope of indirect expropriation. The presence of such annexes in new-wave IIAs is also a crucial detail.

While the claimant's position steers toward an absolute, if not archaic, form of the sole effects doctrine, whereby any interference, regardless of the severity of effects, would render a measure expropriatory; the Canadian position, which attempted to carve out all regulatory measures as long as they were non-discriminatory, were ultimately both rejected by the Tribunal. However, a more refined, further qualified version of this take on the police powers doctrine eventually found its way in the newer IIAsI will address below. It is important to emphasise that Canada, in fact, did not claim that *all* regulatory measures were excluded from the scope, akin to the aforementioned theoretical absolute regulatory carve-out this Chapter addressed earlier - but only the ones that are non-discriminatory. Admittedly, nothing in the relevant NAFTA provision excludes any regulatory measure, which in fact allowed the Tribunal to reject such contention by way of arbitral discretion. Still, reading the Canadian argument as to mean that all regulatory

[400] *Pope & Talbot* (2000), par. 100.

measures are excluded from the scope of Article 1110 would be stretching the meaning of the Canadian position. Likewise, virtually none of the above-mentioned annexed clarifications exclude regulatory measures *per se*, and therefore, the consequential effects of awards such as *Pope & Talbot* on future IIAs should be read carefully and with utmost regard to its nuances.

4.3.4 Final Remarks on the Doctrines and Case Law

The analysis above, following the traditional effect-intent scale often applied to expropriation claims, scrutinised a broad selection of arbitral awards, spanning more than forty years, in detail. In light of Van Harten's assertion that "[a]ny attempt to categorise adjudicative reasoning risks oversimplification",[401] one should accept that arbitral awards often fall somewhere in between the above-presented effect—intent spectrum. The outcome, therefore, is rarely black or white. Even where the effects prevail, they are usually not the exclusive consideration. An unsubstantiated claim of the police powers doctrine will usually fail even before a tribunal receptive of its application, despite the seemingly favourable language in an IIA. An arbitral tribunal expressly applying the effects doctrine will not always contend that the effects are severe enough to find expropriation.

This Chapter engaged in a case law analysis of arbitral tribunals address expropriation claims in light of unqualified, as well as latter, newer, qualified IIAs—and how they apply different doctrinal trends identified in scholarship. Two of the most prevalent doctrines are, as noted above, the (sole) effects doctrine and the police powers doctrine. First arbitral applications of the effects doctrine came under several IUSCT decisions such as *Tippetts*, which also set *de facto* precedent for many subsequent awards. Several other awards, such as *Sea-Land* and *Emmanuel Too*, stand outside this adjudicatory trend. This early acceptance of this doctrine, however, was not uncontroversial. Some scholars attempted to explain the prevalence of this doctrine within the context of IUSCT with reference to the Islamic Revolution, the unpredictable nature of its aftermath and the volatile political tensions which grappled the proceedings.[402]

As for the latter IIA practice, the overall analysis indicates that the application of the sole effects doctrine, while persisting to this day in some form and shape, is no longer the norm. The importance of the effects of a measure, however, is not only relevant, but crucial to finding indirect expropriation. The importance of the economic effects of a measure is expressly incorporated in newer generation IIAs, yet it is counterweighed by the nature of the measure in question. These considerations are typically joined by a regulatory carve-out, enshrining the police powers doctrine

---

[401] Van Harten (*supra* note 30), p. 121.

[402] Heiskanen (2007).

of states for measures that pursue a legitimate public interest and are non-discriminatory.

Ultimately, all cases examined above indicate that the effects, the nature, the scope, and the intent behind a measure; as well as the relationship among these elements are relevant to the indirect expropriation analysis, despite varying degrees of importance attached to them. Where the IIA provides further clarity as to how these considerations relate to one another, the analysis becomes markedly streamlined, as the cases stemming from the Canada – Colombia and Canada – Peru FTAs demonstrate.[403] However, these cases also show that newer generation IIAs are not a silver bullet against erroneous decisions, as *Bear Creek* case shows. These IIAs, as well as several others across the Atlantic Ocean, nonetheless adopt similar clarifications to avoid what they consider as volatile doctrinal oscillations in an effort to maintain consistency and coherence in arbitral decisions. They are directly taking their guidance from arbitral awards, and reacting to them in the form of newer models and blueprints to weed out undesirable outcomes.

I know turn to the new generation IIAs, with a particular focus on regional and plurilateral agreements, to project the conclusions distilled from the case law on the new provisions, and analyse their responsiveness to these emergent trends in treaty interpretation. Reference will also be made to bilateral and model BITs where relevant. The primary reason for this predominant focus on the plurilateral IIAs is their possible far-reaching and sweeping consequences for a multitude of states all at once—if ultimately accepted, the EU agreements examined below will cover all EU Member States. The same goes for plurilateral FTAs like CPTPP and RCEP, as they cover large portions of the world population and global capital flows with possible policy spill-overs into individual BITs of their signatories going forward.

4.4 Expropriation Provisions Under New Generation IIAs

Throughout the first decade of 2000s, only a handful of IIAs were not BITs. As of 2025, a number of comprehensive, plurilateral FTAs and IPAs containing detailed investment chapters are either being negotiated, or have successfully been concluded, especially in the last ten years.[404]

Below, I examine the expropriation provisions found in some of the most outstanding regional and plurilateral IIAs that have been negotiated during 2010s and 2020s so far. These include the new generation FTAs and IPAs negotiated by the EU, which have been referred to above in this Chapter; namely CETA[405] (with

[403] Andreotti (2025), p. 13.

[404] See, for instance, the collection of papers in Bjorklund, Andrea; Gelinas, Fabien; Gaffney, John P; Woss, Herfried (eds.) (2016) Comprehensive Economic and Trade Agreement between the European Union and Canada (CETA) Special Issue (TDM 1); Tung (2015), pp. 19–25.

[405] CETA (2017).

Canada), EUVIPA[406] (with Vietnam), EUSIPA[407] (with Singapore), EUMA[408] (with Mexico), and EUCAFA (with Chile).[409] In addition to these agreements, this Chapter will deepen its analysis with supplementary documents, including the Interpretation of the CETA Joint Committee released in February 2024,[410] providing further clarity for several provisions, including the one on indirect expropriation. For the sake of completeness, I also look at the EU negotiation draft for the TTIP, a failed trade and investment agreement between the EU and the United States. While this particular document has no legal relevance any longer, unlike the other documents referred to here, it contains the only model-like text that has been released unilaterally by the EU with regard to its investment protection policy in the context of its FTA/IIA negotiations. Finally, this section will examine the Annotations to the Model Clauses for Negotiation or Re-negotiation of Member States' Bilateral Investment Agreements with third countries (EU Model BIT), released in 2023.[411]

In addition to the EU agreements above, I look at other notable plurilateral agreements, namely CPTPP, which was adopted on the basis of the text of TPP;[412] as well as RCEP.[413] These two agreements stand as the two largest comprehensive IIAs currently in force, collectively covering nearly the entire Pacific Rim region. In particular, RCEP currently covers about one-third of the world population, and 30% of the global GDP—effectively making it the largest trade deal in history.[414] Despite its extensive reach in terms of key economies, RCEP currently does not include an ISDS mechanism, and its unclear whether or when it will adopt one.[415] The inclusion of its provisions in in this book is nonetheless justified, given the parties' in-build agenda under Article 10.18, which reads that "The Parties shall, without prejudice to their respective positions, enter into discussions on [...] the settlement of investment disputes between a Party and an investor of another Party".[416]

---

[406] EUVIPA (2019).

[407] EUSIPA (2018).

[408] EUMA (2018).

[409] EUCAFA (2023).

[410] CETA Joint Committee, Interpretation of the CETA Joint Committee (9 February 2024) (CETA Interpretative Note), p. 67.

[411] EU Model BIT (2023); Nacimiento P, Scharaw B, Lui J, European Commission Publishes Non-Paper of Model Clauses for Member States' Bilateral Investment Agreements with Third Countries (Kluwer Arbitration Blog, 19 February 2024). https://arbitrationblog.kluwerarbitration.com/2024/02/19/european-commission-publishes-non-paper-of-model-clauses-for-member-states-bilateral-investment-agreements-with-third-countries/.

[412] CPTPP (2018). This agreement is a sequel to TPP, which had been signed on 2016, but was shelved following the 2016 election of Donald Trump as the US President and the subsequent withdrawal of the United States. The remaining signatories revived the TPP text in 2017 under the name CPTPP. The provisions therefore remained the same.

[413] RCEP (2022).

[414] Whiting K, An expert explains: What is RCEP, the world's biggest trade deal? (*World Economic Forum*, 18 May 2021). https://www.weforum.org/stories/2021/05/rcep-world-biggest-trade-deal/.

[415] Lugg et al. (2024), p. 462.

[416] Article 10.18, RCEP (2022).

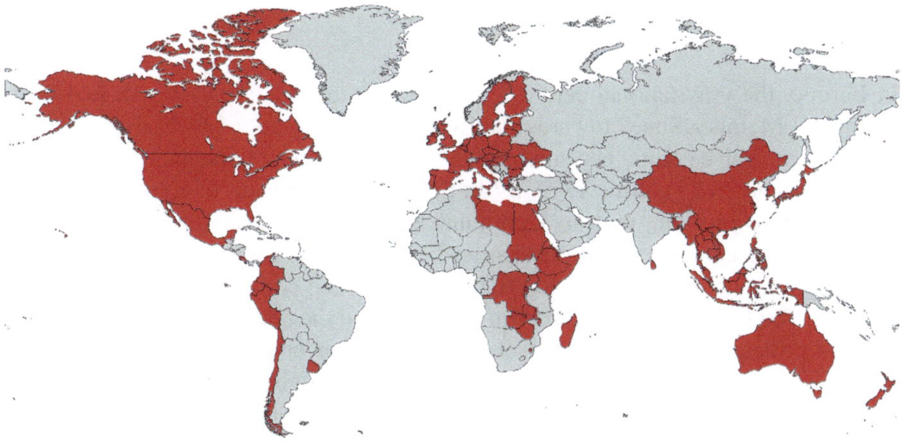

Fig. 4.1 Geographical coverage of the IIAs examined

The Chapter will also examine the expropriation provision under USMCA,[417] which replaced NAFTA as of 2020. As of 1 July 2023, USMCA is the only IIA among the three North American signatories which can form the basis of an ISDS claim, as NAFTA can no longer be used.[418]

Finally, the Chapter will examine the revised version of COMESAIA,[419] which was adopted by the COMESA Council of Ministers in 2017 in order to update the previous 2007 version which never came into force. After many years of stagnation, COMESA Member States reinitiated the process to "validate" the 2017 text and held talks in Cairo in late 2024.[420] In light of this development and its renewed relevance, this text must be revisited and analysed *vis-à-vis* other plurilateral IIAs.

The examination below covers IIAs that are signed by states in all six continents. The Fig. 4.1 gives an aggregate overview of a) the states that are parties to at least one of the abovementioned IIAs, b) the states that have made formal submissions to become a signatory to one of the abovementioned IIAs, and c) the states that expressed interest in joining one or more of the IIAs.

---

[417] USMCA (2020).

[418] Gore KN and Shirlow E (2023) Three Years and Three Decades On: Reflecting on the Final Sunset of NAFTA and USMCA's Sunrise (Kluwer Arbitration Blog, 1 July 2023). https://arbitrationblog.kluwerarbitration.com/2023/07/01/three-years-and-three-decades-on-reflecting-on-the-final-sunset-of-nafta-and-usmcas-sunrise/. Notably, as Canada opted out of the USMCA Chapter 14 on ISDS, Canadian investors can no longer bring ISDS claims against Mexico or the United States, and Mexican and American investors can no longer bring ISDS claims against Canada.

[419] Revised Common Market for Eastern and Southern Africa (COMESA) Investment Agreement (COMESAIA) (2017).

[420] Chibomba M, COMESA Common Investment Agreement set for Validation (COMESA, 29 September 2024). https://www.comesa.int/comesa-common-investment-agreement-set-for-validation/.

4.4.1 The EU IIAs

In Europe, the gravitational centre for investment and trade policies shifted from individual Member States towards the EU, when the Treaty of Lisbon granted the latter the exclusive competence on foreign direct investment pursuant to Article 3(1)(e) and Article 207(1) of the TFEU.[421] In line with this transfer of competences, the European Commission, with its Communication titled "Towards a comprehensive European international investment policy", set out its goals and elaborated on its future action plan with regards to establishing the said common investment policy early on. The Communication, *inter alia*, underlined the necessity to formulate substantive protection principles such as FET in a clear and tangible manner.[422] On several occasions, this goal has been reiterated at the highest level. For instance, in March 2015, the then-Trade Commissioner Cecilia Malmström remarked that "[b]y better defining and narrowing key concepts like 'fair and equitable treatment' and 'indirect expropriation', we are narrowing the scope for abuse. We gave governments, not arbitrators, ultimate control over interpretation of the rules."[423] The European Parliament similarly called for "clear definitions of investor protection standards in order to avoid such problems in the new investment agreements"[424] as early as 2011.

The following provisions reflect the recent iterations of these policy goals. Similar clarifications were also incorporated in the FET provisions, as will be shown in Chap. 5.

4.4.1.1 CETA

Article 8.12 of CETA concerns expropriation. The first paragraph notes that:

> A Party shall not nationalise or expropriate a covered investment either directly, or indirect through measures having an effect equivalent to nationalisation or expropriation [...], except
>
> (a) for a public purpose;
> (b) under due process of law;
> (c) in a non-discriminatory manner, and
> (d) on payment of prompt, adequate and effective compensation.

---

[421] Article 3(1)(e); 207(1), Treaty on the Functioning of the European Union (TFEU) (2009). http://eur-lex.europa.eu/legal-content/EN/TXT/?uri=celex%3A12012E%2FTXT.

[422] European Commission, Communication: Towards a comprehensive European international investment policy (COM (2010)343 (7 July 2010). https://eur-lex.europa.eu/legal-content/EN/ALL/?uri=celex%3A52010DC0343.

[423] Malmström, Cecilia; Discussion on Investment in TTIP at the meeting of the International Trade Committee of the European Parliament (Brussels, 18 March 2015). http://europa.eu/rapid/press-release_SPEECH-15-4624_en.htm.

[424] European Parliament, Resolution on the future European international investment policy (2010/2203(INI)) (6 April 2011). https://www.europarl.europa.eu/doceo/document/TA-7-2011-0141_EN.html.

> For greater certainty, this paragraph shall be interpreted in accordance with Annex 8-A.[425]

The referenced Annex 8-A is as follows:

> The Parties confirm their shared understanding that:
>
> 1. Expropriation may be direct or indirect:
>   (a) direct expropriation occurs when an investment is nationalised or otherwise directly expropriated through formal transfer of title or outright seizure; and
>   (b) indirect expropriation occurs if **a measure or series of measures** of a Party has an effect equivalent to direct expropriation, in that **it substantially deprives the investor of the fundamental attributes of property in its investment, including the right to use, enjoy and dispose of its investment, without formal transfer of title or outright seizure**.
> 2. The determination of whether a measure or series of measures of a Party, in a specific fact situation, constitutes an indirect expropriation **requires a case-by-case, fact-based inquiry** that takes into consideration, among other factors:
>   (a) **the economic impact** of the measure or series of measures, although the sole fact that a measure or series of measures of a Party has an adverse effect on the economic value of an investment does not establish that an indirect expropriation has occurred;
>   (b) **the duration** of the measure or series of measures of a Party;
>   (c) the extent to which the measure or series of measures interferes with **distinct, reasonable investment-backed expectations**; and
>   (d) **the character** of the measure or series of measures, notably their **object, context and intent**.
> 3. For greater certainty, except in the rare circumstance when **the impact of a measure or series of measures is so severe in light of its purpose that it appears manifestly excessive, non-discriminatory measures** of a Party that are designed and applied to protect **legitimate public welfare objectives**, such as health, safety and the environment, do not constitute indirect expropriations.[426]

CETA's final and official text was published in January 2017 at the Official Journal of the EU. Its expropriation provision largely reflects the model adopted by Canada by in its Model FIPAs since 2004,[427] albeit with certain modifications. Whereas the 2004 Canada Model FIPA does not contain express language relating to direct expropriation, CETA's Annex 8-A begins by additionally clarifying what direct expropriation means (Annex 8-A, 1(a)).[428] The elaboration on indirect expropriation (8-A, 1(b)) notes that the measure can be either *a* measure, or *a series of* measures, capturing both single act expropriations and creeping expropriations comprised of a number of measures collectively amounting to expropriation. *Yukos* cases, examined above,[429] pose an accurate example as to the kinds of series of measures this phrase could capture.

---

[425] Article 8.12, CETA (2018).

[426] Annex 8-A, CETA (2017).

[427] Kriebaum (2022), p. 336.

[428] Article 9, Canada Model FIPA (2021), unlike its predecessor, notes that "A direct expropriation under paragraph 1 occurs only when a covered investment is taken by a Party through formal transfer of title or outright seizure." This aligns with the CETA text, which predates the 2021 Model.

[429] *Yukos v. Russia* (2014).

In addition to the measure, the Annex hints at the degree of severity required for a measure or series of measures to amount to expropriation. In reference to another fervently scrutinised issue in expropriation case law, the Annex asks nothing short of substantial deprivation of the fundamental attributes of property, such as using, enjoying, and disposing of the investment. This is in line with the degree of severity generally required in arbitral jurisprudence examined above, regardless of the doctrine or approach adopted by arbitral tribunals. As shown, substantive deprivation has been one of the prevalent and uncontroversial requirements of arbitral reasoning, and its explicit inclusion in the treaty text is therefore unsurprising. What amounts to 'severe', however, notwithstanding the clarifications contained in the provision, is left to the arbitral discretion and requires case-by-case and fact-based analysis. As the cases analysed above indicate, however, it can be said that the degree of deprivation should either be total, or in such a way that the investment can no longer be used or controlled. Cancellation or refusal of mining concessions under the Colombian cases (applying a qualified expropriation provision under the Canada – Colombia FTA very similar to the one in CETA)[430] examined above are relevant here.

The following paragraph concerns the elements to be taken into account while determining whether a measure or a series of measures amounts to indirect expropriation. These considerations are the *economic impact*, the *duration*, and the *character of the measure*; as well as *distinct, reasonable investment-backed expectations*. Three of these elements, namely economic impact, character, and investment-backed expectations have been briefly explained above in the context of the case law examined under this Chapter. They are also included in the 2004 and 2019 Model FIPAs, as well as the 2012 US Model BIT. The duration element, which is added to the CETA text, is absent in the 2004 Canada and 2012 US Models; but was added to the 2021 Canada Model FIPA. It captures temporal features in the *Tippetts* tribunal's reasoning, which noted that the deprivation should not be "merely ephemeral". There is a long string of arbitral awards emphasising this feature.[431]

Sub-paragraph (d) elaborates on what is meant by the 'character' of a measure, by additionally counting object, context, and intent as its 'notable' components. Such elaboration is absent in 2004 and 2021 Canadian FIPAs, as well as the 2012 US Model BIT.

This expatiation had attracted some criticism. Kriebaum called the reference to the 'intent' of the measure "highly problematic", because "to insist on a manifestation of the intention to expropriate on the part of the host State would impose a virtually impossible burden of proof on the investor who would have to demonstrate the motivations behind government action."[432]

---

430 *Eco Oro v. Colombia* (2021); *Red Eagle v. Colombia* (2024); *Montauk v. Colombia* (2024).

431 *Tippetts* (1984); *Wena Hotels Ltd. v. Arab Republic of Egypt*, ICSID Case No. ARB/98/4, Award (8 December 2000); S.D. Myers v. Canada (2000); *LG&E Energy Corp., LG&E Capital Corp., and LG&E International, Inc. v. Argentina*, ICSID Case No. ARB/02/1, Award (25 July 2007).

432 Kriebaum (2014), p. 465.

There are several ways to determine the role of the content, and by extension the *intent*, of a measure. The provision above points out that a tribunal, while conducting case-by-case, fact-based inquiry in order to determine whether indirect expropriation exists, is to take into consideration, *inter alia*, the intent of the challenged measure. This rule prompts several possibilities as to what it means. Kriebaum's reading of the provision, which contends that an investor would have to demonstrate the intention of a host state to expropriate, comprises but one aspect of the broader reading of the same provision. Indeed, a broader reading of the provision could capture intent as an integral part of the balancing analysis implied under the second and the third paragraphs of the Annex. Both collectively and individually, all other elements such as economic impact, duration, and whether or not investor had legitimate expectations, have indicative functions. As pointed out above, there is a difference between looking into whether the government intended to expropriate, and the more general inquiry of what the intent of a measure was, i.e., whether it was for a public goal. Kriebaum's criticism seems to be based on the assumption that the provision entails the former scenario, largely disregarding the broader role of the intent of a measure might have in the analysis prescribed by the Annex.[433] A claimant investor, therefore, may also succeed in a hypothetical claim by asserting that the 'intent' of the measure was not to enact a genuine public purpose, subject to additional requirements referred to above, such as substantial deprivation.[434] Therefore, it can also mean that the investor does not necessarily have to prove that the 'intent' of the measure was to expropriate.

This observation is supported by the last paragraph of the Annex, which includes a carve-out for non-discriminatory measures that are designed and applied to protect legitimate public welfare objectives. When read in conjunction with this paragraph, while considering the economic impact, the duration, object, context, intent of the measure; as well as the extent to which the challenged measure interferes with legitimate expectations, arbitral tribunals are expected to reach to a conclusion on whether this measure has a legitimate public purpose, is excessive and severe *vis-à-vis* its intended purpose. Consideration of intent, in this sense, can benefit a claimant investor in claiming that a measure, claimed to bear a public purpose, is severe and excessive in realising these objectives. Conversely, such consideration can benefit a respondent state by allowing them to argue against indirect expropriation by pointing towards the said government's intention to pursue a public good objective and a proportionate means to achieve this objective. This approach, broader than limiting the arbitral consideration of intent to the question of whether a government intended to expropriate, reflects the arbitral jurisprudence more accurately.[435]

---

[433] Admittedly, the Annex does not clarify in what way the 'intent' would be taken into account while conducting an indirect expropriation analysis.

[434] Annex 8-A (*supra* note 732).

[435] See, for instance, *Montauk v. Colombia* (2024); *Eco Oro v. Colombia* (2021); *ADC v. Hungary* (2006), par. 431; *Metalclad v. Mexico* (2000), par. 108.

The last paragraph of the Annex varies slightly from the 2004 Canadian Model FIPA. Whereas the Annex refers to "manifestly excessive" measures, the 2004 FIPA concerns measures "that […] cannot be reasonably viewed as having been adopted and applied in good faith".[436] While it would be speculative at best to contend what the distinct interpretative difference would be between the two provisions, it is safe to argue that both prompt an implied analysis which is aimed at balancing out the effects of the measure with its intent and means, supplemented by the preceding paragraph. The phrase 'except in rare circumstances' may have a signalling effect: Treaty-makers clearly intended to limit this exceptional situation. In connection, it could be read as guidance to adjudicators with regard to the extent of deference to be accorded to national authorities while assessing excessiveness of a measure *vis-à-vis* its purpose.[437] The determination of a measure being excessive in this regard, then, should only be in 'rare circumstances'.[438] In its 2021 Model FIPA, Canada does not refer to these 'rare circumstances'. Instead, it directly states that "[a] non-discriminatory measure of a Party that is adopted and maintained in good faith to protect legitimate public welfare objectives, such as health, safety and the environment, does not constitute indirect expropriation, even if it has an effect equivalent to direct expropriation."[439] The emphasis on the effects at the end of the provision is also noteworthy.

It should be noted that the CETA text, as well as the 2004 and 2021 Canadian Model FIPAs, differ from the 2012 Model US BIT in terms of the scope of the carve-out. Whereas the 2012 US Model BIT includes a carve-out for "non-discriminatory regulatory actions"; the CETA Annex, the 2004 FIPA, and the 2021 FIPA do not include the word 'regulatory'. It is not clear whether this omission would make any difference in practice, but it is certainly conceivable that the addition of the term 'regulatory' could be argued to limit the scope of the carve-out only to regulatory measures and not, for instance, specific, targeted, administrative measures that go beyond what could be deemed a *bona fide* regulation (such as laws interfering with the investment) in nature.

Previous drafts and negotiation documents of the provision reveal that the expropriation provision had been a point of contention. Bernasconi-Osterwalder's May 2013 analysis of the (non-public) February 2013 Draft Investment Chapter reveals a fundamental divide between the negotiating parties with regards to the construction of the Annex.[440] While Canada's initial proposal was identical to its 2004 Model FIPA, the EU has brought a draft which significantly altered the language of the Annex. The differences are particularly strong in the third paragraph on the carve-out.

---

436 Annex B.13(1), Canada Model BIT (2004).

437 *S.D. Myers v. Canada* (2000). Also see generally, on the issue of deference to states' decision-making authority in international adjudication, Fahner (2022); Shirlow (2021); Shirlow (2014).

438 The implications of this designation leaves the standard applicable to any proportionality analysis unclear. See, Teo et al. (2024), pp. 550–551.

439 Article 9(3), 2021 Canada Model FIPA.

440 Bernasconi-Osterwalder (2013).

First of all, the EU proposal as of February 2013 included three considerations for the determination of whether indirect expropriation occurred: (a) the economic impact, (b) the extent to which the government action interferes with the possibility to own, use or dispose of the property, and (c) the duration of the of the action (or series of actions). In this version, the EU proposal excluded legitimate expectations and the character of the measure as elements of consideration.[441]

Another noteworthy difference between the current text and the EU proposal as of 2013 is the third paragraph of the Annex. The EU proposal, in that regard, read that:

> Subject to the **principle of proportionality**, non-discriminatory measures of general application taken by a Party that are designed to protect legitimate public policy objectives do not constitute indirect expropriation if they are necessary and are applied in such a way that they genuinely meet the public policy objectives for which they are designed.[442]

The EU proposal explicitly refers to the principle of proportionality, as opposed to the implied language of the final text and the Canadian proposal. This language very strongly emphasises on the fact that the tribunals need to balance out the impact and the (public) purpose of a challenged measure. Such strong language, which explicitly prompts a proportionality test to be exercised by the adjudicator has been criticised on the grounds that "it carries the great risk that the analysis by tribunals will not be sufficiently deferential to the democratic and legitimate decisions by state authorities".[443] While this observation has merit, it is not entirely clear how, in practice, the difference between an explicit reference to the proportionality principle, and the language which excludes "measure or series of measures [...] so severe in light of its purpose that it appears manifestly excessive" from the scope of the carve-out would play out. This being said, it could be argued that the CETA parties aimed at retaining a higher threshold by indicating that such situations are "rare" (as opposed to the all-capturing reference to the principle of proportionality in the EU proposal), which may function as a policy signal to adjudicators that they ought to maintain that the challenged measure is not merely 'excessive', but 'manifestly excessive' *vis-à-vis* its purpose. The EU proposal could therefore allow for broader adjudicatory discretion and less deference to states' sovereign prerogatives. The final text of CETA can nonetheless is a balanced effort by the treaty parties to ensure the protection of foreign investors, while drawing the contours of the sovereign's regulatory powers which, in the light of the case law above, is in need of clarification and clear delimitation.

The EU proposal also refers to non-discriminatory measures of *general* application, which would have been markedly similar to the abovementioned position retained in the 2004 Canadian FIPA. Additionally, the EU proposal makes a reference to 'necessity' - a highly controversial concept in international investment law and dispute settlement, and particularly with regard to several arbitral cases in the

[441] CETA Draft (7 February 2013), cited at Bernasconi-Osterwalder (2013), pp. 20–24.

[442] Bernasconi-Osterwalder (2013), p. 22.

[443] Bernasconi-Osterwalder (2013), p. 23.

aftermath of the Argentine crisis, whether or not the governmental measures against the crisis were 'necessary' stirred an immense debate in academia.[444] I will address this concept in Chap. 5.

On 9 February 2024, the CETA Joint Committee, composed of representatives from Canada and the EU, released a note on "Interpretation of the CETA Joint Committee" document, providing further interpretative guidance on, inter alia, Article 8.10 of CETA.[445] According to this note, "an indirect expropriation may only occur if the investor has been radically deprived of the use, enjoyment and disposal of its investment, as if the rights related thereto had ceased to exist."[446] The note also gives further guidance on the temporal aspects of an expropriatory measure: "consideration should be given to whether the interference with the property right is temporary, in which case it is unlikely to amount to an indirect expropriation, or permanent, although the sole fact that a measure is permanent does not establish that an indirect expropriation has occurred."[447]

The note also provides further specifications as what can be considered as "distinct, reasonable investment-backed expectations" pursuant to paragraph (2)(c) of the Annex. It notes that such expectations are those that "a prudent and informed investor could have reasonably formed and that were relied upon in the making of the investment."[448] The note further links the reasonableness of these expectations to factors such as whether the investor was provided "binding written assurances" ,"the nature and extent of governmental regulation" or "the potential for government regulation in the relevant sector."[449]

The note also elaborates on the term "measures of a Party that are designated and applied to protect legitimate public welfare objectives" referred to in paragraph 3 of Annex 8-A, clearly articulating policy considerations such as "measures taken to combat climate change or to address its present or future consequences." It is further noted that these measures will not constitute indirect expropriation, subject to them not being obviously excessive in light of the intended policy objectives.[450] This specification is particularly noteworthy in light of international commitments to combat climate change, such as the Paris Agreement,[451] and its much needed and imminent implementation in national contexts. Finally, in connection with the term "manifestly excessive" under paragraph 3 of the Annex, the note adds that this should be understood as "clearly and obviously excessive". However, the distinction between measures that are clearly, obviously, or manifestly excessive is unclear, as they have similar meanings.

---

[444] Alvarez and Khamsi (2009); Stone Sweet (2010); Reinisch (2011); Martinez (2012).

[445] CETA Interpretative Note (2024).

[446] CETA Interpretative Note (2024), p. 67.

[447] CETA Interpretative Note (2024), p. 67.

[448] CETA Interpretative Note (2024), p. 68.

[449] CETA Interpretative Note (2024), p. 68.

[450] Opinion 2/15 of the Court of Justice of the European Union (16 May 2017), ECLI:EU:C:2017:376, par. 293.

[451] Paris Agreement (2015). https://unfccc.int/sites/default/files/english_paris_agreement.pdf.

4.4.1.2 EU – Singapore IPA (EUSIPA)

The negotiations for the initial version of EUSFTA, which had included an investment protection chapter, were concluded in October 2014. The first EU FTA to rely on the so-called common commercial policy in the post-Lisbon Treaty era, the inclusion of this investment protection chapter soon prompted the question of whether the EU could conclude an FTA encompassing direct and indirect investment, as well as an ISDS mechanism.[452] With its Opinion 2/15, the Court of Justice of the EU decided that the ISDS mechanism fell "within a competence shared between the European Union and the Member States."[453] The Court, while acknowledging that foreign direct investment fell within the common commercial policy of the EU, "non-direct foreign investment" would not.[454]

This finding ultimately resulted in the investment protection provisions of the EUSFTA to be separated. These provisions eventually culminated into the present EUSIPA. EUSIPA was subsequently signed on 19 October 2018. Given the mixity in competence, unlike the EUSFTA (which entered into force in November 2019 following the EU ratification procedure), it will enter into force once it is ratified by all EU Member States. The same observations also apply to the EUVIPA below.

The relevant provision under EUSIPA 2.6, entitled "Expropriation". This article is joined by, inter alia, Annex 1, which is very similar to the Annex under CETA except for two notable differences. First of all, the EUSIPA does not expressly include 'duration' as an element of consideration, unlike CETA. The other difference is that, whereas the CETA text reads "the extent to which the measure or series of measures interferes with *distinct, reasonable investment-backed expectations*", EUSIPA reformulates the element of 'extent' as follows: "the extent to which the measure or series of measures interferes with *the possibility to use, enjoy or dispose of the property*".[455] Legitimate (or reasonable, investment-backed) expectations, therefore, are not explicitly included in indirect expropriation analysis as far as EUSIPA is concerned.

Similar to the CETA text, EUSIPA refers to 'measures', and not 'regulatory measures'.

4.4.1.3 EU – Vietnam IPA (EUVIPA)

EUVIPA was signed on 30 June 2019.[456] Similar to EUSIPA, EUVIPA was initially negotiated under the EU – Vietnam FTA (EUVFTA), but the agreement was subsequently divided due to competence issues explained above. Similar to EUSIPA,

[452] Montanaro and Paulini (2018); Leys (2015), p. 267.

[453] Opinion 2/15 of the Court of Justice of the European Union (16 May 2017), ECLI:EU:C:2017:376, par. 20.

[454] Opinion 2/15, par. 109–110.

[455] Annex 1 on Expropriation, EUSIPA (2018). Emphasis added.

[456] EUVIPA (2019).

EUVIPA also has to be ratified by each EU Member State to enter into force. As of October 2023, 16 Member States had reportedly done so.[457] Its Article 2.7 contains an expropriation provision which identically compares to CETA's and EUSFTA's expropriation clauses. Pursuant to Article 2.7(4), the article is to be interpreted in accordance with Annex 4.[458]

Annex 4 counts the economic impact, the duration, and the character of the measure and entirely omits the paragraph referring to the 'extent' of the measure, which is attached to reasonable investment-backed expectations (CETA) or the possibility to use, enjoy or dispose of the property (EUSIPA) under the agreements examined above.[459]

4.4.1.4 EU – Mexico Agreement (EUMA)

The texts of the trade agreement in principle between the EU and Mexico were published on 21 April 2018. As of 2025, they remain up-to-date, but they may undergo further modifications.

The relevant provisions under EUMA are Article 18, entitled "Expropriation and Compensation", and Annex I on Expropriation.[460] While generally similar to the abovementioned agreements, the Annex contains more examples as to what constitutes legitimate public policy objectives, namely "the protection of public health, social services, public education, safety, and the environment, or public morals, social or consumer protection, privacy and data protection, or the promotion and protection of cultural diversity".[461]

4.4.1.5 EU – Chile Advanced Framework Agreement (EUCAFA)

EUCAFA, together with an Interim Trade Agreement (ITA), will modernise the EU – Chile Association Agreement (EUCAA), which is in force since 2003.[462] Both ITA and EUCAFA were signed on 13 December 2023. The ITA will enter into force when Chile deposits its instrument of ratification, as the EU ratification process was completed. EUCAFA, similar to EUSIPA and EUVIPA, will have to be ratified by each EU Member State.

---

[457] EUVIPA, Legislative Train Schedule (European Parliament), https://www.europarl.europa.eu/legislative-train/theme-international-trade-inta/file-eu-vietnam-ipa.

[458] Article 2.7(4), EUVIPA (2019).

[459] Annex 4, EUVIPA (2019). Although the 'the possibility to use, enjoy or dispose of the property' is referred to within the context of the severity of a measure in the first paragraph.

[460] Article 18(1), EUMA (2018).

[461] Annex I(3), EUMA (2018).

[462] EU – Chile Association Agreement (EUCAA) (2003).

EUCAFA contains an expropriation provision under its Article 10.17.[463] It refers to an unnumbered Annex X entitled "Expropriation". The Annex shares many features with the other annexes above. Its paragraph 2 counts the economic impact, the duration, and the character of the measure identical to EUVIPA. Its paragraph 3, which contains the regulatory carve-out, is identical to EUMA with its articulated examples.

4.4.1.6 TTIP EU Negotiation Text

The only publicly available primary material on the failed TTIP negotiations (*inter alia*, on investment) is the EU negotiation text of November 2015.[464] The TTIP negotiations were indefinitely shelved following the first term election of Donald Trump as the President of the United States in late 2016. While these texts do not include any input from the United States, they nonetheless remain to be important reference points particularly to better understand the EU's position, not only in the context of the TTIP itself, but all current and future EU IIAs.

The proposal's Article 5 is titled 'Expropriation'.[465] Following the same method, it refers to an Annex I, on expropriation.[466] The Annex I is similar to the examples examined above, but shares a striking resemblance to EUVIPA and the most recent IIA, namely EUCAFA.

One notable difference is that whereas the TTIP text includes the phrase "except in the rare circumstance" in reference to manifestly excessive measures,[467] this designation is omitted in both EUVIPA and EUCAFA. The provisions are otherwise virtually identical.

4.4.1.7 EU Model Clauses (EU Model BIT)

In September 2023, the European Commission published a Non-Paper entitled "Annotations to the Model Clauses for negotiation or re-negotiation of Member States' Bilateral Investment Agreements with third countries".[468] These clauses are intended to guide the Member States in their IIA (re)negotiations with non-EU countries, and to ensure that these bilateral negotiations are conducted with internal consistency within the EU.

---

[463] Article 10.17, EUCAFA (2023).

[464] TTIP text (2015). https://policy.trade.ec.europa.eu/eu-trade-relationships-country-and-region/countries-and-regions/united-states/eu-negotiating-texts-ttip_en.

[465] Article 5, TTIP text (2015).

[466] Annex I on Expropriation, TTIP text (2015).

[467] Annex I(3) on Expropriation, TTIP text (2015).

[468] EU Model BIT (2023). The Non-Paper was re-released, *verbatim*, on 31 January 2024, with minor formatting corrections. As of January 2025, the document is available via the following link: https://circabc.europa.eu/ui/group/be8b568f-73f3-409c-b4a4-30acfcec5283/library/9a3525b5-a8cb-47e7-a96a-fe1e7d378809/details?download=true. See, for a review of the Model Clauses, Mavromati and Schubert (2024).

Perhaps expectedly by this point, the provision on Expropriation is similar to those examined above. It is likewise accompanies by an Annex. Both provisions are annotated and contain explanatory commentaries.

The provisions in the Model Clauses themselves, unilateral by their nature, share a striking resemblance to the TTIP negotiation texts examined above, despite having nearly ten years in between their publication dates (late 2023 and late 2015, respectively). The Model Clauses and the TTIP texts represent two temporal checkpoints of the EU investment policy, and two points of reference to observe if, and how, these provisions might have evolved. As for their expropriation provisions, the resemblance is striking.[469]

Both texts omit the reference to 'distinct, reasonable investment-backed expectations'. This overlap strengthens the presumption that the EU does not view the inclusion of legitimate expectations favourable in its IIAs. Juxtaposed with the absence of this proviso in the initial proposal of the EU in the aforementioned February 2013 draft of CETA, it can reasonably be surmised that it was subsequently proposed by Canada.

The regulatory carve-out clause under the expropriation annex is very similar to its counterparts in EUMA and EUCAFA, in addition to its similarity to the TTIP text. The Model Clause embraces the 'the rare circumstance' version of the carve-out clause, which is absent in EUMA and EUCAFA but exists under the TTIP text. Under the commentary for the annex, it is noted that:

> Paragraph 3 reflects the police powers doctrine which is a manifestation of the State's right to regulate. It is a fundamental principle of international law that regulatory activity aimed at achieving legitimate public welfare objectives is not compensable. It is only when the measures are manifestly excessive in light of their objective that a finding of indirect expropriation can be made.[470]

Put together, the abovementioned IIA texts, negotiation documents, as well as the Model Clauses reveal that the EU investment policy on expropriation has mostly stayed the same since at least early 2010s, save for its somewhat expanded regulatory carve-out clause enriched with additional, articulated policy areas. TTIP text counts, for example, public health, safety, environment or public morals, social and consumer protection or promotion and protection of cultural diversity. The Model Clause expands this non-exhaustive list by adding climate change, privacy and data protection as additional examples. While these enumerated policy domains do not limit the adjudicators as to what constitutes a legitimate public goal, it is important that they reflect the topical, imminent and critical policy frameworks as expressly as possible.[471]

---

[469] Article 5 and Annex I of the TTIP text (2015); and the Article and Annex on Expropriation, EU Model BIT (2023), pp. 11–12 and 32–33.

[470] EU Model BIT (2023), p. 33.

[471] The EU Member States are already adhering to these Model Clauses. See, for instance, a series of recent BITs signed by Hungary: Article 6, Hungary – Turkmenistan BIT (2023); Hungary – Oman BIT (2022); Article 7, Hungary – UAE BIT (2021); Hungary – Iran BIT (2017). As per the UNCTAD IIA Database, Hungary signed 8 such BITs, as of September 2024. The last BIT containing an unqualified expropriation provision appears to be the Hungary – Tajikistan BIT (2017).

4.4.2 CPTPP

TPP had been planned as a comprehensive trade deal with 12 parties, including the United States, Japan, Singapore, Mexico, and Canada.[472] Similar to TTIP, following Donald Trump's first term election as President in late 2016, the United States withdrew from TPP, preventing its entry into force. The remaining parties subsequently decided to revive the agreement, and incorporated, by reference, the provisions previously agreed. As such, CPTPP itself is a brief incorporation agreement, and the TPP text itself remains relevant and applicable. The agreement is in force since 30 December 2018.

The relevant provision is Article 9.8, entitled 'Expropriation and Compensation'. The title, through a footnote, refers the reader to an Annex. The first paragraph of the Article, which counts 'public purpose' as an element of lawfulness like the majority of IIAs, contains an additional footnote which reads as follows: "For greater certainty, for the purposes of this Article, the term "public purpose" refers to a concept in [CIL]. Domestic law may express this or a similar concept by using different terms, such as 'public necessity', 'public interest', or 'public use'."[473] It is not entirely clear what is meant by 'a concept of CIL', and how this information may serve as a clarification for adjudicators.

The referenced Annex, namely Annex 9-B, begins by the following paragraph, which does not exist in the EU FTAs above: "An action or a series of actions by a Party cannot constitute an expropriation unless it interferes with a tangible or intangible property right or property interest in an investment."[474] This paragraph, as well as the rest of the Annex, uses the word 'action' instead of 'measure', the word of choice for the EU IIAs. Likewise, the 2012 Model US BIT prefers the word 'action' to 'measure'.

Overall, the contents of the Annex are comparable to that of the CETA and other IIAs above. The elements of consideration include the economic impact, the extent "to which the government action interferes with distinct, reasonable investment-backed expectations", and the character of the government action. A footnote accompanies the phrase "distinct, reasonable investment-backed expectations"; which notes the following:

> For greater certainty, whether an investor's investment-backed expectations are reasonable depends, to the extent relevant, on factors such as whether the **government provided the investor with binding written assurances** and the nature and extent of governmental regulation or the potential for government regulation in the relevant sector.[475]

---

[472] CPTPP (2018). https://www.international.gc.ca/trade-commerce/trade-agreements-accords-commerciaux/agr-acc/cptpp-ptpgp/text-texte/index.aspx?lang=eng. Its parties, as of January 2025, are as follows: Australia, Brunei, Canada, Chile, Japan, Malaysia, Mexico, New Zealand, Peru, Singapore, and Vietnam.

[473] Article 9.8, CPTPP (2018).

[474] Annex 9-B (1), CPTPP (2018).

[475] Annex 9-B, CPTPP (2018).

While the CETA Interpretative Note mentioned above clarifies that distinct, reasonable investment-back expectations may be evidenced by, *inter alia*, written assurances, CPTPP elaborates on the concept within its text. The footnote included in Annex 9-B on the one hand, and the relevant paragraph under the CETA Interpretative Note on the other, are ultimately near-identical.

This clarification found in both CETA and CPTPP also has notable similarities with the expropriation Annex in the ASEAN Comprehensive Investment Agreement (ASEANIA),[476] which refers, besides the economic impact and the character of a measure, to "whether government action breaches the government's prior binding written commitment to the investor whether by contract, licence or other legal document"[477] for the determination of whether a measure amounts to indirect expropriation.

4.4.3 Regional Comprehensive Economic Partnership (RCEP)

RCEP entered into force on 1 January 2022 for its ten original signatories, namely Australia, Brunei, Cambodia, China, Japan, Laos, New Zealand, Singapore, Thailand, and Vietnam.[478]

Its expropriation provision, Article 10.13, refers to Annex 10B. Under its third paragraph, the annex counts the economic impact and the character of the government action, echoing the IIAs examined above. RCEP Annex 10B and the aforementioned ASEANIA contain identical provisions on the relevance of binding written commitments.[479] With respect to 'the character of the government action, including its objective and context', a rather uncommon footnote specifies what that context cook look like for a single signatory, namely Korea:

> For Korea, a relevant consideration could include whether the investor bears a disproportionate burden, such as a special sacrifice that exceeds what the investor or investment should be expected to endure for the public interest.[480]

The regulatory carve-out clause under paragraph 4 notably counts 'real estate price stabilisation' as a legitimate public welfare objective.[481]

---

[476] ASEANIA (2009).

[477] Annex 2, ASEANIA (2009).

[478] Australian Government, Department of Foreign Affairs and Trade, Regional Comprehensive Economic Partnership Agreement (RCEP). https://www.dfat.gov.au/trade/agreements/in-force/rcep.

[479] Annex 10(B)(3)(b), RCEP (2020): "whether the government action breaches the government's prior binding written commitment to the investor, whether by contract, licence, or other legal document".

[480] Annex 10B, RCEP (2020).

[481] Annex 10(B)(4).

4.4.4 USMCA

USMCA is the successor of NAFTA, and contains a Chapter 14 which regulates investment protection. Canada opted-out from this chapter, therefore Canadian investors no longer have the right to resort to arbitration against the United States and Mexico. Similarly, treaty-based arbitral claims cannot be brought against Canada pursuant to USMCA. Article 14.8 and Annex 14-B contain provisions that are identical to their counterparts in the 2012 Model US BIT.[482] The only difference is a footnote added to Annex 14-B(ii), which reads "the extent to which the government action interferes with distinct, reasonable investment-backed expectations". The footnote clarifies, with a language identical to CPTPP and CETA Interpretative Note, that

> whether an investor's investment-backed expectations are reasonable depends, to the extent relevant, on factors such as whether the government provided the investor with binding written assurances and the nature and extent of governmental regulation or the potential for government regulation in the relevant sector.[483]

4.4.5 Revised Investment Agreement for the COMESA Common Investment Area (2017 COMESAIA)

The earlier, 2007 version of the COMESAIA regulated expropriation under its Article 20. Its first paragraph counted public interest, non-discrimination, due process of law, and 'prompt and adequate' compensation as its lawfulness criteria.[484] Under its paragraph 7, it noted that "[a] measure of general application shall not be considered an expropriation of a debt security or loan covered by the Agreement solely on the ground that the measure imposes costs on the debtor that cause it to default on the debt."[485] This paragraph captures a unique provision, whereby the Agreement covered a specific general measure, and situation whereby a foreign investor defaults on its acquired debt and this amount is subsequently repossessed.

Its paragraph 8 is a regulatory carve-out provision. While it generally resembles the ones examined thus far in this Chapter, it contains noteworthy features. It reads that "[c]onsistent with the right of states to regulate and the customary international law principles on police powers, bona fide regulatory measures taken by a Member State that are designed and applied to protect or enhance legitimate public welfare

---

[482] Article 14.8 and Annex 14-B, USMCA (2020); Article 6 and Annex B, Model US BIT (2012).

[483] Annex 14-B, USMCA (2020).

[484] Article 20, Investment Agreement for the COMESA Common Investment Area (2007) (2007 COMESAIA).

[485] Article 20(7), 2007 COMESAIA.

objectives, such as public health, safety and the environment, shall not constitute an indirect expropriation under this Article."[486]

The express recognition of the police powers doctrine as CIL in the text of the agreement itself attracts immediate attention. As discussed above, whether or not the police powers doctrine is or should be accepted as a CIL (or a general international law) rule remains debated.[487] However, its inclusion in the text of a prospective agreement may further augment its perception as such by those who interpret IIAs. Take, for instance, the *Philip Morris v. Uruguay* award[488] mentioned in Chap. 3, which also illustrates an explicit recognition and application of the police powers doctrine to the case at hand. The Tribunal engaged in a detailed analysis of the police powers doctrine and its status within international law.[489] In addition to showing evidence from the 1961 Harvard Draft Convention,[490] as well as the abovementioned Third Restatement of 1987[491] and the 2004 OECD Report;[492] the award notably inferred support from the subsequent inclusion of the principle in CETA and EUSIPA (then cited as EUSFTA).[493] Such express recognition can therefore cumulatively affect and strengthen the overall perception and acknowledgment of the police powers doctrine as part of international law by way of this express language in future IIAs.

Turning now to the revised 2017 COMESAIA text, one is confronted by several important changes. First of all, the new Article 20 omits non-discrimination as a lawfulness criterion.[494] It retains the provision on loan repossession, under Article 20(8) (previously Article 20(7)). The new regulatory carve-out provision, now under paragraph 8, notably omits the phrase "[c]onsistent with the right of states to regulate and the customary international law principles on police powers" but expressly adds "awards by judicial bodies of a Member State" to the scope of the carve-out.[495]

An entirely new addition to the 2017 text is paragraph 10, which contains a clause on the factors to be taken into account while determining whether indirect expropriation occurred. This provision largely echoes what has been laid forth above, in particular the Annex 10B of RCEP, and contains comparable language to the expropriation annexes. For example, paragraph 10(a)(ii) notes that indirect

[486] Article 20(8), 2007 COMESA Agreement.

[487] Titi (2018).

[488] *Philip Morris Brands Sàrl, Philip Morris Products S.A. and Abal Hermanos S.A. v. Oriental Republic of Uruguay*, ICSID Case No. ARB/10/7, Award (8 July 2016) (*Philip Morris v. Uruguay*).

[489] *Philip Morris v. Uruguay* (2006), par. 291 et seq.

[490] The Draft Convention on the International Responsibility of States for Injuries to Aliens (1961) (the Harvard Draft Convention).

[491] Third Restatement of 1987, par. 712.

[492] OECD (2004), p. 5.

[493] *Philip Morris v. Uruguay* (2006), par. 300–301.

[494] Article 20(1), 2017 COMESAIA.

[495] Article 20(8), 2017 COMESAIA.

expropriation occurs if the measures in question "substantially or permanently deprives the investor of the fundamental attributes of property in its investment",[496] and counts the economic impact, the duration, and the character of the measure (with an emphasis on object, context, and intent); as well as whether there has been a breach vis-à-vis prior binding written commitments via contract, licence or other legal documents.[497]

When compared to the 2007 Agreement, the revised text provides more clear-cut guidance on the factors to be taken into account. This addition brings it more in line with the global tendency to articulate various considerations the arbitral tribunals are expected to consider when determining whether indirect expropriation has occurred. On the other hand, the 2017 text retracts the consideration that the police powers doctrine is a right of states pursuant to CIL. Clearly, the express language contained in both texts would render the police powers applicable by virtue of its being in the agreement itself. However, whether or not this retraction reflects a reconsideration of its broader legal status beyond the scope of the COMESA framework is unclear.

4.4.6 Conclusion on the New Generation IIAs

It is evident from the foregoing examination that an immediately recognisable structure for expropriation provisions now dominates newer generation IIAs. Despite some notable differences, such as the role of investment-backed expectations as a factor of consideration; the economic impact, the duration, and the character of a measure are universally recognised sub-elements to be taken into account when determining whether a measure is expropriatory. The inclusion of regulatory carve-out provisions, enshrining the police powers doctrine, is also commonplace. While the overall structure of the carve-out paragraph has remained the same since their inception with the 2004 Canada Model FIPA and the 2004 US Model BIT, more policy domains are now specified in these carve-out clauses. Within the framework of its 2023 Model BIT, the EU and its Member States are consolidating and syncronising the scope of their respective (and prospective) expropriation provisions *vis-à-vis* extra-EU agreements. In the Asia-Pacific context, 'written commitments' appear to have been attached a particular significance.

Reflecting scholarly and case law debates on the subject, some of the texts examined above had attempted to expressly recognise the right to regulate as a rule of CIL.[498] This was subsequently retracted. However, other examples exist where this

[496] Article 20(10)(a)(ii), 2017 COMESAIA.

[497] Article 20(10)(b)(i), (ii), (iii), (iv), 2017 COMESAIA.

[498] 2007 COMESAIA.

recognition remains. For example, 2019 Morocco Model BIT 2019 retains language to that effect, noting that the police powers is "[i]n accordance with the right of States to regulate and the principles of customary international law relating to the police powers of the State".[499]

4.5 Final Remarks

In international law, expropriation is an act consistent with the sovereignty of states. However, given its potential economic consequences for the exposed foreign investor and the host state, international law has strived to strike a balance between the state's sovereign rights and prerogatives on the one hand, and the protection of foreigners abroad on the other. States that focus on inbound flow of investment and capital may be inclined to emphasise the primacy of state sovereignty over individual economic rights to a certain extent. On the other hand, states interested in protecting their investors in other countries might be lean towards protecting private rights against political risk. In the current global regime, states' right to expropriate often comes head-to-head with the deprivation suffered by a foreign investor as a result of such taking. It is a persistent legal and political issue that awaits an eventual resolution.

This Chapter aimed at looking at a state's expropriatory measures from a legal and political perspective, and presented a series of legal and empirical arguments, largely based on case law and a collection of new generation, plurilateral IIAs. Even though each case has its own unique set of facts, most expropriation disputes today concern similar, vague provisions scattered through thousands of IIAs, dating back to the 90s. This being said, as evident that the aforementioned new IIAs have largely taken shape as a result of the accumulated adjudicatory experience as states embedded their adjudicatory experiences to their newer agreements. This is particularly loud and clear with regard to expropriation provisions. Since the proliferation of foreign investor claims throughout 2000s, both the US and Canada brought about their own pro-sovereign approach by adding annexes or additional provisions to their IIAs. These annexes aimed at clarifying what is meant (or not meant) by expropriation. They also articulate several delimitations to otherwise rather vague expropriation provisions that are often incorporated in IIAs. By these delimitations, states have been hoping to prevent unanticipated foreign investor claims. Some treaties even take it a step further and contain carve-outs for legitimate and non-discriminatory acts or measures.

IIAs, and expropriation provisions in particular, have always resembled one another. In this so-called 'recalibration' phase defined by the new generation IIAs, their respective transformations are similar. In most cases, they borrow language

[499] Article 10(8)(c), Morocco Model BIT (2019). The original French text reads as follows: "[c]onformément au droit des États à réglementer et aux principes du droit international coutumier relatifs aux pouvoirs de police de l'Etat …".

from one another. Throughout the 80s and the 90s, a plethora of IIAs were signed which strongly resembled one another in terms of their briefness and vagueness. Arbitral claims stemming from the previous generation of IIAs show that this shared ambiguity in wording did not necessarily transmute into adjudicatory coherence. Even the application of the very same IIA provision on expropriation to several different cases have yielded different results, as different tribunals emphasised on different elements. Whereas some tribunals considered the effects of an act to prevail over its intent, others emphasised the police powers of the host state. All IIAs, vague in a similar fashion, were similarly unclear as to how to tackle this conundrum. This prompted the arbitral tribunals to take the matter into their own hands.

Upon this background, this Chapter attempted to demonstrate the gradual development of a traditionally vague notion, central to the foreign investment protection regime. The analysis throughout the Chapter presented a selection of arbitral disputes, and the instruments upon which these claims are based. It demonstrated the legal (both theoretical and adjudicatory) consequences of different expropriation provisions in the light of different facts and events. It showed the possible extent of the subject of targeted measures such as legislations, regulations, municipal decrees, license refusals, and domestic court decisions. The current case law clearly demonstrates the interpretative divergences of almost identical expropriation provisions as applied to different cases. In investment arbitration, an arbitral tribunal may apply the police powers doctrine to a 'gold standard' Dutch BIT[500] on its own accord. Likewise, the same IIA can be read to give a heightened importance to the effects of a measure *vis-à-vis* the regulatory prerogatives of the host state. While the latter approach, namely the effects doctrine, has been largely confined to earlier cases, it persists and occasionally reappears when the treaty allows for it.[501]

One overarching observation in the Chapter is that the sole effects doctrine will likely lose its residual justification if states stay on course with regards to including explicit references to safeguarding their legitimate, non-discriminatory acts and measures. The current global trend, illustrated by the plurilateral IIAs examined above, indicates as much. Since the emergence of the initial examples of the regulatory carve-out provisions found within the 2004 Canada Model FIPA and the US Model BIT, this tendency has taken over treaty-making practices across the globe. While treaties such as CPTPP and RCEP stand aside from the EU IPAs in several aspects, such as the role of investment-backed expectations, the inclination towards further clarity is the common denominator.

Expropriation provisions in the new-wave IIAs mentioned above show a common concern by states as treaty-makers (and as potential respondents): they do not intend to protect a foreign investor at the expense of their legitimate, non-discriminatory measures and actions aimed at protecting the public health, environment, or other public policy and welfare goals. This is probably the most important 'lesson learned'

[500] *Saluka v. Czech Republic (2006)*. As noted above, the Dutch BITs currently in force are often given as examples for the broad-worded, 'gold standard' IIAs which represent a stream of the so-called 'pro-investor' treaties.

[501] Brower and Blanchard (2014), p. 731; Rockhopper v. Italy (2022).

in the course of the last three decades. The adjudicatory experience demonstrated that a balance between interests was possible, but not inherent, pursuant to the bulk of earlier generation BITs. The new IIAs show that states' concerns are similar. These provisions in treaties such as CPTPP, RCEP, and COMESA further show that this tendency is not limited to the EU and North America. It demonstrates that a global shift in policies with regard to protection of foreign investment converge towards the same goal of minimising, or even abolishing, responsibility merely because a state regulated or acted for public good. This growing compatibility, based on further clarity, will surely affect adjudicatory trends and will possibly result in further coherence in interpretation and application of indirect expropriation provisions. Currently available case law based on qualified expropriation provisions, including but not limited to the above-examined Canada – Colombia FTA, already indicates that an argumentative stream has emerged in arbitral tribunals' interpretation and application of these new provisions. This being said, a word of caution, in light of awards such as *Bear Creek v. Peru*, is necessary. No particular provision renders arbitral tribunals immune to erroneous application of the law. Expecting treaty provisions to bear the entire responsibility for ensuring consistency and correctness of arbitral decisions would be expecting too much from the IIA in question.

The classical, twentieth century context of protectionism often indicated that capital-importing states wished to retain more of their regulatory autonomy mostly due to fear of foreign intervention by richer states. In contrast, the traditional discourse further asserted that capital-exporting countries would rather seek protection for their investors abroad. Today, as adjudicatory experience continues to reveal the true extent and meaning of substantive provisions, the capital-importing and capital-exporting states may be able to find more common ground. The 'modern protectionism' represented by the new generation IIAs makes the distinction between capital-importing and capital-exporting states ever blurrier. The contemporary debates on the matter of protection of foreign investment shows that all states, and not only those classified as capital-importing countries, are susceptible to acting as respondents for their regulatory acts and decisions stemming directly from their sovereign identity. Therefore, it may be argued that such reluctance of facing investor claims, now shared by many states and not just the capital-importing or capital-exporting countries, gives all members of the international community ample opportunity to participate in the recalibration of this still-ongoing international project.

The next Chapter will scrutinise another conspicuously vague principle: FET. It will look into an even more convoluted story of interpretative conflation and evolution.

References

Alschner W (2013) Americanization of the BIT Universe: the influence of Friendship, Commerce and Navigation (FCN) treaties on modern investment treaty law. Göttingen J Int Law 5:455–486

Alschner W (2022) Investment arbitration and state-driven reform: new treaties, old outcomes. Oxford University Press, Oxford

Alvarez JE, Khamsi K (2009) The Argentine crisis and foreign investors: a glimpse into the heart of the investment regime. In: Sauvant KP (ed) The yearbook on international investment law and policy 2008–2009. Oxford University Press, New York, pp 379–478

Andreotti N (2025) The Colombian Santurbán Páramo saga and its contribution to the development of international investment law and arbitration. Arbitr Int (Advance access): 1–15

Bernasconi-Osterwalder N (2013) Commentary to the Draft Investment Chapter of the Canada – EU Comprehensive Economic and Trade Agreement (CETA) IISD Report. https://www.iisd.org/system/files/publications/commentary_investment_chapter_CETA.pdf

Brower CN, Blanchard S (2014) What's in a Meme? The truth about investor-state arbitration: why it need not, and must not, be repossessed by states. Columbia J Transnatl Law 52:689–779

Brownlie I (2003) Public international law, 6th edn. Oxford, Oxford University Press

Brunetti M (2001) The Iran-United States claims tribunal, NAFTA Chapter 11, and the doctrine of indirect expropriation. Chic J Int Law 2:203–212

Bulut ÖE (2022) Drawing boundaries of police powers doctrine: a balanced framework for investors and states. J Int Dispute Settlement 13:583–607

Bungenberg M (2023) (Direct and Indirect) expropriation and the rule of law. In: Reinisch A, Schill SW (eds) Investment protection standards and the rule of law. Oxford University Press, Oxford, pp 61–80

Coe J, Rubins N (2005) Regulatory expropriation and the Tecmed Case: context and contributions. In: Weiler T (ed) International investment law and arbitration: leading cases from the ICSID, NAFTA, bilateral treaties and customary international law. Cameron May, London, pp 597–668

Corey S (2012) But is it just? The inability for current adjudicatory standards to provide "just compensation" for creeping expropriations. Fordham Law Rev 81:973–1012

Cox JM (2019) Expropriation in investment treaty arbitration. Oxford University Press, Oxford

Cremades B (2004) Disputes arising out of foreign direct investment in Latin America: a new look at the Calvo Doctrine and other jurisdictional issues. Dispute Resolut J 59:78

De Luca A (2014) Indirect expropriations and regulatory takings: what role for the "legitimate expectations" of foreign investors? In: Sacerdoti G, Acconci P, Valenti M, De Luca A (eds) General interests of host states in the application of investment treaties. Cambridge University Press, Cambridge, pp 58–75

Demirkol B (2018) Judicial acts and investment treaty arbitration. Cambridge University Press, Cambridge

Dolzer R (2003) Indirect expropriations: new developments? NYU Environ Law J 11:64–93

Dolzer R, Bloch F (2003) Indirect expropriation: conceptual realignments? International Law FORUM du droit international 5:155–165

Dolzer R, Schreuer C (2012) Principles of international investment law, 2nd edn. Oxford University Press, Oxford

Dumberry P (2001) Expropriation under NAFTA Chapter 11 investment dispute settlement mechanism: some comments on the latest case law. Int Arbitr Law Rev 4:96–104

Dupuy PM, Viñuales JE (2015) Human rights and investment disciplines: integration in progress. In: Bungenberg M, Griebel J, Hobe S, Reinisch A (eds) International investment law: a handbook. Nomos, Baden Baden, pp 1739–1767

Edsall RD (2006) Indirect expropriation under NAFTA and DR-CAFTA: potential inconsistencies in the treatment of state public welfare regulations. Boston Univ Law Rev 86:931–962

Escarcena SL (2014) Indirect expropriation in international law (Leuven Global Governance Series). Edward Elgar Publishing, Northampton

Fahner JH (2022) Judicial deference in international adjudication: a comparative analysis. Bloomsbury, London

Fauchald OK (2006) International investment law and environmental protection. Yearb Int Environ Law 17:3–47

Firger DM, Gerrard MB (2012) Harmonizing climate change policy and international investment law: threats, challenges, and opportunities. In: Sauvant KP (ed) Yearbook on International Investment Law & Policy 2010 – 2011. Oxford University Press, New York, pp 517–566

Fontanelli F, Bianco G (2014) Converging towards NAFTA: an analysis of FTA Investment Chapters in the European Union and the United States. Stanford J Int Law 50:211–246

Gazzini T (2010) Drawing the line between non-compensable regulatory powers and indirect expropriation of foreign investment – an economic analysis of law perspective. Manchester J Int Econ Law 7(3):36–51

Giannakopoulos C (2023) Manifestations of coherence and investor-state arbitration. Cambridge University Press, Cambridge

Harbine J (2002) NAFTA Chapter 11 Arbitration: deciding the price of free trade. Ecol Law Q 29:371–394

Harris DJ (2010) Cases and materials on international law, 7th edn. Sweet & Maxwell, London

Heiskanen V (2007) The doctrine of indirect expropriation in the light of the practice of the Iran-United States claims tribunal. JWIT 8:215–232

Helgeson E (ed) (2001) Iran – US Claims Tribunal Reports, no. 31 1995. Cambridge University Press, Cambridge

Henckels C (2012) Indirect expropriation and the right to regulate: revisiting proportionality analysis and the standard of review in investor-state arbitration. J Int Econ Law 15:223–255

Hirsch M (2013) Investment tribunals and human rights treaties: a sociological perspective. In: Baetens F (ed) Investment law within international law. Cambridge University Press, Cambridge, pp 85–105

Hoffmann AK (2008) Indirect expropriation. In: Reinisch A (ed) Standards of investment protection. Oxford University Press, Oxford, pp 151–170

Hoffmeister F, Ünüvar G (2013) From BITs and pieces towards European investment agreements. In: Bungenberg M, Reinisch A, Tietje C (eds) EU and investment agreements: open questions and remaining challenges. Nomos, Baden – Baden, pp 57–85

Howse R, Ünüvar G (2022) Sowing the seeds of an ISDS legitimacy crisis? The notorious first wave of NAFTA Chapter 11 Awards. In: Fabri HR, Stoppioni E (eds) International investment law: an analysis of the major decisions. Bloomsbury Publishing, London, pp 99–117

Kriebaum U (2007) Regulatory takings: balancing the interests of the investor and the state. J World Invest Trade 8:717–744

Kriebaum U (2014) FET and expropriation in the (invisible) EU Model BIT. J World Invest Trade 15:454–483

Kriebaum U (2018) Indirect expropriation: a comparative approach. In: Gattini A, Tanzi A, Fontanelli F (eds) General principles of law and international investment arbitration. Brill, Leiden, pp 429–453

Kriebaum U (2022) Art. 8.12 Expropriation. In: Bungenberg M, Reinisch A (eds) CETA investment law: article-by-article commentary. Baden-Baden, Nomos, pp 300–336

Kucik J, Puig S (2023) Towards an effective appellate mechanism for ISDS tribunals. World Trade Rev 22:562–583

Lauterpacht E, Greenwood CJ (1994) International law reports, vol 95. Cambridge University Press, Cambridge. https://icsidfiles.worldbank.org/icsid/ICSIDBLOBS/OnlineAwards/C3004/CLA-056_Eng.pdf

Lavranos N (2013) In defence of Member States' BITs Gold Standard: the Regulation 1219/2012 establishing a transitional regime for existing extra-EU BITs – a Member State's perspective. Transnatl Dispute Manag 10(2):1–14

Leys D (2015) EU competence in foreign direct investment: will the EU Court of Justice end the controversy? Global Trade Customs J 10(7/8):267–272

Martinez EA (2012) Understanding the debate over necessity: unanswered questions and future implications on annulments in the Argentine gas cases. Duke J Comp Int Law 23:149–186

Mavromati C, Schubert A (2024) The EU model clauses for bilateral investment treaties of EU Member States with third countries. Eur Invest Law Arbitr Rev 9(2):193–216

Miles K (2013) The origins of international investment law: empire, environment and the safeguarding of capital. Cambridge University Press, Cambridge

Montanaro F, Paulini S (2018) United in Mixity? The future of the EU Common Commercial Policy in light of the CJEU's recent case law (EJIL: Talk! 2 February 2018). https://www.ejiltalk.org/united-in-mixity-the-future-of-the-eu-common-commercial-policy-in-light-of-the-cjeus-recent-case-law/

Mostafa B (2008) The sole effects doctrine, police powers and indirect expropriation under international law. Aust Int Law J 15:267–296

Mouri A (1994) The international law of expropriation as reflected in the work of the Iran – US Claims Tribunal. Brill Nijhoff, Dordrecht

Nascimbene J (2024) Creeping expropriation. Jus Mundi. https://jusmundi.com/fr/document/publication/en-creeping-expropriation

Newcombe A (1999) Regulatory expropriation, investment protection and international law: when is government regulation expropriatory and when should compensation be paid? (LL.M. Thesis, Graduate Department of Faculty of Law, University of Toronto). https://utoronto.scholaris.ca/items/20b72958-a1a1-4f08-9695-305010302764

Newcombe A (2005) The boundaries of regulatory expropriation in international law. ICSID Rev 20:1–57

Nicholson FJ (1965) The protection of foreign property under customary international law. Boston Coll Law Rev 6:391–415

OECD (2004) "Indirect Expropriation" and the "Right to Regulate" in International Investment Law (OECD Working Papers on International Investment 2004/4)

OECD (2021) The Future of Investment Treaties (Track 2): The Notion of 'Indirect Expropriation' in Investment Treaties Concluded by 88 Jurisdictions: A Large Sample Survey of Treaty Provisions. https://www.oecd.org/investment/investment-policy/oecd-future-investment-treaties-indirect-expropriation-meeting-background.pdf

OECD (2022) The Future of Investment Treaties (Track 2): Summary of Discussions of the Future of Investment Treaties Track 2 – Meeting of 13 April 2022. https://www.oecd.org/investment/investment-policy/oecd-future-investment-treaties-discussion-summary-track2-april-2022.pdf

Perrone NM (2022) Local communities, extractivism and international investment law: the case of five Colombian communities. Globalizations 19(6):837–853

Rajput A (2018) Regulatory freedom and indirect expropriation in investment arbitration. Wolters Kluwer, Alphen aan den Rijn

Reinisch A (2008) Legality of expropriations. In: Reinisch A (ed) Standards of investment protection. Oxford University Press, Oxford, pp 171–204

Reinisch A (2011) Necessity in investment arbitration. Neth Yearb Int Law 41:137–158

Reinisch A (2012) Expropriation. In: Muchlinski P, Ortino F, Schreuer C (eds) The Oxford handbook of international investment law. Oxford University Press, Oxford, pp 408–456

Rubins N, Kinsella NS (2005) International investment, political risk and dispute resolution. Oceana Publications, Dobbs Ferry

Ruoppo R (2022) Common features of the right to property and international investments: evidence from the use of EctHR case law in investment tribunals' decisions. Ital Rev Int Comp Law 2:347–369

Sauvant KP, Chiswick-Patterson M (eds) (2008) Appeals mechanism in international investment disputes. Oxford University Press, Oxford

Schill SW (2007) Tearing down the Great Wall: the new generation investment treaties of the People's Republic of China. Cardozo J Int Comp Law 15:73–118

Schreuer C (2008) Preliminary rulings in investment arbitration. In: Sauvant KP, Chiswick-Patterson M (eds) Appeals mechanism in international investment disputes. Oxford University Press, Oxford, pp 207–212

Shan W (2007) From north – south divide to private – public debate: revival of the Calvo Doctrine and the changing landscape in international investment law. Northwest J Int Law Bus 27:631–664

Shirlow E (2014) Deference and indirect expropriation analysis in international investment law: observations on current approaches and frameworks for future analysis. ICSID Rev 29:595–626

Shirlow E (2021) Judging at the interface: deference to state decision-making authority in international adjudication. Cambridge University Press, Cambridge

Sornarajah M (1994) The international law on foreign investment. Cambridge University Press, Cambridge

Stone Sweet A (2010) Investor-state arbitration: proportionality's new frontier. Law Ethics Hum Rights 4:47–76

Subedi SP (2008) International investment law: reconciling policy and principle. Hart Publishing, Oxford and Portland

Teo J, Richter J, Kadu S, Khaw T (2024) Rebalancing investment protection standards: analysing the effectiveness of new treaty language in preserving regulatory space for host states. J World Invest Trade 25(4):529–566

Titi C (2014) The right to regulate in international investment law. Nomos, Baden-Baden

Titi C (2018) Police powers doctrine and international investment law. In: Gattini A, Tanzi A, Fontanelli F (eds) General principles of law and international investment arbitration. Brill Nijhoff, Leiden, pp 323–343

Tung K-Y (2015) Investor-state dispute settlement under the trans-pacific partnership. Calif Int Law J 23:19–25

Ünüvar G (2023) A tale of policy carve-outs and general exceptions: Eco Oro v Colombia as a case study. J Int Dispute Settlement 14(4):517–533

Vandevelde KJ (2010) Bilateral investment treaties: history, policy, and interpretation. Oxford University Press, Oxford

Viñuales JE (2012) Foreign investment and the environment in international law. Cambridge University Press, Cambridge

Visser F (1988) The principle of permanent sovereignty over natural resources and the nationalisation of foreign interests. Comp Int Law J South Africa 21(1):76–91

Zarra G (2018) The issue of incoherence in investment arbitration: is there need for a systemic reform? Chin J Int Law 17(1):137–185

Chapter 5
The Fair and Equitable Treatment Principle and Its Thresholds

Abstract This Chapter explores the conceptual evolution and interpretative challenges surrounding the Fair and Equitable Treatment (FET) principle in international investment law. Through a detailed case law analysis, the Chapter examines how arbitral tribunals have approached the persistent and problematic association of FET with the Minimum Standard of Treatment (MST) under customary international law (CIL). Based on this expansive case law analysis, it argues that this association has led to conceptual ambiguity, inconsistencies in arbitral decisions, and circular reasoning, undermining the clarity and predictability of the FET principle. The Chapter critiques the reliance on CIL/MST references, including the arbitrary invocation of precedents like the *Neer* case, and highlights the inadequacy of these references in clarifying the scope of FET. Instead, it notes that some new-generation IIAs increasingly codify specific acts and omissions that constitute violations of FET, reflecting a shift toward more concrete and coherent frameworks. While agreements such as CPTPP and RCEP maintain references to CIL, the EU's practice diverges by articulating detailed obligations, detaching FET from its association with MST. Ultimately, the Chapter advocates for abandoning the MST/CIL linkage to achieve a clearer and more consistent application of FET. It argues that the growing body of arbitral decisions, despite their limitations, provides a foundation for defining specific sub-elements of FET, enabling the principle to evolve into a relatively consistent and transparent standard. This shift, as reflected in emerging treaty practices, signals a step toward a more reliable and fairness-oriented framework in investment law.

G. Ünüvar, *The Transformation of International Investment Law and Its Principles*, European Yearbook of International Economic Law 44,
https://doi.org/10.1007/978-3-032-01110-7_5

5.1 Introduction

The traditional objectives of promotion and protection of investments have driven the development of international investment law and investor-state dispute settlement (ISDS) for decades. Different principles, such as Most-Favoured-Nation (MFN) and National Treatment (NT); as well as the above-analysed provisions on protection against expropriation, are the primary tools that have facilitated the establishment of the treaty-based network of protection for foreign investors available today. Whereas MFN and NT function as *contingent* protection principles[1] which ensure the treatment offered to favoured third party investors and national investors also extend to foreign investors, expropriation provisions objectively aim at ensuring that the investment of a foreigner has not been destroyed by overt or creeping measures by host states. MFN and NT are by no means exclusive to international investment protection regime, as they are also well-established principles in international trade law.[2] Although legal scholarship has thoroughly discussed questions such as the extent of MFN treatment and whether it covers both substantial and procedural rules,[3] when compared to traditionally more vague concepts and given their inherently contingent nature, the controversies related to their application are relatively limited.

Although international law prescribes certain guiding principles,[4] the determination of what amounts to expropriation and what falls within the scope of non-compensable sovereign prerogatives of a host state have been fervently debated for over decades. Chapter 4 above examined this conundrum in detail, and highlighted how arbitral elaborations have shaped treaty-making practices of states in light of competing interests of disputing parties. Despite an increasingly vocal acknowledgment that measures implementing non-discriminatory public objectives do not constitute indirect expropriation in line with the states' police powers, it is nonetheless crucial that a state either destroys, or takes away the effective control or enjoyment, of an investment for expropriation to exist. It is also well-established in international law that expropriation should be accompanied by compensation, despite decades-long disagreements regarding the determination of the amount of compensation. Furthermore, an expropriatory measure has to be for a public purpose, need to observe due process and cannot be discriminatory for it to be lawful. Some of these elements are already featured in the vast majority all IIAs in force—others are slowly being integrated as a new generation of IIAs emerge.

---

[1] Newcombe and Paradell (2009), p. 148; OECD (2004), p. 2.

[2] Article I (General Most-Favoured-Nation Treatment) and Article III (National Treatment on Internal Taxation and Regulation), the General Agreement on Tariffs and Trade ('GATT' - 1947).https://www.wto.org/english/docs_e/legal_e/gatt47.pdf.

[3] Nikièma (2017), p. 10; Cole (2012); Schill (2009).

[4] UN General Assembly, Resolution 1803 (XVII) Permanent Sovereignty over Natural Resources, 14 December 1962, p. 15. https://undocs.org/a/res/1803(xvii).

In terms of its constituent elements and the debates it has thus far invoked as to its correct interpretation, the FET principle is *much* more elusive and complex than the indirect expropriation which, as demonstrated above, has a large number of persistent and highly sensitive controversies itself. According to Dolzer and Schreuer, FET is "the most frequently invoked standard in investment disputes",[5] and it is easily one of the most controversial principles in international investment law.[6] Some commentators described the FET principle as a 'boilerplate' provision: a standard clause that is rarely negotiated in depth.[7] From another perspective, Kill argued that, historically, "states did not view the obligation to provide [FET] as deriving from [CIL]. The assertion [...] that the [FET] requirement is equal to the [IMS] for treatment for aliens should therefore be discounted as representing the view of capital-exporting countries only."[8] Since its first appearance during the mid-twentieth century in early IIAs, states have adopted different methods in order to capture the obligation to accord fair treatment to foreigners, in addition to the abovementioned contingent protection principles borrowed from, *inter alia*, trade law. Part of the analysis above in Chap. 2, in which I examined the concept of fairness in a sovereign's treatment of a foreigner, directly (yet not exclusively) pertains to the emergence of the FET principle in investment law.[9] Indeed, as I argued in Chap. 2, fairness has been conceived and upheld as a contingent notion, often assessed *vis-à-vis* the treatment of another group, and served as a discursive yardstick to establish an MST for foreigners.[10] Chapter 2 further asserted that MFN and NT principles are similarly direct manifestations of this traditional reasoning.[11] FET principle, however, while directly referring to core concepts such as fair (and its semantic substitutes such as 'just' or 'equitable'), spontaneously aspires to a certain degree of normativity, interpreted and applied by adjudicators.[12] Pointing towards this rather perplexing situation, Chap. 2, in retrospect, indicated that the FET principle in contemporary international investment law indeed aims at transcending beyond this traditional, contingent meaning of 'fair', goes beyond its historic and semantic subjectivity, and seeks to conceptualise an objective meaning within the framework of the protection of foreigners and their property. FET is often understood to contain different *subset*; specific types of measures, acts, or omissions committed by states that could potentially violate this principle, such as arbitrary conduct, lack of due process, denial of justice, frustration of legitimate expectations, and so on. Therefore, at this point, 'fair treatment' in general, and 'Fair and Equitable Treatment' in international investment law have different (yet

---

[5] Dolzer and Schreuer (2012), p. 130; UNCTAD (2012), p. 1.

[6] Dolzer and Stevens (1995), p. 58.

[7] Waibel (2019).

[8] Kill (2008), p. 858.

[9] Chapter 2.

[10] This Chapter refers to MST and the International Minimum Standard (IMS) interchangably.

[11] Dolzer and Stevens (1995), pp. 63–65.

[12] Kill (2008), p. 855.

not entirely separate) meanings. The generality of the former notwithstanding, the latter naturally calls for a specific content and context. As opposed to the general analysis conducted under Chap. 2, this Chapter concerns this latter notion and the complex relationship between the two.

Similar to the case study on expropriation conducted in the *supra* Chap. 4, I will first elaborate on the conceptual development of the FET principle as included in consecutive generations of IIAs, and the preceding attempts at including 'equitable' treatment in international trade relations. Then, I will engage in an in-depth case law analysis.

The purpose of this case law analysis is not to lay forth a precise list of the abovementioned subset. There is copious scholarship on the constituent subset of FET, and this Chapter does not seek to duplicate what has already been done in that regard.[13] While the case law analysis will point towards specific subsets identified by arbitral tribunals and ultimately reflect upon the emergent interpretative trends in light of vague provisions, this Chapter's main focus will be on the inexplicably persistent association of the FET principle with the MST, often accepted to reflect CIL. This Chapter will highlight how arbitral tribunals handle this linkage between these two equally elusive concepts, arguing that this long-standing association is more harmful and confusing than it has ever been useful.

In my conclusions, therefore, I will assert that the efforts to determine the contours of CIL and the arbitral references to its content with regard to the treatment of foreigners are largely evasive, incomplete, and inconclusive—yielding conceptually circular results.[14] Therefore, I argue that CIL/MST references are the primary (yet not necessarily the sole) reason for the inconsistency embedded within this principle.[15] In cases which arbitral tribunals explicitly examined the content of MST *vis-à-vis* the content of FET (perceived as *autonomous* or otherwise), the accuracy of references to the origins of CIL in the field are dubious—such as the surprisingly popular, and equally arbitrary, tendency to refer to the *Neer* case.[16] Neither the content of these references, nor the attempts to explain FET through references to CIL/MST in general, hardly clarify and streamline the fairness analysis. Many arbitral tribunals have identified elements of what comprised fair treatment, and the new IIAs, regardless of whether CIL actually existed in this field, seem to have codified what seems to overlap with what has been *perceived* to be CIL.

While several new-wave IIAs, such as CPTPP and RCEP, continue the tradition of including references to CIL within the context of FET, the EU practice seems to have diverted from this association.[17] Opting out of the inconclusive, disjointed

[13] Živković (2023); Sarmiento and Nikièma (2022); Angelet (2022); Dumberry (2018); Kläger (2011); Tudor (2008); Schreuer (2005). See, in particular, Yu (2024), p. 264 et seq, presenting an empirical analysis and breakdown of different elements incorporated in FET provisions until 2020.

[14] Dumberry (2024a), p. 19; Ünüvar (2022), p. 284.

[15] Ünüvar (2022), p. 289.

[16] *LFH Neer and Pauline Neer (U.S.A.) v. United Mexican States* (1926) IV RIAA, pp. 60–66. http://legal.un.org/riaa/cases/vol_IV/60-66.pdf (*Neer v. Mexico*).

[17] *Infra* analysis on the new generation FET Provisions.

associations pervasive across IIAs currently in force, and in light of the famously indeterminate arbitral jurisprudence on FET, the EU and its Member States seem to have completely detached themselves from this method and began articulating specific acts and omissions that would *prima facie* violate this principle. Ultimately, I will argue that, while states are, as argued above, free to negotiate the terms they see fit in their agreements in line with their policy choices; a clear, consistent, and coherent future for the FET case law is only possible through doing away with the MST/CIL references and articulating the specific acts that are considered to be breaches of this principle. While arbitral elaborations thus far do not give a satisfactory answer on the conceptual relationship between FET and CIL/MST, they do provide a wealth of information on what these specific acts may be. It is therefore possible to reconstruct, as is being currently done by a number of new wave IIAs, a more concrete framework of the FET principle as it continues its quest to become an objective, non-contingent, and hopefully a more consistent, clear principle—a carefully designed manifestation of *fairness* itself—assuming FET's existence is desirable to begin with.

5.2 Emergence of FET Provisions

5.2.1 Prototypes of FET

Some historic-legal analyses in the field traces the roots of the FET principle to the inter-war efforts of the League of Nations.[18] According to Article 23(e) of the 1919 Covenant of the League of Nations, the Members of the League "will make provision to secure and maintain freedom of communications and of transit and equitable treatment for the commerce of all Members of the League."[19] The same Article also refers to "just treatment of the native inhabitants of territories under their control",[20] a rule relevant for territories under the control of colonial empires. Pinchis-Paulsen noted that the work of the Economic sub-Commission of the League during the 1933 London conference aimed at addressing "'non-tariff' barriers to trade, including 'administrative' protectionism."[21] The sub-Commission's work acknowledged the fact that some subjects were "so complicated and elusive that it seem[ed] almost impossible to arrive in every important case at a satisfactory special solution" with regard to determining which state measures amounted to 'reinforced protection'.[22] Building upon this perceived impossibility, the League Secretariat suggested that

[18] Pinchis-Paulsen (2014), p. 20; Weiler (2013), p. 18.

[19] Article 23(e), Covenant of the League of Nations (1919) (CLN).http://www.refworld.org/docid/3dd8b9854.html.

[20] Article 23(b), CLN (1919).

[21] Pinchis-Paulsen (2014), p. 40.

[22] Pinchis-Paulsen (2014), p. 47.

the drafting of an 'equitable treatment' clause could potentially protect the balance established between states. In general, it seems almost certain that the drafters had seen the formulation of an equitable treatment clause, in the light of strong past disagreements among states, as a way of compromise regarding the definition of indirect protectionism of states, a perceived obstacle in front of the free trade relations among contracting states.[23] In other words, through this 'equitable treatment' provision, states seem to have agreed to disagree.

Many scholars cite the 1948 Havana Charter as the introduction of the contemporary FET principle in IIAs.[24] Under its Article 11(2), the Havana Charter had given the ITO[25] the role to make recommendations "for and promote bilateral and multilateral agreements on measures designed [...] to assure ***just and equitable treatment*** for enterprise [and] capital [...] brought from one [m]ember country to another [...]".[26]

The Economic Agreement of Bogota refers to "equitable treatment" for foreign capital, and elaborates on what would be understood as equitable under its Article 22: "[t]he States therefore agree not to take unjustified, unreasonable or discriminatory measures that would impair the legally acquired rights or interests of nationals of other countries in the enterprises [and] capital [...] they have supplied."[27] The article continues by specifying a number of other positive and negative duties of states in connection with the above-mentioned "equitable treatment", such as granting facilities and incentives for foreign capital and refraining from unjustifiable restrictions upon the transfer of such capital.

Another important, yet unratified, instrument was the 1949 ICC Code particularly for its elaboration on the scope of fair treatment under Articles 2, 3, and especially 5.[28] As explained in Chap. 2 above, this draft text is one of the earliest contemporary examples of an IIA text that linked the concept of fair treatment with an international standard. The standard was set to be beyond the boundaries set by NT, MFN, or other contingent thresholds.[29]

While the early work of the League of Nations on the notion of equity with regard to indirect barriers to trade might have shed light on the subsequent formulation of the FET provisions, the examples set by the Havana Charter and Economic

---

[23] Pinchis-Paulsen (2014), p. 48.

[24] Yu (2024), p. 261; Waibel (2019); Bonnitcha (2014), p. 143; Dolzer and Schreuer (2012), p. 131; Bronfman (2005), p. 613; Vandevelde (2010), p. 44.

[25] Toye (2012).

[26] Article 11(2), Havana Charter for an International Trade Organization (1948, not in force). https://www.wto.org/english/docs_e/legal_e/havana_e.pdf.

[27] Article 22, The Economic Agreement of Bogota of the Organization of American States (1948). http://www.oas.org/juridico/english/treaties/A-43_Economic_Agreement_of_Bogota.pdf; Also see, Lockwood (1948), p. 618.

[28] International Code of Fair Treatment for Foreign Investment (the 'ICC Code' - 1949), printed in: UNCTAD (2003) International Investment Instruments: A Compendium (Volume I—Multilateral Instruments), p. 273–276, https://unctad.org/system/files/official-document/dtci30vol1_en.pdf.

[29] Ünüvar (2022), p. 279.

Agreement of Bogota, as well as the ICC Code, served as prototypes for contemporary IIAs. In the subsequent decades, FET principle appeared on a number of draft treaties, such as the Abs-Shawcross Draft Convention on Investment Abroad (1959)[30] and the OECD Draft Convention (1967),[31] which had a more direct effect on contemporary IIAs.

Particularly the latter text, which included an OECD commentary, noted that the FET extended "at all times [...] to the property of the nationals of the other Parties" stemmed from "the standard set by international law for the treatment due by each State with regard to the property of foreign nationals."[32] It further asserted that

> the standard may be more exacting where rules of national law or national administrative practices fall short of the requirements of international law. The standard required confirms in effect to the 'minimum standard' which forms part of customary international law.[33]

Unsurprisingly, neither the commentary nor the article itself provides any clarification as to the content of the referenced CIL rule—an omission emulated in the thousands of IIAs in force today.

5.2.2 *FET in European IIAs Until the Twenty-First Century*

Earlier European BITs had either excluded overt references to an FET obligation, or followed a trend of linking the FET standard to a particular contingent principle, such as non-discrimination, MFN, or NT.[34] In 1961, Switzerland signed its first BIT with Tunisia (which has since been replaced by another BIT)[35]; and the agreement contains one of the earliest examples of the FET principle in a European BIT, if not in fact the earliest. Its Article 1 states that investments shall benefit from "fair and equitable" treatment, and at the least, equal treatment accorded to national

[30] Article I: 'Each Party **shall at all times ensure fair and equitable treatment to the property of the nationals of the other Parties**. Such property shall be accorded the most constant protection and security within the territories shall not in any way be impaired by unreasonable or discriminatory measures.' The Draft Convention on Investments Abroad (the 'Abs-Shawcross (Draft) Convention' - 1959), printed in UNCTAD (2003) International Investment Instruments: A Compendium –301—303. https://unctad.org/system/files/official-document/dite2vol5_en.pdf.

[31] The Draft Convention on the Protection of Foreign Property (the 'OECD Model' - 1967).https://investmentpolicy.unctad.org/international-investment-agreements/treaty-files/2812/download.

[32] Notes and Commentary, The OECD Model (1967). https://legalinstruments.oecd.org/api/download/?uri=/public/f20b06a4-f007-4b2e-a624-f161545305d0.pdf&name=Draft%20Convention%201967.pdf, p. 10.

[33] Notes and Commentary, The OECD Model (1967), p. 10.

[34] Vandevelde (2010), p. 46.

[35] Switzerland—Tunisia BIT (1961); Switzerland—Tunisia BIT (2012).

investors.[36] In this particular case, NT principle seems to have set a minimum threshold for what would be considered fair and equitable.

In other instances, where the FET principle was absent in a treaty altogether, other protection provisions espoused its function. The 1959 Germany—Pakistan BIT, the first BIT ever signed, does not overtly mention "fair" and/or "equitable" treatment. However, pursuant to its Article 2, "[n]either Party shall subject to discriminatory treatment any activities carried on in connection with investments including the effective management, use or enjoyment of such investment by the nationals or companies of either Party [...] unless specific stipulations are made in the documents of admission of an investment."[37] Article 3, in addition, specifies that investments shall "enjoy protection and security" in the territory of the other party.[38]

It should be made clear that neither of these articles stipulate FET principle *per se* in its contemporary context, as both principles captured under Article 2 and 3 have their equivalents (namely the principles of non-discrimination[39] and full protection and security[40]) in more recent BITs. Another German BIT, namely the China—Germany BIT of 2009, clearly states under its Article 2 that "[n]either Contracting Party shall take any arbitrary or discriminatory measures against the management, maintenance, use, enjoyment and disposal of the investments by the investors [...]", and its Article 4 guarantees the enjoyment of "full protection and security" in the territory of the other party.[41] In addition to these principles, Article 3 titled 'Treatment of Investment' further specifies that "[i]nvestments of investors of each Party shall at all times be accorded fair and equitable treatment [...]".[42] This initial absence (and consequent proliferation) of an explicit FET articulation strengthens the assessment that FET in fact overlaps with several other standards of treatment included in investment treatments without prejudice to its standalone nature as an autonomous protection principle.[43]

This inclination of establishing an interrelation between the NT and FET principles continued well into mid-1990s—the Barbados—Switzerland BIT, signed in 1995, similarly states that:

> [Parties] shall ensure **fair and equitable treatment** within [their] territory of the investments of the investors of the other [party]. This treatment **shall not be less favourable than** that granted by each [party] to investments made within its territory **by its own investors,**

[36] Article 1, Switzerland—Tunisia BIT (1961). Translated by the author from the authentic French text, which reads as follows: "Les investissements ainsi que les biens, droits et intérêts appartenant à des ressortissants, fondations, associations ou sociétés d'une des Hautes Parties Contractantes dans le territoire de l'autre bénéficieront ***d'un traitement juste et équitable, au moins égal à celui qui est reconnu par chaque Partie à ses nationaux.***" Emphasis added.

[37] Article 2, Germany – Pakistan BIT (1959).

[38] Article 3, Germany – Pakistan BIT (1959).

[39] For example, Article 3, Finland – Türkiye BIT (1995).

[40] For example, Article 5, Japan – Peru BIT (2009).

[41] Article 4, China – Germany BIT (2009).

[42] Article 3, China – Germany BIT (2009).

[43] OECD (2004), p. 25.

> or than that granted by each [party] to the investments made within its territory **by investors of the most favoured nation**, if this latter treatment is more favourable.[44]

For Switzerland, this trend suddenly changed after 1996. Switzerland—Croatia BIT of 1996, unlike the Barbados BIT, splits the FET, NT and MFN principles under different paragraphs of the same article, and seemingly disconnected their determinative link. More specifically, after mid-90s, MFN and NT principles were not used as minimum thresholds for what was considered 'fair and equitable'—certainly not as frequently as it had been done since the 1960s.[45] This may be read as an attempt to underline that they constitute different, autonomous principles; while maintaining at least a causal and contextual overlap between these rules.

The early Swiss practice has also been frequently associated with IMS.[46] This assessment seems accurate according to the Swiss Department of Foreign Affairs, which stated that the FET principle referred to IMS.[47] This being said, it is unclear whether more recent Swiss BITs aim at retaining this interpretation, given Swiss BITs do not in fact explicitly contain language establishing such link.[48] Other European states have comparable practices. France—Malta BIT of 1976 refers not only to NT, but also to MFN, with regard to setting the limits of the FET principle. Its Article 3 states that

> Either Contracting Party binds itself to ensure on its territory a fair and equitable treatment to the investments of the nationals and companies of the other Party and to undertake not to impair the exercise of this right either by way of statute or de facto. This treatment **shall not be less favourable than that which is accorded by each Contracting Party to the nationals and companies of the most favoured nation.**[49]

However, this is not to say that unqualified FET provisions were by any means uncommon in Europe during the first decades of IIA-making. One example of such a provision which does not include any threshold for FET would be Article 1 of the Germany—United States Treaty of Friendship, Commerce and Navigation (FCN) of 1956, which states that "[e]ach Party shall at all times accord fair and equitable treatment to the nationals and companies of the other Party, and to their property,

[44] Article 3, Barbados – Switzerland BIT (1995) Emphasis added; also see, Switzerland – Ukraine BIT (1995); Pakistan – Switzerland BIT (1995). With certain differences in wording, Belgium – Morocco BIT (1965) contains a similar FET clause.

[45] This being said, previous drafting methods have not been completely abolished. For instance, see, Colombia – Switzerland BIT (2009).

[46] Newcombe and Paradell (2009), p. 268; OECD (2004), p. 10.

[47] Swiss Department of Foreign Affairs (FDFA), 1980 Mémoire in 36 Ann. Suisse de Droit Int'l 174, 178. "*On se réfère ainsi au principe classique du droit des gens selon lequel les Etats doivent mettre les étrangers se trouvant sur leur territoire et leurs biens au bénéfice du 'standard minimum' international, c'est-à-dire leur accorder un minimum de droits personnels, proceduraux et économiques.*"

[48] For instance, Switzerland – Trinidad and Tobago BIT (2010) as well as Georgia – Switzerland BIT (2014) contain post-1996 provisions. Interestingly, neither IIA refers to the MST.

[49] Article 3, France – Malta BIT (1976). Emphasis added.

enterprises and other interests."[50] Likewise, the Singapore—UK BIT of 1975 notes that "[i]nvestments of nationals and companies of either Contracting Party shall at all times be accorded fair and equitable treatment" without any explicit delimitation of the principle.[51]

As a predominantly European multilateral treaty, the original ECT includes a distinct reiteration of the FET principle under its Article 10:

> Each [party] shall [...] encourage and create stable, equitable, favourable and transparent conditions for [foreign investors] to make [i]nvestments in its [a]rea. [This] shall include a commitment to accord at all times [...] fair and equitable treatment. [...] In no case shall such [i]nvestments be accorded treatment less favourable than that required by international law, including treaty obligations.[52]

Wälde praised the ECT Article 10 as being the "most advanced text in terms of extensive investor protection" back in 2004.[53] It had been regarded as an elaborate[54] and progressive[55] provision, particularly for its wording on the scope of FET. Yet, despite its relatively articulate wording which includes stability, transparency and favourability as the elements of state responsibility attached to providing FET to investors, the ECT jurisprudence on FET does not point at a clear-cut, coherent pattern in application of the principle or a discernible difference in application vis-a-vis other contemporary BITs. There are a number of landmark arbitral cases under ECT that will be scrutinised below in detail, especially within the context of the scope and extent of FET provisions. This elaboration aside, the uncertainty attached to Article 10 of ECT is chiefly the result of the qualification in the provision: it reads that the treatment accorded to foreign investors shall not be less than what is required by international law, including treaty obligations.[56] What, indeed, is required by international law?

5.2.3 FET in North American IIAs Until the Twenty-First Century

The vague meaning of substantive protection principles in IIAs, the FET principle among them, truly came under spotlight for experts and the public during the late 90 s, following the first NAFTA-based disputes between foreign investors and North

[50] (West) Germany -United States FCN (1956).

[51] Singapore - UK BIT (1975). Other examples include the UK – USSR (Russia) BIT (1991), ChinaSweden BIT (1982).

[52] Article 10, Energy Charter Treaty (1998).

[53] Wälde (2004), p. 196.

[54] Schreuer (2005).

[55] Wälde (2004).

[56] Article 10, Energy Charter Treaty (1998).

American states. Until NAFTA, however, North American landscape had been far from convergent in terms of foreign investment policies and IIA provisions.

The United States had launched a programme for FCNs programme after World War II, due to discontent towards pre-WWII commerce treaties. These treaties were seen as insufficient in terms of their ability to promote and protect foreign investment, and the eventual exclusion of foreign investment protection from the scope of the GATT rules further underlined the necessity of a new stream of international instruments.[57] Between the years 1946 and 1956, sixteen FCNs were signed with countries such as Japan, Ethiopia, Uruguay, (West) Germany, the Netherlands and Greece.[58] The FCN treaties are also widely cited by scholars to have inspired the Abs-Shawcross Draft Convention which, eventually, inspired the first wave of BITs. Some scholars even asserted that FCN treaties were essentially BITs themselves.[59]

The FCNs did not only give the future BITs and investment protection provisions in other trade agreements their initial blueprint. Although the Havana Charter was the first text to refer to it as an over-arching, general protection principle for foreign investors, the FCNs played a crucial role in effectively introducing the FET principle in trade and investment-related protection of foreign capital.[60] For instance, in November 1946, FCN between Taiwan and the United States was signed, and it entered into force 2 years later, in November 1948.[61] It contains the FET principle under its Article XIX and XX, with regards to international transactions, transactions with a state monopoly or agency, as well as concessions and purchase of supplies from foreign nationals, corporations and associations. Similar specific provisions were also present in other, latter, FCN treaties.[62]

However, the US FCN treaties were not based on one uniform model. Their content and shape varied significantly. Take, for instance, the Germany—United States FCN treaty, which contained a broad FET clause that resembled European and subsequent North American BIT articulations. Pursuant to Article I, "[each party] shall at all times accord fair and equitable treatment to the nationals and companies of the other [p]arty, and to their property, enterprises and other interests."[63] Unlike the Taiwan FCN treaty, the German FCN treaty provides for FET 'at all times' and does not limit its application to certain acts such as concessions or purchase of supplies. This practice later found its way into North American BITs, as well as IIAs in general.

The United States began its BIT practice in early 1980s—more than two decades after the emergence of the first European BITs. It is possible to link this delay to the

[57] Walker (1958), p. 63.

[58] Walker (1958), p. 57.

[59] Alschner (2013), pp. 461–463.

[60] For a comprehensive, archival analysis of the United States FCNs and the rationale behind the fair treatment provisions contained therein, see Pinchis-Paulsen (2018).

[61] Taiwan – United States FCN (1948).

[62] Greece – United States FCN (1954).

[63] (West) Germany -United States FCN (1956).

FCN practice, given the common conception of BITs as a new generation of commercial treaties functioning similar to FCNs. The transition from FCNs to BITs has been officially explained by the objective of "[protecting] investment abroad in countries where investor rights are not already protected through existing agreements (such as modern treaties of friendship, commerce, and navigation [FCN] [...])".[64]

The first three BITs that the United States signed were with Panama,[65] Senegal[66] and Haiti.[67] Article II of the Panama—United States BIT states that "[i]nvestment of nationals and companies of [parties] shall at all times be accorded fair and equitable treatment [...] in the territory of the other [p]arty."[68] On his letter of transmittal dated 20 February 1986, George P. Schultz, the Secretary of State of the Reagan Administration, gave a brief overview of the American perspective on the FET principle:

> The model BIT accords the better of national or most-favored-nation (MFN) treatment to foreign investment [...] The BIT also includes **general treatment protections** designed to be **a guide to interpretation and application of the treaty**. Thus, the [p]arties agree to accord investments 'fair and equitable treatment' [...] in no case **'less than that required by international law**.' [...][69]

In 1987, the United States and Canada had finalised the negotiations for the US—Canada FTA (USCFTA).[70] Despite having a dedicated investment chapter, it did not contain an FET provision. While its dispute settlement provisions have been called "relatively robust",[71] CUSFTA did not contain an ISDS mechanism. NAFTA then extended USCFTA to Mexico when it entered into force in 1994. It includes a comprehensive investment chapter (Chapter 11), contains an ISDS mechanism and an FET provision (Article 1105, titled "Minimum Standard of Treatment"). This article, in its first paragraph, states that"[e]ach [p]arty shall accord to investments of investors of another [p]arty treatment in accordance with international investment law, including fair and equitable treatment".[72] A North American lawyer, directly involved in Canadian and Mexican IIA practice in particular, asserted during an interview that Mexico being a party to the treaty had a profound influence on the inclusion of the ISDS and FET provisions to NAFTA.[73]

---

[64] Office of the United States Trade Representative, Bilateral Investment Treaties http://www.ustr.gov/trade-agreements/bilateral-investment-treaties.

[65] Panama – United States BIT (1982).

[66] Senegal – United States BIT (1983).

[67] Haiti – United States BIT (1983 - not in force).

[68] Article II, Panama – US BIT (1982).

[69] Schultz, George P, Letter of Transmittal (to the President of the United States concerning the PanamaUS BIT) (20 February 1986), available at http://www.state.gov/documents/organization/43582.pdf Emphasis added.

[70] United States - Canada FTA (USCFTA) (1987).

[71] Blomstrom and Kokko (1997), p. 20.

[72] Article 1105, NAFTA (1994).

[73] Interview #20. The interviewee wished to remain anonymous.

More broadly, the North American tendency has generally been to link the FET principle to international law,[74] or in the case of the post-2004 IIAs, to CIL.[75] Both qualifiers exist with the purpose of setting the boundaries of state responsibility with regard to what 'fair and equitable' entails, while the latter's addition of 'customary' can be seen as a response and remedy to perceived adjudicatory (mis)interpretations of NAFTA Article 1105 by arbitral tribunals.[76] Article 1105 of NAFTA has sparked great controversy especially in the late 90s and early 2000s, effects of which are still observable and relevant to arbitral practice to this day.[77] As will be shown below in detail, the existence of any meaningful difference between the arbitral applications of these various qualifications, as well as between the existence or lack of any qualification, in application is dubious. These issues will be scrutinised below, particularly within the context of several key NAFTA claims.

5.3 The Vague Content and Scope of FET

As noted above, the content of the FET principle, as well as its consequences, have been thoroughly discussed over the years by investment law experts, practitioners and arbitrators.[78] One of the key discussions on the subject is on the thresholds used to determine its content: is it adjacent to the MST principle, or does it entail a completely separate, or autonomous, criterion that is independent from this perceived minimum threshold?[79] One Canadian lawyer, when asked about the content of the FET, noted the following:

> FET [...] could be anything. In fact, FET could be treatment under international law, which could cover every trade agreement out there. This is a very big fear for governments. One [...] concern is that [...] actions which are completely legitimate from a regulatory perspective [may] bring some sort of liability.[80]

The Chapter will outline different interpretative elements, subsets, and methods incorporated (or omitted) in IIAs in order to give coherence and fluidity to the subsequent case law analysis. It is very important to be able to pinpoint if, and how,

[74] Article II (2), Czech Republic – United States BIT (1992); Article II (3), Tunisia – United States BIT (1993); Article II (2), Argentina – United States BIT (1994).

[75] To recall, the abovementioned (Chap. 3) 2001 FTC interpretative note which reaffirmed that 'international law' under Article 1105 refers to CIL; NAFTA Free Trade Commission (FTC), North American Free Trade Agreement (NAFTA) Notes of Interpretation of Certain Chapter 11 Provisions (FTC Notes, 31 July 2001).

[76] FTC Notes (2001).

[77] Dumberry (2004); Dumberry (2024b).

[78] Yu (2024); Živković (2023); Sarmiento and Nikièma (2022); Angelet (2022); Dumberry (2018); Islam (2018); Paparinskis (2013); Kläger (2011); Tudor (2008); Schreuer (2005).

[79] One of the most outstanding supporters of the 'autonomous' FET is Dr. F.A. Mann. See, Mann (1981), p. 244.

[80] Interview #1.

the adapted wording and interpretation in a particular treaty influenced the decision of an arbitral tribunal.

In Chap. 2, the book elaborated on the historical and political clashes between states in connection with the notions of contingent and non-contingent fairness.[81] In short, the Chapter argued that historically, the vertical relationship between a sovereign and a foreigner has been governed at the former's discretion. The assessment of fairness of any treatment extended to foreigners had exclusively been contingent upon the treatment extended to another person or group. Non-contingent fairness, within the same context, refers to the notion of fairness based on a set of overarching principles and standards. These standards, constituent elements of MST, are claimed to transcend domestic treatment standards and legislation so that states would not be able to justify abusive treatment by using the veil of domestic regulations; and these treatment standards will therefore apply to foreigners even if the state refuses to accord such treatment to its nationals.[82] While scholarship indicates that such standard exists, its construing elements have never been laid out in their entirety, and no satisfying answer as to what such treatment standard refers has been given.

Despite this vagueness, there are a number of elements that have emerged in arbitral practice.[83] Borchard, for instance, counts "police and judicial protection for [property] rights" and excludes bad faith, fraud, outrage resulting in injury and municipal arbitrariness from the scope of IMS.[84] It is also asserted that the equal treatment of the nationals and foreigners is not *per se* sufficient for ISM to be invoked, in line with the divergence between absolute and relative equality. After referring to the "erroneous interference that [IMS] is *definite* and *definable*", Borchard goes on to set a point of reference, by stating that "[t]he international standard is compounded of general principles recognized by the domestic law of practically every civilized country [...]"[85] This vagueness seems to have been perceived as an embedded feature of the notion; in fact, not very different from the FET principle as an inherently vague standard regardless of its relationship to IMS.

While the reality is much more nuanced, it could generally be said that available arbitral practice diverges on the basis of whether IMS equals (or at least is strongly related) to FET on one side, and the idea that FET should be an entirely autonomous principle on the other. Both ends of the spectrum, despite their -ostensibly- demonstrably distinct configurations, in fact invoke a similar uncertainty: if FET is expected to be an autonomous principle, what are the components of its normative identity—or does this autonomy means precisely that it is devoid of a uniform, singular meaning, granting adjudicators a complete freedom in identifying its content? If its link to IMS is accepted, on the other hand, what different outcome would that

[81] Chapter 2.

[82] Stone (2012), p. 81.

[83] Yu (2024); Vandevelde (2010).

[84] Borchard (1940), p. 449.

[85] Borchard (1940), p. 458.

bring about, apart from the legal and jurisprudential consequences of FET being autonomous?

Other benchmarks, such as 'international law', were also used in an attempt to delimit the scope of this principle. A famous example is, as alluded to above, NAFTA. Although the base NAFTA text had no interpretative guide besides a reference to international law, the NAFTA Free Trade Commission (FTC) issued an Interpretative Note on July 2001 in order to reaffirm the correct interpretation of Article 1105. The note reads as follows:

> Article 1105 (1) prescribes the customary international law minimum standard of treatment of aliens as the minimum standard of treatment to be afforded to investments of investors of another [p]arty.
>
> The concepts of "fair and equitable treatment" and "full protection and security" do not require treatment in addition to or beyond that which is required by the customary international law minimum standard of treatment of aliens.
>
> A determination that there has been a breach of another provision of the NAFTA, or of a separate international agreement, does not establish that there has been a breach of Article 1105 (1).[86]

Interestingly, the FTC Interpretative Note is not the first, nor the only, source which reaffirmed that the US intended the phrase 'international law' to mean 'CIL'. There is no doubt that the two have different meanings, as international law *includes* CIL, but is not limited by it.[87] In a Letter of Submittal dated 24 April 2000 (more than a year before the FTC Note) addressed to the then-President of the United States Bill Clinton, the Secretary of State Madeleine Albright noted that:

> Paragraph 3 [of Article 2 of the Bahrain - US BIT of 1999] sets out **a minimum standard of treatment** based on standards found in **customary international law**. The [obligation] to accord 'fair and equitable treatment' [...] [is] explicitly cited [...] The general reference to international law also implicitly incorporates other fundamental rules of customary international law regarding the treatment of foreign investment. However, this provision does not incorporate obligations based on other international agreements.[88]

While the above letter relates specifically to the 1999 US—Bahrain BIT, given its general language and the near-identical language contained in the US BITs

---

[86] FTC Notes (2001).

[87] Brower II (2006).

[88] Albright M, Letter of Submittal (24 April 2000). https://investmentpolicy.unctad.org/international-investment-agreements/treaties/bit/362/bahrain%2D%2D-united-states-of-america-bit-1999-. The transmittal statement of the Albania – US BIT (1995) identically includes this paragraph. In addition, the note elaborates on what is meant by 'other fundamental rules of customary international law': "[...] for example, that sovereignty may not be grounds for unilateral revocation or amendment of a Party's obligations to investors and investments (especially contracts), and that an investor is entitled to have any expropriation done in accordance with previous undertakings of a Party." Tarnoff P, Letter of Submittal (3 August 1995). https://investmentpolicy.unctad.org/international-investment-agreements/treaties/bit/47/albania%2D%2D-united-states-of-america-bit-1995-. Also see, Warren C, Letter of Submittal (7 September 1993), which similarly notes that the relevant provision of the 1997 Ecuador – US BIT "sets out a minimum standard of treatment based on customary international law". https://2009-2017.state.gov/e/eb/ifd/43254.htm.

throughout 90s, it could be argued that a similar reasoning had driven the US treaty practice *vis-à-vis* the required threshold of treatment. It is also clear from the explanation here that the FET is not used synonymously with the minimum standard, but is considered a constituent sub-obligation of this minimum standard. Furthermore, the use of the phrase 'international law' is characterised as an implicit reference to other CIL rules relating to treatment of foreigners in addition to the obligations explicitly mentioned in the provision, while other international agreements are excluded from the scope. This conclusion is supported by the Canadian Statement of Implementation of NAFTA, which stated that NAFTA Article 1105(1) "provides for a minimum absolute standard of treatment, based on the long-standing principles of customary international law",[89] bringing the Canadian position in line with the US.

In their post-2001 BITs and FTAs, the United States and Canada have maintained the position asserted under the FTC Interpretative Note more explicitly, and begun noting that the threshold for the FET principle was CIL. Similar to the methods that have been used to further clarify the considerations in an indirect expropriation test, the tendency has been to be able to further explain what "fair and equitable" meant by annexes. Take, for instance, Article 10.5 of the Colombia - US FTA titled "Minimum Standard of Treatment":

> Each [p]arty shall accord to covered investment treatment in accordance with customary international law, including fair and equitable treatment and full protection and security.[90]

A footnote directs the reader to an Annex 10-A, which reads that this article "shall be interpreted in accordance with Annex 10-A."[91] The referenced annex states that the mentioned "CIL" shall be understood as "*general and consistent practice* of [s]tates that they follow from *a sense of legal obligation*. With regards to Article 10.5, the CIL minimum standard of treatment of aliens refers to all customary international law principles that protect the economic rights and interests of aliens."[92] Similar clarifications, which in their essence fall short of its explanatory purposes due to its rather circular wording (which essentially notes that CIL means all CIL principles), exist in other North American IIAs.[93]

The treaty recognises MST as an overarching rule which also encompasses the FET principle; and in such a setting, the arbitral application of this rule will have to stem from the overarching CIL rule and its components. Similar to the effect of annexes on the indirect expropriation test (i.e., the carve-out of certain measures or series of measures), the annex and the interpretative guidance it provides aim to set the limits for what is considered to be within the boundaries of the provision. The annex appears to declare that the provision should be read somewhat narrower than

[89] Department of External Affairs Canada, North American Free Trade Agreement, Canadian Statement on Implementation, (Canada Gazette, Part I, 1 January 1994), p. 149. Available http://www.international.gc.ca/trade-agreements-accords-commerciaux/assets/pdfs/N11_JAN1994.pdf.

[90] Article 10.5, Colombia – US FTA (2012).

[91] Article 10.5, Colombia – US FTA (2012).

[92] Annex 10-A, Colombia – US FTA (2012). Emphasis added.

[93] Article 11.5, Australia – US FTA (2005).

what may have been the case if it were not tied to CIL. However, and unlike the indirect expropriation annexes, the arbitral tribunals do not have any meaningful interpretative guidance as to *how* their discretion is limited with regards to all CIL principles that protect the economic rights and interests of aliens. Besides generally pointing towards the fact that such principles indeed exist, IIAs rarely elaborate on what is meant by 'all CIL principles' on the subject. IIAs have been systematically mute on these issues—until recently.

While the exact subset of MST may be unclear, there is a generally accepted way to identify whether or not a rule is CIL. The generality and consistency of the state act, and whether or not it stems from *opinio juris,* are prerequisites for a rule or principle to aspire to the level of CIL.[94] If, however, the subject of examination is a provision in an IIA with no qualification or threshold, in accordance with Article 31 of VCLT, CIL will still be relevant to the interpretation of the said provision. In this case, the presence of the general and consistent practice of states based on *opinio juris* is still a supplementary consideration.[95] If the treaty explicitly considers FET as a constituent element of MST like the example above, the outstanding effect will be that the parties, through the treaty, will have demonstrated their doctrinal preference with regards to the role of CIL. The other alternative is to omit the mention of CIL from the provision regarding FET, so that the provision can imply an autonomous, self-standing principle. However, as Porterfield argues, "arbitrators tend to define the [CIL]-linked standard for FET in exactly the same manner as the autonomous standard: by reference to previous arbitral awards and academic writings, without any evidence of either state practice or *opinio juris.*"[96] As the implications of these seemingly different formulations are unsettled at best, it is not granted that all arbitral tribunals will disregard CIL to grant FET autonomy, or even consider the exclusion of the CIL from the analysis as a prerequisite of its autonomous analysis.

5.4 Selected Case Law on FET: Autonomy Vs. Thresholds

As noted above, the vagueness and subjectivity encompassing both MST and FET demonstrate a need for a tangible framework for coherence and consistency. This requires more than simple references to other vague rules. This assertion finds

[94] Thirlway (2010), pp. 102–103; *North Sea Continental Shelf* (*Federal Republic of Germany v. Denmark*). Judgment (20 February 1969). https://www.icj-cij.org/case/51. Also see, Article 4 of the India – Uzbekistan BIT (2025), which specifies under a footnote that "'customary international law' only results from a general and consistent practice of States that they follow from a sense of legal obligation." The main text of the article articulates sub-elements such as "denial of justice in any judicial or administrative proceedings", "fundamental breach of due process", "targeted discrimination on manifestly unjustified grounds, such as gender, race or religious belief", or "manifestly abusive treatment, such as coercion, duress and harassment." Notably, the wording of the BIT indicates that these sub-elements "constitute a violation of customary international law".

[95] Article 31(3), Vienna Convention (1969).

[96] Porterfield (2013).

confirmation in the fragmented and conflicting case law with regards to the FET principle. I identify doctrinal and behavioural inclinations, particularly with regards to the application of relevant CIL, in relation to the nature of facts and the consequent awards.

I aim to demonstrate that a persistent uncertainty and inconsistency exists in arbitral case law regarding the implications of these thresholds. While recent empirical studies indicate that a reference to MST might push tribunals to adopt ostensibly more 'restrictive' readings,[97] the identification of an actual restrictive reading to a particular case requires further evidence to the effect that an arbitral tribunal actually adopts the restrictive reading it said it would. As some cases below demonstrate, it is not uncommon for arbitral tribunals to declare a 'restrictive' approach only to cite cases where an unqualified FET provision was applicable. It is also systemically difficult to compare an ostensibly 'autonomous', therefore 'broad' reading as it applies to a case, and a 'restrictive' reading as it applies to a different set of facts to reach to the conclusion that the former is definitively more lenient than the latter.

The selection of cases below is conducted following a representative geographical allocation as to coincide with the overall coverage of investment arbitration practice. Besides its geographical representation, the analysis takes into account a variety of relevant state measures such as interference with business operations, hindrance of an investment, alleged abusive treatment, and denial of justice. Several relatively new awards, similar to the indirect expropriation case law analysis above, are included to bolster the analysis and strengthen the conclusions as newer IIAs with revised provisions emerge.

Vague qualifiers such as CIL or international law, as well as the lack of such qualifiers, do not guarantee different, discernible streams of interpretation. First group of cases mostly concern the interpretation of different -qualified and unqualified- FET provisions. Second group of cases aim to highlight legitimate expectations arguments presented within the context of FET principle to demonstrate what arbitrators deemed to be 'legitimate'. Finally, a third group of cases will briefly outline the investor's conduct, and how it contributes to the FET analysis conducted by arbitrators. In order to avoid repetition, I do not include factual backgrounds for the cases that have already been addressed under Chap. 4.

As noted above, this Chapter does not seek to provide a list of subset that ought to be included in the FET principle.[98] It will, however, refer to subset identified in scholarship and in arbitral awards to subsequently compare specific elements (legitimate expectations being one controversial element in that regard) specifically in connection with their associations with autonomous and restrictive readings of FET

[97] Dumberry (2024b), pp. 307–308.

[98] Schill (2022), p. 361; also see, Article 13, The Institute of International Law, Eighteenth Commission, Legal Aspects of Recourse to Arbitration by an Investor Against the Authorities of the Host State under Inter-State Treaties (13 September 2013). https://www.idi-iil.org/en/publications/aspects-juridiques-du-recours-a-larbitrage-par-un-investisseur-contre-les-autorites-de-letat-hote-en-vertu-dun-traite-interetatique-version-anglaise/.

respectively. The focus will be on the similarities and divergences between the subset identified pursuant to an autonomous reading on the one hand, and an ostensibly 'restrictive', CIL-bound reading on the other. The identified subset, as will be demonstrated below, differ only marginally, and do not ensure that any qualification has the intended effects of delimiting the scope of protection.

Following the case law analysis, the Chapter will assess how these ambiguous differences in treaty-making throughout 80s, 90s, and even 2000s have been addressed in the new generation of IIAs, and whether or not they present any substantial steps forward in better encapsulating what a normative, non-contingent obligation of FET should look like. The Chapter will ultimately argue that, for FET to attain any semblance of consistency in arbitral case law, references to MST or CIL should ideally be discarded. FET should lay forth specific, articulated subset to inject clarity to the concept. While there is a general tendency in new generation treaty-making towards identifying at least *some* sub-elements, I argue that the EU approach in particular shows promise when compared to IIAs that continue to refer to MST.

5.4.1 *Where It All Began: Earlier NAFTA Awards and the Fine-Tuning of Thresholds*

A logical starting point to any FET case law analysis is certainly the pre-2001 Note case law that originated from NAFTA. In that light, ***Pope & Talbot Inc. v. Canada***[99] award is a key example. It is an oft-cited case, and the most appropriate case with which to start the case analysis for its catalyst effect on the meaning and scope of the NAFTA Article 1105.[100]

The Claimant, *inter alia*, alleged a breach of MST under 1105 NAFTA. The decision on Article 1105 claim predates the FTC interpretation by only a few months. Thus, the content of the term 'international law' had been disputed by the investor, who had claimed that it included all sources of international law found in Article 38 of SICJ; as well as the concept of 'good faith', the guidelines on foreign direct

[99] *Pope & Talbot Inc. v. The Government of Canada, UNCITRAL.* Award on the Merits of Phase 2 (10 April 2001) (*Pope & Talbot v. Canada*). Facts of the case can be found above in Chap. 4.

[100] For ease of reference, Article 1105 of NAFTA is as follows (emphasis added):

1. Each Party shall accord to investments of investors of another Party *treatment in accordance with international law, including fair and equitable treatment* and full protection and security.
2. Without prejudice to paragraph 1 and notwithstanding Article 1108(7)(b), each Party shall accord to investors of another Party, and to investments of investors of another Party, non-discriminatory treatment with respect to measures it adopts or maintains relating to losses suffered by investments in its territory owing to armed conflict or civil strife.
3. Paragraph 2 does not apply to existing measures relating to subsidies or grants that would be inconsistent with Article 1102 but for Article 1108(7)(b).

investment prepared by the World Bank,[101] other treaty obligations of the NAFTA parties and, to a certain extent, relevant domestic law of the NAFTA parties.

Canada opposed to such broadening of the standard, and pointed out that for a violation of international law to be found, the challenged state act needs to be *egregious;* that is, "a denial of fairness would have to be shocking to be a violation of Article 1105."[102] Canadian position suggested that fairness was *inclusive* to MST. Mexico and the United States had also expressed their position on the matter during the proceedings. Along with a number of other cases which involved this discussion, *Pope & Talbot* decision clearly played a role in the shaping of the July 2001 Interpretation by FTC.

The Tribunal, however, submitted to the alternative interpretation and declared fairness to be *additive*; hence granting a perceived autonomy to FET above MST as set by international law. Its line of reasoning is noteworthy:

> It is true that the language of Article 1105 suggests otherwise [as in, the fairness elements being inclusive], since it states that the fairness elements are included within international law. But that interpretation is clouded by the fact [...] that the language of Article 1105 grew out of the provisions of bilateral commercial treaties negotiated by the United States and other industrialized countries.[103]

The Tribunal then went on to cite the FET provision in the 1987 US Model BIT,[104] which contains a different language than Article 1105.[105] The Tribunal expressly acknowledged that the language in NAFTA suggests that the interpretation would be different,[106] yet still argued that given these types of agreements grew out of treaties negotiated by the United States, those treaties must be considered as a 'principle source'. There is no plausible argument as to why the applicable treaty language was completely ignored, and why the clearly divergent language contained in NAFTA, specifying that FET was included in the 'international law' threshold, could suddenly have a different meaning. An added problem was that the Respondent was not the United States, but Canada. Finally, it concluded that "[a] logical corollary to [the language of NAFTA 1105] is that compliance with the fairness elements

---

[101] World Bank, Guidelines on the Treatment of Foreign Direct Investment (1992). https://documents1.worldbank.org/curated/fr/955221468766167766/pdf/multi-page.pdf.

[102] *Elettronica Sicula S.p.A. (United States of America v. Italy)*, Judgment (20 July 1989). https://www.icj-cij.org/sites/default/files/case-related/76/076-19890720-JUD-01-00-EN.pdf (*ELSI*), par. 128.

[103] *Pope & Talbot v. Canada* (2001), par. 109.

[104] US Model BIT (1987); also *see*, Ruttenberg (1987).

[105] Article II(2) of the 1987 US Model BIT reads as follows: "Investment shall at all times be accorded fair and equitable treatment, shall enjoy full protection and security and shall in no case be accorded treatment less than that required by international law."

[106] The Tribunal expressly noted the following: "It is true that the language of Article 1105 suggests otherwise, since it states that the fairness elements are included within international law. But that interpretation is clouded by the fact, as all parties agree, that the language of Article 1105 grew out of the provisions of bilateral commercial treaties negotiated by the United States and other industrialized countries. As Canada points out, these treaties as a "principal source" of the general obligations of states with respect to their treatment of foreign investment." (par. 110).

must be ascertained free of any threshold that might be applicable to the evaluation of measures under the minimum standard of international law."[107] In this light, the Tribunal contended that it would not apply the CIL standard test which, according to the Canadian position and its own conclusion on the meaning of the provision, entails an analysis based on the criteria that a measure had to be "'egregious', 'outrageous' or 'shocking' or otherwise extraordinary."[108]

Free from these so-called thresholds, the Tribunal found that the only successful FET claim by the claimant was under a process called the verification review. Following the claimant's initial arbitration submission, the Softwood Lumber Division ("SLD") of Canada had contacted the investment, requesting further information on why the claimant was unable to reach its quota allocation. As the Tribunal contended, the claimant "[had not] been anything less than fully cooperative with the SLD" with regards to sharing and making available the information. SLD, in return, had invoked a number of unnecessary challenges for the investor, such as requesting the investor to make available relevant documents for the review in Canada instead of Portland, where they were located—the consequences of such request, as the Tribunal asserted, were "substantial and disruptive".[109] No particular explanation or regulatory or legal basis as to why the documents should be made available in Canada was given to the investor, besides the fact that it was somehow deemed not acceptable. The Tribunal reached its decision of an FET violation following its analysis of a number of inconsistent and outright false facts presented by the SLD to the relevant Canadian minister with regards to the quota discrepancy. It was also underlined that "[the] episode goes well beyond the glitches and innocent mistakes that may typify the process [...] the verification review process is nothing less than a denial of the fair treatment [...]".[110]

The Tribunal provided no further explanation on how an examination of the case where fairness elements would be deemed *inclusive* to the international law threshold would differ from the *autonomous* analysis it had conducted. Besides rejecting the above-mentioned thresholds, it does not elaborate on the criteria of this autonomous analysis it undertook. In that sense, the difference between an additive and an inclusive fairness analysis is not discernible. Although the Tribunal may have meant that the international law/CIL benchmark would somehow be more demanding, as in, it has to be 'egregious' or 'shocking'; it is at best dubious to rely on these inherently subjective notions. The Tribunal's erroneous ascertainment of the correct interpretation notwithstanding, even if it had accepted the Canadian position, one could still ask whether a threshold is really higher and lower, or if at all meaningful, if what is 'shocking' or 'egregious' could change from one adjudicator to another given they lack legal, normative meanings. An adjudicatory threshold, in this sense,

---

[107] *Pope & Talbot v. Canada* (2001), par. 111.

[108] *Pope & Talbot v. Canada* (2001), par. 118.

[109] *Pope & Talbot v. Canada* (2001), par. 172.

[110] *Pope & Talbot v. Canada* (2001), par. 181.

needs to be significantly more discernible and concrete, and not reliant entirely on subjective and fluid criteria.

S.D. Myers v. Canada[111] is another pre-FTC Note case, concerning a claim by S.D. Myers, Inc. (SDMI) against the Canadian decision to ban the transfer of a highly toxic substance, polychlorinated biphenyl (PCB), from Canada to the United States, for disposal. The claimant argued that "the promulgation of the export ban by Canada was done in a discriminatory and unfair manner that constituted a denial of justice and a violation of good faith under international law."[112]

The Tribunal, after asserting that it did not "have an open-ended mandate to second-guess government decision making", noted that a breach of Article 1105 "occurs only when it is shown that an investor has been treated in such an unjust or arbitrary manner that the treatment rises to the level that is unacceptable from the international perspective."[113] In its elaboration of the scope of IMS as it is referred to under Article 1105, the Tribunal made a reference to the US—Mexican Claims Commission case *Hopkins*, which reads that "[t]he citizens of a nation may enjoy many rights which are withheld from aliens, and conversely, under international law, aliens may enjoy rights and remedies which the nation does not accord to its own citizens."[114] Having accepted the possibility of preferential treatment for aliens *vis-à-vis* nationals within a domestic law context, the Tribunal further added that "[t]he determination must be made in the light of the high measure of deference that international law generally extends to the right of domestic authorities to regulate matters within their own borders."[115] Applying the same provision as *Pope & Talbot*, the *S.D. Myers* tribunal instead referred to an international *acceptability* criterion, which is not any less vague than terms such as *shocking*, or *egregious*.

Mondev v. United States[116] had been a pending case when the FTC Note was adopted by the NAFTA parties. The award was dispatched to its parties roughly a year and a half after the Note, in October 2002. The dispute concerns the state conduct within the context of a tripartite rehabilitation agreement for an area in Boston. The central claim by Mondev was that granting a government organ, namely the Boston Redevelopment Authority, statutory immunity from tort liability constituted a denial of justice and thus fell below the MST laid forth pursuant to Article 1105(1). The *Mondev* tribunal's analysis is particularly outstanding for its evolutionary, progressive perception of CIL which asserts that CIL "refers to customary international law as it stood no earlier than the time at which NAFTA came into force. It is not limited to the international law of the nineteenth century or even the first half of the

---

[111] *S.D. Myers, Inc. v. Government of Canada,* UNCITRAL, Partial Award (13 November 2000) (*S.D. Myers v. Canada*).

[112] *S.D. Myers v. Canada* (2000), par. 136.

[113] *S.D. Myers v. Canada* (2000), par. 263.

[114] *George W. Hopkins (USA) v. United Mexican States.* Decision (3 June 1927). http://legal.un.org/riaa/cases/vol_IV/218-219.pdf.

[115] *S.D. Myers v. Canada* (2000), par. 263.

[116] *Mondev International Ltd. v. United States of America,* ICSID Case No. ARB(AF)/99/2, Award (11 October 2002).

twentieth century, although decisions from that period remain relevant."[117] Another NAFTA award, namely ***ADF v. United States,***[118] confirmed this dynamism of CIL.

Another notable feature of the Mondev award is the Tribunal's elaboration on the Canadian claim that "the meaning of those provisions in customary international law is that laid down by [...] the Mexican Claims Commission in the *Neer* case",[119] namely the conclusion that "the treatment of an alien [...] should amount to an outrage, to bad faith, to wilful neglect of duty, or to an insufficiency of governmental action so far short of international standards that every reasonable and impartial man would readily recognise its insufficiency."[120] The Tribunal questioned the appropriateness of this case as a basis for the CIL requirements on the matter. The Tribunal aptly observed that the "case [...] concerned not the treatment of foreign investment as such but the physical security of an alien."[121] Furthermore, the Tribunal opined that "what is unfair or inequitable need not equate with the outrageous or the egregious. In particular, a State may treat foreign investment unfairly and inequitably without necessarily acting in bad faith."[122] With this contention, the Tribunal arguably alluded to the fluid character of terms such as 'outrageous' and 'egregious', and further observed that the definitions and perception of these terms were susceptible to time, and contextual differences.[123] The Tribunal then elaborated on its understanding of CIL: "In holding that Article 1105(1) refers to customary international law, the FTC interpretations incorporate current international law, whose content is shaped by the conclusion of more than two thousand bilateral investment treaties and many treaties of friendship and commerce."[124]

The Tribunal further scrutinised the denial of justice claim, as a relevant element of inquiry within the scope of Article 1105. As to the meaning of denial of justice, the Tribunal pointed towards the difference between dealing with "unremedied acts of the local constabulary", and "[second-guessing] the reasoned decisions of the highest courts of a State."[125] It concluded that NAFTA tribunals could not act as a court of appeal. With this in mind, citing the ***Azinian v. United Mexican States***[126] case, the Tribunal identified several examples which could be deemed as denial of justice: (a) refusal by courts to entertain a suit, (b) subjecting such suit to undue delay, (c) administrating justice in a "seriously inadequate way", and (d) clear and

[117] *Mondev v. USA* (2002), par. 125.

[118] *ADF Group Inc. v. United States of America*, ICSID Case No. ARB(AF)/00/1, Award (9 January 2003), par. 179 (*ADF v. USA*).

[119] *Neer v. Mexico* (1926).

[120] *Mondev v. USA* (2002), par. 114.

[121] *Mondev v. USA* (2002), par. 115.

[122] *Mondev v. USA* (2002), par. 116.

[123] *Mondev v. USA* (2002), par. 116–117.

[124] *Mondev v. USA* (2002), par. 125.

[125] *Ibid*, par. 126.

[126] *Robert Azinian, Kenneth Davitian & Ellen Baca v. The United Mexican States*,ICSID Case No. ARB(AF)/97/2, Award (1 November 1999) (*Azinian v. Mexico*).

malicious misapplication of the law. Furthermore, referring to the *ELSI* Case,[127] the Tribunal scrutinised the notion of arbitrariness.[128] In the light of these elaborations, the *Mondev* Tribunal failed to find a breach of Article 1105.

The decision by the *Mondev* tribunal, at least in principle, markedly differs from the *Pope & Talbot* award in terms of its consideration of the 2001 FTC Note. It affirms the North American position which considers FET to be inclusive to CIL, rather than additive. This prompted the Tribunal to engage with the content, the scope, and the nature of CIL/MST framework. This being said, while *Pope & Talbot* gave an autonomous character to FET as opposed to *Mondev*'s contention that it is linked to an ever-evolving CIL, both tribunals ultimately agreed on the fact that an act needed not to be shocking or egregious to amount to an unfair treatment. The *Mondev* Tribunal's analysis, like *Pope & Talbot*, did not elaborate on the differences between the two interpretations, and even highlighted the "long-standing and divisive debate about whether any such thing as a minimum standard of treatment of investment in international law actually exists."[129]

Waste Management v. Mexico[130] was a post-FTC dispute between an American investor and the city of Acapulco in Mexico with regards to a waste disposal concession granted to the former by the latter. FET claim was complementary to the expropriation claim; however, its particular examination by the Tribunal is highly illustrative. First, the Tribunal, taking into account past NAFTA case law,[131] framed the FET breach as follows:

> […] [T]he minimum standard of treatment of fair and equitable treatment is infringed by conduct attributable to the [s]tate and harmful to the claimant if the conduct is **arbitrary**, **grossly unfair**, **unjust** or **idiosyncratic**, is **discriminatory** and exposes the claimant to **sectional or racial prejudice**, or involves a **lack of due process** leading to an outcome **which offends judicial propriety** – as might be the case with **a manifest failure of natural justice** in judicial proceedings or a **complete lack of transparency or candour** in an administrative process. In applying this standard, it is relevant that the treatment is in breach of **representations** made by the [host state] **which were reasonably relied on by the claimant**.[132]

The *Waste Management* tribunal, therefore, asked whether or not the challenged act (a) is arbitrary, (b) is discriminatory and prejudiced; (c) is conducted without due process (which, as a result, is detrimental to judicial propriety); (d) is a manifest failure of natural justice; (e) is transparent. Additionally, the Tribunal considered

[127] *ELSI* (1989).

[128] *Mondev v. USA* (2002), par. 127.

[129] *Mondev v. USA* (2002), par. 120.

[130] *Waste Management, Inc. v. United Mexican States (II),* ICSID Case No. ARB(AF)/00/3. Award (30 April 2004) (*Waste Management v. Mexico*).

[131] *S.D. Myers v. Canada (2000), Mondev v. USA (2002), ADF v. USA (2003), Loewen Group, Inc. and Raymond L. Loewen v. United States of America,* ICSID Case No. ARB(AF)/98/3, Award (26 June 2003) (*Loewen v. USA*).

[132] *Waste Management v. Mexico* (2004), par. 98. This paragraph remains highly popular in arbitral practice to this day. See, for instance, *Interconexión Eléctrica S.A. E.S.P. v. Republic of Chile*, ICSID Case No. ARB/21/27, Award (13 December 2024), par. 755; *Odyssey Marine Exploration, Inc. v. United Mexican States*, ICSID Case No. UNCT/20/1, Final Award (17 September 2024) (*Odyssey v. Mexico*), par. 298.

representations by the host state on which a foreign investor 'reasonably' relied in connection with its investment—alluding to the legitimate (or in this case, reasonable) expectations doctrine. In particular the reference to the latter is important as legitimate expectations are generally not considered to be part of CIL and excluded from the scope of MST.[133]

Along with a number of government organs and associated institutions, the conduct of the city Acapulco was also alleged to have breached the minimum standard as prescribed by Article 1105. The city, in accordance with the concession agreement, was to pay the claimant a monthly fee in exchange for the waste management service. Besides, the city was also claimed to be at fault with regards to the enforcement of the terms between the parties. Both obligations were continuously hindered, and the Tribunal settled this as a fact.

What followed was the consideration of the "countervailing factors" to the reflected failure to comply with contractual obligations. The Tribunal considered the factors which hindered the city of Acapulco to satisfy the duties pursuant to the agreement. "[The city] made at least some attempts to encourage local residents and business groups to contract with [the claimant]", stated the Tribunal, pointing towards the local unrest which came about with the concession granted to the claimant and against the extra fee charged to the residents for waste disposal. "[I]t did bring at least some proceedings against the 'pirates' [unauthorised garbage collectors] and even against its own employees caught moonlighting in the concession area [...] some steps were [also] taken [...] to identify allocation for the permanent waste disposal site [...]".[134]

Furthermore, it was maintained that the claimant was rather 'heavy-handed' with regards to the execution of its concession activities, towards a community not particularly content with the agreement and related activities. Among them was counted "immediate invoices" issued to the residents, accompanied by threats of legal action in the event of non-payment.

Third, the consideration shifted towards the macroeconomic situation in Mexico which, according to the Tribunal, severely affected the city's capacity to perform its obligations.

This being said, the Tribunal contended that it "does not suggest that financial stringency or public resistance are, as such, excuses for breaches of contractual commitments"; nor that it would look into a situation in which the claimant itself is responsible for bad business. However, this should not mean that the scrutiny of each specific case should disregard the social and economic circumstances in which

[133] *Obligation to Negotiate Access to the Pacific Ocean* (*Bolivia v. Chile*), Judgment (1 October 2018), par. 162: "The Court notes that references to legitimate expectations may be found in arbitral awards concerning disputes between a foreign investor and the host State that apply treaty clauses providing for fair and equitable treatment. It does not follow from such references that there exists in general international law a principle that would give rise to an obligation on the basis of what could be considered a legitimate expectation. Bolivia's argument based on legitimate expectations thus cannot be sustained." https://www.icj-cij.org/case/153.

[134] *Waste Management v. Mexico* (2004), par. 110.

the investment is conducted. Indeed, the Tribunal maintained that the city was in "a situation of genuine difficulty" and thus its non-payment *per se* will not amount to a breach of Article 1105. The non-payment, therefore, did not arise from an arbitrary choice or conduct which the state had undertaken—nor was it motivated by 'sectoral or local prejudice'.

The *Waste Management* award is a striking example of the role of public opinion on particular investments, their involvement and function; with regards to a host state's adjudicatory justification of certain acts and failures therewith. As for the financial crisis, it was clearly stated that it is not an 'excuse' for Acapulco's failure to fulfil its contractual obligations; but the conclusion implies that it may counteract the claims of arbitrariness if there is sufficient effort to remedy the failure despite the macroeconomic hardships the country may be suffering. A similar inquiry sits at the core of the Argentine cases examined later in this section. One could argue that if the city had not shown such efforts to fulfil its obligations (despite the eventual failure), the arbitrariness argument could have prevailed despite the economic crisis. In short, the state's attitude towards the perceived hindrance or distress can determine whether or not the challenged conduct is arbitrary—even if the eventual outcome is not ideal for the investor.

With regards to arbitrariness, ***Plama v. Bulgaria***[135] award under the ECT also adds to the above-provided analysis by approximating the term "arbitrary" with "unreasonable".[136] This also seems to be in line with the examination of what arbitrariness is, pursuant to Article 1105 of NAFTA. In fact, the economic and social circumstances of the time, coupled with efforts of ramification, took the conduct (or lack, thereof) from the scope of *arbitrariness*, and placed it under what could be called *inevitability*, which does not *per se* invoke an attributable, unfair and inequitable act conducted in bad faith.

Waste Management is among the most cited arbitral cases for its explicit and influential articulation of the 'subset' of the FET principle.

The ***Methanex v. United States***[137] award presents an important FET analysis with regards to its explanation and elaboration of the interrelation between FET and other protection principles. Although the discussion is highly NAFTA-specific, its results are equally illustrative for the broader IIA regime. Methanex essentially referred to the discrimination clause under Article 1102 and linked it to FET, and claimed that "intentional discrimination is, by definition, inequitable."[138] Through such interpretation, Methanex drew a parallel between Articles 1102 and 1105. It further stated that the FTC interpretation of Article 1105 is a "[...] distinct and [...] important [...] deletion from [NAFTA] to be anything other than an amendment".[139] Methanex

---

[135] *Plama Consortium Limited v. Bulgaria,* ICSID Case No. ARB/03/24, Award (27 August 2008) (*Plama v. Bulgaria*).

[136] *Plama v. Bulgaria* (2008), par. 184.

[137] *Methanex Corporation v. United States of America, UNCITRAL,* Final Award on Jurisdiction and Merits (3 August 2005) (*Methanex v. United States*).

[138] *Methanex v. United States* (2005), Part IV, Chapter C, par. 2.

[139] *Methanex v. United States* (2005), Part IV, Chapter C, par. 4.

argued in favour of disregarding the interpretation, "on the basis that it is nothing more than an attempt by the USA retroactively to suppress a legitimate claim."[140]

Methanex further claimed that California's ban was "arbitrary, grossly unfair, unjust and idiosyncratic in the sense that there was a pandering to a domestic US industry [...] In addition, [...] there was a complete lack of transparency [...]. [W]henever a political official implicitly favours one competitor in return for political contributions and shuts another competitor out of the market, that action is arbitrary, grossly unfair, unjust, and idiosyncratic as the decision is not made on the merits."[141] Reference to the *Waste Management* formulation referred to above is notable.

The Tribunal's decision affirmed the US position, which submitted that the FTC interpretation was binding, and that Article 1102 would not automatically entail an Article 1105 responsibility, since the third paragraph of the FTC Note clearly stated that "[a] determination that there has been a breach of another provision of the NAFTA, or of a separate international agreement, does not establish that there has been a breach of Article 1105(1)."[142]

The Tribunal pointed out that Methanex's discrimination claim pursuant to Article 1102 had already been rejected, and therefore even if there was an automatic fulfilment of both principles, Methanex's claim would still fall short. Besides, the Tribunal contended that the parties to the NAFTA have consciously made a differentiation between the two principles, as evident from the separate wording in Article 1102 and Article 1105, as well as the wording of paragraphs (1) and (2) of the latter. According to the Tribunal, "[w]hen the NAFTA Parties did not incorporate a non-discrimination requirement in a provision in which they might have done so, it would be wrong for a tribunal to pretend that they had", and the FTC interpretation "simply confirmed" this.[143]

With regards to the validity of the FTC Note, the Tribunal rejected the alleged necessity of an official amendment. Indeed, Article 39 of VCLT simply refers to "[amendment] by agreement"[144]; and in the present case, the Note was indeed decided collectively by Mexico, the United States and Canada as parties to the NAFTA.

As the final consideration, the Tribunal rejected Methanex's argument that differential treatment is automatically discriminatory on the grounds that California differentiated between national and foreign investors. It pointed out that "international law [was] clear" on the issue, and it was in fact allowed in CIL to make distinctions between nationals and foreigners, and this fact does not necessarily entail discriminatory treatment *per se*.

Thunderbird v. Mexico,[145] another NAFTA award, was issued after the FTC Note. The claimant was an American entertainment company involved in gaming

---

[140] *Methanex v. United States* (2005), Part IV, Chapter C, par. 5.

[141] *Methanex v. United States* (2005), Part IV, Chapter C, par. 8.

[142] FTC Notes (*supra* note 410); *Methanex v. United States* (2005), Part IV, Chapter C, par. 17.

[143] *Methanex v. United States* (2005), Part IV, Chapter C, par. 17.

[144] Article 39, Vienna Convention (1969).

[145] *International Thunderbird Gaming Corporation v. Mexico*, UNCITRAL, ad hoc, Arbitral Award (26 January 2006) (*Thunderbird v. Mexico*).

machine business with an interest in the Mexican market. Upon their request, the Mexican government had issued an *Officio* stating that it would be possible to operate gaming machines "as long as they do not become, in any manner whatsoever, as gaming or betting machines; provided; however, that [the claimant subsidiary] complies with the states and/or municipal laws or regulations in Mexico."[146] This had been interpreted as a confirmation for their planned business activities. In late 2001, however, Mexican government declared the claimant's activities illegal—a conduct which invoked this arbitral claim.

The Tribunal adopted the FTC interpretation; therefore, the above-mentioned CIL-inspired position prevailed. Thunderbird elaborated on its understanding of FET under three elements: detrimental reliance (legitimate expectations), denial of justice, and abuse of rights. The latter two could be associated with due process and arbitrariness, respectively.

As for the legitimate expectations, the Tribunal discussed the issue as follows:

> [T]he concept of 'legitimate expectations' relates, within the context of the NAFTA framework, to a situation where a [party]'s conduct creates reasonable and justifiable expectations on the part of an investor (or investment) to act in reliance on said conduct, such that a failure […] to honour those expectations could cause the investor (or investment) to suffer damages.[147]

Having thus included the legitimate expectations as a sub-element into the scope of MST, the *Thunderbird* award added to the string of cases where a CIL-qualified FET provision was associated with the legitimate expectations of the investor. The Tribunal then went on to differentiate between "arbitrary and unfair" and "*manifestly* arbitrary or unfair", and linked the latter to MST.[148] It rejected Thunderbird's argument on the bases that Thunderbird "was given a full opportunity to be heard and to present evidence", and that the "administrative irregularities […] were [not] grave enough to shock as sense of judicial propriety."[149]

5.4.2 *Beyond NAFTA: How Other Tribunals Read (or Ignored) Thresholds*

The doctrinal and adjudicatory divergences on the content of the FET principle are not limited with the NAFTA practice. As vague FET provisions exist globally, similar arbitral elaborations have taken place in the context of different IIAs. Given the importance of the NAFTA disputes in setting the scene for the adjudicatory debate on FET and MST early on, however, they were widely cited in cases even when a given dispute did not stem from Article 1105 of NAFTA. Such interaction between

---

[146] *Thunderbird v. Mexico* (2006), par. 59.

[147] *Thunderbird v. Mexico* (2006), par. 147.

[148] *Thunderbird v. Mexico* (2006), par. 197. In the words of the Tribunal, "[…] cannot find sufficient evidence on the record […] that the […] proceedings were arbitrary or unfair, **let alone so manifestly arbitrary or unfair as to violate the minimum standard of treatment.**" Emphasis added.

[149] *Thunderbird v. Mexico* (2006), par. 198; 200.

different treaty regimes allowed cases stemming from other IIAs to contribute to the jurisprudence on FET.

One important example to such influence, ***Saluka v. Czech Republic,***[150] was a dispute regarding the alleged expropriation and unfair treatment by the Czech Republic, with regards to a financial aid programme in banking sector. The claimant claimed that their exclusion from the aid programme damaged their investment.[151] The Czech Republic—Netherlands BIT of 1991, under its Article 3(1) on FET reads as follows:

> Each [c]ontracting [p]arty shall ensure fair and equitable treatment to the investments of investors of the other [c]ontracting [p]arty and shall not impair, by unreasonable or discriminatory measures, the operation, management, maintenance, use, enjoyment or disposal thereof by those investors.[152]

After pointing out that the foregoing wording of the (unqualified) FET principle was inherently in need of an *ad hoc* context, the Tribunal asserted that "[the FET wording in the Treaty] does not set out totally subjective standards" according to which an arbitral tribunal would have full discretion, relaying almost on an *ex aequo et bono* reasoning.[153] The Tribunal then ascertained that the FET principle retained a subjective and general element, yet it also acknowledged the existence of "sufficient legal content to allow the case to be decided on the basis of law."[154]

Saluka argued that "since [the provision] is not in any way qualified, it should be interpreted broadly", indicating that the content of the FET principle is autonomous. However, the claimant refers to the *Waste Management*[155] award and claims that for an FET breach, the treatment should be "arbitrary, 'grossly' unfair, unjust or idiosyncratic". Saluka's choice of reference is noteworthy. The fact that the *Waste Management* award formulated its oft-cited framework against the backdrop of a CIL-qualified (post-2001 Note) provision, namely Article 1105 NAFTA, draws further attention to the approximate nature of what is perceived as the 'broad' and 'narrow' readings of the FET principle. The act should also invoke discrimination, sectional or racial prejudice, and should lack due process.[156] Lack of transparency and candour, as well as failure of the 'natural justice', are also associated with the analysis.

The respondent, on the other hand, had argued that the standard in Article 3(1) in fact referred to a minimum standard by citing the ***Genin v. Estonia***[157] award, as well as the *Neer* case. The respondent had articulated its opinion on what the Tribunal

[150] *Saluka Investments B.V. v. The Czech Republic*, UNCITRAL, Partial Award (17 March 2006) (*Saluka v. Czech Republic*).

[151] Factual background of this case can be found in Chap. 4.

[152] Article 3(1), Czech Republic - Netherlands BIT (1991).

[153] *Saluka v. Czech Republic* (2006), par. 284.

[154] *Saluka v. Czech Republic* (2006), par. 284.

[155] *Waste Management v. Mexico* (2004).

[156] *Saluka v. Czech Republic* (2006), par. 288.

[157] *Alex Genin, Eastern Credit Limited, Inc. and A.S. Baltoil v. Estonia*, ICSID Case No. ARB/99/2, Award (25 June 2001).

should address; namely, whether or not "the governmental action in question was wilfully wrong, actually malicious, or so far beyond the pale that it cannot be defended among reasonable members of the international community."[158]

Despite the seemingly different standpoints, the parties' arguments do not seem to make a tangible or significant difference in application. Indeed, the nuance between what is arbitrary, grossly unfair, unjust or idiosyncratic, discriminatory, prejudiced and devoid of due process; and what is wilfully wrong, actually malicious, and indefensible among the members of international community is not explicitly distinguishable, as both sets of elements will inherently stem from assertions and deductions reflected upon the circumstances of each case. Although it is clear two sets of constituents are not absolutely synonymous, one could argue that they would not necessarily lead to an entirely different, narrower, or broader outcome in each case. The *Saluka* tribunal adopted the same approach: "Whatever the merits of this controversy between parties may be, it appears that the difference between the Treaty standard laid down in Article [3(1)] and the customary minimum standard, when applied to the specific facts of a case, *may well be more apparent than real*."[159] This observation of the Saluka Tribunal sits at the very core of the dissent based on a division leading to two ostensibly competing (yet substantially hollow) sets of considerations. The Tribunal ultimately rejected the MST interpretation, and gave an autonomous character to the principle.[160]

The Tribunal took into account the *ordinary meaning* of the treaty in accordance with Article 31(1) of VCLT. It was specified that Article 3(1) should be analysed in connection with the object and purpose of the Treaty enshrined in its title (promotion and protection), as well as the preamble; which gives a two-fold objective for the BIT: promotion *and* protection. The *Saluka* Tribunal linked the fair and equitable treatment of foreign investors with one of the objectives of the treaty, namely the "[stimulation of] the flow of capital and technology and the economic development of the [parties]".[161]

The outcome is that the treaty gives the state the responsibility to "proactively [stimulate] the inflow of foreign investment capital, [or at the least, refrain from deterring] foreign capital by providing disincentives to foreign investors."[162] The

[158] *Neer v. Mexico* (1926).

[159] *Saluka v. Czech Republic* (2006), par. 291. Emphasis added.

[160] A similar conclusion was reached by the *Rumeli v. Kazakhstan* Tribunal: "The Arbitral Tribunal considers that this precision is more theoretical than real. It shares the view of several ICSID tribunals that the treaty standard of fair and equitable treatment is not materially different from the minimum standard of treatment in customary international law." *Rumeli Telekom A.Ş. and Telsim Mobil Telekomünikasyon Hizmetleri A.Ş. v. Republic of Kazakhstan,* ICSID Case No. ARB/05/16, Award (29 July 2008) (*Rumeli v. Kazakhstan*), par. 611. The applicable Kazakhstan – Türkiye BIT (1992) does not contain an FET provision. It was imported from the Kazakhstan – UK BIT (1995) through the Most-Favoured-Nation provision. The applicable FET rule is unqualified.

[161] *Saluka v. Czech Republic* (2006), par. 298.

[162] *Saluka v. Czech Republic* (2006), par. 301.

FET-specific reflection of these duties is, as the "dominant element of the [FET] standard]", the legitimate expectations of the investor. The Tribunal made a distinction between what has been called "arrangements in reliance upon which the foreign investor was inducted to invest" and "breach of representations [...] which were reasonably relied on by the [investor] on one hand; and the "subjective considerations and motivations" of the investor on the other. It was made clear that the latter was not a relevant factor in deciding on a FET breach—similarly, it was specified that "no investor may reasonably expect that the circumstances prevailing at the time the investment is made remain totally unchanged."[163]

This in mind, the Tribunal also stated that a state's "legitimate right subsequently to regulate domestic matters in the public interest must be taken into consideration" as well, *vis-à-vis* the aforementioned expectations of the investor, to be able to strike a balance between the two.

In the second phase of the analysis and in line with the general explanation of the inquiry, the Tribunal remarked that by conducting "differential treatment without a reasonable justification" and "unreasonably frustrating [...] good faith efforts to resolve the bank's [fiscal] crisis", Czech Republic had violated the FET obligation. It is noted that the government actions "lacked even-handedness, consistency and transparency [...]".[164]

The *Saluka* award is important in terms of its FET analysis and the elements the Tribunal had taken into consideration. Its clear recognition of the relationship between the provisions of a treaty, in particular its preambular clauses; and their interpretative implications on the operative clauses such as the FET principle is noteworthy. The reasoning of the Tribunal also expressly challenges the perceived difference between a CIL-bound FET analysis and an autonomous FET analysis. Furthermore, the Tribunal did not refrain from seeking reference in tribunals, such as *Waste Management*, which had interpreted and applied Article 1105 of NAFTA.

The *Saluka* Tribunal notably sets forth an *ad hoc* list of abstract elements that inherently require a case-by-case analysis with "due regard to all relevant circumstances": the adopted framework of the FET principle includes "manifestly inconsistent, non-transparent, unreasonable (i.e. unrelated to some rational policy), or discriminatory (i.e. based on unjustifiable distinctions)."[165] The Tribunal also counted "due process" and "freedom from coercion or harassment by its own regulatory authorities".[166] As will be shown below, the *Saluka* formula foreshadows what was subsequently included in the EU IPAs and FTAs.[167]

[163] *Saluka v. Czech Republic* (2006), par. 305.

[164] *Saluka v. Czech Republic* (2006), par. 498–499.

[165] *Saluka v. Czech Republic* (2006), par. 308–309.

[166] *Saluka v. Czech Republic* (2006), par. 308.

[167] Article 8.10(2), Comprehensive and Economic Trade Agreement between Canada and the European Union (CETA) (2017). https://policy.trade.ec.europa.eu/eu-trade-relationships-country-and-region/countries-and-regions/canada/eu-canada-agreement_en.

The ***RDC v. Guatemala***[168] Tribunal endorsed the dynamic nature of the FET and the CIL in its entirety. As for the content of the FET, the Tribunal cited *Waste Management,* and maintained that a FET breach should (a) be attributable to the host state, (b) be harmful to the investor, (c) be arbitrary, grossly unfair, unjust or idiosyncratic, (d) be discriminatory and pre-judgmental, (d) be lacking due process and transparency.[169]

It should be noted that CAFTA's FET provision explicitly stems from the North American model and expressly incorporates MST as a ceiling.[170] Despite this seemingly fine-tuned provision with clear indications that the intention was to connect FET and CIL (and therefore to install the stricter standard *vis-à-vis* the autonomous FET interpretation), the *RDC* tribunal, instead of investigating the general practice and *opinio juris* elements to identify the existence of a CIL rule, adopted what it considered to be a "[persuasive integration of] the accumulated analysis of prior [pre-2001] NAFTA Tribunals and [the reflection of] a balanced description of the minimum standard of treatment."[171]

The ***Liman v. Kazakhstan***[172] dispute concerned an ECT claim, *inter alia*, against the Kazakh domestic court decisions regarding a license transfer. The Tribunal stated, and repeated throughout its FET analysis, that the arbitral tribunals "must not function as an appeal body to correct errors, if any, of domestic procedural or

---

[168] *Railroad Development Corporation v. Republic of Guatemala, ICSID Case No. ARB/07/23, Award (29 June 2012) (RDC v. Guatemala).*

[169] *RDC v. Guatemala* (2012), par. 219; in reference to *Waste Management v. Mexico* (2004), par. 98.

[170] Article 10.5: 'Minimum Standard of Treatment', Dominican Republic—Central America FTA (CAFTA-DR) (2006):

1. Each Party shall accord to covered investments treatment in accordance with customary international law, including fair and equitable treatment and full protection and security.
2. For greater certainty, paragraph 1 prescribes the customary international law minimum standard of treatment of aliens as the minimum standard of treatment to be afforded to covered investments. The concepts of **"fair and equitable treatment"** and "full protection and security" **do not require treatment in addition to or beyond that which is required by that standard**, and do not create additional substantive rights. The obligation in paragraph 1 to provide:

    (a) **"fair and equitable treatment" includes the obligation not to deny justice in criminal, civil, or administrative adjudicatory proceedings in accordance with the principle of due process embodied in the principal legal systems of the world**; and

    (b) "full protection and security" requires each Party to provide the level of police protection required under customary international law.

3. A determination that there has been a breach of another provision of this Agreement, or of a separate international agreement, does not establish that there has been a breach of this Article.'

[171] *RDC v. Guatemala* (2012), par. 219.

[172] *Liman Caspian Oil BV and NCL Dutch Investment BV v. Kazakhstan*, ICSID Case no. ARB/07/14, Award (22 June 2010) (*Liman v. Kazakhstan*).

substantive law committed by the host states' national courts.".[173] The reasoning is parallel to the *S.D. Myers* Tribunal's arguments, which had refused to 'second-guess' government acts. After maintaining the existence of such difference between an appeal review and an investment tribunal, it went on to limit its scope of examination by stating that "the only relevant issue [...] is whether the Kazakh courts violated ECT Article 10(1) [...] when making their decisions",[174] and not whether the Kazakh courts applied the Kazakh provisions correctly. It was further maintained that the act did not "[offend] judicial propriety, even if they could be considered surprising."[175]

The FET analysis conducted by the Tribunal sought an impact more severe than merely invoking a sense of surprise, which by itself should not amount to unfair and inequitable treatment of the investment. In this light, the Tribunal's standard review stemmed from the examination of whether or not the acts (court decisions) were *arbitrary, grossly unfair, unjust or idiosyncratic or involving lack of due process.* This articulation, the product of the *Waste Management* Tribunal but commonly used in many arbitral cases beyond NAFTA, established that for a FET breach occur, the challenged act needs a more severe consequence than sheer surprise at the investor's end. This should also be considered differently than the legitimate expectations discussions that relate directly to expectations upon which the investment decision is based.

The ***Vivendi v. Argentina (Vivendi II)***[176] Tribunal's FET analysis began with reflections on the scope of the FET principle under Article 3 of the Argentina—France BIT,[177] which includes a reference to international law. Assessing the correlation between 'international law' and MST, the Tribunal concluded that there was "no basis for equating principles of international law with the minimum standard of treatment" and that it supported "a broader reading that invites consideration of a wider range of international law principles than the minimum standard alone."[178] It has been further maintained that, while interpreting the FET principle, "one should also look to contemporary principles of international law, not only to principles from almost a century ago", referring to the *Neer* case.[179] The similarity between the *Vivendi II*, *ADF* and *Mondev* tribunals' analyses (despite originating from different IIAs) is noteworthy.

The *Vivendi II* Tribunal's reading of the applicable FET provision, which includes a reference to international law, has since found recognition. A reference to 'international law', according to the Tribunal, does not mean that the FET is limited to

---

[173] *Liman v. Kazakhstan (2010)*, par. 324. *Compare*, *S.D. Myers v. Canada* (2000), par 263; *Mondev v. USA* (2002), par. 126.

[174] *Liman v. Kazakhstan (2010)*, par. 326.

[175] *Liman v. Kazakhstan* (2010), par. 348.

[176] *Compania de Aguas del Aconquija S.A. and Vivendi Universal S.A. v. Argentina,*ICSID Case No. ARB/97/3, Second Award (20 August 2007) (*Vivendi II*).

[177] Article 3, Argentina – France BIT (1991).

[178] *Vivendi II* (2007), par. 7.4.7.

[179] *Vivendi II* (2007).

CIL. Its extensive controversy aside, this was deemed possible exclusively in the NAFTA context because of the FTC Note. There are multiple other examples, some of them detailed in this Chapter, where this association is rejected by the Tribunals in the non-NAFTA context.[180]

As for the application of the FET principle to the case at hand, the Tribunal stated the following:

> [W]hile it would have been entirely proper for a new government with a different policy perspective on privatization to seek to renegotiate a concession agreement in a transparent non-coercive manner, it is clearly wrong (and unfair and inequitable in terms of the BIT) to seek to bring a concessionaire to the renegotiation table through threats of rescission based on colourable allegations after having wrongly deprived the concessionaire's billings of formal legitimacy.[181]

The paragraph above summarises the overall application of the prescribed FET analysis succinctly. It lays forth two instances—one hypothetical, one actual—and gives the former a fair and equitable character while excluding the latter from its scope due to coercive behaviour.[182] The *Vivendi II* award stands out in the sense that it includes a tangible, comparable and inferential application of the standard. In addition to this, several other facts such as the rejection of concession being a "politically driven arm-twisting aimed at compelling [c]laimants to agree to new terms" and that the claimant's initial proposal for renegotiating the terms being "immediately rejected" confirmed the fact that the act was against the FET principle.

Some recent awards (as of 2025) rendered pursuant to unqualified FET provisions, as well as those that are qualified with 'international law', demonstrate that arbitral tribunals continue to distinguish between unqualified and qualified FET provisions in terms of their perceived protective scope, noting that the FET provisions under examination are not limited by CIL. In ***Indian Metals v. Indonesia,***[183] the claimant held a coal mining production licence issued by the government. The dispute arose when the claimant's mining concession was rendered 'useless' due to overlapping licences that were issued to other companies.[184]

The Tribunal observed that the applicable BIT, namely the India—Indonesia BIT of 1999,

> does not expressly limit the FET standard to treatment 'in accordance with international law' or analogous formulations. Moreover, the Tribunal also notes that several non-NAFTA

[180] See also, Total S.A. v. The Argentine Republic, ICSID Case No. ARB/04/01, Decision on Liability (27 December 2010), par. 125–127 (*Total v. Argentina*) (applying the Argentina—France BIT (1991)); *Crystallex International Corporation v. Bolivarian Republic of Venezuela*, ICSID Case No. ARB(AF)/11/2, Award (4 April 2016) (*Crystallex v. Venezuela*) (applying the Canada – Venezuela BIT (1996)).

[181] *Vivendi II* (2007), par. 7.4.31.

[182] Harassment and coercion are explicitly mentioned in several new generation FTAs; see new IIAs analysis below.

[183] *Indian Metals & Ferro Alloys Ltd v. Indonesia*, PCA Case No. 2015-40, Award (29 March 2019) (*Indian Metals v. Indonesia*).

[184] *Indian Metals v. Indonesia* (2019), par. 15.

> tribunals that interpreted clauses with such formulations concluded that these formulations should not be understood as limiting the FET to customary minimum standard of treatment.[185]

This is an accurate observation, in the sense that nothing in the BIT limits the FET provision to any CIL benchmark. The Tribunal is correct in showing restraint with regard to extending the NAFTA interpretation to a non-NAFTA instrument. As noted above under the *Vivendi II* award, this is a peculiarity of the NAFTA framework.

The Tribunal appears to have embraced the FET sub-elements articulated by the Claimant, namely the investor's reasonable and legitimate expectations, arbitrariness and non-discrimination, transparency and consistency, good faith, due process and procedural propriety, and the principle of proportionality.[186] The Tribunal did not consider these sub-elements to be exhaustive. It further accepted that "not every inconsistency or lack of transparency of the host state will automatically result in an FET breach."[187]

The Tribunal subsequently endorsed the FET elements identified by the ***Lemire v. Ukraine*** Tribunal[188] which, despite an 'international law' qualifier, declares the FET provision to be 'autonomous' and the 'international law' benchmark to reflect a floor, as opposed to a ceiling.[189] The provision indeed reads that investors "shall in no case be accorded treatment *less than that required by international law*."[190]

The *Lemire v. Ukraine* Tribunal is justified in its assertion that the formulation of the 'international law' qualifier in question is a floor and not a ceiling. This impression may be strengthened when one examines other ways this 'international law' qualifier is inserted in other FET provisions. Take, for instance, Article II(2), of Canada—Venezuela BIT, which reads that "each contracting Party shall, *in accordance with the principles of international law*, accord investments or returns of investors of the other Contracting Party fair and equitable treatment and full protection and security."[191] This being said, despite the arguably distinct method of incorporation and the positioning of international law as a benchmark, the ***Crystallex v. Venezuela*** Tribunal nonetheless considered the Canada—Venezuela BIT provision to reflect an autonomous FET obligation[192] which includes protection of legitimate expectations, protection against arbitrary and discriminatory treatment, transparency and consistency, among others.[193] In identifying the sub-elements of this

[185] *Indian Metals v. Indonesia* (2019), par. 225.

[186] *Indian Metals v. Indonesia* (2019), par. 226.

[187] *Indian Metals v. Indonesia* (2019), par. 228.

[188] *Joseph Charles Lemire v. Ukraine*, ICSID Case No. ARB/06/18, Decision on Jurisdiction and Liability (14 January 2010), par. 284 et seq (*Lemire v. Ukraine*).

[189] *Lemire v. Ukraine* (2010), par. 253.

[190] Article II(3), Ukraine – US BIT (1994).

[191] Article II(2), of Canada – Venezuela BIT (1996).

[192] *Crystallex v. Venezuela* (2016), par. 530.

[193] *Crystallex v. Venezuela* (2016), par. 543.

autonomous standard, the Tribunal liberally cited arbitral awards that had applied unqualified and MST-qualified provisions, including *S.D. Myers*, *Mondev*, *Saluka*, and *Lemire*.

Another illustrative award in that regard is ***Gardabani v. Georgia***.[194] According to the claimants, Georgia adjusted the tariffs applicable to the energy sector as well as the claimants' investments in accordance with a new tariff-setting method, which ultimately caused the claimants losses in their investments. The applicable BIT was the Georgia—Netherlands BIT which, under its Article 3, contains an unqualified FET provision.[195] In its analysis of the content and nature of the FET principle, the Tribunal observed that "[u]nlike other treaties, the BIT makes no reference to the minimum standard of treatment at international law nor to treatment 'in accordance with principles of international law' or any similar formulation", eventually noting that "the FET standard embodied in the BIT constitutes an autonomous treaty standard which is not limited to the minimum standard of treatment at customary international law."[196]

On that point, the Tribunal sought guidance from the abovementioned *Crystallex* award which, as noted above, interpreted a provision with an 'international law' qualifier and contended that it had no limiting effect on the FET provision. Furthermore, in further asserting the autonomous character of the FET provision at hand, the *Gardabani* Tribunal articulated the sub-elements of the FET standard to include legitimate expectations, protection against arbitrary and discriminatory treatment, transparency, due process and good faith[197]—declaring this list to reflect a 'consensus' between arbitral awards. It further cites the *Mondev* award (through the *Crystallex* award)[198] above in setting the limits of severity of a challenged measure. Given that *Mondev* award reflects an interpretation of the post-FTC Notes CIL threshold pursuant to NAFTA, it is an interesting choice to rely on in determining the severity threshold of an autonomous standard. The Tribunal further reinforced this threshold with the abovementioned conclusions reached by the *Saluka* Tribunal in ascertaining that the treatment should be "unacceptable from the international perspective."[199]

---

[194] *Gardabani Holdings B.V. And Silk Road Holdings B.V. V. Georgia*, ICSID Case No. ARB/17/29, Award (27 October 2022) (Gardabani v. Georgia).

[195] Georgia – Netherlands BIT (1998).

[196] *Gardabani v. Georgia* (2022), par. 498.

[197] *Gardabani v. Georgia* (2022), par. 499; citing *Electrabel S.A. v. Republic of Hungary*, ICSID Case No. ARB/07/19, Decision on Jurisdiction, Applicable Law and Liability (30 November 2012) (*Electrabel v. Hungary*), par. 7.74. This award was based on the ECT, which includes a floor 'international law' qualifier under its Article 10(1). Cf. to the sub-elements noted above under *Crystallex v. Venezuela* (2016), par. 543.

[198] *Gardabani v. Georgia* (2022), par. 501.

[199] *Gardabani v. Georgia* (2022), par. 501.

The ***Cairn Energy v. India*** award is another example where the Tribunal found that the applicable FET provision was autonomous.[200] The dispute concerned India's tax measures as they applied to certain transactions of the claimants in 2006, when they underwent a corporate reorganisation. These tax measures were specifically applied to some share transfers, and the claimants argued that the retroactive application of a 2012 Amendment made to the Income Tax Act of 1961 to a series of transactions which took place in 2006 breached India's obligations under the India—UK BIT.[201]

Despite its finding that the FET provision was "broadly worded",[202] the Tribunal also acknowledged that the provision had "independent legal content"[203] and, in fact might share elements with MST despite its autonomous character. It further points towards a historic link between the FET standard and MST, noting that the latter inspired the former.[204] In further unpacking this somewhat cautious autonomy it had attached to the FET provision, the Tribunal cited the *Mondev* and *ADF* awards, like several examples above analysing autonomous FET provisions, in limiting the scope of the applicable provision.[205] In particular the reference to the latter is noteworthy. As both awards stem from NAFTA and interpret CIL-qualified provisions, the *ADF* Tribunal's contention that the scope of FET must be "disciplined by being based on State practice and judicial or arbitral case law or other sources of customary or general international law", one could argue, is not a broad starting point for an ostensibly autonomous FET provision.[206]

In its subsequent analysis in identifying the FET subset, the Tribunal counted the following as the 'core principles' of the FET standard: stability, predictability, and consistency of the legal framework; the principle of legality; the protection of investor confidence or legitimate expectations; procedural due process and denial of justice; substantive due process or protection against discrimination and arbitrariness; transparency; as well as reasonableness and proportionality.[207] In identifying these core principles, the Tribunal cited a number of awards, among them ***Bayındır v. Pakistan***, which was rendered on the basis of the Pakistan—Türkiye BIT[208] contain-

[200] *Cairn Energy PLC and Cairn UK Holdings Limited (CUHL) v. India*, PCA Case No. 2016-07, Final Award (21 December 2020) (*Cairn Energy v. India*), par. 1701 et seq.

[201] India – UK BIT (1994); *Cairn Energy v. India* (2020), par. 1–2.

[202] *Cairn Energy v. India* (2020), par. 1706.

[203] *Cairn Energy v. India* (2020), par. 1707.

[204] *Cairn Energy v. India* (2020), par. 1704.

[205] *Cairn Energy v. India* (2020), par. 1707.

[206] *ADF v. USA* (2003), par. 184. It is even more interesting that the Tribunal expressly notes that "[h]ere again the discussion was on NAFTA Article 1105 and the Tribunal considers that the same reasoning applies to the interpretation of Article 3(2) of the [India – UK BIT]", essentially equating the NAFTA provision and the autonomous FET provision applicable to the case vis-à-vis their implications. *Cairn Energy v. India* (2020), p. 478 (footnote 2150).

[207] *Cairn Energy v. India* (2020), par. 1721.

[208] *Bayındır İnşaat Turizm Ticaret ve Sanayi A.Ş. v. Islamic Republic of Pakistan* (I), ICSID Case No. ARB/03/29, Award (27 August 2009) (*Bayındır v. Pakistan*).

ing an FET provision with an MST qualifier, "including fair and equitable treatment".[209]

The Tribunal, despite its acknowledgment that the FET provision in question is autonomous, nonetheless sought to establish a normative link between MST and the autonomous FET as it understood the principle. Accordingly, the Tribunal observed that MST represented the base of the FET standard. Citing the *S.D. Myers* award, the Tribunal noted that the MST standard was "the floor below which treatment of foreign investors must not fall".[210] At this point, no further elaboration was made as to what an autonomous FET would *additionally* entail, following their analogy, to build upon this 'floor'. Both in its conceptualisation of the principle and in its choice of cited case law, the Cairn Energy Tribunal's overall deference and attention to MST in identifying the contours of an autonomous FET is therefore pertinent.

Three cases examined under Chap. 4, namely ***Eco Oro v. Colombia,***[211] ***Red Eagle v. Colombia,***[212] and ***Montauk v. Colombia,***[213] further provide useful examples as to how more recent tribunals dealt with a CIL-qualified FET provision. All three tribunals interpreted Article 805 of the Canada—Colombia FTA.[214] In *Eco Oro*, the Tribunal emphasised the dynamic and evolving nature of the CIL benchmark, noting that "actions that infringe a sense of fairness, equity and reasonableness will fall afoul of Article 805."[215] It further identified that "transparency, stability and the protection of the investor's legitimate expectations play a central role in defining the FET standard, as does procedural or judicial propriety and due process and fairness, refraining from taking arbitrary or discriminatory measures, or from frustrating the investor's reasonable expectations with respect to the legal framework affecting the investment."[216] It further contended that the investor was entitled to a predictable business environment to balance the promotion of foreign investment and enforcement of environmental regulations.[217] The Tribunal ultimately found a breach of Article 805, due to Colombia's failure to act coherently in its management and preservation of the *páramos*.[218]

---

[209] Article 3(2), Pakistan – Türkiye BIT (1995), reads as follows: "Investments of investors of each Contracting Party shall at all times be accorded treatment in accordance with international law minimum standard of treatment, including fair and equitable treatment and full protection and security in the territory of the other Contracting Party."

[210] *S.D. Myers v. Canada* (2000), par. 259.

[211] *Eco Oro Minerals Corp. v. Republic of Colombia*, ICSID Case No. ARB/16/41, Decision on Jurisdiction, Liability and Directions on Quantum (9 September 2021) (*Eco Oro v. Colombia*).

[212] *Red Eagle Exploration Limited v. Republic of Colombia*, ICSID Case No. ARB/18/12, Award (28 February 2024) (*Red Eagle v. Colombia*).

[213] *Montauk Metals Inc. (formerly known as Galway Gold Inc.) v. Republic of Colombia*, ICSID Case No. ARB/18/13, (7 June 2024) (*Montauk v. Colombia*).

[214] Canada – Colombia FTA (2008).

[215] *Eco Oro v. Colombia* (2021), par. 747; also see, Ünüvar (2023), p. 525.

[216] *Eco Oro v. Colombia* (2021), par. 754.

[217] *Eco Oro v. Colombia* (2021), par. 748.

[218] *Eco Oro v. Colombia* (2021), par. 821.

Professor Philippe Sands' now-famous (partial) dissent to the *Eco Oro* decision in 2021 also deserves mention.[219] His rejection of legitimate expectations as a sub-element of MST is particularly important. He further argued that, even if they were relevant, any frustration of expectations should amount to egregious and shocking behaviour.[220] He further disagreed that 'stability and predictability' were subset of MST.[221]

In *Red Eagle v. Colombia*, the Tribunal examined at the outset whether legitimate expectations formed part of MST. It is one of the few Tribunals to expressly (and accurately) refer to the general state practice and *opinio juris* as required evidence to ascertain that such sub-element exists under MST. To that end, it noted that "[t]he Claimant has not provided the Tribunal with any evidence of either state practice or *opinio juris* to support the existence of such a rule, and the Tribunal is aware of none."[222] Having failed to identify any 'quasi-contractual relationship' or any relevant expectation, the Tribunal then proceeded to examine whether a lack of transparency, or arbitrary, unreasonable, disproportionate, or discriminatory conduct existed *vis-à-vis* the investor.[223]

The *Montauk v. Colombia* Tribunal distilled four sub-elements from the parties' submissions and examined them in turn: good faith, arbitrariness, legitimate expectations, and transparency.[224] As for the first, the Tribunal rejected that good faith constituted a stand-alone sub-element of the FET standard as MST: "it would be better for the Tribunal to [analyse] Respondent's compliance with other obligations derived from MST and, afterwards, determine if they were performed in good faith."[225] As for the second sub-element, citing the *Waste Management* award, the Tribunal ascertained that protection against arbitrariness was 'undisputedly' covered by MST.[226] The Tribunal further acknowledged that legitimate expectations were included under the sub-elements of MST by some tribunals.[227] It also

---

[219] *Eco Oro v. Colombia* (2021), Partial Dissent of Professor Philippe Sands QC (9 September 2021).

[220] *Eco Oro v. Colombia* (2021), Partial Dissent of Professor Philippe Sands QC (9 September 2021), p. 13.

[221] *Eco Oro v. Colombia* (2021), Partial Dissent of Professor Philippe Sands QC (9 September 2021), p. 18.

[222] *Red Eagle v. Colombia* (2024), par. 293.

[223] *Red Eagle v. Colombia* (2024), par. 283–316.

[224] Montauk v. Colombia (2024), par. 911.

[225] *Montauk v. Colombia* (2024), par. 914.

[226] *Montauk v. Colombia* (2024), par. 918.

[227] *Montauk v. Colombia* (2024), par. 924; see also, *William Richard Clayton, Douglas Clayton, Daniel Clayton, and Bilcon of Delaware, Inc. v. Government of Canada*, PCA Case No. 2009-04, Award on Jurisdiction and Liability (17 March 2015) (*Bilcon v. Canada*), par. 427 et seq. The Bilcon Tribunal, interpreting Article 1105 of NAFTA, asserted that "the international minimum standard exists and has evolved in the direction of increased investor protection precisely because sovereign states-the same one constrained by the standard-have chosen to accept it." (par. 438) The Tribunal then overtly accepted that 'reasonable' expectations were a sub-element of the contemporary MST (par. 455).

considered transparency and consistency to be included in MST.[228] The Tribunal subsequently rejected the claim, referring to the abovementioned dissenting opinion of Prof. Sands in the *Eco Oro* decision, who asked: "did the process of delimitation cross the line of departing from the rule of law, or proceed on a basis that shocks our sense of juridical propriety? In my view it did not, and the heart of the Decision makes it clear, premised as it is on the view that the Respondent acted in good faith."[229]

The abovementioned cases reflect a large variety of instruments and FET formulations. They also span more than two decades—whereas some are the so-called 'trailblazers' in setting the normative foundations of what an autonomous FET principle looks like vis-à-vis one that is qualified by MST, some of them build upon this accumulated arbitral and scholarly knowledge and experience. Despite their differences, they all share an undeniable commonality: they are all unclear on what autonomy means for the FET principle, or how CIL/MST delimits it. Most of the Tribunals above rendered their decisions with an evident awareness of a difference between the two conceptualisations. However, the case law above, besides articulating certain emergent sub-elements which may stem from both CIL-bound and autonomous readings of the FET, do not reveal a pattern as to how these two differ. It does not suffice to call MST a 'floor' for the FET; or to declare, as some IIAs indeed do, treatment should be accorded in accordance with MST, "including fair and equitable treatment", hinting at the possibility that MST is indeed *broader* than FET.

While the case law so far demonstrates that a pattern has emerged as to what kinds of sub-elements are considered part of FET as an autonomous or otherwise qualified principle,[230] what the case law analysis in this Chapter primarily seeks to demonstrate is that a systemic, normative, and conceptual conflation has emerged alongside this pattern. This normative confusion has been ossifying within case law—even after decades of arbitral elaborations.

This being said, one particular sub-element warrants further scrutiny due to its uncertain, outlier position between different reiterations of FET. Some examples above reveal that while legitimate expectations are often included in the autonomous FET provisions, it is not uncommon to see it under other reiterations of the principle.

---

[228] *Montauk v. Colombia* (2021), par. 932 et seq.

[229] *Montauk v. Colombia* (2024), par. 937; *Eco Oro v. Colombia* (2021), Partial Dissent of Professor Philippe Sands QC (9 September 2021), p. 15.

[230] Vandevelde (2010), p. 105.

5.4.3 Legitimate Expectations as a Sub-Element of FET

Several awards, in addition to examining various sub-elements of FET *vis-à-vis* various thresholds adopted in applicable IIAs, focused specifically on the expectations of investors. A number of them have already been referred to above in their broader context.

The evaluation of foreign investors' expectations and their role in identifying an FET breach is one of the most contentious subjects in FET case law.[231] While the Tribunals that interpret 'autonomous' FET provisions often count legitimate expectations among relevant sub-elements; as awards such as *Waste Management* and *Thunderbird* demonstrate, several NAFTA Tribunals have explicitly incorporated legitimate expectations as a sub-element of the CIL framework.

The ***Tecmed v. Mexico***[232] Tribunal was one of the first arbitral tribunals to elaborate on the expectations of foreign investors. Deciding on an FET breach claim along with its aforementioned expropriation claim, the Tribunal elaborated on the principle as follows, in the context of other subset of FET:

> [FET principle] requires the Contracting Parties to provide to international investments treatment that does not affect **the basic expectations** that were taken into account by the foreign investor to make the investment. The foreign investor expects the host State to act in **a consistent manner**, **free from ambiguity** and **totally transparently** in its relations with the foreign investor, so that it may know beforehand any and **all rules and regulations that will govern its investments**, as well as **the goals of the relevant policies and administrative practices or directives**, to be able to plan its investment and comply with such regulations. [...] The foreign investor also expects the host State to **act consistently**, i.e. without **arbitrarily** revoking any preexisting decisions or permits issued by the State that were **relied upon by the investor** to assume its commitments as well as to plan and launch its commercial and business activities. The investor also expects the State to use the legal instruments that govern the actions of the investor or the investment in conformity with the function usually assigned to such instruments, and not to deprive the investor of its investment without the required compensation.[233]

The applicable BIT, namely the Mexico—Spain BIT of 1995, includes the qualifier "in accordance with international law".[234] The paragraph above contains a number of sub-elements of FET, all of which seem to revolve around (and more importantly, directly originate from) the impressions and expectations the host state leaves with regards to the conduct of the investment. Indeed, the *Tecmed* Tribunal overtly emphasised the importance of the investors' expectations with regards to FET, and went on to specify that the investor was entitled to consistent, unambiguous and

[231] Laryea (2021); Potestà (2013); Zeyl (2011), p. 219.

[232] *Tecnicas Medioambientales Tecmed S.A. v. Mexico,* ICSID Case No. ARB (AF)/00/2, Award (29 May 2003) (*Tecmed v. Mexico*).

[233] Tecmed v. Mexico (2003), par. 154.

[234] Mexico – Spain BIT (1995); this agreement has since been replaced by the Mexico – Spain BIT (2006). The latter instrument includes a reference to "customary international law, including fair and equitable treatment" (translated from the original Spanish text which reads, "trato acorde con el derecho internacional consuetudinario, incluido trato justo y equitativo").

transparent treatment and clarity with regards to the policy goals and administrative practices as their *basic expectations*. This would allow the investor to conduct its investment in an anticipatable and streamlined manner. It is further stated that investor's knowledge on the rules and procedures according to which its investment would be realised was also crucial. States are responsible for providing an accessible environment as to avail investors to know the rules of which they should be aware.

The Tribunal then specified and illustrated some other elements of FET—such as general consistency in sovereign acts (i.e., not arbitrarily revoking permits crucial for the realisation of the investment) giving rise to an expectation at the investor's end that their investment would be aptly protected. Finally, in reference to due process, the Tribunal underlined states' responsibility to refer to appropriate legal instruments that govern the actions of the foreign investor.

With regard to the relocation agreement of the claimant's landfill operations to another site, the Tribunal asserted that there had been an agreement to proceed with the said relocation after the new facilities were operable. This was not possible, however, following the taking of the landfill by the government without any relocation. The Tribunal rejected the claims that such action was prompted by "community pressure", and maintained that the authorities were "fully aware" of the potential problem prior to agreeing to the relocation. It is contended that the claimant "*may* have reasonably trusted"[235] the state to avail the permit to continue until the time of relocation. Other relevant indications that the above-mentioned *Tecmed* standard was not duly observed include: (a) failure to "unequivocally and clearly [specifying] the deadlines, terms and conditions that would apply to the relocation", (b) "[denial of the renewal of the permit] without any compensation whatsoever", and (c) ambiguity with regards to its intentions to close the landfill.[236] The Tribunal was convinced that the officials had not been consistent and clear, as "the contradiction and uncertainty [was] inherent".[237] It is also stated that the proximity of the landfill's location to an urban area, which was considered to have resulted from Mexican government's neglect, did not necessarily challenge the legality or legitimacy of the landfill operation by the claimant. Given the claimant did not seem to be at fault due to such erroneous land allocation for the landfill, the Tribunal argued that the closure of the landfill should have been accompanied by "the payment of the appropriate compensation".[238] Collectively, these actions were considered to have "frustrated [the claimants'] fair expectations upon which [its] actions were based".[239]

[235] Tecmed v. Mexico (2003), par. 160. Emphasis added.

[236] Tecmed v. Mexico (2003), par. 163.

[237] Tecmed v. Mexico (2003), par. 170.

[238] Tecmed v. Mexico (2003), par. 164.

[239] Tecmed v. Mexico (2003), par. 173.

The *Tecmed* tribunal's FET analysis has attracted criticism.[240] While it counts consistency, transparency, and due process as among constituent elements of FET similar to some awards examined above, the real controversy comes from the alleged origin of these articulated elements. The Tribunal attached those elements not to a normative obligation under the applicable treaty, but rather to the *basic* expectations of an investor.[241] Firstly, it is important to distinguish between basic and legitimate expectations—it is the latter, and not the former, that are often protected. Secondly, the FET obligation or its sub-elements, as the *Tecmed* Tribunal implied, do not originate from the expectations of investors; if anything, investor's expectations may invoke unfair treatment only if they satisfy certain criteria (such as the expectations being investment-backed, or even formal and written, under some IIAs).

The *Tecmed* Tribunal's FET analysis has nonetheless inspired many subsequent tribunals. Possibly one of the most outstanding awards in that regard is the wording in ***Cargill v. Mexico***, a NAFTA dispute. Referring to the *Tecmed* award, the claimant in *Cargill* argued that "[Tecmed case is] not only [...] a statement of the autonomous meaning, but also of the current content of the [CIL] as to the duty to provide [FET]."[242] The respondent's counter-argument stemmed from the *Neer* decision.[243] While it accepted that MST could evolve, it did not accept that the standard was "identical to the meaning some tribunals have given to the obligation as a matter of

---

[240] An exceptional criticism came from the *Red Eagle v. Colombia* (2024) Tribunal (par. 295) Emphasis added: "In its submissions, the Claimant has relied heavily on the award of the tribunal in *Tecmed v. Mexico*. In that case, the tribunal suggested that the investors have a wide range of legitimate expectations relating to the stability and consistency of a host State's regulatory framework, without the need to show the existence of a representation, the existence of a reasonable expectation or reliance on that representation. The *Tecmed* tribunal also stated that a State's failure to fulfil such expectations would amount to a breach of the customary MST. It is not a surprise that the award in Tecmed is often cited by claimants in investorstate disputes, in seeking to claim the broadest possible protection under the relevant investment treaty. With respect to the tribunal that sat in *Tecmed*, however, ***the majority of this Tribunal is very far from being persuaded that this view of the MST is correct or even plausible***. As explained above, ***that award relied on no evidence of state practice or opinio juris to support its conclusion as to the existence of such a customary rule, and it appears there is none***. It is striking that ***the Tecmed standard is now rarely (if ever) followed by tribunals and has been strongly criticized in explicit terms by the annulment committee in MTD v. Chile***. The Tecmed award is not one on which reliance may be placed." Also see, *MTD Equity Sdn. Bhd. and MTD Chile S.A. v. Republic of Chile*, ICSID Case No. ARB/01/7, Decision on Annulment (12 March 2007) (*MTD v. Chile*), par. 67: "The obligations of the host State towards foreign investors derive from the terms of the applicable investment treaty and not from any set of expectations investors may have or claim to have. ***A tribunal which sought to generate from such expectations a set of rights different from those contained in or enforceable under the BIT might well exceed its powers***, and if the difference were material might do so manifestly."

[241] Potestà (2013), p. 92.

[242] *Cargill, Incorporated v. Mexico,* ICSID Case No. ARB(AF)/05/2, Award (18 September 2009), par. 242.

[243] *Neer v. Mexico* (1926).

autonomous treaty interpretation."[244] Notwithstanding the lack of clarification as to what Mexico's position on the content of CIL was (given it asserted the content reflects the *Neer* decision and *may* have evolved past it), it seems evident that the parties had differing positions. The Tribunal eventually referred to the *Waste Management* and *ADF* [245] awards, and considered FET bound by the content of CIL as articulated under these awards.[246]

Several other tribunals conducted FET analyses with an emphasis on the legitimate expectations. ***Occidental Petroleum v. Ecuador***[247] concerns the dispute between the American oil exploration company Occidental and Ecuador, concerning the modifications to a partnership contract, and the relevant law in Ecuador related to VAT reimbursements to which Occidental claimed to be entitled. Following Ecuador's refusal to continue its periodical reimbursement of VAT payments made by Occidental on behalf of Petroecuador, the state-owned oil company; Occidental brought, *inter alia*, an FET claim.

The relevant FET provision is Article II (3) (a) of the Ecuador—United States BIT,[248] which grants the investor the right to be accorded FET at all times. It is also supplemented by a 'floor' threshold, which states that the treatment "shall in no case be [...] less than that required by international law."[249]

The Tribunal went on to scrutinise whether Ecuador "has frustrated [Occidental]'s legitimate expectations on the basis of which the investment was made". Overall, the Tribunal traced individual objectives of the treaty in order to give the FET principle a concrete context in terms of possible legitimate expectations. With a reference to the preamble, the Tribunal put the emphasis on "[maintaining] a stable framework" as among the objectives of the BIT. The Tribunal clearly saw this objective as a defining feature of the FET principle, as the remainder of the analysis revolves around this particular purpose of the treaty, identified as the expectation that VAT reimbursement would continue unhindered in this particular case.

This, however, did not mean that *any* change in the legal and business framework would result in a treaty breach. The Tribunal did not associate the challenged measure with a breach before further delving into the state interpretation of the modified agreement, which, according to Ecuador, included a VAT reimbursement scheme. The Tribunal found no evidence to this end, as VAT reimbursement was not mentioned anywhere in the modified contract. Therefore, Ecuador was found to have misinterpreted the modified agreement. Occidental's subsequent attempts to clarify such exclusion of VAT reimbursement from the new agreement were "wholly unsatisfactory and thoroughly vague". The Tribunal contended that such alteration of the

---

[244] *Cargill v. Mexico* (2009), par. 244.

[245] *Waste Management v. Mexico* (2004); *ADF v. USA* (2003).

[246] *Cargill v. Mexico* (2009), par. 283–284.

[247] *Occidental Petroleum Corporation and Occidental Exploration and Production Company v. Ecuador*, ICSID Case No. ARB/06/11, Award (5 October 2012) (*Occidental v. Ecuador*).

[248] Ecuador – US BIT (1997).

[249] Article II(3)(a), Ecuador – US BIT (1997).

legal and business framework constituted a breach, since the abovementioned modification in the form of VAT reimbursement exclusion "was [done] without providing any clarity about its meaning and extent that the practice and regulations were also inconsistent with the changes."[250]

The Tribunal pointed towards the rule of "maintaining stable legal and business framework" in international law. As can be understood from its examination of several treaties (WTO instruments), decisions (Andean community decisions), as well as customary rules (according to the Tribunal, evidenced by arbitration case law), it seems that the Tribunal, at least in principle, included all relevant international law instruments to its analysis, rather than solely observing whether or not the qualification referred only to CIL.

AES v. Hungary[251] concerned a dispute over pricing modifications done over the years, in the course of AES' investment in Hungary. An ECT-based arbitration, the claim included the breach of Article 10(1).

The award looked into a number of substantive issues related to the scope and extent of the FET principle. With regards to legitimate expectations, the Tribunal contended that "legitimate expectations can only be created at the moment of investment".[252] In addition, citing the *Duke Energy v. Ecuador*[253] and *Tecmed v. Mexico* awards, the *AES* Tribunal established that the expectations must be taken into account by the foreign investor to make the investment. Therefore, the expectations should emerge at the time of the investment, and their consideration should be associated with the decision of making the investment.[254]

The *AES* Tribunal also elaborated on the meaning of creating "stable" conditions for foreign investors pursuant to Article 10(1). It was stated that

> [t]he stable conditions that the ECT mentions relate to the framework within which the investment takes place. Nevertheless, **it is not a stability clause**. A legal framework is by definition subject to change as it adapts to new circumstances day by day and a state has the sovereign right to exercise its powers which include legislative acts. [...] [T]he [t]ribunal observes that no specific commitments were made by Hungary that could limit its sovereign right to change its law (such as a stability clause) or that could legitimately have made the investor believe that no change in the law would occur.[255]

In that connection, the *AES* Tribunal appropriately considered the promise of stable conditions to be different from a specific promise of legislative *standstill*—in the light of the sovereign rights of states, the latter would be very broad in favour of a

[250] *Occidental v. Ecuador* (2012), par. 184.

[251] *AES Summit Generation Limited and AES-Tisza Eromu Kft v. Hungary,* ICSID Case No. ARB/07/22, Award (23 September 2010) *(AES II).*

[252] *AES II* (2010), par. 9.3.7; On when the legitimate expectations exist in general, see Schreuer and Kriebaum (2009).

[253] *Duke Energy Electroquil Partners & Electroquil S.A. v. Ecuador*, ICSID Case No. ARB/04/19, Award (18 August 2008) (*Duke v. Ecuador*).

[254] Schreuer and Kriebaum (2009).

[255] *AES II* (2010), par. 9.3.31.

foreign investor, given it would have a decisive and direct impact on any legislative act on the state's end, regardless of its necessity or purpose.

With regards to allegations of politically motivated modifications of the law, the Tribunal stated that "any reasonably informed business person or investor knows that laws can evolve in accordance with the perceived political or policy dictates of the times."[256] Given the dispute coincided with Hungarian accession process to the EU, laws and regulations were reportedly undergoing a rigorous transformation. The *AES* Tribunal, therefore, acknowledged the fact that politically motivated acts, simply because they are political, cannot be considered arbitrary.

ExxonMobil v. Venezuela[257] concerned a set of claims arising out of a number of association and concession agreements to Mobil, which brought a claim against Venezuela seeking compensation for its losses due to, *inter alia*, Venezuelan curtailments to production and export, additional taxation and alleged coercion and expropriation of investment during the presidency of late Hugo Chavez.

Among others, this very dispute has been credited as a contributor to Venezuela's frustration with the investment protection structure for its loopholes with regards to the so-called *nationality shopping*.[258] Venezuela had challenged the jurisdiction of the Tribunal, stating that "the restructuring of the Mobil Corporation through the creation [...] of the Dutch holding constituted an abuse of rights, which deprived the [t]ribunal of jurisdiction under the [Venezuela – Netherlands] BIT."[259]

The Tribunal rejected this claim:

> As stated by the [c]laimants, the aim of the restructuring of their investments in Venezuela through a Dutch holding was to protect those investments against breaches of their rights by the Venezuelan authorities by gaining access to ICSID arbitration through the BIT. The [t]ribunal considers that **this was a perfectly legitimate goal** as far as it concerned future disputes.[260]

With regards to ExxonMobil's FET breach claims, the Tribunal examined the claim for the FET breach in more general terms. It was maintained that "this standard may be breached by frustrating the expectations that the investor may have legitimately taken into account when making the investment [...] [They] may result from ***specific formal assurances*** given by the host state in order to induce investment."[261] The Tribunal did not concern itself with a discussion on the implications of an autonomous FET and its sub-elements by articulating an exhaustive or illustrative

[256] *AES II* (2010), par. 9.3.34.

[257] *Venezuela Holdings, B.V., Mobil Cerro Negro Holding, Ltd., Mobil Venezolana de Petroleos Holdings, Inc., Mobil Cerro Negro, Ltd. And Mobil Venezolana de Petroleos, Inc. v. Venezuela*, ICSID Case No. ARB/07/27, Award (9 October 2014) (*ExxonMobil v. Venezuela*).

[258] Villegas-Ruiz (2020), p. 522; Knottnerus and Van Os (2012) https://www.iisd.org/itn/2012/01/12/the-netherlands-treaty-shopping/.

[259] *ExxonMobil v. Venezuela* (2014), par. 185. There is no BIT or another IIA between Venezuela and the United States.

[260] *ExxonMobil v. Venezuela*, Decision on Jurisdiction (10 June 2010), par. 204. Emphasis added.

[261] *ExxonMobil v. Venezuela* (2014), par. 256. Emphasis added.

list of conditions needed in order to maintain an FET breach. Instead, a rather isolated 'legitimate expectations' analysis was conducted *vis-à-vis* the facts of the case.

The Tribunal, before looking into specific facts, maintained that Mobil was "reasonably and legitimately" entitled to expect to produce "at least 120,000 barrels per day of extra-heavy crude oil", with an exception set in case Venezuela's "international commitments" compelled the parties to reduce the production under the agreement conditions. It was also agreed that such cut would only be done on a *pro rata* basis. The Tribunal then examined the two groups of curtailments: one in October 2006, concerning all oil producers in Venezuela (thus, *pro rata*) yet not arising out of an international commitment; and the second group, undertaken from November 2006 to March 2007, which was not done on a *pro rata* basis yet arising out of an international commitment.[262]

Both groups, given neither arose out of international commitments *and* were conducted on a *pro rata* basis at the same time, were considered to have breached the FET principle. The Tribunal further stated that "[it is not] necessary to separately examine whether [Venezuela]'s conduct was also arbitrary and/or discriminatory [because] the [c]laimants would not be entitled to a greater relief even if the [t]ribunal were to establish a breach of these BIT protections."[263]

Article 3(1) of the Netherlands—Venezuela BIT, in addition to the FET requirement, forbids arbitrary or discriminatory measures.[264] Arbitrariness, as it is linked to the necessity and proportionality of (as well as the rationale behind) a state act, is a key consideration both as an autonomous breach and as a subset of the FET analysis.[265] The parties, in their contract, clearly regarded international commitments as a justification for such curtailments (albeit to a certain extent), which is commonly seen as an indication that a state act (the curtailment in this case) is not, at least in its entirety, arbitrary.

Generally speaking, any possible arbitrary (or justifying) motivation on the host state's end should be scrutinised in the context of FET—regardless of its autonomous or MST-qualified wording in an IIA. This is particularly important when FET's inherently *ad hoc* nature is considered regardless of its qualification. An analysis limited to contract-bound legitimate expectations might miss other potentially arbitrary elements, or an otherwise contract breach might have another compelling justification. Admittedly, this is not an immediate factual concern of this particular case since Venezuela did not have any further justifications for the curtailment, however this does not seem to be the decisive reason for the Tribunal's disregard of arbitrariness. Instead, it was seen as a potential additional responsibility. This is a general methodological concern in order to establish terminological

[262] *ExxonMobil v. Venezuela* (2014), par. 260–263.

[263] *ExxonMobil v. Venezuela* (2014), par. 273.

[264] Article 3(1), Netherlands – Venezuela BIT (1993).

[265] For an elaborate analysis of arbitrariness as a subset of the FET principle, *see,* Stone (2012); Schreuer (2009).

coherence and arbitral justice, rather than maintaining a particular adjudicatory method solely based on the prospective relief or the investor.

Mohammad Ammar al-Bahloul v. Tajikistan Tribunal[266] addressed several FET breach claims, including claims related to (a) inconsistency and lack of transparency with regards to the issuance licenses and visas, (b) failure to meet legitimate expectations, (c) failure to observe due process, and (d) unfair treatment. While the legitimate expectations analysis was conducted separately from the preceding inconsistency and lack of transparency analysis, both strands of the Tribunal's analysis touch upon what foreign investors can and cannot legitimately expect.

With regards to consistency and transparency claims, the Tribunal provided for a formulation which, similar to the *AES* Tribunal's contention, aimed at striking a balance between regulatory assurance of host states and safety of foreign investors. On transparency, the Tribunal adopted the ***Metalclad***[267] criteria, which proposes that "all relevant legal requirements" should be clear and open to the investor and all other 'affected' investors, "for the purpose of initiating, completing and successfully operating investments made, or intended to be made".[268] As for consistency, the *Tecmed* formulation was adopted.

The Tribunal further pointed out that "[n]either of these criteria [i.e. transparency and consistency] is intended however to go so far as to require the [s]tate to freeze its framework but rather to act in an open manner and consistent with commitments it has undertaken."[269] Similar to *AES*, the difference between a 'framework standstill' and a '*stable* framework' was underlined. Same principle has also been affirmed in the ***CMS v. Argentina*** award.[270]

As for the allegations of the lack of due process, the Tribunal counted a number of obligations which collectively constitute the due process requirement: (a) "the obligation to notify an investor of hearings and not to decide about a claim in his absence"[271]; (b) "the obligation not to maliciously misapply the substantive law"[272]; (c) "the obligation not to use powers for improper purposes"[273]; (d) "the obligation

[266] *Mohammad Ammar Al-Bahloul v. Tajikistan*, SCC Case No. 064/2008, Partial Award on Jurisdiction and Liability (2 September 2009) and Award (8 June 2010) (*Al-Bahloul v. Tajikistan*).

[267] *Metalclad Corporation v. The United Mexican States,* ICSID Case No. ARB(AF)/97/1, Award (20 August 2000) (*Metalclad v. Mexico*).

[268] *Metalclad v. Mexico* (2000), par. 76.

[269] *Al-Bahloul v. Tajikistan* (2009), par. 185.

[270] *CMS Gas Transmission Company v. Argentina,* ICSID Case No. ARB/01/8, Award (12 May 2005) (*CMS v. Argentina*), par. 277 (see below analysis); cited in *Al-Bahloul v. Tajikistan*: "It is not a question of whether the legal framework might need to be frozen as it can always evolve and be adapted to changing circumstances, but neither is it a question of whether the framework can be dispensed with altogether when specific commitments to the contrary have been made."

[271] Paulsson (2005), p. 160.

[272] *Mondev v. USA* (2002), par. 127.

[273] *Saluka v. Czech Republic* (2006), Partial award, par. 307.

not to act intentionally against the investor to harm his investment"[274]; and (e) "not to exercise unreasonable pressure on an investor to reach certain goals."[275]

As for the legitimate expectations, the Tribunal cited the *Thunderbird v. Mexico* and ***Parkerings-Compagniet AS v. Lithuania***[276] awards to frame the principle and its scope of protection. The latter award had inquired "whether Parkerings had any legitimate expectation in the stability of the legal system and whether its expectation has been frustrated."[277] This early, *Tecmed*-inspired conceptualisation of investor's expectations, in retrospect, appears to merge two possible sub-elements of FET, namely legitimate expectations and regulatory stability. This also appears to be the view of the Tribunal as it contended that legitimate expectations would arise only where "explicit promise[s] or [guaranties]" and "[implicit] assurances and representations that the investor took into account in making the investment" existed.[278] If no such explicit or implicit representation was present, the Tribunal considered that the circumstances surrounding the conclusion of the agreement are decisive to determine the legitimacy of the investor's expectations. The Tribunal carefully separated the issue of any expectations an investor might have with regard to regulatory changes from the framework of *legitimate* expectations:

> It is each State's undeniable right and privilege to exercise its sovereign legislative power. A State has the right to enact, modify or cancel a law at its own discretion. Save for the existence of an agreement, in the form of a stabilisation clause or otherwise, there is nothing objectionable about the amendment brought to the regulatory framework existing at the time an investor made its investment. As a matter of fact, any businessman or investor knows that laws will evolve over time. What is prohibited however is for a State to act unfairly, unreasonably or inequitably in the exercise of its legislative power.[279]

The *Parkerings* award was rendered pursuant to Norway—Lithuania BIT of 1992, which, under its Article III, assures "equitable and reasonable treatment and protection"[280] with no further qualifiers. Pursuant to such open-ended drafting, and taking stock of the arbitral case law analysis conducted so far, the arbitral tribunals appear likely to include legitimate expectations in their analysis, and to elaborate on what kinds of representations constitute legitimate expectations, in light of their prevalence in party submissions. In that sense, if IIA parties intend to include legitimate expectations as a sub-element of the FET principle, further clarification on what types of acts or representations are considered 'legitimate' will likely be useful.

---

[274] *Waste Management v. Mexico* (2004), par. 138.

[275] *Pope & Talbot v. Canada* (2001), par. 68.

[276] *Parkerings – Compagniet AS v. Lithuania,* ICSID Case No. ARB/05/8, Award (11 September 2007) (*Parkerings v. Lithuania*).

[277] *Parkerings v. Lithuania* (2007), par. 329.

[278] *Parkerings v. Lithuania* (2007), par. 331. It should be noted that the *Parkerings* award cited the *Tecmed* award and accepted its coverage of 'basic expectations', yet interpreted this as a reference to 'legitimate expectations' (par. 330).

[279] *Parkerings v. Lithuania* (2007), par. 332.

[280] Article III, Lithuania – Norway BIT (1992) (*supra* note 449).

Another Tribunal that broadly embraced the legitimate expectations as a sub-element of the FET principle was ***Devas v. India***.[281] The dispute arose following the cancellation of a frequency allocation agreement between Devas, the claimant; and Antrix, an Indian state-owned company. The reason behind the cancellation was India's policy decision "to reserve a part of the electromagnetic spectrum known as the S-Band 'for national needs, including for the needs of defence, para-military forces, railways and other public utility services as well as for societal needs, and having regard to the needs of the country's strategic requirements."[282] The applicable IIA was the India—Mauritius BIT.[283]

The Tribunal was generally of the opinion that little difference existed between an autonomous or a qualified reading of the FET principle.[284] It adopted the view expressed by the ***El Paso v. Argentina*** award, which had declared that "the legitimate expectations of the investors have generally been considered central in the definition of FET, whatever its scope."[285] The subsequent analysis almost exclusively focuses on Devas' legitimate expectations, and specifically its connection to the sub-element of good faith: "the Claimants were entitled to legitimate expectations that, in accordance with the text of the Treaty as well as under a general obligation under international law, the *Respondent would deal with them in good faith*."[286]

Furthermore, it is also possible to consider legitimate expectations as a *supplementary* element and only in the context of other sub-elements, similar to the *Montauk* Tribunal's handling of the good faith element as a secondary consideration. The recent ***Odyssey v. Mexico*** award appears to have given the claimant's legitimate expectations such a supplementary role.[287]

The dispute arose as a result of the denial of relevant permits for an off-shore phosphate seabed mining project in Baja California Sur due to environmental concerns and the potential harmful effects of the project on the local ecosystem.[288] The Tribunal, after acknowledging the binding effect of the FTC Note on (and the CIL qualification of) Article 1105 of NAFTA, took note of the fact that both parties had

---

[281] *CC/Devas (Mauritius) Ltd., Devas Employees Mauritius Private Limited, and Telcom Devas Mauritius Limited v. Republic of India* (I), PCA Case No. 2013-09, Award on Jurisdiction and Merits (25 July 2016) (*Devas v. India*). Another recent award, namely *GPF v. Poland*, similarly places the legitimate expectations of an investor at the center of its (autonomous) FET analysis: "a consensus emerges about the core components of FET, which include the protection of legitimate expectations, the protection against conduct that is arbitrary, unreasonable, disproportionate and lacking in good faith, and the principles of due process and transparency." GPF GP S.à.r.l v. Republic of Poland, SCC Case No. V 2014/168, Award (29 April 2020), par. 543.

[282] *Devas v. India*, par. 5.

[283] India – Mauritius BIT (1998).

[284] *Devas v. India*, par. 456–457.

[285] *El Paso Energy International Company v. The Argentine Republic*, ICSID Case No. ARB/03/15, Award (31 October 2011) (*El Paso v. Argentina*), par. 348.

[286] *Devas v. India*, par. 465. The Tribunal subsequently explained that the 'good faith' obligation 'under international law' stemmed directly from the Vienna Convention (1969).

[287] *Odyssey v. Mexico* (2024).

[288] *Odyssey v. Mexico* (2024), par. 81 et seq.

agreed on the *Waste Management* Tribunal's articulation of the content of CIL. It found that "there are no reasons to deviate from the reasoning set out in *Waste Management v. Mexico* […] as the position of both parties is that the applicable customary international law standard of [FET] is properly reflected in that award."[289] In its efforts to further identify the contours of MST, the Tribunal admitted that "[t]he standard sought is universal and not a specific concept limited to NAFTA. Therefore, non-NAFTA decisions, to the extent they seek to reflect customary international law, may be of assistance."[290]

The Tribunal subsequently considered arbitrariness, due process, and legitimate expectations as the three prongs of its FET analysis. For the latter, the Tribunal notably accepted the parties' shared understanding that "legitimate expectations are not a stand-alone element within the FET standard under NAFTA Article 1105(1). Rather, such expectations are a factor that may be considered in determining whether a conduct violates the FET standard."[291] It is unclear what is meant by the second sentence: are legitimate expectations only relevant when examined within the context of other sub-elements; or are they secondary, facultative considerations for tribunals?

In his dissenting opinion, Prof. Sands heavily criticised the majority's handling of the FET analysis. He argued that, in reaching the conclusion that the two environmental permit denials were arbitrary, the majority largely ignored Mexico's extensive and well-reasoned scientific reports.[292] He also considered the majority's "observations" on the claimant's legitimate expectations to be inconclusive and superficial.

5.4.3.1 Post-Crisis Argentine Cases and the Importance of Context in Ascertaining Legitimate Expectations

Following its infamous 2001 economic crisis, a plethora of investor claims were filed against Argentina by, *inter alia*, US and Spanish investors. As a result of its 1990s privatisation programme (particularly in the energy sector), Argentina had attracted substantial foreign investment by a series of stabilisation guarantees with regards to the tariff returns, including the pegging of the Argentine peso to the US dollar with a fixed *one-to-one* rate.[293] The government had also granted certain concessions to the license holders with regard to future license modifications.

In spite of its ongoing recession, in order to restore competitiveness and improving its insolvency, the country attempted to acquire large financial packages. It also

[289] *Odyssey v. Mexico* (2024), par. 299.

[290] *Odyssey v. Mexico* (2024), par. 304.

[291] *Odyssey v. Mexico* (2024), par. 317.

[292] Odyssey v. Mexico (2024), par. 25–28.

[293] Argentina's Crisis Explained (*Time*, 20 December 2001). http://content.time.com/time/world/article/0,8599,189393,00.html..

attempted to refinance its national debt through private banks, but to minimal effect.[294] As a result, in early 2002, the Argentine government abolished the pegging of pesos to dollar with its *Public Emergency and Foreign Exchange System Reform Law (*hereinafter 'Public Emergency Law' or 'PEL'*),* eventually causing peso to plummet in value *vis-á-vis* the US dollar. Many concessions and rights with regard to licenses were also terminated, and many domestic and foreign investors were affected.

A number of arbitral claims with regard to the energy sector, such as *CMS*,[295] ***Continental Casualty,***[296] El Paso,[297] ***Enron,***[298] ***Sempra,***[299] and ***LG&E***[300] (*v. Argentina*) have been under spotlight ever since, and their content has been scrutinised in detail.[301] Their context has been described as "a Rorschach test of attitudes toward the worldwide network of investment treaties".[302] One particularly noteworthy aspect was the handling of the concept of 'necessity' by arbitral tribunals as laid forth pursuant to Article 25 of the Draft Articles on Responsibility of States for Internationally Wrongful Acts (ARSIWA).[303] The Chapter, however, will not look into the question of necessity in its entirety and limit itself to the FET analyses in these awards.[304] Since the facts that had given rise to these disputes (as briefly provided above) were virtually identical, the text will refrain from repetition.

---

[294] Kiguel (2011).

[295] *CMS Gas Transmission Company v. The Republic of Argentina*, ICSID Case No. ARB/01/8, Award (12 May 2005) (*CMS v. Argentina*).

[296] *Continental Casualty Company v. The Argentine Republic*, ICSID Case No. ARB/03/9, Award (5 September 2008) (*Continental Casualty v. Argentina*).

[297] *El Paso v. Argentina* (2011).

[298] *Enron Corporation and Ponderosa Assets, L.P. v. Argentine Republic*, ICSID Case No. ARB/01/3, Award 22 May 2007) (*Enron v. Argentina*).

[299] *Sempra Energy International v. The Argentine Republic*, ICSID Case No. ARB/02/16, Award (28 September 2007) (*Sempra v. Argentina*).

[300] *LG&E Energy Corp., LG&E Capital Corp., and LG&E International, Inc.v. Argentine Republic*, ICSID Case No. ARB/02/1, Decision on Liability (3 October 2006) and Award (25 July 2007) (*LG&E v. Argentina*).

[301] Grigera (2024); Reinisch and Tropper (2022); Mola (2016), p. 371; Alvarez and Khamsi (2009).

[302] Alvarez and Khamsi (2009), p. 381.

[303] Draft Articles on Responsibility of States for Internationally Wrongful Acts (2001) (ARSIWA). https://legal.un.org/ilc/texts/instruments/english/draft_articles/9_6_2001.pdf.

[304] On this, see Paddeu and Waibel (2022), p. 162. In particular, the discussion relating to the CIL origins of the state of 'necessity' has sparked debates among academics. Some tribunals, like *CMS*, have adopted the wording in Article 25 of ARSIWA (2001), which reads that "Necessity may not be invoked by a State as a ground for precluding the wrongfulness of an act not in conformity with an international obligation of that State unless the act [...] **is the only way** for the State to safeguard an essential interest" (Emphasis added). Some tribunals interpreted the phrase 'only way' literally, and found Argentina to be responsible, because the measures undertaken by the state were literally 'not the only way' to tackle the economic problems the country had faced.

Following their analysis, the Chapter will also briefly examine ***Metalpar v. Argentina,***[305] which concerned the effects of the state measures on the automobile sector, and analyse this award's take on the FET principle vis-à-vis the energy sector decisions to better understand how factual-contextual differences (for instance with regard to applicable concessions and regulatory framework) may affect the legitimate expectations analysis. All disputes examined below, except for the Metalpar case, are based on the Argentina—US BIT of 1991, which notes that "Investment shall at all times be accorded fair and equitable treatment, shall enjoy full protection and security and shall in no case be accorded treatment less than that required by international law."[306]

Despite the parallel FET analyses conducted by all tribunals mentioned above, their framing of the FET principle, their application of the legitimate expectations, and the eventual finding of a breach differ. Given their factual and analytical similarities, it is most appropriate to consider these cases in connection with one another.

The *LG&E v. Argentina* Tribunal's decision on liability referred to a number of constituent elements of the FET. After pointing out that Article 31 VCLT was the interpretative point of reference, the Tribunal identified the nature of the FET principle as a concept highly dynamic in terms of its temporal and factual circumstances: "Due to the fact that such international standards have a generic nature and that their interpretation varies with the course of time and with the circumstances of each case, it becomes difficult to establish an unequivocal and static concept of these notions."[307]

In the *Enron* award, the Tribunal argued that in certain situations, FET may be equated to MST; but in other situations, it might differ from it. It observed that "at least in the context of the Treaty applicable to this case, [FET] can also require a treatment additional to, or beyond that of, customary law".[308] The *CMS* Tribunal, conversely, equated the FET principle to MST, noting that

> While the choice between requiring a higher treaty standard and that of equating it with the international minimum standard might have relevance in the context of some disputes, the Tribunal is not persuaded that it is relevant in this case. In fact, the Treaty standard of fair and equitable treatment and its connection with the required stability and predictability of the business environment, founded on solemn legal and contractual 83 commitments, is not different from the international law minimum standard and its evolution under customary law.[309]

Similar to the *CMS* Tribunal, the *Sempra* Tribunal did not consider the FET principle in the BIT to require protection beyond CIL: "[FET] standard imposed under a treaty can also eventually require a treatment additional to or beyond that of

[305] *Metalpar S.A. and Buen Aire S.A. v. The Argentine Republic*, ICSID Case No. ARB/03/5, Award on the Merits (6 June 2008) (*Metalpar v. Argentina*).

[306] Article II(2)(a), Argentina – US BIT (1991).

[307] *LG&E v. Argentina* (2006), par. 123. Emphasis added.

[308] *Enron v. Argentina* (2007), par. 258.

[309] *CMS v. Argentina* (2005), par. 284.

customary law. Such does not appear to be the case with the present dispute".[310] Despite their different takes on the FET-CIL connection, the subsequent analyses do not have notable differences stemming from this issue. Finally, neither the *Continental Casualty* nor the *El Paso* Tribunals considered this issue important, with the latter calling the discussion of FET-CIL interrelationship "somewhat futile"—instead drawing attention to the importance of ascertaining "the content" of the FET standard.[311]

On the specific sub-elements of FET, there are also some differences among the awards. The *LG&E* Tribunal listed stability of the legal and business framework, even-handedness and justness, consistency and transparency, and "investor's expectations when making its investment in reliance on the protections to be granted by the host [s]tate" as sub-elements of FET.[312] It was also explicitly stated that bad faith was not a pre-requisite for a FET breach.[313]

The Tribunal paid close attention to what it subsequently called 'fair expectations' of investors, and drew its contours as follows:

> they are based on the conditions offered by the host State at the time of the investment; they may not be established unilaterally by one of the parties; they must exist and be enforceable by law; in the event of infringement by the host State, a duty to compensate the investor for damages arises except for those caused in the event of state of necessity; however, the investor's fair expectations cannot fail to consider parameters such as business risk or industry's regular patterns.[314]

Two notable features of this elaboration are that first, an investor's unilateral expectations would not qualify as legitimate expectations according to the Tribunal. This differs markedly from the broader conceptualisation under the *Tecmed* award cited by the Tribunal. Tecmed's 'basic expectations' model arguably opened way for unilateral 'expectations' of an investor vis-à-vis the conduct of the government to be protected. Indeed, the exclusion of unilateral impressions from the scope implies that some form of representation on the state's end is necessary for these expectations to properly form. An added limitation alludes to the investor's own due diligence, as business risk and know-how relating to a specific industry might also affect the legitimacy of an investor's expectations.

However, according to the Tribunal, these representations did not have to be specific in the sense that they did not have to be targeted at the investors *directly* and *personally*. It considered *sectoral specificity* sufficient in that regard. It provided further context in light of the background of the dispute, and defined the post-80 s economic crisis remedies and market liberalisation policies put in place by Argentina

[310] *Sempra v. Argentina* (2007), par. 302.

[311] *El Paso v. Argentina* (2011), par. 335; The Tribunal nonetheless noted that "it is the view of the Tribunal that the position according to which FET is equivalent to the international minimum standard is more in line with the evolution of investment law and international law" (par. 336).

[312] *LG&E v. Argentina* (2006), p. 127; referring to the T*ecmed v. Mexico* (2003) and *Waste Management v. Mexico* (2004) awards.

[313] *LG&E v. Argentina* (2006), par. 129.

[314] *LG&E v. Argentina* (2006), par. 130.

as "mainly dependent upon foreign capital".[315] It was pointed out that the concession laws and regulations were specifically aimed at mitigating the "country risks" in Argentina for foreign investors. Given the claimants had in fact relied upon these guarantees and concessions while investing in Argentina, for the purposes of the adjudication, this new privatisation scheme was considered within the context of "specific expectations among investors", which in return bound Argentina to its guarantees.

Having also endorsed the *Tecmed* formula on legitimate/basic expectations, the *Sempra* Tribunal similarly noted that "[t]his requirement becomes particularly meaningful when the investment has been attracted and induced by means of assurances and representations"[316] In *Enron*, the Tribunal drew attention to the importance of these expectations being derived from "the conditions that were offered by the State to the investor at the time of the investment and that such conditions were relied upon by the investor when deciding to invest."[317] The *El Paso* Tribunal noted that "the legitimate expectations of the investors have generally been considered central in the definition of FET, *whatever its scope*."[318] It further emphasised that (a) legitimate expectations can be breached even in the absence of bad faith; (b) legitimate expectations resulted from a confrontation of the objective expectations of investors and the right of the state to regulate; and (c) the legitimacy of expectations depended on the circumstances.[319]

The *Continental Casualty* Tribunal generally acknowledged that legitimate expectations were relevant,[320] but pointed out a key contextual difference between the case at hand and the others examined here with regard to legitimate expectations: unlike the others, Continental "had entered in that market" before the sectoral concessions and general legislative assurances were put in place.[321] Because of the absence of 'specific undertakings' *vis-à-vis* Continental, the Tribunal conducted a different analysis with regard to the investor's legitimate expectations. Eventually, the Tribunal found that no legitimate expectations existed. Furthermore, it noted that the claimant "should have maintained a reduced trust [...] as the worsening of the crisis was evident".[322]

Like the *LG&E* Tribunal, the *Sempra* Tribunal drew attention to the importance of the stability of the legal and business framework. It then observed that the measures in question have substantially changed this framework under which the investment was decided and implemented.[323] The *Enron* tribunal reached a near-identical

[315] *LG&E v. Argentina* (2006), par. 133.

[316] *Sempra v. Argentina* (2007), par. 298.

[317] *Enron v. Argentina* (2007), par. 262.

[318] *El Paso v. Argentina* (2011), par. 348.

[319] *El Paso v. Argentina* (2011), par. 356 et seq.

[320] *Continental Casualty v. Argentina* (2008), par. 260.

[321] *Continental Casualty v. Argentina* (2008), par. 259.

[322] *Continental Casualty v. Argentina* (2008), par. 262.

[323] *Sempra v. Argentina* (2007), par. 303.

conclusion on the relevance of stability.[324] Citing the *LG&E* decision, it stated that "a key element of fair and equitable treatment is the requirement of a 'stable framework for the investment'".[325]

The *CMS* Tribunal reached the same conclusion (subsequently inspiring the *LG&E* Tribunal) and stated that "one principle objective of the protection envisaged [in the preamble of the BIT] is that fair and equitable treatment is desirable 'to maintain a stable framework for investments and maximum effective use of economic resources.'" the *CMS* Tribunal further elaborated that:

> It is not a question of whether the legal framework might need to be frozen as it can always evolve and be adapted to changing circumstances, but neither is it a question of whether the framework can be dispensed with altogether when specific commitments to the contrary have been made.[326]

It then noted:

> In fact, the [FET standard] and its connection with the required stability and predictability of the business environment, founded on solemn legal and contractual commitments, is not different from the international law minimum standard and its evolution under customary law.[327]

The *Continental Casualty* Tribunal, however, took a different view on the issue of stability of the legal framework, noting that

> [i]t is not a legal obligation in itself for the Contracting Parties, nor can it be properly defined as an object of the Treaty. It is rather a precondition for one of the two basic objects of the Treaty ... it would be unconscionable for a country to promise not to change its legislation as time and needs change, or even more to tie its hands by such a kind of stipulation in case a crisis of any type or origin arose.[328]

The *El Paso v. Argentina* Tribunal was also cautious towards reading too much into the stability of the legal and business framework as a requirement:

> Such a standard of behaviour, if strictly applied, is not realistic, nor is it the BITs' purpose that States guarantee that the economic and legal conditions in which investments take place will remain unaltered ad infinitum.[329]

As the foregoing analysis reveals, even in light of the same set of facts and the same applicable BIT, arbitral tribunals can and will diverge on how to interpret the FET principle—provided the provision allows the sufficient interpretative leeway for them to do so. All tribunals underlined the relevance of legitimate expectations to the FET analysis. In the face of the severe changes in the legal and business framework, all tribunals maintained that there was a breach of the FET principle, save for the partial finding by the *Continental Casualty*. The *Enron* tribunal further took note

[324] *Enron v. Argentina* (2007), par. 261.

[325] *Enron v. Argentina* (2007), par. 260.

[326] *CMS v. Argentina* (2005), par. 277.

[327] *CMS v. Argentina* (2005), par. 284.

[328] *Continental Casualty v. Argentina* (2008), par. 259.

[329] *El Paso v. Argentina* (2011), par. 350.

of the Argentine "international marketing" and "the statutory enshrinement of the tariff regime"[330] to bolster Enron's legitimate expectations and its reliance on the Argentine incentives.

All tribunals, at least briefly, refer to the FET—CIL relationship. None, however, attach any substantial importance to this connection. Whereas the *Enron* Tribunal considered Article II of the BIT to reflect a protection beyond MST, the *CMS* and *Sempra* Tribunals disagreed. The *Continental Casualty* and *El Paso* Tribunals did not consider the discussion to be important to the outcome. All in all, the analyses conducted resemble one another, despite ostensibly different views on the threshold. Finally, the Tribunals notably differed in the importance they attached to the stability of the legal and business framework.

This being said, even within the context of such a controversial bundle of cases which had adopted differing benchmarks and interpretations, in particular on the connection between FET and MST,, the FET analyses ultimately stem from the same subset and, ultimately, adopt a similar reasoning. It must also be underlined that these cases, given their factual overlap, clearly influenced one another; as latter Tribunals typically referred to earlier cases such as *CMS* and *LG&E*. In particular, such cross-referencing is evident in how they all maintained that the stability of the legal and business framework is relevant to some degree. They also appear to rely on other cases similarly, such as *Tecmed* and *Waste Management*, and adopt the approaches contained within them to varying degrees—for example, while all cases refer to the *Tecmed* award, none of them subscribed to the unilateral, broad reading it had adopted on the 'basic' expectations of investors as a source of responsibility.

Another post-2001 case in Argentina was *Metalpar v. Argentina,*[331] which concerned the claims of a Chilean investor in the automobile sector. Facts related to the economic crisis naturally remain the same; however, the domestic legal framework and the conduct of the investment differ from the license-based guarantees granted to the claimants referred to above under the Gas Law (with the exception of Continental). This case is thus illustrative for the overall FET analysis and how a contextual shift affects the legitimate expectations analysis.

The claimant argued that the Argentine response to the crisis was not coherent; it was ambiguous, unpredictable and lacking in transparency, which prevented investors from being able to plan their activities. Argentina, in response, maintained that "[the claimant] cannot argue that it had any legitimate expectation that, in the face of the most serious economic, social and institutional collapse in the history of the country, its investment would not be affected at all and that the legal framework governing the contractual relationships between private persons would not be readjusted."[332]

---

[330] *Enron v. Argentina* (2007), par. 265.

[331] *Metalpar S.A. and Buen Aire S.A. v. Argentina*, ICSID Case No. ARB/03/5, Award on the Merits (6 June 2008) (*Metalpar v. Argentina*).

[332] *Metalpar v. Argentina* (2008), par. 123.

The Tribunal ultimately decided that Argentina did not breach the FET principle. It has been contended that Argentina did not deny access to justice or acted in a discriminatory manner—in fact, it was the claimant that refrained, on its own discretion, from using the judicial and extra-judicial mechanisms that Argentina put in place following the crisis.[333]

The Tribunal, furthermore, was not convinced by the legitimate expectations argument used by the claimant. It explored case law in order to conduct a comparative analysis of the principle and the facts. It accurately and succinctly laid forth the principal difference between the case at hand and, *inter alia*, some of the cases mentioned above:

> [...] [The awards provided][334] asserted that investors' expectations were related to fair and equitable treatment. However, in all of them, the conflict arose out of a state of facts different to the one under analysis in this case: in some of them, the relevant governments had invited the foreign investors to participate in a bidding process that was awarded to each of those investors and ended with the signing of a contract. In other cases, there were other types of contractual relations which created legitimate expectations; in all of them, the [g]overnment refused to renew or to comply with the contract, license or permit. In this specific case, there was no bid, license, permit or contract of any kind between Argentina and [c]laimants, and the [t]ribunal considers that there were no legitimate expectations entertained by [Metalpar] that were breached by Argentina.[335]

Therefore, in this particular case, The Tribunal found that Metalpar had no representation similar to those present under the energy cases referred to above. It was, therefore, not entitled to the rights the tribunals granted to them. It is further asserted that the claimants had business experience in Argentina as well as in Chile, and that they had known that the automobile industry in Argentina was in decline since 1997. In line with this fact, the Tribunal assessed the possibility of Metalpar in fact having legitimate expectations, and contended that "it is unlikely that [Metalpar] legitimately expected that their investments would not be subject to the ups and downs of the country in which they were made or that the crisis that could already be foreseen would not make it necessary to issue legal measures to cope with it."[336]

Despite the identical macro-economic situation, the analysis produced a completely different outcome with regard to FET due to stark differences in representations given and concessions granted by Argentina to foreign investors. The main difference was the absence of any form of representation, save the issuance of a license or tariff agreements. The direct impact of an investor's position, intent, knowledge, degree of negligence, and the legal framework to which and investor is subject also played a determinative role.

---

[333] *Metalpar v. Argentina* (2008), par. 180–181.

[334] It counts *LG&E v. Argentina* (2006) and *Enron v. Argentina* (2007), among others.

[335] *Metalpar v. Argentina* (2008), par. 185–186.

[336] *Metalpar v. Argentina* (2008), par. 187.

5.4.4 Investor's Conduct and Its Impact on FET

Before I conclude the FET case law analysis and move on to the new generation IIAs to identify if, and how, the case law shaped these new instruments, a brief illustration on how investor's own conduct or negligence has affected the findings of FET can prove to be useful. While the application of the contributory fault principle in investment arbitration has been criticised for not being sufficiently coherent,[337] the purpose here is not to provide a comprehensive examination. Nonetheless, for the purposes of our dissection of the FET principle, the premise that an investor's own misconduct is a relevant sub-element is a useful consideration which may guide future IIAs.

MTD v. Chile[338] concerned a claim arising out of a real estate contract of a large-scale community project to be undertaken in Pirque, Chile, pursuant to the Chile—Malaysia BIT of 1992 which contains an unqualified FET provision.[339] Following the signing and approval of the project, MTD submitted an application in order to commence the process for zoning changes for some agricultural lands included in the project description. Initially suffering from a slow process, the zone change application was ultimately discarded, despite alleged endorsements of the project by government officials including the Mayor of Pirque, and the then-President of Chile, Eduardo Frei Ruiz-Tagle. Following the rejection of the zone change, MTD initiated arbitral proceedings.

The *MTD* Tribunal conducted a thorough FET analysis, first by laying forth the standards of its examination of the facts. The Tribunal cited Judge Steven Schwebel, who describes the FET principle as "a broad and widely-accepted standard encompassing such fundamental standards as good faith, due process, non-discrimination, and proportionality."[340] Following a consideration of the NAFTA-inspired, MST interpretation, the Tribunal maintained that the BIT according to which the Tribunal has been established did not include any references to CIL.[341] Then, it went on to conduct an interpretation of the relevant provision on FET in accordance with Article 31 of VCLT—in good faith, in accordance with its ordinary meaning within the scope of the treaty context as well as its object and purpose. The Tribunal took into account the ordinary meaning of the words "fair" and "equitable", and approximated them with "just", "even-handed", "unbiased" and "legitimate". The Tribunal also elaborated on the pro-active nature of the preamble, consequentially allocating the state's responsibility to conduct an "even-handed and just" treatment through

---

337 Marcoux and Bjorklund (2020), p. 905; see also generally Jarrett (2019), p. 43 et seq.

338 *MTD Equity Sdn. Bhd. and MTD Chile S.A. v. Republic of Chile, ICSID Case No. ARB/01/7*, Award (25 May 2004).

339 Article 2, Chile – Malaysia BIT (1992).

340 *MTD v. Chile* (2004), par. 109; cited Opinion of Judge Steven Schwebel, par. 23.

341 Article 3, Chile – Malaysia BIT (1995).

means of promotion, creation and stimulation of a favourable investment environment.[342]

The Tribunal cited the *Tecmed* tribunal's definition on "fair and equitable" treatment,[343] declaring it the "standard that the Tribunal will apply to the facts of the case."[344] It then moved on to the analysis of the facts of the case. Eventually, the analysis of the FET broke down to three contested events: (a) an alleged meeting, as claimed by the Chilean government and refused by the claimant, during which the claimant was clearly informed that such project would be risky; (b) the scope of the Foreign Investment Commission's competence, which is described as merely approving the inflow of investment to Chile by the government; and (c) the responsibility of the claimants as "diligent investors", implying the responsibility of the investor to properly inform themselves with regards to an unanticipated event that might damage or destroy the investment.[345] In that sense, the attributability of such event to the state, and not the misconduct or negligence of the investor itself, rises to a whole new level of significance.

As for the alleged meeting, the Tribunal, after mentioning the limited evidence of the meeting ever taking place, went on to analyse the subsequent conduct of the parties. One crucial evidence seemed to be the endorsement of the project by the Chilean President and his subsequent refusal to attend to the inauguration of the project due to a scheduling conflict—however, the Tribunal asserted that if the reason for the cancellation of attendance was due to the lack of feasibility of the project, as the respondent claimed, it should have been made clear. Therefore, "the Respondent does not seem to have acted in accordance with the allegedly clear warnings given to representatives of the Claimants [at the alleged meeting]."[346] Similarly, the Tribunal argued that "if the statements made to [the investor] by [the government officials] had been as clear as alleged, the Claimants would have protected themselves accordingly by looking for another site or cancelling the proposed investment altogether."[347]

As for the competences of the Foreign Investment Commission, the Tribunal concluded that the applications made would include the location of the investment; and given that the Commission was composed at a ministerial level, its attributed importance should be indeed high. It is also stated that the Commission is "required to carry out a minimum of diligence internally and externally. Approval of a Project in a location would give *prima facie* to an investor the expectation that the project is feasible in that location".[348]

[342] *MTD v. Chile* (2004), par. 113.
[343] *MTD v. Chile* (2004), par. 114.
[344] *MTD v. Chile* (2004), par. 115.
[345] *MTD v. Chile* (2004), par. 149.
[346] *MTD v. Chile* (2004), par. 157.
[347] *MTD v. Chile* (2004), par. 158.
[348] *MTD v. Chile* (2004), 163.

The Tribunal made clear the perceived responsibilities of each party. Before elaborating further on the diligence of the investor, it maintained that "it is the responsibility of the investor to assure itself that it is properly advised, particularly when investing abroad in an unfamiliar environment. However, [...] Chile is not a passive party and the coherent action of [its] officials [...] is the responsibility of Chile, not of the investor."[349]

The Tribunal finally stated that "based on the evidence presented [...] approval of an investment by [the Commission] for a project that is against the urban policy of the [g]overnment is a breach of the obligation to treat an investor fairly and equitably [...] This conclusion of the [t]ribunal does not mean that Chile is responsible for the unwise business decisions for the lack of diligence of the investor."[350]

As arguably the most important section of the FET examination, the diligence analysis shed light on how important the investor's own conduct can be for the outcome. The Tribunal agreed with Chile's argument that if the investor had made "even the most rudimentary of inquiries", it would be undisputedly clear to them that the location of the project was in fact a "high-quality agricultural land and plays and important role in the environmental health of the Metropolitan Region. They would have also learned about the [decision] adopted just two years earlier which 'expressly prohibited urban development in Pirque and designated it as an exclusive [agricultural area].'"[351] The Tribunal then rendered its view on the scope of protection and the FET:

> The BITs are not an insurance against business risk and the [t]ribunal considers that the [c]laimants should bear the consequences of their own actions as experienced businessmen. Their choice of partner, the acceptance of a land valuation based on future assumptions without protection themselves contractually in case the assumptions would not materialize, including the issuance of the required development permits, are risks that [MTD] took irrespective of Chile's actions.[352]

The award therefore included the consideration of a contributory fault[353] at MTD's end. The Tribunal, taking into account that Chile had nonetheless acted against FET principle in its subsequent conduct in accordance with the adopted method of analysis (as described in and quoted from the Tecmed award), and that MTD is to bear the consequences of its own negligence as a diligent investor. As a result, the Claimant received only 50% of the assessed damages.[354]

The ***Biwater v. Tanzania*** case[355] also relates to the discussion of the investor's own misconduct and negligence and its impact on a tribunal's decision, and how

[349] *MTD v. Chile* (2004), par. 164.

[350] *MTD v. Chile* (2004), par. 167.

[351] *MTD v. Chile* (2004), par. 169.

[352] *MTD v. Chile* (2004), par. 178.

[353] Burgstaller and Galagan (2024); Marcoux and Bjorklund (2020), p. 883.

[354] *MTD v. Chile* (2004), par. 242–243.

[355] *Biwater Gauff (Tanzania) Ltd. v. United Republic of Tanzania,* ICSID Case No. ARB/05/22, Award (24 July 2008) (*Biwater v. Tanzania*).

such misconduct tips the balance in determining whether an act can be deemed unfair. The applicable treaty, the Tanzania—UK BIT, contains an unqualified FET provision under its Article 2.[356] It concerned a dispute between Biwater Gauff, an Anglo-German joint venture which had undertaken the operation of water and sewage services in Dar-es-Salaam via a lease agreement. Following a period of poor performance by the investor, the agreement was terminated.

The Tribunal, after conducting an in-depth examination of the FET principle and its context, pinpointed several components for FET as distilled from the case law and academia: legitimate expectations, good faith, transparency, consistency, and non-discrimination.[357] It had been subsequently pointed out that there were other, in this case not relevant, components of the FET principle such as denial of justice.[358] The Tribunal eventually concluded that several acts of the state in fact constituted a breach of the FET principle, such as a public speech given by a Tanzanian minister, the withdrawal of VAT exemption, and the seizure of the investor's offices and infrastructure.

One of the highlights of this award was definitely the *causation* analysis conducted by the Tribunal. Despite the initial contention that Tanzania had breached its obligations under the FET principle, the analysis continued in order to determine whether or not the damages suffered by the investor were in fact caused by the host state through the challenged acts. The point of reference on which the parties had agreed as "the general principles governing [s]tate responsibility and the attribution of acts and omission to the [s]tate" was ARSIWA.[359] Despite never being transformed into a treaty, it has been acknowledged as the CIL on state responsibility by some tribunals, including the ICJ.[360] This being said, as pointed out by Kurtz, there are a number of questions related to its legitimacy as the "final expression of the customary law".[361]

As was also cited by the Tribunal, Crawford's commentary on Article 31 of ARSIWA provides for an elaboration of the constituent elements of the causation analysis. Two very important, yet not exhaustive, elements stand out: (a) attributability of the damage to a state act, and (b) a threshold which sets the limits for an act to be deemed too indirect or remote. As for the application of these criteria, Crawford pointed out a very important detail with regards to what attributable act

356 Tanzania – UK BIT (1994).

357 *Biwater v. Tanzania* (2008), par. 586–603.

358 *Biwater v. Tanzania* (2008), par. 602.

359 Draft Articles with Commentary (2001) (*supra* note 1004).

360 *Biwater v. Tanzania* (2008), par. 479; *Legal Consequences of the Construction of a Wall in the Occupied Palestinian Territory*, Advisory Opinion (9 July 2004). https://www.icj-cij.org/case/131, par. 140–142 (according to which the ICJ rejected the argument that the construction of a wall within the Palestinian territory could be justified with the necessity doctrine). For a general discussion on the Draft Articles as customary law *see*, Kurtz (2010).

361 Kurtz (2010), p. 207.

actually means: "[i]n some cases, the criterion of 'directness' may be used, in others 'foreseeability' or 'proximity'."[362]

Before continuing with the application of its analysis to the case at hand, the Tribunal also pointed out the difference between establishing a causal link between the damage and the act *per se*, and establishing a causal link between the damage and the 'underlying' or 'dominant' cause.[363] On this matter, the *ELSI* case was taken as the point of departure: "[...] there were several causes acting together that led to the disaster to ELSI. No doubt the effects of the requisition might have been one of the factors involved. But the underlying cause was ELSI's headlong course towards insolvency; which state of affairs it seems to have attained even prior to the requisition."[364] ELSI's 'underlying cause' analysis, taken into account in conjunction with Professor Crawford's commentary, produces the following conclusion: the mere fact that a causal link was established between the act and the outcome is not necessarily accompanied by the state's liability to compensate. If the dominant or the primary cause[365] of the damage or suffering, despite being side by side with a lesser contribution by the state, is the investor's own misconduct and not the breach of a BIT principle (in this case, a FET breach), then the state will not necessarily be liable.

The application of this prescribed analysis maintained that it was predominantly investor's own conduct that actually stripped the investment from its economic value in its entirety even before the investor's claims arose. Among the counted (mis)conducts were the poor preparation for the sewage and waterworks bid, negligence in benefitting from accurate methods to re-calibrate existing data inconsistencies, failure to generate projected income due to management and implementation difficulties and the subsequent need for a renegotiation which eventually failed.

The following paragraph summarises the application of these elaborated principles:

> [T]he [tribunal] concludes in all the circumstances that the actual, proximate or direct causes of the loss and damage for which [the Claimant] now seeks compensation were acts and omissions that had already occurred [before the claims arose]. In other words, none of [Tanzania]'s violations of the BIT [after the claims arose] in fact caused the loss and damage in question, or broke the chain of causation that was already in place.[366]

The conclusion, therefore, converged upon the idea that the act or acts that constitute a *prima facie* breach of the FET principle will not necessarily transform themselves into a BIT-based liability if there is no causal link. Despite their unfair and inequitable nature *per se*, the fact that if the state conduct is not the dominant cause for the loss of economic value of the investment, this will mean that the state will not be liable. It was not the state's measure that rendered the investment worthless,

[362] *Biwater v. Tanzania* (2008), par. 785 citing James Crawford, ARSIWA (2001), p. 93.

[363] *Biwater v. Tanzania* (2008), par. 786.

[364] *Biwater v. Tanzania* (2008), par. 786; citing *ELSI* (1989).

[365] Jarrett (2019), p. 45. This can also be referred to as the 'operative' or 'effective' cause.

[366] *Biwater v. Tanzania* (2008), par. 798.

because the investment was already essentially worthless when the alleged harmful acts were conducted by the state.

5.4.5 Observations on How the Case Law and IIA Provisions on FET Interact

The case law analysis above sought to illustrate the interpretative trends and the arbitral elaborations on the scope of the FET principle. All cases examined above relate to a variety of sectors, different types of FET provisions, respondent states, claimants, as well as different kinds of state conduct. They reveal a complicated, at times conflated, landscape of legal reasoning and application of the FET principle.

As noted at the beginning of this Chapter, my primary aim was to demonstrate that the long-standing, perceived differences between different types of qualified or unqualified FET provisions do not have a substantial bearing on the content of the FET analyses conducted by arbitral tribunals. Even those tribunals who act with the conviction that a CIL-qualified FET sets a different threshold than a so-called autonomous reading are unable to articulate this distinction in actionable terms. Numerous tribunals, such as Saluka and El Paso, outright declare this distinction 'more apparent than real' and 'fictitious'. Therefore, the current treaty-making practice of attaching CIL or international law qualifiers remains largely ineffective with regard to defining the content and scope of the FET principle, as there are compelling examples of both 'qualified' and 'unqualified' FET clauses giving rise to near-identical legal applications of the principle.

This is particularly evident when NAFTA cases rendered before and after the July 2001 FTC Interpretative Notes are compared. The *Pope & Talbot* tribunal analysed the FET principle with an assumption that it was an autonomous standard and not a mere manifestation of CIL, therefore refusing to be bound by criteria that the act needed to be 'egregious' or 'shocking'. The *Mondev* tribunal, on the other hand, explicitly linked its analysis to CIL, yet linked a dynamic and evolutionary character to FET. This eventually lead the Tribunal to the conclusion that an act need not be 'egregious', given the applicable CIL have evolved beyond the *Neer* definition.

More generally, disputes stemming from the so-called qualified provisions, such as *Waste Management* (NAFTA) and *RDC* (CAFTA), prescribe that for an FET breach, the state measure or measures need to be arbitrary, grossly unfair, unjust and idiosyncratic; discriminatory and lacking due process. In particular, the Waste Management award is popular among all types of cases, and tribunals interpreting qualified or unqualified FET provisions often refer to it for its clear articulation of the FET sub-elements.

The case law analysis also shows that arbitral tribunals tend to treat 'international law' qualifiers as unqualified FET provisions, refusing to 'limit' the scope of these provisions to CIL, as awards like *Indian Metal* and *Lemire* demonstrate.[367] On the other hand, other disputes such as *Saluka* (, prescribe the same, or at least a comparable, list of considerations. A number of other tribunals, regardless of their autonomy (or attachment to IST), laid forth overlapping interpretative factors: *Tecmed* and *MTD* tribunals list consistency, transparency, freedom from ambiguity, good faith, and due process; the *Thunderbird* tribunal mentions denial of justice and abuse of rights. *Mondev, Mohammad Ammar* and *Azinian* tribunals also elaborated on denial of justice as a constituent element of FET. Awards like *Cairn Energy*, interpreting autonomous FET provisions, seek guidance in reference to awards such as ADF, where qualified FET provisions were applied.

Almost all tribunals, some almost exclusively, highlighted the 'legitimate expectations of the investor' while examining whether the FET obligation was breached. Among others, *ExxonMobil, Occidental, Tecmed, Eco Oro, CMS, LG&E, Sempra, Enron,* and *Thunderbird* all emphasised the role and importance of the legitimate expectations of the investor to the outcome and liability of the host state, regardless of the FET provision's relationship to CIL. A number of tribunals contended that a stable legal and business framework also formed a part of the FET analysis—a distinguishing between a *stable* framework and a framework *standstill.* Regardless of the qualifiers utilised in the specific provision, ordinary meaning of the words 'fair' and 'equitable' were common references. Tribunals also sought guidance from Article 31 of VCLT in conjunction with the preamble of the respective investment treaty.

Whether an act or measure of a state can be deemed fair also directly relates to the attributability of the measure to the host state. In fact, legitimate expectations and attributability of the measure stand at the two ends of the same argumentative spectrum. On one hand, as the *MTD* and *Biwater* tribunals demonstrated, if the investor's own conduct or negligence is the dominant or the underlying cause, a state may see its liability diminished.

This Chapter examined more than 40 awards, spanning from 2000 to late 2024. Given there were 207 ISDS cases where "FET was interpreted in awards on the merits"[368] as of 2020, and with the obvious caveat that this number has definitely increased in the past 5 years, this still corresponds to approximately 15–18% of all awards where FET was interpreted by an arbitral tribunal. Hidden in this multitude of awards, the bits and pieces of an overarching FET principle has emerged independently from the confounds of any qualifier. Despite the traditionally vague wording in most treaties, the FET principle has gradually evolved into a set of considerations, *de facto* detaching itself from the ineffective autonomy—CIL duality. Take, for instance, the ***Merrill & Ring*** award:

> A requirement that aliens be treated fairly and equitably in relation to business, trade and investment is the outcome of this changing reality and as such it has become sufficiently

[367] This appears to correlate with recent empirical studies reaching a similar conclusion. See, Dumberry (2023), p. 25.

[368] Yu (2024), p. 262.

> part of widespread and consistent practice so as to demonstrate that it is reflected today in customary international law as opinio juris. **In the end, the name assigned to the standard does not really matter. What matters is that the standard protects against all such acts or behavior that might infringe a sense of fairness, equity and reasonableness**. Of course, the concepts of fairness, equitableness and reasonableness cannot be defined precisely: they require to be applied to the facts of each case.[369]

This observation can be considered in parallel to the dynamic character of FET *and* CIL. At this point, their evolutionary processes—assuming they were separate processes to begin with—are very much intertwined. Linking FET to CIL or considering it autonomous is, given their ever-changing, evolving character, does not reveal much about their content at any given time. In practice, their development and content is in a visible overlap. One or the other interpretation does not guarantee one or another threshold, treatment, or behaviour.

Some scholars have expressed more assertive positions. For instance, Vandevelde argued that "virtually all of the awards" stem from uniform interpretations. He went on to identify (a) reasonableness, (b) non-discrimination, (c) consistency, (d) transparency, and (e) due process as constituent elements of what he calls the 'unified FET theory'.[370] He further loosely utilised from Dworkin's integrity principle[371] in an attempt to explain the role of the legitimate expectations in FET analysis.[372]

He referred to reasonableness in connection with the rule of law. He noted that the concept has "a substantive and a procedural dimension", the latter of which largely referred to due process.[373] Given due process, *inter alia*, includes a requirement that the investors are accorded impartial treatment before local courts and administrative justices, the denial of due process emerges as denial of justice.[374] As for the substantial aspect of due process, one may refer to arbitrariness.[375] In short, Vandevelde explained the prohibition of denial of justice and arbitrariness under what he referred to as reasonableness.[376] According to his argument, this requires a host state's treatment of foreign investors to "be reasonable related to a legitimate public policy objective."[377]

---

369 *Merrill and Ring Forestry L.P. v. Canada,* ICSID Case No. UNCT/07/1, Award (31 March 2010), par. 210.

370 Vandevelde (2010), p. 53.

371 Dworkin (1986), p. 176. He refers to a legislative integrity which "asks lawmakers to try to make the total set of laws morally coherent".

372 Yu expands the sub-element glossary by empirically examining 569 publicly available investment treaties signed before 2020. In addition to Vandevelde's sub-elements, namely reasonableness, non-discrimination, consistency, transparency, and due process/denial of justice; she counts legitimate expectations, coercion/harassment, bad faith, and stability. See, Yu (2024), p. 264.

373 Vandevelde (2010), p. 49.

374 Vandevelde (2010), p. 50.

375 Vandevelde (2010), p. 51.

376 Vandevelde (2010), p. 54.

377 Vandevelde (2010); *S.D. Myers v. Canada* (2000).

Vandevelde's analysis aims at drawing a coherent framework for this collective arbitral experience. His conclusion is that arbitrators, even when unguided by the treaty text due to obscure or outright non-existent references, tend to draw analytical support from preceding arbitral awards. It follows that the arbitral experience has now reached a degree of substance, and this substance presents a tangible framework for states and their policy makers who, in turn, enhance the previous generation provisions by addressing the shortcomings exposed through the adjudicatory practice.

The foregoing case law study can be interpreted in at least two ways. The *first way* would be to declare, unequivocally, that an autonomous FET is identical to an FET conceptualised within the framework of CIL. While it is extremely cumbersome to identify any meaningful, systemic, consistently applied distinction between (multiple reiterations of) the two, it might still be useful to consider that some arbitral tribunals, at least in theory, consider the CIL principle to be more stringent and extend more deference to a host state. Accordingly, it is important not to discard the possibility that *some* difference *might* exist –but this is yet to be demonstrated, after more than two decades of intense arbitral practice. On that point, the *Red Eagle* Tribunal's observations and accurate (and equally rare) position on the identification of a CIL rule is important. If arbitral tribunals will continue to interpret CIL-qualified rules, which they certainly will if some newer IIAs are any indication, they might as well begin treating them as such: by looking closer at the question of whether the alleged CIL rule carries with it a) consistent and general practice and b) *opinio juris* as two conditions *sine qua non* of a CIL rule.

The focus, therefore, can certainly be on continuing the dissection of these differences and insisting on this dichotomy between autonomy and CIL. I disagree that this is the right path to take. As such, the *second way* to read the foregoing case law study would be to simply move *beyond* this dichotomy and embrace the knowledge the case law has thus far provided. This would only be possible by dissociating the sub-elements with any perceived, broad, vague threshold; and instead building the normative framework directly around these sub-elements. Vandevelde's conclusions support that assertion, and in hindsight, appear to have foreshadowed how certain treaty-makers have changed their treaty-making practices today.

This is what this Chapter will finally address. It is important to carry our conclusions into prospective applications of this emergent pattern; and demonstrate how different, new generation IIAs capture them. Having made its case that engaging with vague qualifications in reference to international law and CIL do not provide any interpretative clarification or guarantee a specific set of subset, the Chapter will now turn its attention to the FET provisions under the new generation IIAs examined under Chap. 4 to pinpoint different ways treaty-makers responded to this complicated, incremental, adjudicatory norm-building process.

5.5 FET Provisions Under New Generation FTAs

In conjunction with the doctrinal and case law analysis conducted above and in parallel to the examination of expropriation provisions under new generation IIAs in Chap. 4, the book will now turn to the new FET provisions to complete its analysis. The accumulation of the adjudicatory experience outlined above has attracted several divergent reactions from all around the world especially in the recent years. Understanding the variety of reactions to this ambiguity is extremely important to reflect upon the future of FET provisions in new generation IIAs.

The analysis below will follow the sequence under Chap. 4. I will therefore begin the examination below by looking at the FET/MST provisions under CETA[378] (with Canada), EUVIPA[379] (with Vietnam), EUSIPA[380] (with Singapore), EUMA[381] (with Mexico), and EUCAFA (with Chile).[382] I will then focus on the Interpretation of the CETA Joint Committee released in February 2024[383] which, similar to the indirect expropriation rule, expands and clarifies certain interpretative points concerning CETA's FET provision. I will conclude the section on the EU agreements with a close-up of the EU negotiation draft for the TTIP,[384] as well as the Annotations to the Model Clauses for Negotiation or Re-negotiation of Member States' Bilateral Investment Agreements with third countries (EU Model BIT), released in 2023.[385] Where relevant, I will refer to Member State Model BITs to draw parallels between national practices and the EU-level framework.

---

[378] Comprehensive and Economic Trade Agreement between Canada and the European Union (CETA) (2017). https://policy.trade.ec.europa.eu/eu-trade-relationships-country-and-region/countries-and-regions/canada/eu-canada-agreement_en.

[379] EUVIPA, Signed in 2019, not in force as of January 2025). https://policy.trade.ec.europa.eu/eu-trade-relationships-country-and-region/countries-and-regions/vietnam/eu-vietnam-agreement/texts-agreements_en.

[380] EUSIPA (Signed in 2018; not in force as of January 2025). https://policy.trade.ec.europa.eu/eu-trade-relationships-country-and-region/countries-and-regions/singapore/eu-singapore-agreements/texts-agreements_en.

[381] EUMA, Agreement reached in principle, published in 2018. https://circabc.europa.eu/ui/group/09242a36-a438-40fd-a7af-fe32e36cbd0e/library/0cc57f29-63bc-476f-80f9-4516a0b0b739/details.

[382] EUCAFA. Signed in February 2023; the European Parliament gave its consent in February 2024). https://circabc.europa.eu/rest/download/6a47b636-0dbd-4537-8544-cdb01b6e80a3?.

[383] CETA Joint Committee, Interpretation of the CETA Joint Committee (9 February 2024) (CETA Interpretative Note), p. 67.

[384] TTIP Negotiating Directives. https://circabc.europa.eu/ui/group/09242a36-a438-40fd-a7af-fe32e36cbd0e/library/8c193123-2084-4231-9e71-bed0d034bb9c/details?download=true.

[385] EU Model BIT (2023); Nacimiento P, Scharaw B, Lui J, European Commission Publishes Non-Paper of Model Clauses for Member States' Bilateral Investment Agreements with Third Countries (Kluwer Arbitration Blog, 19 February 2024). https://arbitrationblog.kluwerarbitration.com/2024/02/19/european-commission-publishes-non-paper-of-model-clauses-for-member-states-bilateral-investment-agreements-with-third-countries/.

I will then proceed with CPTPP, which was, as noted above in Chap. 4, adopted on the basis of the text of TPP.[386] I will then examine RCEP,[387] USMCA,[388] and Finally, the revised, 2017 edition of COMESAIA.[389]

5.5.1 *The EU IIAs*

In the course of the negotiations for new generation IIAs of the EU and in line with goal, the European Commission has prescribed what kinds of treatment shall be considered to be a breach of the FET principle very early on. As noted above in Chap. 4, in its Communication "Towards a comprehensive European international investment policy", the European Commission had already laid forth its intentions to clarify and specify substantive protection principles. This push for further clarity covers indirect expropriation and relevant clarifications examined in the previous Chapter. The convergence between the identified sub-elements under the case law on the one hand, and the sub-elements expressly incorporated in the EU IIA on the other, is also noteworthy. The Chapter will elaborate on this convergence in the course of this section and the conclusions of the Chapter.

5.5.1.1 CETA

Pursuant to Article 8.10 of CETA, entitled "Treatment of Investors and Covered Investments", "[e]ach Party shall accord in its territory to covered investments of the other Party and to investors with respect to their covered investment fair and equitable treatment [...] in accordance with paragraphs 2 and 7." The following paragraph 2 contains a negative list of acts:

> A Party breaches the obligation of fair and equitable treatment referenced in paragraph 1 where a measure or series of measures constitutes:
>
> **denial of justice** in criminal, civil or administrative proceedings;
>
> **fundamental breach of due process**, including a **fundamental breach of transparency**, in judicial and administrative proceedings;
>
> **manifest arbitrariness**;
>
> **targeted discrimination** on **manifestly wrongful grounds**, such as gender, race or religious belief;

[386] CPTPP (2018). This agreement is a sequel to TPP, which had been signed on 2016, but was shelved following the 2016 election of Donald Trump as the US President and the subsequent withdrawal of the United States. The remaining signatories revived the TPP text in 2017 under the name CPTPP. The provisions therefore remained the same.

[387] RCEP (2022).

[388] USMCA (2020).

[389] Revised COMESAIA (2017).

> **abusive treatment** of investors, such as coercion, duress and harassment; or
>
> a breach of any further elements of the fair and equitable treatment obligation adopted by the Parties in accordance with paragraph 3 of this Article.[390]

In accordance with the final sentence of this paragraph, the following paragraph 3 gives way for the parties to "regularly, or upon request of a Party, review the content of the obligation to provide fair and equitable treatment."[391] It tasks the Committee on Services and Investment to "develop recommendations in this regard, and submit them to the CETA Joint Committee for decision."[392]

Paragraph 4 notes that,

> When applying the above fair and equitable treatment obligation, a Tribunal **may take into account whether a Party made a specific representation** to an investor to induce a covered investment, that created **a legitimate expectation**, and upon which the investor relied in deciding to make or maintain the covered investment, but that the Party subsequently frustrated.[393]

While the provision allows a tribunal to take into account legitimate expectations of an investor, it seems to have left the discretion of whether such consideration is relevant to the adjudicators. The provision further notes that, for an expectation to qualify as 'legitimate', it needs to stem from a specific representation upon which an investment was made. This formulation is generally in line with the understanding of legitimate expectations as it stems from the case law analysis, where specific representations which existed at the time of the investment and upon which the investor relied are covered by this wording. Unsurprisingly, it is narrower than the *Tecmed* formulation, which includes basic, unilateral expectations and simple frustrations on the investors' side.[394]

Paragraph 6 notes that "a breach of another provision of [CETA], or of a separate international agreement, does not establish a breach of this Article."[395] The final paragraph 7 further clarifies that "the fact that a measure breaches domestic law does not, in and of itself, establish a breach of this Article."[396]

Earlier drafts of CETA reveal some interesting details. For instance, in February 2013, the parties seem to have diverged over the issue of the title of the article. Canada seems to have proposed the title "Minimum Standard of Treatment" in line with the North American practice which pertains to the CIL threshold examined

[390] Article 8.10(2), CETA (2017); Ünüvar (2020).

[391] Article 8.10(3), CETA (2017).

[392] Article 8.10(3), CETA (2017).

[393] Article 8.10(4), CETA (2017).

[394] Potestà (2013); *Waste Management v. Mexico* (2004), par. 98; *LG&E v. Argentina* (2006), par. 130; *EDF (Services) Limited v. Romania, ICSID Case No. ARB/05/13*, Award (8 October 2009), par. 219.

[395] Article 8.10(6), CETA (2017).

[396] Article 8.10(7), CETA (2017).

above, while the EU had proposed "Treatment of Investment".[397] The parties agreed on the current title between February and November 2013.

Another very important disagreement, which is also associated with the divergence regarding the title, was the extent of the clarifications contained within the article. Earlier drafts indicate that the parties had intended the aforementioned elements (in paragraph 2) to be non-exhaustive; and Canada had further proposed that a CIL qualifier is added.[398] Both proposals were eventually dropped in favour of the current, exhaustive and relatively clear-cut version.

The CETA Interpretative Note of 9 February 2024 contains a number of important clarifications regarding Article 8.10.[399] First of all, the Note emphasises that the sub-elements under Article 8.10.2 are indeed exhaustive.[400] While this can be inferred from the text itself, it is an important reaffirmation. Furthermore, it notes that a denial of justice claim "requires prior exhaustion of local remedies except if there are no reasonably available local remedies to provide effective redress, or if the local remedies provide no reasonable possibility of such redress."[401] Furthermore, the Note contains a word of caution to the tribunal that "it is not a court of appeal of domestic court decisions and should not engage in reviewing the merits of domestic court decisions."[402]

The Note further unpacks the assessment method for 8.10.2(a) and (b), namely denial of justice and a "fundamental breach of due process, including a fundamental breach of transparency, in judicial and administrative proceedings" as follows:

> For there to be a denial of justice and a fundamental breach of due process within the meaning of Article 8.10.2(a) and (b), there must be **improper and egregious procedural conduct** in judicial or administrative proceedings, which does not **meet the basic internationally accepted standards of administration of justice and due process**, and which **shocks or surprises a sense of judicial propriety** such as the unfounded refusal of access to courts or legal representation, failure to provide an opportunity to be heard, discriminatory treatment by the courts, clearly biased and corrupt adjudicators, or a **complete or unjustifiable lack of transparency** in the proceedings, such as a failure to provide notice of the proceedings or reasons for the decision.[403]

---

[397] Cited in Bernasconi – Osterwalder (2013), p. 17.

[398] Bernasconi – Osterwalder (2013), pp. 17–20.

[399] CETA Joint Committee, Interpretation of the CETA Joint Committee (9 February 2024) (CETA Interpretative Note).

[400] CETA Interpretative Note, p. 64.

[401] On the condition of the exhaustion of local remedies and its significance within international investment arbitration pracice, see *Loewen v. USA* (2003). More generally, see, *ELSI* (1989). Both of these decisions also exmaine whether the exhaustion of local remedies was a possibility. Brauch (2017).

[402] CETA Interpretative Note, p. 64; in that connection see *S.D. Myers v. Canada* (2000); *Mondev v. USA* (2002); *Liman v. Kazakhstan* (2010).

[403] CETA Interpretative Note, p. 65.

The elaboration above, at least in part, appears to be inspired by some of the cases referred to above, such as *ELSI*,[404] *Mondev*,[405] and *Waste Management*[406] in its choice of wording.

The Note further elaborated on 'arbitrariness', a sub-element included under Article 8.10.2(c), as follows: "[a] measure is manifestly arbitrary within the meaning of Article 8.10.2(c) when it is evident that the measure is not rationally connected to a legitimate policy objective, such as where a measure is based on prejudice or bias rather than on reason or fact." This language appears to have been imported from the 2021 Canada Model FIPA.[407]

According to the Note, Article 8.10.2(d), which counts 'targeted discrimination on manifestly wrongful grounds such as gender, race or religious belief', covers "measure or series of measures single out the investor in providing differential treatment based on illegitimate grounds such as gender, race or religious belief."[408] It should, however, not be understood so as to prevent "the Parties from granting preferential treatment to promote gender or racial equality or to otherwise address under-representation of socio-economically disadvantaged groups."[409]

The Note clarifies that the finding of an 'abusive treatment of investors, such as coercion, duress and harassment' requires "a finding of serious misconduct".[410] The following situations may serve as illustrations: "the harm or threatened harm to the investor such as whether the episodes of alleged harassment or coercion were repeated and sustained; and the rationale for the Party's actions, such as whether the authorities were acting within the scope of their authority or whether there was an abuse of power."[411]

Last but not least, the Note contains some important clarifications and specifications as to how the legitimate expectations of an investor may be taken into account by adjudicators. First of all, it is noted that "representations made to an investor may only be taken into account to the extent that they are relevant as a factor in

---

[404] *ELSI* (1989), par. 128, referring to "an act which shocks, or at least surprises, a sense of juridical propriety".

[405] *Mondev v. USA* (2002), p. 114, referring to "insufficiency of governmental action so far short of international standards that every reasonable and impartial man would readily recognise its insufficiency".

[406] *Waste Management v. Mexico* (2004), par. 98, referring to "complete lack of transparency".

[407] See, Article 8, Canada Model FIPA (2021), footnote 1: "A measure is manifestly arbitrary when it is evident that the measure is not rationally connected to a legitimate policy objective, such as when a measure is based on prejudice or bias rather than on reason or fact." In turn, the 2021 Model FIPA may have borrowed this expression from the *Lauder v. Czech Republic* award, which stated, citing Black's Law Dictionary (seventh edn, 1999), "arbitrary means 'depending on individual discretion; (...) founded on prejudice or preference rather than on reason or fact'". *Ronald S. Lauder v. The Czech Republic*, UNCITRAL, Award (3 September 2001) (Lauder v. Czech Republic), par. 221.

[408] CETA Interpretative Note, p. 66.

[409] CETA Interpretative Note, p. 66.

[410] CETA Interpretative Note, p. 66.

[411] CETA Interpretative Note, p. 66.

determining a breach of fair and equitable treatment as set out in Article 8.10.2."[412] This clarification bears a striking resemblance to the language used in the above-mentioned case *Odyssey v. Mexico*, where the Tribunal noted that "legitimate expectations are not a stand-alone element within the FET standard under NAFTA Article 1105(1). Rather, such expectations are a factor that may be considered in determining whether a conduct violates the FET standard.[413] While the Tribunal's (or, for that matter, the Note's) meaning is not precisely clear, Article 8.10.4 seems to be a secondary, *dependent* element which can only be read in conjunction with the main elements referred under Article 8.10.2. For instance, a tribunal may rely on an investor's legitimate and investment-backed expectations to the extent that it is useful to determine if a particular revocation or denial of permit is arbitrary. However, a tribunal cannot consider the frustration of an expectation *per se* as a breach of this provision.

The Note introduces further limitations to legitimate expectations, namely that they

> cannot arise from representations if **a prudent and informed investor would not have reasonably relied upon the representations** in making the investment, notably because the representations were **not sufficiently specific and unambiguous** and **did not have the requisite degree of formality** for example because they were **not made in writing** by the competent authority of a Party.[414]

Insofar as this clarification allocates a certain degree of responsibility and duty of diligence to the investor, it can be considered as a countervailing factor in favour of host states. Several tribunals referred to above have reached similar conclusions, such as *Metalpar* and *MTD*, where the alleged expectations were not deemed 'legitimate' because they were not genuine, specific or unambiguous. The paragraph also clarifies that the representations may be deemed inadmissible if they are not done formally, for example in writing; but this does not appear to be an exhaustive criterion for assessing formality.

5.5.1.2 EUSIPA

While the EUSIPA Article 2.4, entitled "Standard of Treatment", is comparable to the CETA Article 8.10, it differs notably in certain aspects. The first paragraph ensures FET, and it is accompanied by a footnote which reads as follows: "Treatment in this Article includes treatment [...] which directly or indirectly interferes with the covered investors' operation, management, conduct, maintenance, use, enjoyment and sale or other disposal of their covered investments."[415]

---

[412] CETA Interpretative Note, p. 67.

[413] *Odyssey v. Mexico* (2024), par. 317.

[414] CETA Interpretative Note, p. 67.

[415] Article 2.4(1), EUSIPA (2018).

The second paragraph, which includes a negative list of acts similar to CETA Article 8.10, contains the *following elements:*

(a) *denial of justice in criminal, civil and administrative proceedings;*
(b) *a fundamental breach of due process;*
(c) *manifestly arbitrary conduct;*
(d) *harassment, coercion, abuse of power or similar bad faith conduct.*[416]

Both the CETA and the EUSIPA include denial of justice and fundamental breach of due process in their first and second sub-paragraphs. On denial of justice, EUSIPA includes a footnote clarification which reads that "the sole fact that the covered investor's claim has been rejected, dismissed or unsuccessful does not in itself constitute a denial of justice".[417] Whereas CETA elaborates that a fundamental breach of due process includes "a fundamental breach of transparency", the EUSIPA refrains from such articulation. Manifest arbitrariness (CETA) and manifestly arbitrary conduct (EUSIPA) are, in effect, equivalent; as they would arguably both include arbitrary conduct and omissions that may be deemed arbitrary in the circumstances. For CETA language that reads "abusive treatment of investors, such as coercion, duress and harassment", the EUSIPA includes, under its sub-paragraph (d), harassment, coercion, abuse of power or similar bad faith conduct.[418] What stands out *vis-à-vis* the CETA text is the absence of the non-discrimination element in EUSIPA.

The previous, FTA version of EUSIPA included a fifth stand-alone sub-element on legitimate expectations.[419] In the IPA version, a new paragraph 3 was included, and the legitimate expectations provision was brought in line with the CETA approach. Article 2.4(3) now reads:

> In determining whether the fair and equitable treatment obligation, as set out in paragraph 2, has been breached, a Tribunal **may** take into account, where applicable, whether a Party made **specific or unambiguous representations** to an investor so as to induce the investment, that created legitimate expectations of a covered investor and which **were reasonably relied upon by the covered investor**, but that the Party subsequently frustrated.[420]

A clarificatory footnote is added to paragraph 3, which clearly attaches a secondary and dependent role to legitimate expectations, possibly confirming the reading under CETA as well. According to this footnote, "the frustration of legitimate expectations as described in this paragraph does not, by itself, amount to a breach of

[416] Article 2.4(2), EUSIPA (2018).

[417] Article 2.4(2), EUSIPA (2018).

[418] Article 2.4(2)(d), EUSIPA (2018).

[419] The fifth sub-element of the previous version read: "a breach of legitimate expectations of a covered investor arising from specific or unambiguous representations from a Party so as to induce the investment and which are reasonably relied upon by the covered investor".

[420] Article 2.4(3), EUSIPA (2018).

paragraph 2, and such frustration of legitimate expectations must arise out of the same events or circumstances that give rise to the breach of paragraph 2."[421]

The subsequent paragraph4, like CETA Article 8.10(3), notes that the parties can extend the exhaustive list included in the preceding paragraph.[422]

Paragraph 6 of Article 2.4 has no corresponding provision in CETA. It covers "specific and clearly spelt out commitment[s] in a contractual written obligation",[423] and prohibits the treaty parties to "frustrate or undermine the said commitment[s] through the exercise of [their] governmental authority".[424] This paragraph arguably layers the coverage of legitimate expectations in the IPA, and defines a special category of protected expectations that stem directly from 'contractual written obligation'. This seems to be a distinct type of expectation: whereas Article 2.4(3) generally regulates legitimate expectations as may have originated from specific representations that were reasonably relied upon by the investor, Article 2.4(6) concerns a legally binding situation whereby the investor would have the expectation that the host state would comply with its written, contractual obligations.

This is a notable distinction, and it is arguably also reflected in case law. Whereas some legitimate expectations had originated from regulatory concessions and incentives[425]; in other cases, they had originated from specific rights that investors possessed—for instance by virtue of an operation license they held, or their expectation that a license would be issued, renewed, would not be revoked or interfered with.[426]

The last paragraph of Article 2.4 maintains that a breach of another provision of EUSIPA or another international agreement does not entail an automatic breach of Article 2.4.

5.5.1.3 EUVIPA

Article 2.5 of the EUVIPA is entitled "Treatment of Investment", and it contains seven paragraphs in total. Its first paragraph establishes that FET analysis shall be conducted in accordance with "paragraphs 2 to 7 and Annex 3 (Understanding on

---

[421] Article 2.4(3), EUSIPA (2018).

[422] Article 2.4(3), EUSIPA (2018).

[423] According to a footnote, "'contractual written obligation' means an agreement in writing, entered into by a Party, itself or through any entity mentioned in paragraph 7 of Article 1.2 (Definitions), with a covered investor or a covered investment whether in a single instrument or multiple instruments, that creates an exchange of rights and obligations, binding both parties."

[424] Article 2.4(5), EUSIPA (2018). A footnote further unpacks 'the exercise of governmental authority': "For the purposes of this Article, a Party frustrates or undermines a commitment through the exercise of its governmental authority when it frustrates or undermines the said commitment through the adoption, maintenance or non-adoption of measures mandatory or enforceable under domestic laws."

[425] *CMS v. Argentina* (2005); *Enron v. Argentina* (2007).

[426] *Waste Management* (2004); *Indian Metals v. Indonesia* (2019).

the Treatment of Investments)"[427] Paragraph 2, like CETA and EUSIPA, contains a negative list, which includes the following: (a) denial of justice in criminal, civil or administrative proceedings, (b) fundamental breach of due process in judicial and administrative proceedings, (c) manifest arbitrariness, (d) targeted discrimination on manifestly wrongful grounds, such as gender, race or religious belief, (e) abusive treatment such as coercion, abuse of power or similar bad faith conduct, or (f) "a breach of any further elements [...] adopted by the parties" in accordance with the subsequent paragraph 3.[428] The said paragraph, like the two IIAs outlined above, prescribe the method according to which the parties may extend this exhaustive list.

The provision on legitimate expectations, Article 2.5(4), is in essence equivalent to those mentioned above. Likewise, the same ancillary, dependent nature of legitimate expectations *vis-à-vis* the articulated sub-elements (under paragraphs 1 to 3) is emphasised.[429]

Article 2.5(6) includes a specific provision which resembles the EUSIPA Article 2.4(6) regarding written agreements.[430]

5.5.1.4 EUMA

Article 15 of EUMA, entitled "Treatment of Investors and of Covered Investments", generally follows the same structured outlined above under CETA and other IIAs.[431] The provision includes further considerations that a tribunal shall *inter alia* take into account pertaining to the four sub-elements counted: a) denial of justice in criminal, civil or administrative proceedings; b) fundamental breach of due process; c) manifest arbitrariness, *including* targeted discrimination on manifestly wrongful

[427] Article 2.5(1), EUVIPA (2019).

[428] Article 2.5 (2), EUVIPA (2019).

[429] Article 2.5(4) reads as follows: "When applying paragraphs 1 to 3, a dispute settlement body under Chapter 3 (Dispute Settlement) may take into account whether a Party made a specific representation to an investor of the other Party to induce a covered investment that created a legitimate expectation, and upon which the investor relied in deciding to make or maintain that investment, but that the Party subsequently frustrated." In the previous, FTA version of this agreement, 'will' was used instead of 'may'.

[430] *Article* 2.5(5), EUVIPA (2019). It prohibits parties from breaching such agreements, provided that (a) they are concluded and take effect after the date of entry into force of EUVIPA; (b) the investor relies on that written agreement in deciding to make or maintain an investment as defined by EUVIPA; (c) the written agreement creates an exchange of right and obligations in connection to the said investment, binding on both parties; and (d) the written agreement does not contain a clause on settlement of disputes between its parties by international arbitration.

[431] Article 15, EUMA (2018).

grounds,[432] such as gender, race or religious belief; and d) harassment, coercion, or abuse of power.[433]

The first clarification concerns denial of justice and due process:

> whether the measure or series of measures involves gross misconduct **that offends judicial propriety**. The mere fact that an investor's challenge of the impugned measure in domestic proceeding has been rejected or dismissed or has otherwise failed does not in itself constitute a denial of justice[434]

A further clarification, which is partly similar to the CETA Interpretative Note above, was made with regard to Article 15(2)(c) concerning manifest arbitrariness: "With regard to the subparagraph 2 (c), whether the measure or series of measures were **patently not founded on reason or fact**, or were patently founded on illegitimate grounds such as **prejudice or bias**."[435] It further adds that

> The mere illegality, or a merely inconsistent or questionable application of a policy or procedure, does not in itself constitute manifest arbitrariness as referred to in the subparagraph 2 (c), while **a total and unjustified repudiation of a** law or regulation, or **a measure without reason**, or **a conduct that is specifically targeted to the investor or its covered investment with the purpose of causing damage** are likely to constitute manifest arbitrariness as referred to in the subparagraph 2 (c).[436]

These clarifications give further context to the assessment of tribunals examining whether or not a measure is arbitrary. One noteworthy feature of this clarificatory note is that in addition to exemplifying types of acts that cannot be deemed arbitrary, it also illustrates what kinds of measures are *likely to be* manifestly arbitrary. These clarifications also aim to contextualise specifically what 'manifest' arbitrariness means, as opposed to a measure that may be arbitrary at a lower degree of severity. It is also noted that bad faith *vis-à-vis* foreign investor or their investment, specifically if the measure is intended to cause harm, is an example of manifest arbitrariness.

A final clarification concerns Article 15(2)(d) on harassment, coercion, or abuse of power. Accordingly, the Tribunal shall consider whether a host state acted ultra vires, or "whether the episodes of alleged harassment or coercion were repeated and sustained."[437]

Article 15(4), concerning legitimate expectations, is generally similar to those under CETA, EUSIPA, and EUVIPA. EUMA, however, adds another sentence, which is distinct in character at first glance: "However, the mere fact that a Party

---

[432] EUMA merges the arbitrariness and discrimination subsets into one, deeming the latter to be included to the former. In CETA, EUVIPA and EUCAFA, arbitrariness and discrimination are referred to separately.

[433] Article 15(2)(a) to (d), EUMA (2018).

[434] Article 15, EUMA (2018) Footnote 16. The phrase 'offends judicial propriety' is also used in *Waste Management v. Mexico* (2004), p. 98.

[435] Article 15, EUMA (2018) Footnote 16.

[436] Article 15, EUMA (2018) Footnote 16.

[437] Article 15, EUMA (2018) Footnote 16.

takes or fails to take an action that may be inconsistent with an investor's legitimate expectations does not constitute a breach of this Article, even if there is loss or damage to the covered investment as a result."[438] Despite its different wording, this addition is similar to the clarifications in above IIAs that legitimate expectations *per se* cannot be considered as a stand-alone sub-element, and will not constitute breaches.

5.5.1.5 EUCAFA

EUCAFA is the most recent EU IIA to date. Its Article 10.15, entitled "Treatment of Investors and of Covered Investments", does not have any notable differences to the agreements examined above.[439] It most closely resembles EUMA, and contains the same clarifications regarding the sub-elements listed under 10.15(2)(a) to (d). The legitimate expectations provision under paragraph 3 is notably shorter than EUMA's corresponding paragraph, but the EUCAFA provision is still in line with other EU IIAs such as CETA, EUSIPA, EUVIPA, and the below-examined TTIP Text.

5.5.1.6 TTIP EU Negotiation Text

The EU's TTIP proposal contains its FET provision under Article 3 entitled "Treatment of Investors and of covered investments".[440]

Article 3 is near identical to Article 8.10 of CETA, with slight modifications. Its paragraph 1 contains the general FET obligation which points at "paragraphs 2 to 5".[441] Paragraph 2, the exhaustive list of elements, contains all those under CETA Article 8.10.[442] Article 3(2)(b), which includes the only additional element, reads "fundamental breach of due process, including a fundamental breach of transparency *and obstacles to effective access to justice*, in judicial and administrative proceedings".[443] In sub-paragraph (e) of Article 3, the TTIP text notes "harassment, coercion, abuse of power or similar bad faith conduct", instead of CETA's subparagraph (e) which reads "[a]busive treatment of investors, such as coercion, duress and harassment".[444] The subparagraph (f), as is the case in the CETA text, gives way to parties to modify the list. One apparent difference is that while the CETA Article 8.10 indicates that the parties may modify the list either regularly or upon the request of one of the parties, the TTIP proposal allows this only upon request.[445]

---

[438] Article 15(4), EUMA (2018).

[439] Article 10.15, EUCAFA (2023).

[440] Article 3, TTIP text (2015).

[441] Article 3(1), TTIP text (2015).

[442] Article 3(2), TTIP text (2015).

[443] Article 3(2)(b), TTIP text (2015).

[444] Article 3(2)(e), TTIP text (2015).

[445] Article 3(2)(f), TTIP text (2015).

5.5.1.7 EU Model Clauses (EU Model BIT)

The EU Model BIT[446] prepared by the European Commission to guide Member States in their extra-EU BIT negotiations and re-negotiations also contains an FET provision. The overall structure aligns with the IIAs above. Its paragraph 2 containing the FET sub-elements, and its paragraph 3 on legitimate expectations, are identical to those under CETA.

The commentary on the FET provision contains similar clarifications to CETA's Interpretative Note analysed above. It specifies that paragraph 2 presents a 'closed list of improper and reprehensible State conduct', and adds that "legitimate expectations may only be treated as a relevant consideration when assessing an allegation of violation of the FET standard through any of the (a)-(e) elements, and not as a standalone element that in itself would give rise to a violation of the FET standard."[447]

5.5.2 *CPTPP*

As explained in Chap. 4, CPTPP refers directly to TPP provisions, including its Article 9.6, entitled "Minimum Standard of Treatment".[448] is as follows:

1. Each Party shall accord to covered investments treatment in accordance with applicable customary international law principles, including fair and equitable treatment and full protection and security.
2. For greater certainty, paragraph 1 prescribes the customary international law minimum standard of treatment of aliens as the standard of treatment to be afforded to covered investments. The concepts of "fair and equitable treatment" and "full protection and security" do not require treatment in addition to or beyond that which is required by that standard, and do not create additional substantive rights. The obligations in paragraph 1 to provide:

    (a) "fair and equitable treatment" includes the obligation not to deny justice in criminal, civil or administrative adjudicatory proceedings in accordance with the principle of due process embodied in the principal legal systems of the world; and
    (b) "full protection and security" requires each Party to provide the level of police protection required under customary international law.

---

[446] EU Model BIT (2023). The Non-Paper was re-released, *verbatim*, on 31 January 2024, with minor formatting corrections. As of January 2025, the document is available via the following link: https://circabc.europa.eu/ui/group/be8b568f-73f3-409c-b4a4-30acfcec5283/library/9a3525b5-a8cb-47e7-a96a-fe1e7d378809/details?download=true.

[447] EU Model BIT (2023), p. 10.

[448] Article 9.6, CPTPP (2018). The title of the Article refers to Annex 9-A, which reads as follows: "The Parties confirm their shared understanding that "customary international law" generally and as specifically referenced in Article 9.6 (Minimum Standard of Treatment) results from *a general and consistent practice of States* that they follow from *a sense of legal obligation*. The customary international law minimum standard of treatment of aliens refers to *all customary international law principles* that protect the investments of aliens."

3. A determination that there has been a breach of another provision of this Agreement, or of a separate international agreement, does not establish that there has been a breach of this Article.
4. For greater certainty, the mere fact that a Party takes or fails to take an action that may be inconsistent with an investor's expectations does not constitute a breach of this Article, even if there is loss or damage to the covered investment as a result.
5. For greater certainty, the mere fact that a subsidy or grant has not been issued, renewed or maintained, or has been modified or reduced, by a Party, does not constitute a breach of this Article, even if there is loss or damage to the covered investment as a result.

The FET provision in CPTPP is strikingly different from all of the above FTAs examined. The US influence is observable due to similarities of the text with the US Model BIT,[449] as well as the general North American IIA configurations examined throughout this Chapter.

Article 9.6(1) includes the obligation to accord "to covered investments treatment in accordance with applicable customary international law principles, *including* fair and equitable treatment [...]". Paragraph 2 notes that "[FET does] not require treatment in addition to or beyond that which is required by [IMS], and do not create additional substantive rights."[450] Several elements of FET, such as denial of justice and due process, are counted under the same paragraph in a non-exhaustive, illustrative manner. Paragraphs 4 and 5 specify that "the mere fact" that a party's actions may be inconsistent with an investor's expectations and that "a subsidy or grant has not been issued, renewed or maintained, or has been modified or reduced [...] does not constitute a breach of [Article 9.6]."[451]

CPTPP Article 9.6 clearly follows in the footsteps of its North American predecessors in attaching CIL as a threshold and the determinant of what is fair and equitable. Even though the inclusion of 'due process' and 'denial of justice' in the provision may be seen as adjudicatory guidance, the fact that they are not part of an exhaustive arguably list curbs their effectiveness as clarifications. Besides, even the articulated non-exhaustive elements have their own vague qualifiers: it is not entirely clear which legal systems are counted amongst "the principle legal systems of the world".[452]

This being said, the Annex 9-A may be seen as a positive step forward in its express acknowledgment that CIL requires the identification of "a general and consistent practice of States that they follow from a sense of legal obligation."[453]

Sub-paragraphs 4 and 5 introduce some tangible clarifications and resemble their counterparts in the EU IIAs examined above. Notably, paragraph 4 of CPTPP contains near-identical language to Article 15(4) of EUMA, noting that "the mere fact that a Party takes or fails to take an action that may be inconsistent with an investor's

[449] US Model BIT (2012).

[450] Article 9.6(2), CPTPP (2018).

[451] Article 9.6(4) and (5), CPTPP (2018).

[452] Article 9.6(2)(a), CPTPP (2018).

[453] Annex 9-A, CPTPP (2018).

expectations[454] does not constitute a breach of this Article, even if there is loss or damage to the covered investment as a result."[455] In specifying that certain administrative prerogatives, such as denying grants or subsidies are not *per se* FET violations might also provide interpretative guidance to arbitral tribunals.

5.5.3 RCEP

Article 10.5 of RCEP, entitled "Treatment of Investment", notes that "Each Party shall accord to covered investments fair and equitable treatment and full protection of security, in accordance with the customary international law minimum standard of treatment of aliens."[456] The only sub-element articulated under Article is denial of justice, under paragraph 2(a). Under its paragraph 2(c), it notes that "the concepts of fair and equitable treatment and full protection and security do not require treatment to be accorded to covered investments in addition to or beyond that which is required under the customary international law minimum standard of treatment of aliens, and do not create additional substantive rights."[457] The provision contains no further clarifications or specific provisions on, for example, legitimate expectations.

5.5.4 USMCA

USMCA's Article 14.6, entitled "Minimum Standard of Treatment", is another provision heavily influenced by the 2012 US Model BIT.[458] As such, it is near-identical to the CPTPP provision examined above with the exception that it does not include a provision corresponding to CPTPP Article 9.6(5) on subsidies and grants.

---

[454] In EUMA, it reads '*legitimate* expectations'.

[455] Article 9.6(4), CPTPP (2018).

[456] Article 10.5(1), RCEP (2020). The provision refers to an Annex 10A, which is very similar to CPTPP Annex 9-A, which reads as follows: "The Parties confirm their shared understanding that 'customary international law' generally and as specifically referenced in Article 10.5 (Treatment of Investment), including in relation to the customary international law minimum standard of treatment of aliens, results from a general and consistent practice of States that they follow from a sense of legal obligation."

[457] Article 10.5(2)(c), RCEP (2020).

[458] Article 14.6, USMCA (2020).

5.5.5 2017 COMESAIA

The 2007 version of COMESAIA regulated 'Fair and Equitable Treatment' under its Article 14. Roughly based on the North American model at the time, it stated that "Member States shall accord fair and equitable treatment to COMESA investors and their investments, in accordance with customary international law",[459] and counted denial of justice and due process as sub-elements. Similar to the CPTPP provision, it also noted that "the customary international law minimum standard of treatment of aliens as the minimum standard of treatment to be afforded to covered investments and does not require treatment in addition to or beyond what is required by that standard."[460]

A distinct feature of this text was its paragraph 3, which factored in different levels of development among COMESA Member States and the subsequent assessment of what was fair and equitable and, consequently, suggesting that this article did not establish a unitary understanding of FET: "Member States understand that different Member States have different forms of administrative, legislative and judicial systems and that Member States at different levels of development may not achieve the same standards at the same time. Paragraphs 1 and 2 of this Article do not establish a single international standard in this context."[461]

In its revised 2017 version, COMESAIA completely overhauled its Article 14. Now uniquely entitled "Fair judicial and administrative treatment", it contains a list of sub-elements analogous to the EU IIAs examined above: (a) denial of justice in criminal, civil or administrative proceedings; (b) un-remedied and egregious violations of due process; (c) targeted discrimination on manifestly unjustified grounds, such as gender, race or religious belief; or (d) manifestly abusive treatment, such as coercion, duress and harassment.[462] It has notably removed its CIL references altogether, as well as its distinct paragraph 3 factoring in different levels of development.

---

[459] Article 14, 2007 COMESAIA.

[460] Article 14(2), 2007 COMESAIA.

[461] Article 14(3), 2007 COMESAIA.

[462] Article 14(1)(a) to (d), 2017 COMESAIA.

5.6 Concluding Remarks: Adjudicatory Experience, New Generation IIAs, and the Construction of 'Objective' Fairness in Investment Law

5.6.1 How Do New Generation IIAs Compare?

The agreements examined here collectively represent some of the most prominent examples of the new generation IIAs, which aim at remedying the vague nature of the FET principle. Several policy considerations, such as regulatory authority, arbitral discretion, and injecting at least some degree of predictability, are shared rationales. Despite these common goals, the ways they go about tackling these issues are different from one another. While the EU IIAs relate closely, they too have differences among themselves. However, the CPTPP, RCEP, AND USMCA, reflecting their predominantly American-inspired roots and structures,[463] reflect an entirely different approach. The initial, 2007 version of COMESAIA followed a basic American model as well. However, its 2017 model adopts a distinct EU-style drafting with its articulated, exhaustive list of elements.

The EU seeks to define of the FET principle by including an exhaustive list of negative acts. This allows for a 'checklist' style examination, according to which the adjudicators would test a challenged act or acts against the items identified, such as denial of justice, fundamental breach of due process, and manifest arbitrariness.[464] These items, which function as explicit clarifications, create a bundle of subset facilitated by the arbitral tribunals over the years. A remarkable feature of these draft texts is that there are no references to CIL or any other general threshold pinned on expansive and vague concepts.[465] Instead, the provisions in the EU IIAs codify what has been often perceived to be sub-elements of the FET principle as they have accumulated in particular in the past two decades and a half. These sub-elements were either identified as constituent elements of the ever-ambiguous MST/CIL, or as autonomous manifestations of what a state's unfair treatment may look like. The goal has been to transmute them into treaty law in order to expressly ascertain their formative and normative relevance to the principle. In other words, the list approach allows tribunals to use these considerations, such as coercion, arbitrariness and denial of justice not as presumptive constituents of CIL; but tangible, undisputed elaborations of what the parties objectively consider as 'fair'. While they are still subject to adjudicatory interpretation, they go a long way with regard to precision vis-à-vis IMS/MST.

The EU texts also make references to a *review* procedure for expanding these sub-elements. This clause ascertains that the FET principle does not depend on a certain collection of subset, confined to a temporal snapshot. By providing such a

[463] Alschner (2013).

[464] Ünüvar (2022), p. 292.

[465] Dumberry (2024a).

possibility to review and modify the interpretative sub-elements of the principle, the parties embraced FET as an ever-transforming principle. This feature is a recurring team in case law, starting from the *Mondev* award.[466] Subsequent tribunals also perceived FET as a dynamic, evolving concept.[467] Indeed, if parties agree explicitly on other reference points, the EU texts ascertain that they can be incorporated into the text, and will be equally binding. Such a provision should be considered a positive step towards more clarity, as it allows a dynamic, cumulative adjudicatory tradition to emerge. It could also be seen as a precautionary measure against interpretative loopholes that might arise during an arbitral dispute and can be helpful in minimizing contradictory outcomes in arbitral applications due to vaguely drafted provisions, in line with the EU's overall policy of clarifying the FET standard and incorporating key lessons learned from case-law. One such initiative was, indeed, the CETA Interpretative Notes that revisited the CETA provisions and provided useful clarifications, even before its full entry into force.

The recognisable efforts towards further clarity notwithstanding, these FET provisions still contain many subjective elements. It seems rather evident that the EU and its treaty partners have been building this framework in order to highlight regulatory sovereignty and the right to regulate by limiting arbitrators' discretion without entirely discarding its neutral, third-party judiciary status. Despite this framework, it could be claimed that adjudicators will nonetheless use a certain degree of discretion to grant a context to terms such as 'manifest' arbitrariness or 'fundamental' breach of due process.[468] When asked about the new generation FET provisions, a prominent arbitrator had the following to say:

> I think it is a good idea [to try to define FET] [...] But, it is an illusion to believe that you can list everything. It is like a contract – doesn't matter if it is a hundred pages, or a thousand pages. You will always have issues which come up that are not exactly written down. Writing down ten or so examples [in reference to the list under the FET provision] – I believe it clarifies FET to an extent, but it is not the end of the story. It could be considered a step forward, but [you cannot] eliminate every possible dispute.[469]

Therefore, while it may be possible to provide for a lengthy and more specific list of acts, it is not granted that precise foreseeability is agreeable or beneficial, let alone possible.[470] The level of specificity in a treaty is less about absolute precision, and more about striking a sustainable balance between the policy space to states on the one hand, and granting adjudicatory and interpretative discretion to arbitral tribunals on the other. The current stage of the evolution demonstrates that policy-makers have been receptive of the arbitral elaborations. As new generation IIAs remain largely untested, it is yet to be seen whether their response to this arbitral experience

[466] Mondev v. USA (2002), par. 125.

[467] *LG&E v. Argentina* (2007); *RDC v. Guatemala* (2012).

[468] *Thunderbird v. Mexico* (2006), par. 197.

[469] Interview #6.

[470] Alschner (2022); Dolzer and Schreuer (2012), p. 133; Van Aaken (2009), p. 517.

will effectively address perceived shortcomings and the normative ambivalence surrounding FET.

One criticism towards the list approach adopted by the EU has been the lack of a reference to the 'stable framework' sub-element.[471] The case law indicates that this is a common consideration for arbitral tribunals.[472] While a direct reference to stable framework may be absent in the treaties, there are numerous references to transparency, predictability, and legitimate expectations under the FET provision, all of which may prompt the question of whether the establishment of a stable framework forms part of the FET principle. The case law further reveals that arbitral tribunals, usually with a reference to the 'object and purpose' of a treaty through Article 31 of VCLT, refer to the preambles of IIAs for interpretative guidance. These preambles sometimes contain references to the establishment of a stable framework between treaty parties.[473] The new IIAs contain preambular references to a stable framework: for instance, CETA's preambles note that the parties resolve to "[e]stablish clear, transparent and predictable mutual advantageous rules to govern their trade and investment".[474] While the 'stable framework' subset is not articulated as such, the constituent features of a stable legal and business framework can be extracted from the EU IIAs, using different formulations.

All IIAs examined above except for RCEP and COMESAIA refer to the legitimate expectations of investors. They also elaborate on what types of expectations can be 'legitimate'. This acknowledges the role these expectations play in determining whether an FET breach had occurred, and this is likely to continue. This broad acknowledgment, however, also curbs their force: they are given a secondary role *vis-à-vis* the other sub-elements. In 2005, In his *Thunderbird v. Mexico* dissenting opinion, Wälde wrote that "[o]ne can observe over the last years a significant growth in the role and scope of the legitimate expectation principle, from an earlier function as ***a subsidiary interpretative principle*** to reinforce a particular interpretative approach chosen, to its current role as ***a self-standing subcategory and independent basis*** for a claim under the 'fair and equitable standard'".[475] Twenty years on, arbitral tribunals still consider legitimate expectations to be an important element, regardless of the qualifiers (CIL, international law, or otherwise) in IIAs. Whether this repossession of interpretative authority embedded within these newer generation IIAs will successfully reverse the development of legitimate expectations as a self-standing subcategory of FET is yet to be seen.

When evaluated on the basis of the EU model, CPTPP, RCEP, and USMCA are less assertive and progressive with regard to the overall framework they present. Their primary shortcoming is ultimately their persistent reliance on CIL. The

[471] Kriebaum (2016).

[472] See, for instance, the Argentine cases above.

[473] For instance, see the Preamble in BLEU (Belgium – Luxembourg Economic Union) – Croatia BIT (2003).

[474] Preamble, CETA (2017); Preamble, EUVIPA (2020): "this Agreement will create **[...] a stable and predictable environment for investment**". Emphasis added.

[475] *Thunderbird v. Mexico* (2006), Separate Opinion (1 December 2005), par. 37.

two-prong method of CIL identification in their respective annexes, namely identifying general and persistent practice and *opinio juris*, is a positive step forward, and arbitral tribunals would be bound by it. This is not a novelty, however. Some of the IIAs examined under the case law analysis, such as CAFTA-DR, already incorporate this clarification, yet it did not necessarily prompt the arbitral tribunals to engage with it.[476] As examined above, the *Red Eagle v. Colombia*[477] Tribunal is one (rare) example of an arbitral tribunal doing so. In Canada—Colombia FTA, Article 805 makes a direct reference to Article 38 of the SICJ,[478] which counts "international custom, as evidence of a general practice accepted as law". Other cases interpreting Article 805, like *Eco Oro* and *Montauk*, ultimately did not engage with this method, despite it being prescribed. Annex 9-A ultimately prescribes the same test more overtly, and it is yet to be seen whether arbitral tribunals will engage with it more directly.

In addition to prescribing the above-mentioned two-prong test, these IIAs nonetheless mention some sub-elements, namely due process and/or denial of justice. These, however, are not exhaustive sub-elements. To a large extent, therefore, they retain the early 2000s North American, post-FTC NAFTA-inspired approach, and insist on maintaining the MST as a benchmark. Whereas the EU IIAs collectively form a novel drafting method, CPTPP, RCEP, and USMCA embrace the current conceptual ambiguity and refrain from extensive concretisation of FET in favour of arbitral discretion. The framework thus has not changed much since the first strand of modified IIAs the US negotiated in early to mid-2000s. For instance, the United States—Uruguay BIT of 2005, under its Article 5(2)(b), states that "[FET] includes the obligation not to deny justice in criminal, civil, or administrative adjudicatory proceedings in accordance with the principle of due process in the principle legal systems of the world."[479] This provision bears a striking resemblance to the CPTPP text as it stands today.[480]

Finally, the transformation and development of the COMESAIA is unique. The 2007 version was mainly based on the US Model, however the 2017 version expressly embraces the list method developed by the EU. While the current version is not as elaborate as the EU IIAs themselves, I believe this brings about more clarity as to the intentions of the negotiating parties. Still, it would be beneficial to further specify the meaning and the role of investors' expectations in the FET analysis

---

[476] Annex 10-B, CAFTA-DR (2006); *Corona Materials LLC v. Dominican Republic*, ICSID Case No. ARB(AF)/14/3, Award (31 May 2016) (*Corona v. Dominican Republic*), par. 248 et seq. Parties, as well as non-disputing Party submissions in disputes routinely point towards the Annex.

See, for instance, *RDC v. Guatemala* (2012), par. 207; Michael Ballantine and Lisa Ballantine v. The Dominican Republic, PCA Case No. 2016-17, Final Award (3 September 2019), par. 408 et seq; 413 et seq.

[477] *Red Eagle v. Colombia (2024).*

[478] Article 38, SICJ (1945).

[479] Article 5(2)(b), Uruguay – US BIT (2005); Article 10.5 (2)(a), CAFTA-DR (2006).

[480] It is important to reiterate that while the US is not a party to CPTPP at the moment, its predecessor and current legal-textual foundation TPP would have included the US as a party.

similar to those that exist under the EU agreements to pin down its normative use to adjudicators.

5.6.2 Does the Adjudicatory Practice Construct an 'Objective' Fairness?

In Chap. 2, I elaborated on the historic-political development of the notion of fairness as a constituent notion of a sovereign's conduct towards foreigners. I laid down the framework based on the premise that fairness has retained its contingency throughout history. In other words, it has been defined and contextualised in reference to other principles, subjects, or objects. In Chap. 2, I turned my attention to how sovereigns use their prerogatives to limit themselves as it stems from their sovereign powers in the context of foreign investment protection.

Chapters 4 and 5, collectively detailed two very specific, yet important, illustrations as to how this sovereign prerogative to self-restrain played out in the context of two key substantive protection principles found under IIAs: indirect expropriation and FET. Their constituent principles and sub-elements are the result of decades-long legal, political, economic, and philosophical elaborations by adjudicatory *rule-makers* on what is, or should be, fair, egregious, shocking, or arbitrary. Beyond general and vague insinuations that an international standard existed, no forum, authority, or polity could tangibly ascertain what that standard required. No consistent guidance existed as to what such non-contingent fairness could look like.

The question of whether considerations such as due process, denial of justice, non-arbitrary conduct, transparency, legitimate expectations, stability of legal and business frameworks, or non-discrimination stem from a minimum standard, at least in light of the intensified efforts to include them in the treaty texts, dilutes the efforts to clarify the meaning of fairness. While states naturally retain the ability to add any qualifier they want in their treaties as they see fit, if the objective is to narrow, broaden, or otherwise clarify a meaning, CIL/MST/IMS benchmarks do not ensure any predictable scope or framework. As one Canadian legal scholar and legal counsel involved in ISDS practice since the 90s, referring to the 'narrow' interpretation implied by the CIL qualification, noted: "[w]hen I say narrower, I mean [the parties'] intent to narrow it, not their success in narrowing it."[481]

The new generation EU IIAs clearly want to evade this inquiry, and instead focus on the genuine, underlying question of what is actually *meant* by this otherwise vague concept. This method has not appeared out of thin air and its implementation does not take place in a vacuum. The elements to be taken in consideration by the arbitral tribunals pursuant to new-wave IIAs are pinpointed as a result of a long adjudicatory tradition which has gradually informed the policy and treaty-makers,

[481] Interview #7.

consultants and lawyers, and even investors. The new EU IIAs seem to reflect a parallel understanding.

I believe the FET provisions advocated by the EU are a solid step towards the codification and consolidation of written, as well as unwritten, rules that have somehow guided the doctrine and adjudication in international investment law, and a clear indication of the developing, transforming nature and content of IIAs. Through such codification of the accumulated subset of what is 'fair' in international investment law, the construction of an objective notion of 'fairness' is therefore in the making.

References

Alschner W (2013) Americanization of the BIT universe: the influence of friendship, commerce and navigation (FCN) treaties on modern investment treaty law. Göttingen J Int Law 5:455–486

Alschner W (2022) Investment arbitration and state-driven reform: new treaties, old outcomes. Oxford University Press, Oxford

Alvarez JE, Khamsi K (2009) The Argentine crisis and foreign investors: a glimpse into the heart of the investment regime. In: Sauvant KP (ed) The yearbook on international investment law and policy 2008–2009. Oxford University Press, New York, pp 379–478

Angelet N (2022) Fair and equitable treatment. Max Planck Encycl Int Law (MPIL), 1–30

Bernasconi – Osterwalder N (2013) Commentary to the Draft Investment Chapter of the Canada – EU Comprehensive Economic and Trade Agreement (CETA) IISD Report. https://www.iisd.org/system/files/publications/commentary_investment_chapter_CETA.pdf

Blomstrom M, Kokko A (1997) Regional Integration and Foreign Direct Investment: A Conceptual Framework and Three Cases. *World Bank Policy Research Working Paper Series* No. 1750

Bonnitcha J (2014) Substantive protection under investment treaties: a legal and economic analysis. Cambridge University Press, Cambridge

Borchard E (1940) Minimum standard of the treatment of aliens. Mich Law Rev 38:445–461

Brauch MD (2017) Exhaustion of Local Remedies in International Investment Law (IISD Best Practices Series – January 2017). https://www.iisd.org/system/files/publications/best-practices-exhaustion-local-remedies-law-investment-en.pdf

Bronfman MK (2005) Fair and equitable treatment: an evolving standard. Max Planck UNYB 10:609–680

Brower CH II (2006) Why the FTC notes of interpretation constitute a partial amendment of NAFTA article 1105. Va J Int Law 46:347–363

Burgstaller M, Galagan D (2024) Contributory fault in international investment arbitration. J Int Arbitr 41(4):397–438

Cole T (2012) The boundaries of Most Favored nation treatment in international investment law. Mich J Int Law 33:537–586

Dolzer R, Schreuer C (2012) Principles of international investment law, 2nd edn. Oxford University Press, Oxford

Dolzer R, Stevens M (1995) Bilateral investment treaties. Martinus Hijhoff Publishers, The Hague

Dumberry P (2004) An empirical study of the fair and equitable treatment standard clause: how tribunals have examined its relationship with the minimum standard. Wolters Kluwer, Alphen aan den Rijn

Dumberry P (2018) Fair and equitable treatment: its interaction with the minimum standard and its customary status. Brill Nijhoff, Leiden

Dumberry P (2023) The Cost of Inaction: Arbitral Practice in Respect of Earlier Generation FET Clauses and Current Approaches to FET Clauses. OECD: The Future of Investment Treaties (Track 2). https://oecd.org/investment/investment-policy/Expert-contribution-Prof-Dumberry-on-FET.pdf

Dumberry P (2024a) The ‘minimum standard of treatment’ in international investment law: the fascinating story of the emergence, decline and recent resurrection of a concept. In: Merkouris P, Kulick A, Álvarez-Zarate JM, Żenkiewicz M (eds) Custom and its interpretation in international investment law. Cambridge University Press, Cambridge

Dumberry P (2024b) NAFTA'S FET clause is (practically) dead! Long live its legacy!: an empirical survey of how tribunals have interpreted FET clauses linked to the minimum standard of treatment. Eur Invest Law Arbitr Rev 9(2):277–308

Dworkin R (1986) Law's empire. Harvard University Press, Cambridge

Grigera A (2024) Necessity in Investment Arbitration: Boosting the ICSID System's Legitimacy (The American Review of International Arbitration Blog, 25 March 2024). https://aria.law.columbia.edu/necessity-in-investment-arbitration-boosting-the-icsid-systems-legitimacy/

Islam R (2018) The fair and equitable treatment (FET) standard in international investment arbitration: developing countries in context. Singapore, Springer Nature

Jarrett M (2019) Contributory fault and investor misconduct in investment arbitration. Cambridge University Press, Cambridge

Kiguel M (2011) Argentina's 2001 Economic and Financial Crisis: Lessons for Europe. Think Tank 20: Beyond Macroeconomic Policy Coordination Discussions in the G-20. https://www.brookings.edu/wp-content/uploads/2016/06/11_argentina_kiguel.pdf.

Kill T (2008) Don't cross the streams: past and present overstatement of customary international law in connection with conventional fair and equitable treatment obligations. Mich Law Rev 106:853–880

Kläger R (2011) ‘Fair and equitable treatment’ in international investment law. Cambridge University Press, Cambridge

Knottnerus R, Van Os R (2012) The Netherlands: A Gateway to ‘Treaty Shopping’ for Investment Protection (*Investment Treaty News,* 12 January 2012). https://www.iisd.org/itn/2012/01/12/the-netherlands-treaty-shopping/

Kriebaum U (2016) FET and Expropriation in the Comprehensive Economic Trade Agreement between the European Union and Canada (CETA). *TDM 1—Comprehensive Economic and Trade Agreement between the European Union and Canada (CETA).* https://www.transnational-dispute-management.com/article.asp?key=2320.

Kurtz J (2010) The paradoxical treatment of the ILC articles on state responsibility in investor-state arbitration. ICSID Rev 25:200–217

Laryea ET (2021) Legitimate expectations in investment treaty law: concept and scope of application. In: Chaisse J, Choukroune L, Jusoh S (eds) Handbook of international investment law and policy. Springer Nature, Singapore, pp 97–120

Lockwood JE (1948) Economic agreement of Bogota. Am J Int Law 42:611–620

Mann FA (1981) British treaties for the promotion and protection of investments. Br Yearb Int Law 52:241–254

Marcoux JM, Bjorklund AK (2020) Foreign investor' responsibilities and contributory fault in investment arbitration. Int Comp Law Quart 69(4):877–905

Mola L (2016) International investment arbitration and serious economic crises: lessons learned in the Argentinean crisis of 2000-2001. In: Tanzi A, Asteriti A, Lazo Polanco R, Turrini P (eds) International investment law in Latin America/ Derecho Internacional de las Inversiones en América Latina. Brill Nijhoff, Leiden, pp 370–399

Newcombe A, Paradell L (2009) Law and practice of investment treaties. Wolters Kluwer, Alphen aan den Rijn

Nikièma SH (2017) The Most-Favoured-Nation Clause in Investment Treaties: IISD Best Practices Series

OECD (2004) Fair and Equitable Treatment Standard in International Investment Law (OECD Working Papers on International Investment 2004/3). https://www.oecd.org/content/dam/oecd/en/publications/reports/2004/09/fair-and-equitable-treatment-standard-in-international-investment-law_g17a166b/675702255435.pdf.

Paddeu F, Waibel M (2022) Necessity 20 years on: the limits of article 25. ICSID Rev 37(1–2):160–191

Paparinskis M (2013) The international minimum standard and fair and equitable treatment. Oxford University Press, Oxford

Paulsson J (2005) Denial of justice in international law (Hersch Lauterpacht Memorial Lectures No. 17). Cambridge University Press, Cambridge

Pinchis-Paulsen M (2014) The ancestry of 'equitable treatment' in trade: lessons from the league of nations during the inter-war period. J World Invest Trade 15:13–72

Pinchis-Paulsen M (2018) Resolving challenges to historical research: developing a project to define fair and equitable treatment. In: Schill SW, Tams CJ, Hofmann R (eds) International investment law and history. Edward Elgar, Cheltenham, pp 179–212

Porterfield MC (2013) A Distinction Without a Difference? The Interpretation of Fair and Equitable Treatment Under Customary International Law by Investment Tribunals (*IISD, Investment Treaty News, 22 March 2013*). https://www.iisd.org/itn/2013/03/22/a-distinction-without-a-difference-the-interpretation-of-fair-and-equitable-treatment-under-customary-international-law-by-investment-tribunals/

Potestà M (2013) Legitimate expectations in investment treaty law: understanding the roots and the limits of a controversial concept. ICSID Rev 28:88–122

Reinisch A, Tropper J (2022) The Argentinian crisis arbitrations. In: Ruiz Fabri H, Stoppioni E (eds) International investment law: an analysis of the major decisions. Hart Bloomsbury, London, pp 119–134

Ruttenberg VH (1987) The United States bilateral investment treaty program: variations on the model. J Int Law 9:121–143

Sarmiento F, Nikièma S (2022) Fair and Equitable Treatment: What it matters and what can be done https://www.iisd.org/system/files/2022-11/fair-equitable-treatment-en.pdf

Schill SW (2009) The multilateralization of international investment law. Cambridge University Press, Cambridge

Schill SW (2022) Landmark cases on fair and equitable treatment: empowering and controlling arbitrators as law-makers. In: Ruiz Fabri H, Stoppioni E (eds) International investment law: an analysis of the major decisions. Hart Bloomsbury, London, pp 359–379

Schreuer C (2005) Fair and equitable treatment in arbitral practice. J World Invest Trade 6:357–386

Schreuer C (2009) Protection against arbitrary or discriminatory measures. In: Rogers CA, Alford PA (eds) The future of investment arbitration. Oxford University Press, New York, pp 183–198

Schreuer C, Kriebaum U (2009) At what time must legitimate expectations exist? In: Werner J, Ali AH (eds) A liber Amicorum: Thomas Wälde. Cameron May, London, pp 265–276

Stone J (2012) Arbitrariness, the fair and equitable treatment standard, and the international law of investment. Leiden J Int Law 25:77–107

Thirlway H (2010) The sources of international law. In: Evans MD (ed) International law, 3rd edn. Oxford University Press, Oxford, pp 95–121

Toye R (2012) International trade organization. In: Daunton M, Narlikar A, Stern RM (eds) The Oxford handbook on the World Trade Organization. Oxford University Press, Oxford, pp 85–100

Tudor I (2008) The fair and equitable treatment standard in the international law of foreign investment. Oxford University Press, Oxford

UNCTAD (2012) Fair and Equitable Treatment (UNCTAD Series on Issues in International Investment Agreements II). https://unctad.org/system/files/official-document/unctaddiaeia2011d5_en.pdf

Ünüvar G (2020) Is CETA the promised breakthrough? Interpretation and evolution of fair and equitable treatment and (indirect) expropriation provisions. In: Andenas M, Pantaleo L, Happold M, Contartese C (eds) EU external action in international economic law. Springer, Berlin, pp 193–219

Ünüvar G (2022) The vague meaning of fair and equitable treatment principle in investment arbitration and new generation clarifications. In: Lam J, Kjær AL (eds) Language and legal interpretation in international law. Oxford University Press, Oxford, pp 271–292
Ünüvar G (2023) A tale of policy carve-outs and general exceptions: eco Oro v Colombia as a case study. J Int Disp Settlement 14(4):517–533
Vandevelde KJ (2010) A unified theory of fair and equitable treatment. Int Law Polit 43:43–106
Villegas-Ruiz JA (2020) Oil & gas International Dispute Resolution in context: the example of Exxon Mobil v. Venezuela AMDIPC No 2:495–527
Waibel M (2019) Fair and equitable treatment as boilerplate. Am Rev Int Arbitr 30(1):85–111. https://papers.ssrn.com/sol3/papers.cfm?abstract_id=3401770
Wälde T (2004) Investment arbitration under the energy charter treaty: an overview of selected key issues based on recent litigation experience. In: Horn N (ed) Arbitrating foreign investment disputes: procedural and substantive legal aspects. Kluwer Law International, The Hague, pp 193–236
Walker H Jr (1958) The post-war commercial treaty program of the United States. Polit Sci Quart 73:57–81
Weiler T (2013) The interpretation of international investment law: equality, discrimination and minimum standards of treatment in historical context. Leiden, Brill Nijhoff
Yu C (2024) International adjudication as interactional law-making: the incorporation of fair and equitable treatment elements in investment treaties. J Int Econ Law 27:259–277
Zeyl T (2011) Charting the wrong course: the doctrine of legitimate expectations in investment treaty law. Alberta Law Rev 49(1):203–235
Živković V (2023) Fair and equitable treatment and the rule of law. Elgar Publishing, Cheltenham

Chapter 6
Conclusion

Abstract International investment law has rapidly evolved from a relatively recent field grounded in longstanding legal and political traditions. The rise of investor-state dispute settlement (ISDS) mechanisms has significantly shaped the interpretation and development of key protection principles, creating a feedback loop between arbitration and treaty-making. This book examined how new-generation international investment agreements (IIAs) reflect lessons learned from arbitral practice, especially regarding indirect expropriation and Fair and Equitable Treatment (FET). Through detailed case studies, it highlighted the ongoing balancing act between state sovereignty, investor protections, and public interests. Ultimately, the book underscored the dynamic process of legal evolution and the challenges ahead in achieving clarity and fairness in international investment law.

International investment law is one of the fastest-developing fields in international law. Despite its relatively short history spanning from the second half of the twentieth century to today, it builds upon a centuries-old legal, political, social, and economic conjuncture. *Vis-à-vis* the general subject of the treatment of foreigners in a host country, the subject-matter of international investment regime is a key tributary. It forms but a single but remarkable constituent of a much larger structure. It feeds and transforms this grand image, as it interacts with other tributaries and engages in a reciprocal process of growth and enrichment.

For most of their existence, IIAs and the dispute settlement mechanisms they have provided had been fairly underutilised. Now, however, with its unprecedented popularity especially in the past twenty-five years, ISDS is an important part of the international investment law discipline and a direct component of its norm-building process. Treaty and policy-making on the one hand, and dispute settlement on the other, are two sides of this transformation. They form an effective feedback loop to emphasise each other's strengths and shortcomings.

G. Ünüvar, *The Transformation of International Investment Law and Its Principles*, European Yearbook of International Economic Law 44,
https://doi.org/10.1007/978-3-032-01110-7_6

The so-called new generation IIAs are the natural continuation of this adjudicatory law-making process, whereby judicial elaborations and articulations inform newer generation legal instruments and push policy-makers to reflect upon the tools in their legal and political arsenal. This has perhaps been the most evident for more open-ended, vague principles such as indirect expropriation and FET. Addressing key policy discussions such as the distinction between a non-compensable regulatory measure and an indirect expropriation, as well as the constituent sub-elements of the FET principle, this book provided an extensive case study as to what lessons the arbitral experience has provided for policy-makers, practitioners, and academics thus far. Clarity can only be truly achieved through experience; and ISDS, despite all of its vices and shortcomings, has provided invaluable know-how.

This discussion is not cut off from its historical and political origins. Chapter 2 provided an in-depth examination of the notion of fairness and its transformation from a contingent principle to a non-contingent and allegedly objective notion. Chapter 3 then turned its attention to state as sovereign, examining its ability to self-restrict as a particular manifestation of this sovereign power. Bringing IIAs into focus as tools for such self-restriction, the book then highlighted the need for balancing competing interests and paradigms driving the very existence of the international investment regime. Fairness is a concept which undergirds these different, competing paradigms; and it fulfils a key role in establishing the balance between them.

Two principles, namely indirect expropriation and FET, are two reiterations of what the book called 'non-contingent' fairness. Chapter 4 delved into the principle of indirect expropriation: its definition, sub-elements, its defining characteristics as well as the fundamental clashes which drive its normative transformation. Focusing on a broad selection of cases that spans more than two decades, the book demonstrated how arbitral tribunals have been constructing a distinction between what a state could do without pecuniary ramifications, and what it could not do without violating a treaty obligation. As earlier IIAs did not attempt to answer this key conundrum, arbitral tribunals took the matter into their hands. This incremental adjudicatory 'action' found its 'reaction' in how states revisited the scope of indirect expropriation, universally embracing the idea that a certain policy space had to be carved out for legitimate, non-discriminatory measures enacted for the benefit of the public.

As for FET, the divide runs deeper. In Chap. 5, the book provided another case study, examining generations of arbitral tribunals interpreting what 'fair and equitable' treatment entailed. It generally identified two things. First, it found that earlier attempts to draw the contours of this principle on the basis of equally ambivalent concepts such as the 'minimum standard of treatment' have proven to be ineffective. Second, and despite the ineffectiveness of these so-called 'thresholds', this arbitral experience gradually accumulated into a series of sub-elements that are now easily identifiable. It further contended that some IIAs, such as those being negotiated and signed by the EU, understood and captured the implications of these two important lessons more accurately than its counterparts such as CPTPP, RCEP, and USMCA.

This book's ultimate goal was to weave a narrative on how legal fields learn from experience, and react to such experiences. There are few better examples than international investment law in this regard. Despite their potential, it is yet to be seen whether the new generation approaches will be able to advance the objectives of coherence, clarity, and certainty; as well as balancing what is at stake for states as sovereigns, foreign investors as private entities and, maybe most importantly, the public as the most vulnerable of all.

Annex 1: *List of Interviews*

(Name (where available), date, time, identifiers, location of interview):

- **Interview #1**, 19 May 2015 (14:31): North American lawyer experienced in NAFTA (trade and investment disputes) practice (Copenhagen, Denmark)
- **Interview #2**, 11 August 2015 (12:46): Turkish lawyer experienced in oil and gas, as well as investment law (Ankara, Türkiye)
- **Interview #3**, 12 August 2015 (11:00): Turkish lawyer experienced in banking & finance, energy, investment, infrastructure, mergers and acquisitions and competition law (Ankara, Türkiye)
- **Interview #4**, 13 August 2015 (12:05): Turkish lawyer experienced in energy, investment, infrastructure, mergers and acquisitions and administrative law (Ankara, Türkiye)
- **Interview #5**, 27 August 2015 (17:35): European government official, working on negotiations of trade and investment treaties (Stockholm, Sweden)
- **Interview #6**, 28 August 2015 (12:00): European lawyer, arbitrator, professor. Practice and academic focus: international economic law (Stockholm, Sweden)
- **Interview #7**, 23 September 2015 (19:00): North American lawyer, arbitrator, and academic in international investment and trade law (online)
- **Interview #8**, 23 September 2015 (21:00): North American lawyer and arbitrator (online)
- **Interview #9**, 28 September and 26 October 2015: North American lawyer, former government official experienced in investment and trade matters (phone call)
- **Interview #10**, 19 November 2015 (12:00): Singaporean lawyer working on investment and trade disputes (Singapore)
- **Interview #11**, 20 November 2015 (16:30): Korean lawyer working on investment and trade disputes (Singapore)
- **Interview #12**, 21 November 2015 (12:00): *Hugo Perezcano Diaz, former head of Trade Remedy Authority of Ministry of Economy; former lead legal counsel for Ministry of Economy (previously Ministry of Trade and Industrial Promotion),*

G. Ünüvar, *The Transformation of International Investment Law and Its Principles*, European Yearbook of International Economic Law 44,
https://doi.org/10.1007/978-3-032-01110-7

Mexico. He actively participated in the NAFTA and Uruguay Round negotiations, and was Mexico's lead counsel in disputes brought under trade and investment agreements until the end of 2006. He provided consent to all references by e-mail on 15 May 2025.

- **Interview #13**, 22 November 2015 (12:30): Oceanian professor and lawyer, experienced in international investment arbitration (Singapore)
- **Interview #14**, 23 November 2015 (13:30): North American lawyer, academic and administrator, involved in NAFTA practice and international investment arbitration (Singapore)
- **Interview #15**, 23 November 2015 (15:00): North American lawyer and professor (Singapore)
- **Interview #16**, 24 November 2015 (12:30): Southeast Asian academic and government official involved in the IIA negotiations and the preparation of the national Model BIT (Singapore)
- **Interview #17**, 24 November 2015 (12:30): Southeast Asian academic and government official involved in the IIA negotiations and the preparation of the national Model BIT (Singapore)
- **Interview #18**, 25 November 2015 (17:00): Southeast Asian government official, ministry of trade (Singapore)
- **Interview #19**, 25 November 2015 (17:00): Southeast Asian government official, ministry of economy (Singapore)
- **Interview #20**, 26 November 2015 (16:00): North American arbitrator, lawyer and professor (Singapore)
- **Interview #21**, 4 April 2016 (14:00): EU official (Copenhagen, Denmark)

Annex 2: *Ethical Principles and Guidelines on Interviews*

This addendum describes the procedure followed in this thesis to gain access to the experts interviewed for this book, to secure their consent for the use of their statements, and to protect their anonymity.

The recruitment of the informants followed the general principles which prescribe that each interviewee must be recruited by means of a formal letter. The letter was sent to the interviewees by e-mail, and it contained the following elements: (a) a brief presentation of the researcher (Güneş Ünüvar), (b) the nature of the project and the reasons why I was seeking interviewees, and (c) a presentation of the researcher's home institute (at the time, the Centre of Excellence on International Courts, University of Copenhagen), including a description of its overall purpose, namely the study of international adjudicatory bodies. The letter also informed the interviewees that the interviews would be conducted for the sole purpose of gathering data for academic works, such as future scholarly publications and the PhD dissertation which forms the basis of this book.

In the letter, the interviewees were also made aware that they were chosen because of their prominent professional positions relating to the practice of international investment law and arbitration. The letter was signed by the researcher and it provided the necessary contact information (phone, e-mail, address).

Before the beginning of each interview, the content of the introduction letter was briefly repeated in order to remind them of the key points of the project and of the overall scope of the interview. Subsequently, I would make the interviewees aware of the manner in which the interview would be conducted and the nature of the questions they would be asked. In some instances, the interviewees had requested the questions or topics in advance, which were provided. At this stage, I also asked the informants if I could record the interview session. If the interviewee agreed, in order to avoid ambiguities, I would record the entire interview on a tablet device. I also added that the recording would discontinue at any time during the interview, if the interviewee so wished. When consent to the use of recording device was not

G. Ünüvar, *The Transformation of International Investment Law and Its Principles*, European Yearbook of International Economic Law 44,
https://doi.org/10.1007/978-3-032-01110-7

present either written or oral, the researcher considered the silence on the matter as lack of consent.

Before the beginning of each interview, the interviewees were also informed that they would be granted maximum anonymity by default. It was made clear to the interviewees that they would not, under any circumstance, referred to by name or any specific feature that would allow direct identification without written or recorded consent. This was a deliberate choice made after having considered the nature of the people interviewed for the purpose of this work. Given the prominence of all interviewees in the field, I also considered the possibility of them being identifiable by others merely on the basis of their statements. Furthermore, the interviewees are often public figures, whose ideas and life events may be of public domain. To avoid this kind of indirect or even speculative identification, this book refers to the interviewees as generally as possible, so as to balance the necessity to demonstrate their professional relevance on the one hand, and respect their anonymity to the extent possible on the other. When written consent for direct quotation was present (by way of, including but not limited to, e-mail) I referred to the interviewee by name. The files containing the records of the interviews had been stored with protective passwords, and were available only to me. After the completion of the PhD thesis upon which this book is generally based, I immediately disposed of all the audio recordings relating to the interviews.

GPSR Compliance

The European Union's (EU) General Product Safety Regulation (GPSR) is a set of rules that requires consumer products to be safe and our obligations to ensure this.

If you have any concerns about our products, you can contact us on ProductSafety@springernature.com

In case Publisher is established outside the EU, the EU authorized representative is:

Springer Nature Customer Service Center GmbH
Europaplatz 3
69115 Heidelberg, Germany

Batch number: 09106840

Printed by Printforce, the Netherlands